THE CONSTITUTION, THE COURTS, AND HUMAN RIGHTS

An Inquiry into the Legitimacy of Constitutional Policymaking by the Judiciary

MICHAEL J. PERRY

Yale University Press   New Haven and London

Designed by Nancy Ovedovitz and set in VIP Melior type by Northeast Typographic Services, Inc.
Printed in the United States of America by The Murray Printing Co., Westford, Mass.

Library of Congress Cataloging in Publication Data

Perry, Michael J.
    The Constitution, the courts, and human rights.

    Includes bibliographical references and index.
    1. Civil rights—United States. 2. United States—Constitutional law—Interpretation and construction. 3. Judicial review—United States. 4. United States. Supreme Court. I. Title.
KF4749.P43   1982   342.73'085   82-40164
ISBN 0-300-02745-1   347.30285   AACR2

10   9   8   7   6   5   4   3   2   1

For my Father

Come, you whom my Father has blessed, take for your heritage the kingdom prepared for you since the foundation of the world. For I was hungry and you gave me food; I was thirsty and you gave me drink; I was a stranger and you made me welcome; naked and you clothed me, sick and you visited me, in prison and you came to see me.

Lord, when did we see you hungry and feed you; or thirsty and give you drink? When did we see you a stranger and make you welcome; naked and clothe you; sick or in prison and go to see you?

I tell you solemnly, in so far as you did this to one of the least of these brothers of mine, you did it to me.

Matthew 25:34–40

You said to me: "The greatness of my country is beyond price. Anything is good that contributes to its greatness. And in a world where everything has lost its meaning, those who, like us young Germans, are lucky enough to find a meaning in the destiny of our nation must sacrifice everything else." I loved you then, but at that point we diverged. "No," I told you, "I cannot believe that everything must be subordinated to a single end. There are means that cannot be excused. And I should like to be able to love my country and still love justice. I don't want just any greatness for it, particularly a greatness born of blood and falsehood. I want to keep it alive, by keeping justice alive."

Albert Camus, *Letters to a German Friend*

CONTENTS

PREFACE

In this book, which is an essay in constitutional theory, I address a wide range of issues. There are two basic issues that I do not address, however, and I think it will clarify my argument if I indicate, here at the outset, what those two issues are.

First. I am concerned with the legitimacy of constitutional policymaking (by the judiciary) that goes *beyond* the value judgments established by the framers of the written Constitution (extraconstitutional policymaking). I am not concerned with the distinct issue of the legitimacy of constitutional policymaking that goes *against* the framers' value judgments (contraconstitutional policymaking). The former is an issue in democratic theory. Moreover, it is an issue that might engage any society, even one without a written constitution and therefore without framers, if that society (1) is committed, at the level of its political-legal culture, to democratic government but (2) has a politically unaccountable judiciary that opposes itself, in the name of some "fundamental" but unwritten law, to the politically accountable branches and agencies of government.

The latter is a different sort of issue. There the problem is not the legitimacy, in terms of democratic theory, of an activist but politically unaccountable judiciary, but the legitimacy of any governmental institution, including the judiciary, acting contrary to (some aspect of) the written fundamental law, understood as norms constitutionalized by framers. Only a society with a written constitution could be engaged by the latter issue.

I am concerned here exclusively with the former issue—indeed, contemporary constitutional theory is concerned almost exclusively with that issue—because virtually no constitutional doctrine (regarding freedom of expression, equal protection, etc.) established by the modern Supreme Court represents a value judgment contrary to any of the framers' value judgments. Nonetheless, because it is possible that enforcement, by the federal judiciary against the governments of the fifty states, of value judgments *beyond* those constitutionalized by the framers is itself a contraconstitutional practice—a practice *contrary to* the *federal* character of American government established by the framers—the legitimacy of contraconstitutional (judicial) practice is a basic issue that ought to be addressed and that I shall address in a later essay.*

*For an important recent essay that attends to the distinction between (what I am calling) extraconstitutional and contraconstitutional policymaking, see Sandalow, *Constitutional Interpretation,* 79 MICH. L. REV. 1033 (1981).

Second. In my view, which I elaborate in chapter 4, a necessary but not sufficient condition of a successful defense of constitutional policymaking by the judiciary in human rights cases is that there be right answers to political-moral questions. That is a necessary condition, because if there are not right answers, one cannot justify constitutional policymaking in human rights cases;* but it is not a sufficient condition, because even if there are right answers, it might still be impossible to justify constitutional policymaking.†

My defense of constitutional policymaking in human rights cases presupposes that there are right answers, and I have some things to say about the matter of right answers, and of moral skepticism, in chapter 4. But I do not pretend to defend the claim that there are right answers. This is not an essay in metaethics. However, the problem of objectivity in ethics is a fundamental issue that constitutional theory cannot ignore if it hopes to make a genuine intellectual advance. I shall address that problem too in a later essay.‡

*   *   *   *   *   *

Thus, there is more, and fundamental, work to be done. This essay is simply my beginning. I hazard to publish it now, not because I have addressed all the relevant issues, nor because I have made up my mind, once and for all, on the issues I have addressed. Most assuredly I have done neither. I hope to be thinking and writing about the various relevant issues for another thirty or forty years. (I may even be forced, from time to time, to change my mind!) I publish this essay now because I want to help advance the conversation of constitutional theory.

---

*See Nagel, *The Supreme Court and Political Philosophy,* 56 N.Y.U. L. REV. 519, 519 (1981): "[E]ven some skeptics about ethical truth may nevertheless be willing to allow the Court to make decisions or to create results . . . when those results do not exist in advance, waiting to be discovered." My claim, however, developed in chapter 4, is that no defense of judicial activism can succeed that does not presuppose that there are right answers. (I doubt that to say that there are right answers in ethics is to say that those answers "exist in advance, waiting to be discovered.")

†*Cf. id.* at 519: "[E]ven a believer in the existence of objectively discoverable ethical truth will not want to assign to the Court general jurisdiction over the determination and enforcement of that truth."

‡Lawrence Sager, commenting on an earlier version of chapter 4 (Perry, *Noninterpretive Review in Human Rights Cases: A Functional Justification,* 56 N.Y.U.L. REV. 278 (1971)), has written that "Professor Perry . . . [is] very much a rights skeptic." Sager, *Rights Skepticism and Process-Based Responses,* 56 N.Y.U.L. REV. 417, 420 n. 6 (1981). If by rights skeptic Professor Sager means (as he seems to) one who doubts that very much modern constitutional doctrine regarding human rights can be grounded in the *written* Constitution (*see id.* at 419), then I am certainly a rights skeptic. But this book, in particular chapter 4, should make it clear that I reject moral skepticism. (For a frontal assault on contemporary moral skepticism, see

A final prefatory word: Some constitutional theorists have recently suggested that the conversation in which I and others are engaged is a dead-end. Paul Brest, for example, has claimed that "the controversy over the legitimacy of judicial review in a democratic polity—the historic obsession of normative constitutional law scholarship—is essentially incoherent and unresolvable."* I flatly reject any such claim. I hope this book demonstrates that the controversy is both coherent and resolvable (although, to be sure, the eventual resolution may be other than I imagine it to be).

I want to express my deep gratitude to several individuals. For moral support, and for translating that support into a most congenial work environment: Dean James E. Meeks. For generous financial support: The Ohio State University and its College of Law. For critical evaluations of earlier versions of the essay, but for which I would surely be in even bigger trouble than I am: Larry Alexander, Dan Conkle, Kent Greenawalt, Lou Jacobs, Bill Nelson, Jerry Reichman, Rich Saphire, Greg Stype, Jack Weinstein, Steve Wineman, Larry Zacharias, and the students in my 1980 autumn-quarter seminar in constitutional theory. For help in getting the manuscript ready for publication: Gayle Swinger, Jeff Page, and Pat Schirtzinger. I owe a special word of thanks to a dear friend, Susan Kuzma, whose unstinting aid on a number of fronts was simply invaluable.

R. UNGER, KNOWLEDGE AND POLITICS (1975), in particular chaps. 1 and 5; H. Putnam, REASON, TRUTH AND HISTORY (1981). *See also* J. Finnis, NATURAL LAW AND NATURAL RIGHTS (1980).

*Brest, *The Fundamental Rights Controversy: The Essential Contradictions of Normative Constitutional Scholarship*, 90 YALE L. J. 1063, 1063 (1981). *See also* Tushnet, *Darkness on the Edge of Town: The Contributions of John Hart Ely to Constitutional Theory*, 89 YALE L. J. 1037 (1980).

PROLOGUE

Over a quarter century ago, in *Brown v. Board of Education*,[1] the Supreme Court of the United States ruled that racially segregated public schooling violates the United States Constitution.[2] More recently, in *Roe v. Wade*,[3] the Court ruled that restrictive abortion legislation violates the Constitution.[4] In neither case was the Court's ruling authorized, much less required, by the Constitution as written and understood by the framers of that document;* neither ruling, as we will later see, was really the outcome of "interpretation" or "application" of any value judgment made by the framers and embodied by them in the Constitution. In each case the Court's ruling represented the Court's own value judgment:[5] the Court struck down a policy choice made by an electorally accountable branch of government—in *Roe*, for example, a state legislature—and supplanted it with a policy choice of its own.

Constitutional theorists continue to regard *Roe v. Wade* as one of the most controversial constitutional cases in recent times precisely because the Court's ruling cannot be explained by reference to any value judgment constitutionalized by the framers.[6] Many critics of the Court think that *Roe* represents the Court at its worst.[7] *Brown v. Board of Education*, by contrast, is generally thought to represent the Court at its best.[8] And yet, if the

---

*By the "framers," I mean, primarily, those persons—sitting in the original Constitutional Convention or, in the case of amendments to the Constitution, in Congress—who voted to propose the relevant constitutional provision and, secondarily, those persons in the individual state conventions or legislatures who voted to ratify the provision. The framers' understanding of a particular provision is what I mean by the "original understanding" of the provision. Ascertaining the *precise* contours of the original understanding of any given provision may be difficult, sometimes even impossible. See P. BREST, PROCESSES OF CONSTITUTIONAL DECISIONMAKING 139–45 (1st ed. 1975); Brest, *The Misconceived Quest for the Original Understanding*, 60 B.U.L. REV. 204, 209–17 (1980); Tenbroek, *Use by the United States Supreme Court of Extrinsic Aids in Constitutional Construction*, 27 CALIF. L. REV. 399, 405–06 (1939).

Still, it is usually possible to ascertain the rough contours of that understanding. And once the rough contours have been ascertained, it is frequently possible to say: Although we do not know exactly what the framers thought this provision *would* accomplish, there is strong evidence they thought it would *not* accomplish X; or strong evidence they did not think it would accomplish X; or no evidence, or wholly inadequate evidence, they thought it would accomplish X. The historian's ability to ascertain the rough contours of the original understanding of the various constitutional provisions discussed or mentioned in this book is sufficient for purposes of the claims about the original understanding on which I rely. *Cf.* J. ELY, DEMOCRACY AND DISTRUST: A THEORY OF JUDICIAL REVIEW 16 (1980): "I [am not] endorsing for an instant the nihilist view that it is impossible ever responsibly to infer from a past act and its surrounding circumstances the intentions of those who performed it." (I address the matter of the framers' intentions at greater length in chap. 3.)

Court's ruling in *Roe* were illegitimate—as many of the Court's critics insist it is—on the ground that it is not explicable by reference to any of the framers' value judgments, the Court's ruling in *Brown* would have to be deemed illegitimate too, since *neither* ruling was the outcome of interpretation or application of any value judgment constitutionalized by the framers.*

The rulings in *Brown* and *Roe* are not unique in that regard. To the contrary, they are typical of the Supreme Court's modern constitutional workproduct. Virtually all of modern constitutional decision making by the Court—at least, that part of it pertaining to questions of "human rights,"† which is the most important[9] and controversial part, and the part with which I am mainly concerned in this book—must be understood as a species of policymaking, in which the Court decides, ultimately without reference to any value judgment constitutionalized by the framers, which values among competing values shall prevail and how those values shall be implemented. In the modern period of American constitutional law—which began in 1954, with *Brown v. Board of Education*[10]—the United States Supreme Court has played a major and unprecedented role in the formulation of human rights.[11] Most first amendment doctrine regarding political and religious liberty; most equal protection doctrine regarding racial, sexual, and other forms of discrimination; all due process doctrine regarding rights pertaining to contraception, abortion, and sexual behavior; and various constitutional doctrines regarding the rights of inmates of prisons and mental health facilities—this list is far from exhaustive—reflect not value judgments, or interpretations or applications of value judgments, made and embodied in the Constitution by the framers, but value judgments made and enforced by the Court against other, electorally accountable branches of government. Thus, in America the status of constitutional human rights is almost wholly a function, not of constitutional interpretation, but of constitutional policymaking by the Supreme Court.

Growing recognition of that fact has occasioned a major debate in contemporary constitutional theory.[12] Many theorists contend that constitutional policymaking by the Supreme Court is illegitimate, in whole or significant part, on the ground that it is fundamentally inconsistent with

---

*Later, in chap. 3, I amplify and defend my claim that neither ruling is explicable by reference to any of the framers' value judgments. I also argue, in chap. 4, that the constitutional theory that succeeds in justifying the judicial activism underlying the Court's decision in *Brown* also serves to justify the activism underlying its decision in *Roe*. (It does not follow, and would be absurd to maintain, that one who approves the Court's ruling in *Brown* must also approve its ruling in *Roe*.)

†By "human rights," I mean simply the rights individuals have, or ought to have, against government under the "fundamental"—constitutional—law.

our societal commitment to democracy. The Court, it is said, is not a democratic institution, and so may not legitimately engage in constitutional *policymaking*, as opposed to constitutional *interpretation*. This book is an extended inquiry into the legitimacy of constitutional policymaking by the Supreme Court, especially in the area of human rights. It bears mention, here at the outset, that the problem of the legitimacy of constitutional policymaking by the Court is important not merely as an issue in contemporary political-constitutional theory. So it is not at all surprising that judicial policymaking in constitutional cases provokes deep and widespread controversy not only among lawyers and lawyer-academics, but among the lay public as well.[13]

Democracy is a freighted term. Some constitutional theorists have tried to resolve the tension between constitutional policymaking by the Supreme Court and our societal commitment to democratic government more at the level of definition than of theory. They define democracy in terms of certain substantive ideals and then contend that, because (or to the extent that) the Court's constitutional policymaking serves to effectuate those ideals, it is democratic. But that strategem cannot work unless the audience to which it is addressed accepts, or can be persuaded to accept, the controversial claim that the concept of democracy entails the particular substantive ideals stipulated by the theorists, and the further claim, also controversial, that the particular exercise of constitutional policymaking in question serves to effectuate one or more of those ideals. Moreover, the definitional argument simply overlooks the fact that, whatever the character of particular decisions rendered by the Court in the course of constitutional policymaking, the Court itself is plainly not an electorally accountable institution;[14] that fact, as I explain at the beginning of chapter 1, is precisely what gives rise to the debate about the legitimacy of the Court's constitutional policymaking in the first place. Consequently, the definitional argument is destined to exert, and in fact has exerted, very little influence in current constitutional debate.[15]

The notion of democracy on which I rely is primarily procedural, not substantive. With Brian Barry, "I follow . . . those who insist that 'democracy' is to be understood in procedural terms. That is to say, I reject the notion that one should build into 'democracy' any constraints on the content of the outcomes produced, such as substantive equality, respect for human rights, concern for the general welfare, personal liberty or the rule of law."* The following rough definition captures the procedural notion of democracy I have in mind:

*Barry, *Is Democracy Special?*, in PHILOSOPHY, POLITICS AND SOCIETY (FIFTH SERIES) 155, 156 (P. Laslett & J. Fishkin eds. 1979.) *See also* W. NELSON, ON JUSTIFYING DEMOCRACY 3 (1980):

I regard democracy as a system for making governmental decisions. "Democracy" is to be

A democracy is rule by the people where "the people" includes all adult citizens not excluded by some generally agreed upon and reasonable disqualifying factor, such as confinement to prison or to an asylum for the mentally ill, or some procedural requirement, such as residency within a particular electoral district for a reasonable length of time before the election in question. "Rule" means that public policies are determined either directly by vote of the electorate or indirectly by officials freely elected at reasonably frequent intervals and by a process in which each voter who chooses to vote counts equally . . . and in which a plurality is determinative.[16]

Because the word *democracy* is so freighted and misused, suggestive of vague substantive ideals as well as procedural forms, in the remainder of this book I use it only sparingly. In its stead I use a different term, set forth and amplified in chapter 1: *electorally accountable policymaking*.

Throughout this book, as in this prologue, I frequently write as if the chief question were the legitimacy of constitutional policymaking by the Supreme Court of the United States. The question actually addressed, however, is broader: the legitimacy of constitutional policymaking by the American judiciary generally, which includes the lower federal courts and the courts of the individual states.[17] Still, the controversy surrounding the problem of the legitimacy of judicial policymaking in constitutional cases naturally tends to focus on the Supreme Court, which, among all courts, has the last word on federal constitutional matters.[18] Moreover, by virtue of its preeminent position in the American judiciary—a position of formal leadership with respect to certain matters, but also of informal leadership with respect to many more—the Supreme Court sets a highly visible standard of judicial behavior that many other courts tend to emulate.[19]

I should emphasize, by way of caveat, that this book deals much more with the legitimacy of a policymaking process than with the soundness of

---

defined in terms of procedures, not in terms of substantive policy. . . . While there are many legitimate questions to be answered in political philosophy, one good question, certainly, is how the various institutions affecting governmental decisionmaking should be structured.

But see H. Thomas, A History of the World 388 (1979): "Winston Churchill is believed to have said, 'Democracy means that if the door bell rings in the early hours, it is likely to be the milkman.' "

Barry adds: "The only exceptions . . . are those required by democracy itself as a procedure." Barry, *supra* this note, at 156. (For examples of such exceptions, see text accompanying note 16 *infra*.) Barry, therefore, probably would not deny, and in any event I readily concede, that the concept of democracy entails the principle of freedom of expression; after all, for government to manipulate the flow of information is for it to manipulate, to some extent, the choices people make in casting their ballots. But that concession has very limited consequences, as we will see in chap. 3, where I discuss the matter at some length.

any particular substantive constitutional doctrines* generated by that process. The relationship between those two issues deserves clarification. In an important respect the issue of the legitimacy of constitutional policymaking is linked to the issue of the soundness of substantive doctrine. That linkage is explored in chapter 4, where I indicate that the legitimacy of constitutional policymaking by the Supreme Court is *in part* a function of the soundness of substantive doctrine generated by such policymaking. However, the issue of the soundness of substantive doctrine is distinct from the issue of the legitimacy of constitutional policymaking. Although one can fault substantive doctrine on the ground that the policymaking process that generated the doctrine is illegitimate,† to do so is not to take issue with any particular doctrine on the merits, but to dispute the legitimacy of the policymaking process. Whether or not one disputes the legitimacy of constitutional policymaking by the Supreme Court, one can nonetheless inquire into the soundness of a particular substantive doctrine on the merits by asking whether the particular doctrine—say, the rule that government may not interfere with a woman's decision to have an abortion—is sound as *political-moral doctrine*. Again, however, in this book I am only peripherally concerned with the soundness of particular substantive doctrines.

The particular categories of substantive constitutional doctrine to which I mainly refer in this book (when I refer to any) are those concerning: (1) freedom of expression; (2) the equal protection of the laws; and (3) a family of matters subsumed under the rubric "substantive due process." The first two categories are, by consensus, among the most important in the whole corpus of constitutional law. The third category is, again by consensus, the most controversial. But the relevance of what I have to say about the issue of the legitimacy of constitutional policymaking by the Supreme Court is by no means confined to those particular categories of doctrine. I might have referred instead to categories of doctrine concerning, for example, freedom of religion,[20] or the fair administration of criminal justice (although those references, I suspect, would be somewhat less dramatic). Note that *any* substantive doctrine generated by judicial policymaking in constitutional cases is fatally tainted if, as many theorists claim, all such policymaking is illegitimate.[21]

---

*By substantive constitutional doctrine, I refer mainly to the principles and rules fashioned by the Supreme Court and other courts to resolve constitutional disputes on the merits.

†The notion, of course, is that if the process is illegitimate, any outcome generated by that process is fatally tainted. Even if one is sympathetic to a particular policy choice on the merits, one may oppose that policy choice if it has been made—"imposed"—by an institution believed to lack legitimate authority to make the choice.

Georges Sorel is reported to have said that he "always wrote by reading, that is, by reacting to the ideas of others."[22] This book is, in that sense, an exercise in writing by reading. No one who hopes to do productive work in constitutional theory can fail to take account of the important work already carried out in this century. Especially relevant are works on the modern period of American constitutional law, during which the Supreme Court has served as a principal architect of important human rights, many quite controversial. As I hope this book makes clear, I am particularly indebted to Robert Bork, the most effective critic of constitutional policymaking by the Supreme Court,[23] and John Ely, a much more conservative defender of such policymaking than I[24]—even though I vigorously dissent from the constitutional theories of both men.

An overview of chapters that follow might be helpful. In chapter 1, by way of clearing the ground and constructing a framework for the remainder of my essay, I discuss several preliminary but nonetheless fundamental matters. One such matter is the crucial distinction between "interpretive" judicial review*—constitutional interpretation—the legitimacy of which is not a particularly difficult problem, and "noninterpretive" review— constitutional policymaking—the legitimacy of which is the central problem of contemporary constitutional theory.

Chapter 2 focuses on noninterpretive review, but not, like the rest of the book, noninterpretive review with respect to human rights issues. Rather, the focus of chapter 2 is on noninterpretive review with respect to the other two principal sorts of constitutional issues: "federalism" issues—issues concerning the proper division of power between the federal government and the governments of the states—and "separation of powers" issues —issues concerning the proper allocation of power among the branches of the federal government. In chapter 2, I establish that no consideration presented by either federalism or separation-of-powers issues undermines the claim, put forth by certain constitutional theorists, that all noninterpretive judicial review is illegitimate.

In chapter 3 (and throughout the remainder of the book), the focus is on noninterpretive review with respect to issues of human rights—issues concerning the proper relationship between the individual and the collectivity *qua* government. There I detail the implications of the claim that all noninterpretive review is illegitimate for two major areas of modern constitutional doctrine: freedom of expression and equal protection. And I argue that one recent, quite prominent attempt, by John Ely, to defend noninterpretive review with respect to both freedom of expression and equal protection issues is wholly unsuccessful.

---

*"Judicial review" refers to the judicial practice of reviewing governmental action (or inaction) to see if it is, as it is claimed to be by the party challenging the action, unconstitutional.

In chapter 4, which is the heart of this book, I attempt to show that even though no justification for noninterpretive review can be predicated on the Constitution as written or even as understood by the framers, there is nonetheless a persuasive functional justification for noninterpretive review with respect to human rights issues—that is, a justification predicated on the crucial function such review serves in American government and also on the particular manner in which it serves that function—and that therefore the claim that all noninterpretive review is illegitimate should be rejected. Along the way, I argue that the only constitutional theory that serves to justify, if any serves to justify, noninterpretive review with respect to either freedom of expression or equal protection issues is one that also serves to justify noninterpretive review with respect to substantive due process issues. (Professor Ely has articulated a theory that purports to justify noninterpretive review with respect to both freedom of expression and equal protection issues but that condemns it with respect to substantive due process issues[25]—a theory I criticize partly in chapter 3 and partly in chapter 4). Essential to my attempt to articulate a functional justification for noninterpretive review with respect to human rights issues is my effort to reconcile such review with our societal commitment to democratic—that is, electorally accountable—policymaking.

One of the most important recent developments in constitutional law is "institutional reform litigation"—cases in which inmates of prisons or of institutions for the mentally disabled challenge, on constitutional grounds, the degrading, brutal conditions in which they are frequently made to live. In the final chapter, against the background of the functional justification offered in chapter 4, I discuss the issue of the legitimacy of noninterpretive review in institutional reform cases. In particular I take issue with much recent commentary, by Nathan Glazer and others,[26] critical of the activist role the lower federal courts have assumed—appropriately, in my view—in reviewing complaints brought by prisoners and the institutionalized mentally disabled.*

In one sense, of course, the fundamental problem addressed in this book—the legitimacy of constitutional policymaking by the judiciary—is old, even if certain terms, such as *interpretive* and *noninterpretive,* are of recent coinage (and, in my view, quite useful). But the problem is also

---

*A court is *activist,* in my use of the term, if, and to the extent that, it exercises noninterpretive review (supplanting policy choices made by electorally accountable governmental officials with policy choices of its own), and *passivist* if, and to the extent that, it confines itself to interpretive review (making no policy choices of its own, but simply safeguarding policy choices constitutionalized by the framers). Of course, there are degrees of activism and passivism, and a court that is activist, to some degree, with respect to one matter—freedom of expression, say—may be passivist, to some degree, with respect to another. For a different use of the terminology, *see* J. ELY, DEMOCRACY AND DISTRUST: A THEORY OF JUDICIAL REVIEW 1–2 & n.* (1980).

perennial. What Woodrow Wilson said of the question of the proper relationship between the federal government and the governments of the states
we can certainly say of the question addressed throughout this book—that
it "cannot . . . be settled by the opinion of any one generation, because it is a
question of growth, and every successive stage of our political and
economic development gives it a new aspect, makes it a new question."[27]
The challenge faced by the contemporary constitutional theorist is to
discuss the perennial, fundamental problem of legitimacy in a manner that
escapes this relentless judgment by Robert McCloskey:

> American constitutional history has been in large part a spasmodic running
> debate over the behavior of the Supreme Court, but in a hundred seventy years
> we have made curiously little progress toward establishing the terms of this
> war of words, much less toward achieving concord. . . . [T]hese recurring
> constitutional debates resemble an endless series of re-matches between two
> club-boxers who have long since stopped developing their crafts autono-
> mously and have nothing further to learn from each other. The same generali-
> zations are launched from either side, to be met by the same evasions and
> parries. Familiar old ambiguities fog the controversy, and the contestants
> flounder among them for a while until history calls a close and it is time to
> retire from the arena and await the next installment. In the exchange of asser-
> tions and counter-assertions no one can be said to have won a decision on the
> merits, for small attempt has been made to arrive at an understanding of what
> the merits are.[28]

CHAPTER ONE

The Problem
of Legitimacy

We in the United States are philosophically committed to the political principle that governmental policymaking—by which I mean simply decisions as to which values among competing values shall prevail, and as to how those values shall be implemented[1]—ought to be subject to control by persons accountable to the electorate.[2] As a general matter, a person is accountable to the electorate *directly* if he holds elective office for a designated, temporary period and can remain in office beyond that period only by winning reelection; accountability is *indirect* if he holds appointive office and can remain in office only at the discretion of his appointer (who in turn is electorally accountable)[3] or, if his office is for a designated, temporary period, by securing reappointment after that period has expired. (I do not for a moment suppose that electorally accountable policymaking invariably generates policies supported by a majority of the electorate. Frequently it is difficult to know whether a particular policy choice enjoys such support, and not infrequently safe to say that it does not.[4]) If judicial review does not run counter to the principle of electorally accountable policymaking, it is at least in serious tension with it. (Whether judicial review—or at least *some* judicial review—runs counter to that principle is the subject of this book.) In constitutional cases, the Supreme Court, which designedly is not accountable to the electorate,[5] stands ready to strike down policy choices made by electorally accountable persons—officials of the legislative or executive branches of government, whether federal or state. The problem thus arises whether, given the principle of electorally accountable policymaking, judicial review is legitimate. In our political culture, the principle of electorally accountable policymaking is axiomatic;[6] it is judicial review, not that principle, that requires justification.[7]

Of course, one could begin the effort to justify judicial review by rejecting the principle of electorally accountable policymaking. (Every year I have several students who refuse to take the principle seriously.[8]) The justificatory enterprise is certainly much simpler if one begins that way. However, any constitutional theory predicated on a rejection of the principle of electorally accountable policymaking is destined to have little currency, since, as far as I can tell, the vast majority of the audience to whom theories of judicial review are directed regard the principle as axiomatic. Therefore, my strategy is not to reject the principle but, on the contrary, to accept it as a given and then to defend judicial review—in particular, constitutional policymaking—as not inconsistent with the principle.*

Let us begin with a fundamental distinction. There are two basic sorts of judicial review. I will refer to them, respectively, as interpretive review and noninterpretive review.[9] The legitimacy of interpretive review is not a particularly difficult problem, as we will see shortly. The legitimacy of noninterpretive review is the central problem of contemporary constitutional theory.

The distinction between interpretive and noninterpretive review can best be elaborated in terms of a particular conception of the United States Constitution. The Constitution consists of a complex of value judgments the framers wrote into the text of the Constitution and thereby constitutionalized.[10] The important such judgments—the ones that will concern us here—fall into two categories. One category of judgments defines the structure of American government by specifying the division of authority, first, between the federal government and the governments of the states and, second, among the three branches of the federal government— legislative, executive, and judicial. The other category defines the limits of governmental authority vis-à-vis the individual; this category of value judgments specifies certain aspects of the relationship that shall exist between the individual and government.[11]

The Supreme Court engages in *interpretive* review when it ascertains the constitutionality of a given policy choice by reference to one of the value judgments of which the Constitution consists—that is, by reference to a value judgment embodied, though not necessarily explicitly, either in some particular provision of the text of the Constitution or in the overall structure of government ordained by the Constitution.[12] Such review is "interpretive" because the Court reaches decision by interpreting —deciphering—the textual provision (or the aspect of governmental structure) that is the embodiment of the determinative value judgment. The

---

*If I were unable to defend constitutional policymaking by the judiciary as consistent with the principle of electorally accountable policymaking, then, given my commitment to constitutional policymaking by the judiciary, I would have to question the axiomatic character of the principle of electorally accountable policymaking. *Cf.* Fiss, *Foreword: The Forms of Justice,* 93 HARV. L. REV. 1, 42 (1979):

I realize that it may not be appropriate to demand justification of an axiom, for it is offered as a starting point, a proposition that you cannot look behind. Yet there must be more that can be said about it. Acceptance of an axiom must turn on something more than a momentary flash of intuition. . . . [T]he axiom can be assessed in terms of its consequences and its underlying social vision. An axiom might at first glance seem attractive enough, but its appeal may decline radically once its full implications are understood.

effort is to ascertain, as accurately as available historical materials will permit, the character of a value judgment the framers constitutionalized at some point in the past.

The Court engages in *noninterpretive* review when it makes the determination of constitutionality by reference to a value judgment other than one constitutionalized by the framers. Such review is "noninterpretive" because the Court reaches decision without really interpreting any provision of the constitutional text (or any aspect of governmental structure)[13] —although, to be sure, the Court may explain its decision with rhetoric designed to create the illusion that it is merely "interpreting" or "applying" some constitutional provision.[14] (I shall have more to say about the distinction between interpretive and noninterpretive review—in particular I shall defend the distinction—in chapter 3.)

Interpretivism refers to constitutional theory that claims that only interpretive judicial review is legitimate and, in particular, that all noninterpretive review is illegitimate. *Noninterpretivism* describes constitutional theory that claims that at least *some* noninterpretive review— noninterpretive review with respect to at least some categories of constitutional questions, with the categories specified by the noninterpretivist theory in question—is legitimate too. (No contemporary constitutional theorist seriously disputes the legitimacy of interpretive review.)

That the Court rarely acknowledges that it exercises noninterpretive review[15]—a matter addressed later when we consider the problem of candor—is presently beside the point. What matters is that many, indeed most constitutional decisions and doctrines of the modern period (concerning human rights issues), as we will see later, cannot fairly be understood as the products of anything but noninterpretive review,[16] and therefore cannot be deemed legitimate unless the noninterpretive review that generated them can be justified. It is also beside the point that one can imagine cases in which there would be room for a reasonable difference of opinion as to whether the framers constitutionalized a particular value judgment,* thereby making it impossible to say that the Court's decisions (in such cases), striking down challenged governmental policy choices, must be explained in terms of noninterpretive rather than interpretive review.[17] The decisions in virtually all modern constitutional cases of consequence, again, cannot plausibly be explained except in terms of noninterpretive review, because in virtually no such case can it plausibly be maintained that the framers constitutionalized the determinative value judgment.[18]

I indicated a moment ago that the legitimacy of interpretive judicial

---

*Or even cases in which there would be room for a reasonable difference of opinion as to whether a value judgment concededly constitutionalized by the framers calls for a decision sustaining or for one striking down the challenged governmental policy choice.

review is not a difficult problem. Let us first consider interpretive review of action by a state government (as opposed to action by the federal government.)* We should begin by inquiring whether interpretive review of state action is authorized by the constitutional text, because if it is, the practice is legitimate. Indeed, if mandated and not merely authorized by the text, the practice is obligatory. No one, after all, contends that our commitment to the principle of electorally accountable policymaking is exclusive. We are committed as well to the principle that electorally accountable policymaking is constrained by the value judgments embodied in the constitutional text, including judgments about what practices the various institutions of government may or must undertake.

Interpretive review by the courts of the state whose action is under review is plainly mandated by the constitutional text. The supremacy clause of Article VI provides: "This Constitution . . . shall be the supreme law of the land; and the judges in every state shall be bound thereby, anything in the constitution or laws of any state to the contrary notwithstanding." But does the text mandate or even authorize interpretive review of state action by the federal courts, in particular by the Supreme Court? There is a plausible textual justification for interpretive review of state action by the Supreme Court: Under Article III,[19] the Court is vested with appellate jurisdiction, "with such exceptions, and under such regulations as the Congress shall make," over "all cases . . . arising under this Constitution," including, therefore, cases in which a state court has determined whether challenged state action is constitutional. But the justification is merely plausible, because one cannot be certain what is meant by "all cases . . . arising under this Constitution." Hence, Alexander Bickel's conclusion was sound that

> [t]he bare text of Article III and of the Supremacy Clause is . . . equivocal. The Supremacy Clause, addressing itself to state judges alone, does put them on a different plane than state legislators and other officials. Yet it says nothing of federal judges, and hence it would not foreclose a system in which the sole reliance for the integrity and supremacy of the federal Constitution as against contravening state enactments would be on the conscientious performance of duty by state judges, subject to no other control.[20]

Although Bickel was right that the bare constitutional text is equivocal, it matters little. Indeed, even if there were no plausible textual justification

---

*The paradigmatic state action, of course, is action by a state legislature, in the form of statutory enactments. But action by any state official (acting in his or her official capacity)—a municipal policeman, say—is state action too. Moreover, under certain circumstances, action by persons who are not state officials is deemed state action for constitutional purposes. See generally L. TRIBE, AMERICAN CONSTITUTIONAL LAW 18.1–.7 (1978).

for interpretive review of state action by the Supreme Court, it would matter little. For there is a compelling functional justification—that is, a justification based on the essential function the practice serves. Under the supremacy clause, state courts are obligated to enforce and so to interpret the Constitution, and, as Bickel argued:

> There is surely ... a strong interest ... in the uniform construction and application of the Constitution as against inconsistent state law throughout the country. This is an interest fairly to be imputed to states which formed a federal union, and it is an interest that can be vindicated only by a federal institution. Congress can and in fact does from time to time perform this function, both as to statute and as to constitutional law; but, if for no other reason than that the instances in which performance of this function is necessary are extremely numerous, it is obviously sensible to lodge the function as well, and indeed chiefly, in the federal judiciary. This is not compelled by the language of the Constitution; it is implied from desirable ends that are attributed to the entire scheme. But most assuredly there is nothing in the language that forbids it. And Congress has so provided—consistently, from the first Judiciary Act of the first Congress onward—and it has done so unambiguously.[21]

Given that the interpretive review of state action the Supreme Court exercises in the course of reviewing judgments of state courts is justified on functional grounds, there is no sensible reason to oppose interpretive review of state action by the lower federal courts, so long as the judgments of those courts are subject, as they are, to revision by the Supreme Court.[22] For whether the initial judgment as to the constitutionality of challenged state action is rendered by a state court or a federal court, in either case the ultimate judgment is that of the Supreme Court.[23]

Let us now consider interpretive review of the federal government's policy choices ("federal action"). Is that practice authorized by the constitutional text? Herbert Wechsler thinks so.[24] Under the supremacy clause, says Wechsler, state courts must determine whether challenged federal action is constitutional, because it is only "laws of the United States which shall be made in pursuance" of the Constitution, which Wechsler takes to mean federal action not inconsistent with any constitutional value, that bind state courts. Under Article III, continues Wechsler, the Supreme Court is vested with appellate jurisdiction ("with such exceptions, and under such regulations as the Congress shall make") over "all cases ... arising under this Constitution," which Wechsler takes to include cases in which state courts have determined whether challenged federal action is constitutional. If, as Wechsler argues, interpretive review of federal action by state courts is authorized, indeed mandated, by the supremacy clause, and if such review is itself subject to appellate review by the Supreme

Court, it makes no sense to oppose interpretive review of federal action by the lower federal courts. The judgments of those courts are subject to revision by the Supreme Court,[25] and so whether the initial judgment as to the constitutionality of challenged federal action is rendered by a state court or a federal court, the ultimate judgment is the Supreme Court's. Indeed, if one accepts Wechsler's premises regarding the supremacy clause and Article III, it makes eminent sense to support interpretive review of federal action by the lower federal courts, which, after all, are *at least* as appropriate a forum as the state courts for the resolution of questions concerning the constitutionality of *federal* action—a point captured in the following rhetorical question by Wechsler:

> Is it a possible construction of the Constitution . . . that if Congress opts, as it has opted, to create a set of lower courts, those courts in cases falling within their respective jurisdictions and the Supreme Court when it passes on their judgments are less or differently constrained by the supremacy clause than are the state courts, and the Supreme Court when it reviews their judgments?[26]

But there is a problem with Wechsler's textual justification. It is by no means clear that the supremacy clause does in fact authorize state courts to determine whether challenged federal action is constitutional.[27] Nor is it clear what is meant, in Article III, by "all cases . . . arising under this Constitution." Once again, then, the bare text is equivocal. In response to Wechsler's attempted textual justification, Bickel asked: "Why is the power to declare federal statutes unconstitutional conceded to state courts?"[28] Bickel's answer:

> In order to enable one to lodge it in the federal courts also, and for no other reason. We have seen the need for judicial authority to construe federal statutes and treaties, and the reason for subjecting state courts to federal appellate jurisdiction when they do so. We have also seen, however, that there is no similar exigency dictating similar judicial authority and similar appellate jurisdiction when the validity of a federal statute under the Constitution is in question, because neither state nor federal courts need to decide that for themselves in the first instance; they can take it as settled for them by the federal legislature and President. The ends of uniformity and of the vindication of federal authority are served in this fashion, without recourse to any power in the federal judiciary to lay down the meaning of the Constitution.[29]

If the bare text does not supply an unequivocal justification for interpretive review of federal action, perhaps the text read in the light of history does so. The framers of the 1789 Constitution, like the framers of amendments to the Constitution, sought to communicate their value judgments by means of provisions written into the constitutional text, and where a textual provision—the supremacy clause, say, or Article III—does not by itself disclose precisely what the framers' value judgment was, one naturally turns to historical materials that might clarify what the framers meant by the provision in question.[30] Did the framers of the 1789 Constitution intend that federal action be subject to interpretive review, in particular by the Supreme Court?

There is perhaps no more disputed historical question in constitutional theory. Some, like Charles Beard[31] and, more recently, Raoul Berger,[32] have answered yes.[33] Others, like Louis Boudin,[34] William Winslow Crosskey,[35] and Learned Hand,[36] have rejected the claim that interpretive review of federal action was intended by the framers.[37] Indeed, one eminent constitutional historian, Edward Corwin, vacillated on the issue: in 1913 he argued that the framers had not intended the practice; in 1914 he changed his mind and argued that they had; and in 1937 he concluded that there is "great uncertainty" as to whether the framers intended it.[38] The record of this debate lends credibility to the conclusion of a respected contemporary constitutional historian, Leonard Levy, that the justification for the practice rests neither on the text of the 1789 Constitution nor on the intentions of the framers of the text.[39]

On what, then, does it rest? Perhaps one might try to argue that the framers of the Bill of Rights—which, unlike the provisions of the 1789 Constitution, was proposed subsequent in time to Alexander Hamilton's defense of judicial review in *Federalist #78*[40] (and ratified in 1791) —presupposed judicial review of federal action and in that sense impliedly authorized it.[41] But beyond any such historical argument, which is fated to be controversial, there is a compelling functional justification for interpretive review of federal action, and therefore the inconclusive nature of the historical debate is inconsequential, and it is regrettable that so much energy has been spent on the debate. Interpretive review of federal action serves an indispensible function, which constitutes the justification for the practice. The Constitution imposes limits on federal power that—and no one disputes this—were intended to have the force of law. Article VI says as much: "This Constitution . . . shall be the supreme law of the land."[42] Because the limits are a part of the supreme law, some institution must enforce them. Otherwise the limits are not legal norms in any meaningful sense but, at best, political-moral norms. For the generation of the framers,[43] and probably for most of us today, the concept of legality entails the notion of enforceability.

But—and this is the key question—why should the enforcing institution be the judicial rather than the legislative or the executive branch? That courts traditionally enforce—and, in enforcing, interpret—law[44] is not an adequate answer. The Constitution is not just another species of law; as the "supreme" law, it has a status superior to that of any other positive law.[45] Another answer, however, is dispositive: the judiciary is that branch of the federal government[46] with the greatest institutional capacity to enforce the legal norms of the Constitution in a disinterested way. Congress and the President, as the principal federal policymakers, have many more incentives than the judiciary to ignore constitutional limits on federal power. The classic statement in that regard, of course, is Alexander Hamilton's observation in *Federalist #78* that of the three branches of government,

> the judiciary, from the nature of its functions, will always be the least danger-ous to the political rights of the Constitution; because it will be least in a capacity to annoy or injure them. The executive not only dispenses the honors, but holds the sword of the community. The legislature not only commands the purse, but prescribes the rules by which the duties and rights of every citizen are to be regulated. The judiciary, on the contrary, has no influence over either the sword or the purse; no direction either of the strength or of the wealth of the society; and can take no active resolution whatever. It may truly be said to have neither FORCE nor WILL but merely judgment; and must ultimately depend upon the aid of the executive arm even for the efficacy of its judgments.[47]

None of this is controversial. Bear in mind that at the moment we are discussing interpretive review, which is to say the enforcement of the value judgments constitutionalized by the framers. While today it is common-place to insist that the contemporary federal judiciary, in exercising *noninterpretive* review, is no longer the passive institution Hamilton en-visioned it to be, no constitutional theorist contends that the legislative or the executive branch of the federal government has as great an institutional capacity as the judicial branch, much less a greater capacity, to exercise *interpretive* review, to enforce the framers' value judgments.

So, although the framers of the 1789 Constitution might not have specifically authorized interpretive review of federal action, they plainly did intend that the Constitution be the supreme law, and interpretive review of federal action best serves the function of fulfilling that intention, of completing the framers' vision of the Constitution as supreme law.[48] The framers sitting in the constitutional or the ratifying conventions might not themselves have thought all this through, at least, not enough of them that we can say that the framers specifically authorized interpretive review of federal action. But that fact is not particularly important, because the functional justification for interpretive review of federal action very soon thereafter became apparent:

> The legitimacy of judicial review does rest on history, but not on the words of the Constitution nor of the framers during the 1787–89 period. It was an historical outgrowth of the constitutional theory of the era of the American Revolution. *Federalist #78* and Marshall's *Marbury* opinion[49] were, sig-nificantly, arguments from general principles. . . . [J]udicial review is "the last word, logically and historically speaking, in the attempt of a free people to

establish and maintain a nonautocratic government. It is the culmination of the essentials of Revolutionary thinking, and, indeed, of the thinking of those who a hundred years and more before the Revolution called for a government of laws and not of men." . . . [J]udicial review was "the natural outgrowth of ideas that were common property when the Constitution was established." . . .[50]

The foregoing functional justification has force especially with respect to interpretive review of federal action by the Supreme Court, but it has force as well with respect to interpretive review of federal action by state and lower federal courts. Under Article III the Supreme Court may concern itself with questions regarding the constitutionality of federal action only (or virtually only) in the course of exercising its *appellate* jurisdiction over cases ("arising under this Constitution") decided in the first instance by state or lower federal courts. Consequently, some courts other than the Supreme Court must exercise judicial review of federal action if the Supreme Court is to have an opportunity to do so.[51]

Although the legitimacy of interpretive review of state and federal action is not a difficult problem, an interesting issue arises in connection with interpretive review that merits brief mention. One who believes that only interpretive review is legitimate contends that the only proper constitutional question for a court is whether the challenged governmental action is inconsistent with any value judgment constitutionalized by the framers.[52] (One who believes that at least some noninterpretive review is legitimate argues that a further question is appropriate: Notwithstanding the fact that the challenged action is not inconsistent with any of the framers' value judgments, ought it to be struck down on the basis of some other value judgment, one not attributable to the framers?)

But there are two different ways to ask that question, or, rather, two different questions: (1) Do I, the judge, think that the challenged action is inconsistent with any of the framers' value judgments?; and (2) Even if I, the judge, think that the challenged action is inconsistent with one of the framers' value judgments, can a reasonable person conclude that the challenged action is not inconsistent? Obviously those different questions are capable of generating different decisions as to the constitutionality of the challenged action. Which question ought the judge to ask who rejects noninterpretive review and so is committed solely to interpretive review?

The constitutional theorist whom Felix Frankfurter characterized as "our great master of constitutional law,"[53] James Bradley Thayer, argued that the second question was the proper one:

> If [the judges'] duty were in truth merely and nakedly to ascertain the meaning of the text of the constitution and of the impeached Act of the legislature, and to determine as an academic question, whether in the court's judgment the two

were in conflict, it would, to be sure, be an elevated and important office, one dealing with great matters, involving large public considerations, but yet a function far simpler than it really is. Having ascertained all this, yet there remains a question—the really momentous question—whether, after all, the court can disregard the Act. It cannot do this as a mere matter of course —merely because it is concluded that upon a true and just construction the law is unconstitutional. . . . It can only disregard the Act when those who have the right to make laws have not merely made a mistake, but have made a very clear one—so clear that it is not open to rational question. That is the standard of duty to which the courts bring legislative acts; that is the test which they apply—not merely their own judgment as to constitutionality, but their conclusion as to what judgment is permissible to another department which the constitution has charged with the duty of making it.[54]

Thayer's rationale was that by asking the first question, a court intrudes on the legislative function, thereby violating the separation of powers:[55]

This rule recognizes that, having regard to the great, complex, ever-unfolding exigencies of government, much which will seem unconstitutional to one man, or body of men, may reasonably not seem so to another; that the constitution often admits of different interpretations; that there is often a range of choice and judgment; that in such cases the constitution does not impose upon the legislature any one specific opinion, but leaves open this range of choice; and that whatever choice is rational is constitutional.

. . . .

[A] court cannot always . . . say that there is but one right and permissible way of construing the constitution. When a court is interpreting a writing merely to ascertain or apply its true meaning, then, indeed, there is but one meaning allowable; namely, what the court adjudges to be its true meaning. But when the true question is not that, but whether certain acts of another department, officer, or individual are legal or permissible, then this is not true. In the class of cases which we have been considering, *the ultimate question is not what is the true meaning of the constitution, but whether legislation is sustainable or not.*[56]

In a later piece, Thayer also contended that

the exercise of [judicial review], even when unavoidable, is always attended with a serious evil, namely, that the correction of legislative mistakes comes from the outside, and the people thus lose the political experience, and the moral education and stimulus that comes from fighting the question out in the ordinary way, and correcting their own errors. The tendency of a common and easy resort to this great function, now lamentably too common, is to dwarf the political capacity of the people, and to deaden its sense of moral responsibility.[57]

Thayer's position does not take adequate account of the fact that the legislative and executive branches of government cannot always be trusted to resolve in an impartial way, or, indeed, even to deliberate about, questions concerning the consistency of their actions with the framers' value judgments. As noted previously, the institutional capacity of the legislative and executive branches is not great in that respect.

Why, then, should a court defer *as a matter of course*—which is how Thayer would have it—to each and every legislative or executive opinion as to the nature of each and every one of the framers' value judgments, especially where, first, the particular opinion in question, while "not irrational," is one with which the court disagrees and, second, there is reason to doubt the other branch's institutional capacity to formulate opinions of the sort at issue in an impartial, good faith manner, unaffected by considerations of institutional or political self-interest?[58] (This is not to suggest that there are no sorts of legislative or executive opinions as to constitutionality with respect to which such deference is appropriate, merely that such deference is not proper with respect to every such "not irrational" opinion.[59]) Further, our experience with the Supreme Court in the modern period suggests that judicial review, rather than deadening, can stir the polity's sense of moral responsibility. Consider, for example, the Court's decisions in the 1950s and 1960s disestablishing racial segregation. At any rate, virtually no notable modern theorist or judge committed solely to interpretive review has endorsed Thayer's extreme position.[60] Such theorists and judges seem content to have courts ask the first question and forgo the second.[61]

The legitimacy of interpretive review of state and federal action is not only not a difficult problem, it is, as well, a largely irrelevant one. The Supreme Court's actions in virtually none of the important constitutional cases of the modern period—certainly in none of the controversial cases involving issues of human rights, including, for example, *Brown v. Board of Education*—can be explained as exercises of interpretive review. (And so the Thayerian issue that arises in connection with interpretive review is largely irrelevant too.) The Court's actions in virtually all of these cases must be explained, as I later demonstrate, as exercises of noninterpretive review. Thus the truly relevant problem is the legitimacy of noninterpretive review. That, the central and most difficult problem of contemporary constitutional theory, is the subject of the rest of this book.

Is noninterpretive review, whether of state or federal action, authorized by the constitutional text? (Again, although we are committed to the principle of electorally accountable policymaking, we are no less committed to the principle that such policymaking is constrained by the value judgments embodied in the constitutional text.) The bare text is equivocal with respect even to most interpretive review. No one has claimed, or could claim, that by itself the text authorizes and thereby legitimates noninterpretive review—the enforcement of value judgments *other than* those the framers constitutionalized.

Does any provision of the constitutional text read in the light of history authorize noninterpretive review? That is, did the framers—*any* framers, whether those of the 1789 Constitution, the Bill of Rights (1791), or, for example, the fourteenth amendment (1868)—intend that state or federal action be subject to noninterpretive review, in particular by the Supreme Court? Bear in mind what it means to claim that the framers authorized noninterpretive review: the claim is necessarily that at some point (or points) in American history governmental officials delegated to the judiciary, in particular to the Supreme Court, authority to enforce against government, not particular value judgments the framers had deliberated and constitutionalized, but unspecified value judgments not constitutionalized or even always foreseen by the framers. That would have been a remarkable delegation for politicians to grant to an institution like the Supreme Court, given the electorate's long-standing commitment to policymaking—to decisions as to which values shall prevail, and as to how those values shall be implemented—by those accountable, unlike the Court, to the electorate. It is difficult enough to defend even interpretive review by reference to the intentions of the framers. It is most unlikely that noninterpretive review can be defended in that fashion.

Note, however, that to say that the framers did not intend the judiciary to undertake a noninterpretive function is not necessarily to say that the framers intend the judiciary not to undertake such a function.* Raoul Berger argues that the framers of the 1789 Constitution intended the

---

*If the framers intended that the judiciary not undertake noninterpretive review of any sort, the exercise of noninterpretive review by the modern Supreme Court would be not merely *extraconstitutional*—beyond any value judgment the framers constitutionalized—which it is, but *contraconstitutional*—contrary to one of those judgments. For an example of reliance on this distinction, see J. CHOPER, JUDICIAL REVIEW AND THE NATIONAL POLITICAL PROCESS: A FUNCTIONAL RECONSIDERATION OF THE ROLE OF THE SUPREME COURT xvii–xviii (1980) "At various points throughout this book, I have made reference to statements by the framers of the Constitution. ... I have not used these materials to suggest that the major propositions advocated in the book were originally ordained. Rather, ... I mean only to show that my proposals are not at war with original intent [not, *i.e.*, contraconstitutional]." For other examples see J. ELY, DEMOCRACY AND DISTRUST: A THEORY OF JUDICIAL REVIEW 123, 236 n. 37 (1980).

Arguably, the Supreme Court's decision in Home Building & Loan Association v. Blaisdell, 290 U.S. 398 (1934), was contraconstitutional and so poses a problem of legitimacy distinct from the problem posed by constitutional policymaking that generates (merely) extraconstitutional decisions. My concern in this book, however, is the legitimacy of extraconstitutional policymaking, not contraconstitutional policymaking. Virtually none of the modern Court's constitutional policymaking is contraconstitutional.

judiciary not to undertake policymaking in constitutional cases. His rationale is that the framers specifically rejected a proposal that the judicial branch of the federal government participate in a Council of Revision, the responsibility of which would have been "to examine every act of Congress and by its dissent to constitute a veto."[62] According to Berger, the framers "drew a line between the judicial reviewing function, that is, *policing* grants of power to insure that there were no encroachments beyond the grants, and legislative policymaking *within* those bounds.[63] The historical record Berger examines does in fact establish that the framers decided against giving the judiciary any part of a certain sort of veto over acts of Congress, a negative to be used, like the presidential veto, on any ground whatsoever.[64] Nonetheless, Berger's argument must be rejected. Noninterpretive review need not constitute such an all-purpose veto, and if it does not, if instead its character is much more circumscribed, and if further the framers did not even contemplate noninterpretive review thus circumscribed, of course it cannot be said that the framers intended the judiciary not to exercise such review.[65]

One of the most distinctive recent efforts to justify noninterpretive review by reference to the intentions of the framers is that of John Ely. Interpretivists argue that the judiciary should enforce, as constitutional constraints against government, only value judgments constitutionalized by the framers and therefore must not enforce constraints the framers did not specify. But, says Ely, two constitutional provisions—the ninth amendment and the privileges or immunities clause of the fourteenth amendment—disclose the framers' judgment that individuals shall be deemed to have constitutional rights beyond merely those specified by the framers.[66] The ninth amendment, which, like the rest of the Bill of Rights, was intended to constrain only the federal government,[67] provides that "[t]he enumeration in the Constitution, of certain rights, shall not be construed to deny or disparage others retained by the people." The privileges or immunities clause provides that "[n]o State shall make or enforce any law which shall abridge the privileges or immunities of citizens of the United States." Neither the language nor the legislative history of the ninth amendment, nor the language nor, according to Ely,[68] the legislative history of the fourteenth amendment, indicates what those unspecified rights might be. Thus, concludes Ely, if the judiciary should enforce, as interpretivists argue it should, value judgments constitutionalized by the framers, it must enforce the value judgments disclosed by the ninth amendment and the privileges or immunities clause and therefore must somehow define and enforce constraints the framers did not specify—the unenumerated norms to which the ninth amendment and the privileges or immunities clause refer.[69] For that reason, says Ely, interpretivism—the theory that the judiciary may not enforce constraints not specified by the framers—is an impossible position to maintain.[70]

Ely's argument is infirm. Consider first Ely's ninth amendment point. Even if the ninth amendment discloses the judgment that individuals shall be deemed to have rights against the federal government beyond those specified by the framers, that judgment does not itself authorize noninterpretive review of federal action—it does not authorize the judiciary to define what those rights shall be and enforce them. Ely anticipates this criticism, but his response is flawed:

> It would be a cheap shot to note that there is no legislative history specifically indicating an intention that the Ninth Amendment was to receive judicial enforcement. There was at the time of the original Constitution little legislative history indicating that *any* particular provision was to receive judicial enforcement: the Ninth Amendment was not singled out one way or the other.[71]

But, as I suggested earlier, even if the framers did not authorize interpretive review of federal action—judicial enforcement of norms specified by the framers—it matters little, for there is a compelling functional justification for such review. Ely's response, however, completely overlooks the fact that the functional considerations that explain and justify *interpretive* review of federal action under the first or fourth amendment, say, have utterly no force with respect to *noninterpretive* review under the ninth amendment.

The justification for interpretive review of federal action is that without it, constraints specified by the framers would not have the status of "supreme law" that the framers plainly intended them to have. But that cannot be the justification for noninterpretive review under the ninth amendment. Unlike interpretive review, noninterpretive review does not secure the status of *existing* constraints—constraints previously specified by the framers—as supreme law, but entails judicial creation of *new* constraints—constraints not previously specified or, for the most part, even foreseen by the framers. There is, after all, a radical difference between judicial enforcement of existing constitutional constraints, which is interpretive review, and judicial creation of new ones, which is noninterpretive review. If the judiciary does not exercise noninterpretive review under the ninth amendment, the status of existing constraints as supreme law is not imperiled; the judiciary simply declines to fashion new constitutional constraints. Thus, not only does the legislative history of the ninth amendment disclose no judgment by the framers that the judiciary should exercise noninterpretive review of federal action, but, significantly, the functional considerations that justify interpretive review of federal action under other constitutional provisions simply have no force with respect to noninterpretive review under the ninth amendment.[72]

Of course, if the ninth amendment had been intended to consti-tutionalize a determinate set of constraints on the federal govern-ment—albeit unenumerated constraints, such as the dictates of "natural justice"—it would then be possible to maintain that judicial enforce-ment of the ninth amendment *does* secure the status of existing constraints—constraints previously constitutionalized (but not enumer-ated or otherwise specified) by the framers—as supreme law. But history does not disclose that the framers intended to incorporate by reference into the ninth amendment a determinate set of constraints. And Ely does not claim otherwise. (If it did disclose such an intention, there would still remain the problem that history does not disclose what those constraints might be.[73])

Consequently, an interpretivist can easily reply to Ely that whereas functional considerations fairly compel the judiciary to enforce constraints specified by the framers, those same considerations do nothing to under-write judicial creation of constraints not specified or even foreseen by the framers. So far as the ninth amendment is concerned, Ely is wrong: inter-pretivism is *not* an impossible position to maintain.[74]

The fatal problem with Ely's privileges-or-immunities-clause point is that it rests on an inaccurate reading of the intentions of the framers of the fourteenth amendment. We will consider the matter of the original under-standing of the fourteenth amendment in chapter 3. For now, suffice it to say that substantial evidence supports the conclusion that the framers, in using the phrase "privileges or immunities of citizens of the United States," meant only to protect, against state action discriminating on the basis of race, a narrow category of "fundamental" rights: those pertaining to the physical security of one's person, freedom of movement, and capac-ity to make contracts and to acquire, hold, and transfer chattels and land—"life, liberty, and property" in the original sense.[75]

But if that historical conclusion is controversial—indeed if I am wrong in believing that the original understanding of the fourteenth amendment was so narrow—no matter. My error would in no way strengthen Ely's position. Even if the original understanding was somewhat broader, the fact remains that there is simply no credible evidence to support Ely's claim that "the Privileges or Immunities Clause . . . was a delegation to future constitutional decision-makers [that is, the judiciary] to protect certain rights that the [Constitution] neither lists, at least not exhaustively, nor even in any specific way gives directions for finding."[76] It was simply not the intention of the framers of the fourteenth amendment to authorize the judiciary to exercise noninterpretive review under any open-ended provision.[77]

At the close of his effort to root noninterpretive review in the language and original understanding of both the ninth amendment and the privileges or immunities clause, Ely sounds a curious note. He suggests that the legitimacy of noninterpretive review

> is a question on which history cannot have the last word, at least not the last affirmative word. If a principled approach to judicial enforcement of the Constitution's open-ended provisions cannot be developed, one that is not hopelessly inconsistent with our nation's commitment to representative democracy, responsible commentators must consider seriously the possibility that courts simply should stay away from them.[78]

First, Ely is wrong. History could have had the last affirmative word. If in fact the framers had authorized the judiciary to exercise (some sort of) noninterpretive review, there would be no problem of legitimacy. To the contrary, there would be a serious question as to the legitimacy of the judiciary's forsaking that office. Again, our societal commitment is not simply to the principle of electorally accountable policymaking; we are committed as well to the coequal principle that such policymaking shall be constrained by the value judgments the framers constitutionalized, including, as I said earlier, judgments about what practices the various institutions of government may or must undertake.

But, second, what difference does it make that in fact the framers did not authorize the judiciary to exercise noninterpretive review, if a principled approach to noninterpretive review can be developed, one that is consistent with our nation's commitment to representative democracy? For in that case the problem of legitimacy will have been solved: it will have been shown that noninterpretive review need not be inconsistent with our commitment to the principle of electorally accountable policymaking. Therefore, given that in his book Ely argues that a principled approach, consistent with the commitment to representative democracy, *can* be developed,[79] it is puzzling why Ely even tries (struggles?) to establish the implausible historical proposition that the intentions of the framers ordain (at least some) noninterpretive review: The contrary proposition—that the intentions of the framers do not warrant noninterpretive review—should be, for Ely, inconsequential.

There is no plausible textual or historical justification for constitutional policymaking by the judiciary—no way to avoid the conclusion that noninterpretive review, whether of state or federal action, cannot be justified by reference either to the text or to the intentions of the framers of the Constitution. The justification for the practice, if there is one, must be functional. If noninterpretive review serves a crucial governmental function that no other practice realistically can be expected to serve, and if it serves that function in a manner that somehow accommodates the principle of electorally accountable policymaking, then that function constitutes the justification for noninterpretive review. Those who seek to defend noninterpretive review—"judicial activism"—do it a disservice when they resort to implausible textual or, more commonly, historical arguments; nothing is gained but much credibility is lost when the case for noninterpretive review is built upon such frail and vulnerable reeds.

Before we turn to the question of whether there is a functional justification for noninterpretive review, a preliminary issue merits consideration. If there is a functional justification, it is affirmative in character, consisting in the main of a claim or complex of claims about the importance of the function the practice serves, the incapacity of other practices to serve the function, and desirability, therefore, of maintaining the practice. There is, however, a negative justification for noninterpretive review, or rather a "negative requirement,"[80] to which I will refer as the requirement of *principled explanation*. That negative requirement is, more precisely, a necessary but not sufficient condition for the legitimacy of noninterpretive review—and, indeed, of judicial review generally, including interpretive review.[81] No exercise of judicial review, which is to say no constitutional decision or, more broadly, doctrine, that fails to comply with the requirement of principled explanation can be deemed legitimate. But compliance with that *negative* requirement does not by itself establish legitimacy, since there might be no *affirmative* justification for the sort of judicial review being exercised, especially if that review consists of policymaking with respect to an issue of a sort—a federalism issue, say—with which the judiciary, in its constitutional-policymaking capacity, probably ought not to concern itself.

Why is there a requirement of principled explanation, and what does it entail? Consider what judicial review involves: the judiciary, once it concludes that challenged governmental action is constitutionally infirm, strikes down a policy choice made by officials accountable to the electorate and thereby substitutes a different policy choice, a different value judgment, whether one constitutionalized by the framers (interpretive review) or some other one (noninterpretive review). Such judicial invalidation ought to be explained; ought to be accompanied by reasons. What could conceivably justify a failure to give reasons? A failure to explain frustrates political dialogue, essential in a representative democracy. Relatedly, by concealing its reasons from scrutiny and criticism the court maximizes the chances of unsound judgment. Most importantly, while no policymaker *should* fail to give reasons, if in our political community any policymaking institution *may* fail to explain, it is certainly not the judiciary. To suggest that courts are not obligated to proffer principled explanations, that instead they may make policy (or do anything else) by fiat, is to suggest that "courts are free to function as a naked power organ," in which case "it is an empty affirmation to regard them . . . as courts *of law*."[82] (By contrast, "[n]o legislature or executive is obligated by the nature of its function to support its choice of values by the type of reasoned explanation that I have suggested as intrinsic to judicial action—however much we may admire such a reasoned exposition when we find it in those other realms."[83])

Obviously not just any explanation—any set of reasons—will do the trick. What conditions must an explanation satisfy if it is to comply with the requirement of principled explanation? Herbert Wechsler's answer is as sound as it is classic:

> [T]he main constituent of the judicial process is precisely that it must be genuinely principled, resting with respect to every step that is involved in reaching judgment on analysis and reasons quite transcending the immediate result that is achieved. To be sure, the courts decide, or should decide, only the case they have before them. But must they not decide on grounds of adequate neutrality and generality, tested not only by the instant application but by others that the principles imply? Is it not the very essence of judicial method to insist upon attending to such other cases, preferably those involving an opposing interest, in evaluating any principle avowed?
>
>   . . . .
>
> A principled decision . . . is one that rests on reasons with respect to all the issues in the case, reasons that in their generality and their neutrality transcend any immediate result that is involved.[84]

In Wechsler's view, then, an explanation must invoke only norms deemed by the court to have force apart from the particular result they ordain in the case at hand—that is, norms that are both neutral and general. A court "gives a neutral principle, in Wechsler's sense, if [it] states a basis for a decision that [it] would be willing to follow in other situations to which [the principle] applies."[85] And a principle is "adequately general," in Wechsler's sense, if it reaches "out beyond the narrow circumstances of the case."[86] An explanation that does not comply with the requirement of principled explanation—an explanation in which the desired result is determinative ("We reach result X because we prefer result X, period")—is essentially an exercise in sheer will, in fiat, and no one suggests that a court of law may frustrate electorally accountable policymaking, or do anything else, on the basis of simple fiat.[87]

Let us be clear, as too many commentators have not been, about what the requirement of principled explanation, in particular Wechsler's articulation of it, does and does not involve.[88] First: Contrary to the claim of some,[89] the requirement is not that judicial review be "value neutral," which obviously it cannot be, since judicial review entails the enforcement of value judgments. Wechsler does not "deny that constitutional provisions are directed to protecting certain values or that the principled development of a particular provision is concerned with the value or the values thus involved."[90] Rather, the requirement—in Wechsler's terms, "[t]he demand of neutrality"—

is that a value and its measure be determined by a general analysis that gives no weight to accidents of application, finding a scope that is acceptable whatever interest, group, or person may assert the claim. So, too, when there is a conflict among values having constitutional protection, calling for their ordering or their accommodation, . . . the principle of resolution must be neutral in a comparable sense (both in the definition of the individual competing values and in the approach that it entails to value competition).[91]

Second: Contrary to the claim of others,[92] the requirement of principled explanation is not inconsistent with the common-law method of developing constitutional doctrine incrementally and even tentatively. Addressing the problem of "how the court's reasons must 'indicate to us how future cases are to be decided,' " Wechsler says:

> [T]he court decides the case at hand and not the cases that have not arisen. . . . But it is one thing to anticipate such future cases that perhaps may be distinguishable, without deciding the sufficiency of the distinction. It is quite another thing to judge the instant case in terms that are quite plainly unacceptable in light of other cases that it is now clear are covered by the principle affirmed in reaching judgment and indistinguishable upon valid grounds. . . . [T]he principle of the decision must be viable in reference to applications that are now foreseeable; and that viability implies a similar decision or the existence of a possibly acceptable distinction. Nothing less will satisfy the elements of generality and of neutrality implicit in the concept of a legal judgment as distinguished from the fiat of a court.[93]

Third, and most important for present purposes: The requirement of principled explanation is not the whole game, or even the most important part of it. While each and every exercise of judicial review must comply with the requirement in order to be legitimate,[94] compliance is not sufficient for purposes of legitimacy. The question whether an explanation invokes only norms deemed by the court to have force apart from the particular result they ordain is distinct from the question whether the norm or norms invoked are the proper ones under all the circumstances. In particular, it is distinct from the question of whether the source of norms from which the invoked norms are derived—for example, "conventional morality"—is an appropriate one for constitutional adjudication.[95] Which brings us back to the central problem of contemporary constitutional theory: Whether—and, if so, in what respects and to what extent—the judiciary may enforce, as constitutional norms, values beyond those constitutionalized by the framers.

My principal aim in this book is to elaborate a functional justification for noninterpretive review with respect to human rights issues. I now want to set forth the essential position of those who argue that only interpretive review is legitimate and that no functional justification for noninterpretive review is adequate—that the judiciary may not legitimately enforce any values not constitutionalized by the framers. That position, interpretivism, is the one to which any functional justification must respond and with which it must deal. And it makes sense to sketch the basic features of interpretivism here at the outset. However, I do not want to criticize interpretivism in this chapter. That comes later, in the course of elaborating the functional justification.

For the interpretivist, as for others, it is axiomatic that governmental decisions as to which values, among competing values, shall prevail, and as to how those values shall be implemented, should be subject to control by persons accountable, directly or indirectly, to the electorate. The interpretivist does not overlook the fact that there are constitutional constraints on electorally accountable policymaking. But those limits consist solely of the value judgments constitutionalized by the framers. The will and judgment of persons accountable to the electorate should be limited not by the countervailing will and judgment of the judiciary, but only by the will and judgment of the framers, which it is the judiciary's office to enforce.[96] Interpretivism reflects a popular—"civics book"—understanding of the division of governmental authority in the American political system, and that, of course, is part of its appeal: In the United States, the basic function of the legislature is to make policy, sometimes in conjunction with the other electorally accountable branch of government, the executive; the basic function of the executive is to administer policy; and the sole function of the judiciary, in constitutional cases, is to police policymaking and administration by keeping it within constitutional bounds.*

According to interpretivism, it is illegitimate, in terms of the "democratic" norms of American political culture, for legislative policymaking and executive policy administration to exceed constitutional bounds. But it is also illegitimate for the judiciary to engage in constitutional

---

*In nonconstitutional cases, of course, the judiciary exercises concededly legitimate policymaking functions, those of legislating the "common law" and of fleshing out, or filling in the interstices of, statutory law. (There is no sharp line between those two functions. See P. BATOR, P. MISHKIN, D. SHAPIRO, & H. WECHSLER, HART & WECHSLER'S THE FEDERAL COURTS AND THE FEDERAL SYSTEM 770 (1973)). Both functions, however, are undertaken by the judiciary in its role as delegate of the legislature; whatever policy choices the judiciary makes in nonconstitutional cases are subject to revision by the ordinary processes of electorally accountable policymaking. In that sense, nonconstitutional policymaking by the judiciary is electorally accountable, even if the judges themselves are not. See J. CHOPER, JUDICIAL REVIEW AND THE NATIONAL POLITICAL PROCESS: A FUNCTIONAL RECONSIDERATION OF THE ROLE OF THE SUPREME COURT 132 (1980); J. ELY, DEMOCRACY AND DISTRUST: A THEORY OF JUDICIAL REVIEW 4 (1980); SANDALOW, Judicial Protection of Minorities, 75 MICH. L. REV. 1166 (1977). Cf. J. ELY, supra this note, at 68: "All too often commentators working in fields other than constitutional law, fields where appeals to this sort of filtered consensus may make sense, seek to transfer their analytical techniques to the constitutional law area without dropping a stitch."

policymaking—noninterpretive judicial review—as opposed to constitutional *interpretation*. The question of the precise constitutional bounds that legislative policymaking and executive policy administration may not exceed must be answered by interpretation, not policymaking—that is, answered by reference to the value judgments constitutionalized by the framers. When the judiciary invokes the Constitution to invalidate challenged governmental action not contrary to any of those judgments, it frustrates the will of electorally accountable officials acting within their constitutional bounds and, moreover, exceeds its own constitutional bounds and thus acts lawlessly.

Interpretivism has many proponents and many more adherents. Among the better known contemporary proponents are William Rehnquist[97] and Raoul Berger.[98] Perhaps the most able and articulate proponent of interpretivism—and therefore opponent of noninterpretivism—is Robert Bork. Throughout this book I take Bork's views to constitute an exemplar of contemporary interpretivism.[99] Therefore, I want to quote some key passages of Bork's provocative lecture on "the proper role of the Supreme Court under the Constitution":[100]

Society consents to be ruled undemocratically within defined areas by certain enduring principles believed to be stated in, and placed beyond the reach of majorities by, the Constitution.

. . . [I]t follows that the Court's power is legitimate only if it has, and can demonstrate in reasoned opinions that it has, a valid theory, derived from the Constitution, of the respective spheres of majority and minority freedom. If it does not have such a theory but merely imposes its own value choices, or worse if it pretends to have a theory but actually follows its own predilections, the Court . . . abets the tyranny either of the majority or of the minority.

. . . .

. . .[N]o argument that is both coherent and respectable can be made supporting a Supreme Court that "chooses fundamental values" because a Court that makes rather than implements value choices cannot be squared with the presuppositions of a democratic society.

. . . .

. . .Where constitutional materials do not clearly specify the value to be preferred, there is no principled way to prefer any claimed human value to any other. The judge must stick close to the text and the history, and their fair implications, and not construct new rights.

. . . .

. . . Where the Constitution does not embody the moral or ethical choice, the judge has no basis other than his own values upon which to set aside the community judgment embodied in the statute. That, by definition, is an inadequate basis for judicial supremacy.

. . . Courts must accept any value choice the legislature makes unless it clearly runs contrary to a choice made in the framing of the Constitution.

. . . .

... There is no principled way in which anyone can define the spheres in which liberty is required and the spheres in which equality is required. These are matters of morality, of judgment, of prudence. They belong, therefore, to the political community. In the fullest sense, these are political questions.[101]

Using Professor Wechsler's requirement of neutral principles as a point of departure, Bork continues:

Recognition of the need for principle is only the first step, but once that step is taken much more follows. Logic has a life of its own, and devotion to principle requires that we follow where logic leads.

. . . .

... We have not carried the idea of neutrality far enough. We have been talking about neutrality in the *application* of principles. If judges are to avoid imposing their own values upon the rest of us, however, they must be neutral as well in the *definition* and the *derivation* of the principles.

It is easy enough to meet the requirement of neutral application by stating a principle so narrowly that no embarrassment need arise in applying it to all cases it subsumes, a tactic often urged by proponents of "judicial restraint." But that solves very little. It certainly does not protect the judge from the intrusion of his own values.[102]

Bork suggests that his view is the professed (though not the actual) view of the Supreme Court,[103] and he seizes on that profession as evidence that his view is—or that the Court thinks it is—the prevailing popular view:

The Supreme Court regularly insists that its results, and most particularly its controversial results, do not spring from the mere will of the Justices in the majority but are supported, indeed compelled by a proper understanding of the Constitution of the United States. Value choices are attributed to the Founding Fathers, not to the Court. The way an institution advertises tells you what it thinks its customers demand.[104]

Critics of interpretivism—who typically, of course, are defenders of noninterpretivism—achieve nothing by pretending that interpretivism is not a forceful theory. Several lines of attack on interpretivism, which I will briefly mention now, should be rejected outright. Interpretivism posits a commitment to the principle of "majoritarian" policymaking in the sense of policymaking that is electorally accountable. The anti-interpretivist claim that, in the United States, policymaking is not all that majoritarian, in the sense that often it is not nearly as reflective of the sentiments of actual majorities as some persons think, is beside the point even if true—and doubtless it is true.[105] For example, Geoffrey Hazard has recently written that most legislation emanating from legislatures in modern times is chiefly the product of committees and experts, and sometimes committees of experts. The same is true of administrative agencies, which produce the bulk of contemporary legislation. . . . [I]f . . . neither Congress nor the agencies adequately express public sentiment, it is hard to see why the Supreme Court should be subject to special criticism because it also does not express that sentiment.[106]

But Hazard is wrong. It is not at all hard to see why. What is crucial about majoritarian policymaking, unlike constitutional policymaking by the Supreme Court, is that policy decisions are made by those *accountable,* even if not always *responsive,* to electoral majorities. True, as I indicated at the very beginning of this chapter, that accountability may be only indirect. But it is electoral accountability nonetheless, and that fact, which has crucial theoretical significance,[107] has great practical importance as well. As Robert Dahl has put it in his classic study:

> [T]he radical democrats who, unlike Madison, insist upon the decisive importance of the election process in the whole grand strategy of democracy are essentially correct. To be sure, if the social prerequisites of polyarchy do not exist, then the election process cannot mitigate, avoid, or displace hierarchical government. But if the social prerequisites of polyarchy do exist, then the election is the critical technique for insuring that governmental leaders will be relatively responsive to non-leaders; other techniques depend for the efficacy primarily upon the existence of elections and the social prerequisites.[108]

Professor Hazard also notes that "it can be said that through various mechanisms internal to legislatures and external to administrative agencies, the 'general will' is somehow made to infuse statutes and administrative regulations so that they are withal the product of a democratic process."[109] "But," he says, "even if that is so, it has to be demonstrated why, by some comparable mechanism, the 'general will' does not also infuse decisional lawmaking in courts."[110] Again Hazard misses the point. What is crucial is electoral accountability, not degree of responsiveness to majority sentiments. Beyond that, as an intuitive matter electoral accountability makes for greater responsiveness; certainly the burden is on Hazard to demonstrate the contrary. And, if the foregoing passage by Dahl is accurate, it makes for greater responsiveness as an experiential matter as well.[111]

The anti-interpretivist claim that nonjudicial policymakers are not always accountable in any very meaningful sense[112]—a lame-duck or second-term President, for example, or the members of the Federal Reserve Board—is very weak. First, the principal such policymakers, that is, legislators, are meaningfully accountable—at least, all those seeking reelection, the vast majority, are. Second, whatever nonjudicial policymakers are not meaningfully accountable hold office only for comparatively short periods of time and so (1) are not likely to be out of touch with dominant political sentiments and in any event (2) can frustrate such sentiments only for short periods; moreover—and this is crucial—their decisions are subject to revision by the ordinary processes of electorally accountable policymaking.[113] Finally, and most important, given our commitment to the principle of electorally accountable policymaking, the claim that not all nonjudicial policymakers are meaningfully accountable counts less as a reason to applaud the existence of electorally unaccountable judicial policymakers, than to make nonjudicial policymakers who are not meaningfully accountable, truly accountable.[114] (The claim that the judiciary is not significantly less accountable than many other governmental policymakers is simply not true. The Supreme Court and the lower federal courts, which are the chief constitutional policymakers in the United States, are not *electorally* accountable at all.)

Nor will it do to attack interpretivism by confusing it with what is essentially a straw man, "literalism," and then demonstrating the obvious infirmity of the latter. No notable constitutional theorist, to my knowledge, has ever contended that the judiciary should enforce constitutional provisions according to their "plain meaning" and should studiously ignore all else, including the original understanding of the provisions. First, many important provisions—for example, "due process of law," "equal protection of the laws," "freedom of speech"—have no *plain* meaning. Second, even the most ardent interpretivists recognize that what has priority is not the particular configuration of words the framers used in drafting a constitutional provision, but rather the value judgment the framers meant to embody in those words.[115] Ascertaining the precise character of the framers' value judgments often requires reference to historical materials that disclose the framers' intentions.[116]

Similarly, so far as I am aware no theorist has ever argued that the judiciary should invalidate only political practices that were present to the minds of the framers and the framers meant to ban. The interpretivist concedes that the judiciary may, even should, strike down political practices that were not present to the minds of the framers and that, therefore, the framers could not have specifically intended to ban. But invalidation of such a political practice is legitimate, according to interpretivism, only if the practice is the analogue of a practice the framers did contemplate and mean to ban, different in no constitutionally significant respect from the practice the framers specifically intended to ban.[117] After all, enforcing value judgments the framers constitutionalized certainly requires invalidation of practices different in no significant respect from those the framers banned.[118] Thus, for example, the interpretivist need not oppose Supreme Court decisions subjecting wiretaps and electronic surveillance to the same fourth amendment standards as physical "searches and seizures."[119] On the other hand, the interpretivist must oppose the Court's decisions invalidating racially segregated public schooling and antimiscegenation laws,[120] because those practices were present to the minds of the framers but the framers chose not to ban them; those decisions cannot fairly be characterized as enforcing value judgments the framers constitutionalized.[121] At any rate, interpretivism is not literalism of any sort; to demonstrate the patent inadequacy of the latter is not to attack the former.[122]

There are two final, preliminary matters I want to address in this chapter. The first concerns the relationship between interpretivism and the claim that generally constitutional provisions should be construed broadly, generously, because, as Chief Justice Marshall declared in one of the most frequently quoted statements in all of constitutional law, "we must never forget that it is *a constitution* we are expounding."[123] The Constitution, said Marshall, is "intended to endure for ages to come, and, consequently, to be adapted to the various *crises* of human affairs. . . . It would have been an unwise attempt to provide, by immutable rules, for exigencies which, if foreseen at all, must have been seen dimly, and which can be best provided for as they occur."[124] The very nature of the Constitution, an *organic* charter of government, the argument runs, is not congenial to interpretivism, which would confine all later generations of Americans to the value judgments of the framers' generation. Moreover, the argument continues, the framers doubtless did not mean to confine posterity to their own late-eighteenth-century vision, for that would have been a cautious, conservative intention, not at all characteristic of the framers, who were bold men, architects of an ambitious new government.[125]

Although in some respects that argument has merit, as a response to interpretivism it is wholly inadequate. It is one thing to construe broadly a constitutional provision granting a particular power to government, in the sense and with the consequence of sustaining an electorally accountable—typically, a legislative—policy choice that the framers might not have contemplated government would make or need to make. That is what Marshall did in *McCulloch v. Maryland*, in which he made the statements quoted above. It is a radically different thing to construe broadly a constitutional provision limiting the power of government, in the sense and with the consequence of striking down an electorally accountable policy choice on the basis of no value judgment fairly attributable to the framers. Interpretivism opposes the latter, not the former.[126] The latter is countermajoritarian and thus poses the problem of legitimacy, which, in the interpretivist's view, is insoluble. The former is not countermajoritarian; in fact it does not even involve the judiciary's broad construction of a power-granting provision of the Constitution so much as the judiciary's deference to the electorally accountable policymaker's impliedly broad construction of the provision. Listen again to Marshall in *McCulloch*, sustaining a congressional act by reasoning that the new federal government could not hope to function effectively without some latitude under the power-granting provisions of the Constitution:

> The subject is the execution of those great powers on which the welfare of a nation essentially depends. It must have been the intention of those who gave these powers, to insure . . . their beneficial execution. This could not be done by confiding the choice of means to such narrow limits as not to leave it in the power of Congress to adopt any which might be appropriate, and which were conducive to the end. This provision[127] is made in a constitution intended to endure for ages to come, and, consequently, to be adapted to the various *crises* of human affairs. To have prescribed the means by which government should, in all future time, execute its powers, would have been to change, entirely, the character of the instrument, and give it the properties of a legal code. It would have been an unwise attempt to provide, by immutable rules, for exigencies which, if foreseen at all, must have been seen dimly, and which can be best provided for as they occur.[128]

Quite likely, then, for the compelling reason Marshall suggested, the framers did design the power-granting provisions of the Constitution to be, to some extent, organic. The framers likely expected that posterity, in the sense of later generations acting through the processes of electorally accountable policymaking, would give shape to certain aspects of the constitutional order that were, in 1789, somewhat indeterminate.[129] If one accepts such premises—and I see no reason not to—it is appropriate, for example, for the Supreme Court to defer to Congress's impliedly expansive reading of the commerce clause* by sustaining modern federal regulatory legislation.[130] But, again, to sustain is one thing, to strike down quite another. There is no historical evidence that the framers expected, much less intended, that the Supreme Court would frustrate electorally accountable policymaking by rendering its own expansive readings of the *power-limiting* provisions of the Constitution. Nor can the organic nature of the *power-granting* provisions explain such a practice. To invoke, in support of such a practice, and therefore in opposition to interpretivism, the organic nature of those provisions, or the intentions of the framers, or Marshall's statements in *McCulloch,* is to betray a fundamental confusion of one mode of judicial activity—invalidation of challenged policy choices

---

*The commerce clause provides that "Congress shall have power . . . to regulate commerce . . . among the several states." U.S. CONST. art. I, § 8, cl. 3.

on the basis of expansive judicial readings of power-limiting provisions—with a palpably different mode—validation of challenged policy choices on the basis of judicial deference to impliedly expansive nonjudicial (electorally accountable) readings of power-granting provisions.[131] And it is an evasive confusion, one that begs a central question:

> It is no answer to argue . . . "we cannot have our government run as if it were stuck in the end of the eighteenth century when we are in the middle of the twentieth," because . . . the real issue is *who is to make the policy choices* in the twentieth century: judges or the combination of legislature and electorate that makes constitutional amendments.[132]

The final matter I want to address here concerns Charles Black's emphatic and persistent counsel that, when discussing the legitimacy of judicial review, it is imperative to distinguish review of state from review of federal action. Let me explain why I do not heed that counsel in much of what follows. Black's position is that judicial review of federal action, in particular of congressional acts, "may be thought to pose a problem [of legitimacy]—a problem to which the right solution was found [in *Marbury v. Madison*[133]], I think, but a problem nonetheless."[134] But, continues Black,

> there simply is no problem about the fundamental legitimacy of judicial review of the actions of the states for federal constitutionality. Article VI [of the Constitution] says as much, literally and directly. . . . [T]here is nothing in our entire governmental structure which has a more leak-proof claim to legitimacy than the function of the courts in reviewing state acts for federal constitutionality. . . . [The legitimacy of this function] is not so much as fairly debatable.[135]

Along the way, Black faults his (then) colleague, Alexander Bickel, for "indicating summarily that he perceives the problem [of the legitimacy of review of state action] as much the same [as that of review of federal action]. . . ."[136] Black's reference is to this closing passage of chapter 1 of Bickel's *The Least Dangerous Branch:*

> The foregoing discussion of the origin and justification of judicial review has dealt for the most part indiscriminately with the power of the federal courts to strike down deferral legislation and the power of those courts to pass on actions of the states. There are, of course, differences. . . . Yet it remains true that when the Court invalidates the action of a state legislature, it is acting against the majority will within the given jurisdiction; what is more, it also promises to foreclose majority action on the matter in issue throughout the country. The court represents the national will against local particularism; but it does not

represent it, as Congress does, through electoral responsibility. The need to effectuate the superiority of federal over state law is not a sufficient justification for judicial review of state actions in those instances in which the federal law in question is constitutional and hence judge-made. In this respect also, therefore, the function must be supported by the [functional] reasons we have surveyed.[137]

Whose position is sounder—Black's or Bickel's? Black, who faults Bickel and others[138] for failing to heed what Black sees as the critical distinction, overlooks a distinction at least as critical—that between interpretive review and noninterpretive review. If the question under discussion is the legitimacy of *interpretive* review, Black is right that one must distinguish review of state from review of federal action. There is a plausible—and in Black's view much more than plausible[139]—textual justification for the former but probably not the latter. (Recall that there is a compelling, but different, functional justification for each.) But if instead the question being discussed is the legitimacy of *noninterpretive* review, the distinction between review of state and review of federal action is not at all crucial.[140] Both are "countermajoritarian," as Bickel's passage makes clear; both entail constitutional policymaking—as opposed to interpretation—by the judiciary; and, as we will later see, the necessary functional justification is really no different for one than for the other. Which question is Black addressing—the legitimacy of interpretive or, instead, of noninterpretive review? All the cases Black mentions—"the school prayer and Bible-reading decisions, . . . the decisions desegregating the state school systems, . . . The decisions reapportioning the state legislatures, . . . the series of decisions imposing more stringent rules on police and prosecutorial misconduct"[141]—must be understood as instances of noninterpretive review. (Why that is so is explained in chapter 3.) And in any event the principal question addressed in this book is the legitimacy of noninterpretive review. Thus the distinction between review of state and review of federal action does not loom large in the chapters that follow.[142]

CHAPTER TWO

Noninterpretive Review, Federalism, and the Separation of Powers

There are three basic sorts of constitutional issues, as I indicated in the prologue, and, correspondingly, it is useful to conceive of three basic types of constitutional policymaking, or noninterpretive review: the noninterpretive review the Court exercises in resolving human rights issues; the noninterpretive review it exercises in resolving federalism issues; and the noninterpretive review it exercises in resolving separation-of-powers issues.

The essential argument of interpretivist constitutional theory is that, given the principle of electorally accountable policymaking, *all* noninterpretive judicial review is illegitimate; the Supreme Court ought never to strike down challenged governmental action as unconstitutional, unless the challenged action is inconsistent with a value judgment attributable to the framers of the Constitution. Because interpretivism admits of no significant distinctions among different sorts of noninterpretive review but holds all such review illegitimate, if even one sort of noninterpretive review can be justified, interpretivism will have been undermined. The issue will then have become simply what other sorts of noninterpretive review, if any, are legitimate too.

The principal concern of this book is the problem of the legitimacy of the noninterpretive review the Court exercises in resolving issues of human rights. The resolution of human rights issues is the most important constitutional function of the Court, and of the judiciary generally, in the modern period. And it is also the most controversial function, because frequently the positions the Court takes on the human rights issues that come before it are so widely and hotly disputed. But the Court resolves other sorts of constitutional issues as well, and before turning to the problem of the legitimacy of noninterpretive review with respect to human rights issues, I want to test interpretivism by inquiring into the possibility of justifying either, or both, of the other two basic sorts of noninterpretive review: noninterpretive review with respect to federalism issues, and that with respect to separation-of-powers issues.*

---

*Some readers may think that this chapter, because it does not deal with constitutional adjudication in human rights cases, does not belong in this book. But any theory of judicial review that aspires to completeness must address the issue of the legitimacy of noninterpre-

The Constitution consists of a complex of value judgments constitutionalized by the framers, and one category of such judgments defines the structure of American government by specifying the division of authority, first, between the federal government and the governments of the states and, second, among the three branches of the federal government. The basic issue in a *federalism* case is whether challenged action by one government, state or federal, exceeds the scope of its constitutional authority and thereby invades the authority (or autonomy) of the other government, federal or state. Under the Constitution, certain legislative authority is delegated to the federal government—for example, Congress has authority "to regulate commerce . . . among the several states"[1]—and authority not so delegated is reserved to the states.[2]

The sort of constitutional case in which the Court most frequently strikes down challenged *state* action on federalism grounds—and thus the sort of federalism case that can usefully serve as our frame of reference at this point—is one in which the challenged action has an adverse impact on the flow of commerce—raw materials, finished products, transportation, or the like—into or out of the state in question.[3] The Court's decisions in many such cases cannot be characterized and defended as products of interpretive review. The constitutional text—here, the commerce clause—and the intentions of the framers are simply too indeterminate[4] to explain the Court's rulings. In many, perhaps most such cases, the Court strikes down the challenged action—the policy choice made by an electorally accountable agency of state government, typically the legislature—not on the basis of a determinate value judgment constitutionalized by the framers, but rather on the basis of the Court's own judgment as to the exigencies of national commerce.[5]

Is there any justification for such a practice? There is a plausible textual justification for interpretive review of state action, and also a compelling functional one. Both, however, are irrelevant, because what is presently at issue is not interpretive review—not judicial invalidation of challenged governmental action on the basis of a value judgment constitutionalized by the framers.

Compelling functional considerations justify the practice of striking down certain challenged state action on the basis of the Court's own judgment as to the requirements of national commerce. The material well-being of the country requires that national commerce not be balkanized by multifarious and parochial state regulations that disrupt the free flow of commerce among the states. Because it has unquestioned constitutional authority "to regulate commerce . . . among the several states," Congress

---

tive review in both federalism and separation-of-powers cases. Of course, the reader who is not particularly interested in that topic may want to skip this chapter.

can act to displace any state regulation that, in its view, improvidently affects interstate commerce. But Congress rarely acts for the purpose of displacing particular state regulations; more commonly it enacts a regulatory provision to deal with a perceived problem, which provision, under the supremacy clause, has the consequence of "preempting" any state regulation inconsistent with the national policy explicit or implicit in the federal provision. Frequently a court must decide whether a challenged state regulation is inconsistent with and thus preempted by a federal regulatory provision.[6] Often, however, there is no preemptive federal provision; at the same time, there is no federal law ratifying explicitly or implicitly the state regulation as consistent with national policy regarding interstate commerce. Then the court, and ultimately the Supreme Court, will decide whether the challenged state regulation is consistent with the requirements, as the Court sees them, of national commerce. Should the Court proceed differently; should it, in the face of congressional silence, presume congressional acquiescence[7] and simply sustain the state regulation as a matter of course?

The answer is no. There must be national policy regarding many aspects of interstate commerce—a policy that is nonparochial and, moreover, uniform throughout the country—if that commerce is to retain its national character and not be balkanized. Consequently, there must also be a national policymaking body to fashion that policy and, incident thereto, to supervise state regulations adversely affecting interstate commerce to determine whether such regulations are consistent with the requirements of national commerce. Under the Constitution, ultimate supervisory authority rests with Congress as a part of its power "to regulate commerce . . . among the several states." But Congress lacks the institutional capacity to attend to the details of hundreds if not thousands of local laws adversely affecting interstate commerce. As Ernest Brown has observed:

> [The] mechanisms of our government . . . give to Congress [no] opportunity or duty of reviewing, to test for compatibility with the federal system, state statutes even in their skeletal form as enacted, much less as fleshed out by application, interpretation and administration. Nor has Congress been so idle that such matters could be assured a place on its agenda without competition from other business which might often be deemed more pressing; in Justice Jackson's phrase, the inertia of government would be heavily on the side of the centrifugal forces of localism.[8]

Therefore, it has fallen to the judiciary, and hence to the Supreme Court, to attend to the details and to determine whether local laws brought before it are consistent with the demands of national commerce.[9]

This functional justification for the judicial practice of reviewing, and sometimes invalidating, challenged state action on the basis of the Court's own judgment as to the requirements of national commerce is widely accepted.[10] Does that mean the conventional wisdom accepts as legitimate at least one sort of noninterpretive review—of state action on federalism grounds—with the consequence that interpretivism is undermined? The answer is plainly no. Although the cases in which the Court undertakes that practice are nominally "constitutional" cases—or, more narrowly, "federalism" or "commerce clause" cases—in reality they are not constitutional cases at all—at least, not in the usual sense—*and do not involve noninterpretive judicial review.*

In such cases, the Court acts not as a constitutional policymaker but only as a legislative policymaker. The Court fashions aspects of national policy regarding interstate commerce essentially as the delegate of Congress, which has ultimate legislative authority over national policy regarding interstate commerce. What policy the Court fashions in such cases is not constitutional policy subject to revision only by the extraordinary processes of constitutional amendment, but legislative policy subject to revision by the ordinary processes of electorally accountable lawmaking. Specifically, it is subject to revision by Congress, an electorally accountable policymaking body.[11] Although I am making this point—that the cases in which state action is challenged on federalism grounds are not really constitutional cases—with particular reference to "commerce clause" cases, it has a more general force, as the following comment by Herbert Wechsler would suggest:

> [The] question whether state enactments shall be stricken down as an infringement on the national authority . . . is . . . primarily a matter for congressional determination in our system as it stands. For while the Court has an important function in this area, . . . the crucial point is that its judgments here are subject to reversal by Congress, which can consent to action by the states that otherwise would be invalidated. *The familiar illustrations in commerce and in state taxation of federal instrumentalities do not exhaust the field.* The Court makes the decisive judgment only when—and to the extent that—Congress has laid down the resolving rule.[12]

Thus far, therefore, the essential argument of interpretivism—that all noninterpretive judicial review is illegitimate—remains intact. True, in many, perhaps most, of the federalism cases in which it invalidates state action, the Court does not exercise interpretive review—does not, that is, base its decision on a value judgment constitutionalized by the framers—but rather acts as a policymaker. And true, compelling functional considerations justify that policymaking. But the Court's policymaking in such cases is plainly something quite distinct from noninterpretive judicial review.[13] In acting as Congress's delegate, the Court functions much as an administrative agency, also Congress's delegate, would function—subject to ultimate congressional control. And so the Court's policymaking, in such cases, is fully consistent with the principle of electorally accountable policymaking and does not give rise to the problem of legitimacy.[14]

Let us now test interpretivism by inquiring into the possibility of justifying noninterpretive review in the other basic type of federalism case—in which the Court is asked to determine whether *federal* action, typically congressional legislation, invades the authority (or autonomy) of state government. Only twice since the late 1930s has the Court invalidated congressional legislation on federalism grounds; one of those cases is particularly controversial and is considered later in this chapter.[15] In none of the important federalism cases of the controversial 1895–1936 period[16] (all of which have since been explicitly or implicitly overruled)[17] did the Court's decisions striking down congressional legislation represent exercises of interpretive review—applications of value judgments constitutionalized by the framers.

The constitutional grants of legislative authority to Congress—certainly those grants that have proven most important: the power to regulate interstate commerce, to tax, and to spend[18]—are, as a matter both of constitutional text and of the intentions of the framers, quite indeterminate in scope. And deliberately indeterminate too, for the framers intended to grant Congress a great deal of legislative authority—perhaps all the legislative authority Congress would likely need, in the framers' late-eighteenth-century view, to deal effectively with whatever problems might arise which the states individually would not be competent to handle.[19] So the framers, as Chief Justice Marshall early noted, designed the power-granting provisions of the Constitution to be organic.

Consequently, it is difficult to imagine enactment of congressional legislation so far afield as to justify the conclusion that the legislation is *ultra vires* even under a latitudinarian construction of the relevant power-granting constitutional provision.[20] It is not surprising, therefore, that the consensus of constitutional commentary is that in the pre-1937 period the Court's decisions striking down congressional legislation on federalism grounds were the product of what we now call noninterpretive review; the Court, or rather a majority of the Court, acted on the basis of its own—not the framers'—judgments as to the proper division of legislative authority between the federal government and the governments of the states.

Is it possible to justify noninterpretive review of congressional legislation on federalism grounds? As I indicated in the previous chapter, there is no textual or historical justification for any sort of noninterpretive review, and so none exists for noninterpretive review of congressional legislation on federalism grounds (or any other grounds for that matter). But what about *Federalist #78*, in which Alexander Hamilton emphasized that the federal judiciary would have authority under the proposed Constitution, indeed would be obligated, to declare void, in a case properly before it, any act of Congress in excess of its delegated powers:

> [E]very act of a delegated authority, contrary to the tenor of the commission under which it is exercised, is void. No legislative act, therefore, contrary to the Constitution, can be valid. To deny this would be to affirm that the deputy is greater than his principal; that the servant is above his master; that the representatives of the people are superior to the people themselves; that men acting by virtue of powers may do not only what their powers do not authorize, but what they forbid.[21]

First, Hamilton's discussion is, at best, evidence that the framers authorized *interpretive* review of congressional legislation on federalism grounds, since what Hamilton defended was judicial enforcement of the value judgments—here, judgments as to the proper division of legislative authority between federal and state government—constitutionalized by the framers in their capacity as representatives of "the people".[22]

But, second, *Federalist #78* is at best equivocal evidence that the framers of the 1789 Constitution—at least, the men who, in 1787, drafted the document—authorized even interpretive review of congressional legislation. Leonard Levy's argument to that effect is sound:

> [*Federalist #78*] was a response to Robert Yates's "Letters of Brutus," an antiratificationist series which sought to discredit the Constitution by magnifying the powers of the federal judiciary into an engine for consolidating national powers at the expense of the states. *Federalist #78*, in other words, was an attempt to quiet the fears stimulated by Yates; turning the latter's argument against him, Hamilton tried to convince his readers that the Court's power was intended to hold Congress in check, thereby safeguarding the states against national aggrandizement. A few other advocates of the Constitution, like Oliver Ellsworth and John Marshall, sought in the same manner to allay popular apprehensions that Congress might exceed its power, especially in the absence of a Bill of Rights to protect the people. Their remarks, like Hamilton's in *Federalist #78*, are evidence of shrewd political tactics, not of the framers' intention to vest judicial review in the Supreme Court over acts of Congress.[23]

Levy's reconstruction gains support from the fact that

> Hamilton offered to the [Constitutional] Convention a complete plan for a new constitution no part of which remotely provided for any sort of judicial review. In *Federalist #33*, where he discussed the necessary and proper clause,[24] which antiratificationists regarded as vesting carte blanche powers in Congress, Hamilton asked who was to judge if Congress "should overpass the just

bounds of its authority." Not once in his answer did he allude to the Supreme Court. Congress in the first instance and the people in the last would judge.[25]

But this is a digression. The present issue is not whether interpretive review of federal action was authorized by the framers, but whether noninterpretive review of federal action on federalism grounds can be justified. Certainly it cannot be justified on the basis of either the constitutional text or the intentions of the framers.

Is there a functional justification for such review? In an influential essay on "The Political Safeguards of Federalism,"[26] Herbert Wechsler has developed a thesis that in effect constitutes a compelling argument that no such justification exists. Wechsler's thesis is that:

> [T]he national political process in the United States—and especially the role of the states in the composition and selection of the central government—is intrinsically well adapted to retarding or restraining new intrusions by the center on the domain of the states. Far from a national authority that is expansionist by nature, the inherent tendency in our system is precisely the reverse, necessitating the widest support before intrusive measures of importance can receive significant consideration, reacting readily to opposition grounded in resistance within the states. Nor is this tendency effectively denied by pointing to the size or scope of the existing national establishment. However useful it may be to explore possible contractions in specific areas, such evidence points mainly to the magnitude of unavoidable responsibility under the circumstances of our time.[27]

If Wechsler's thesis is substantially sound, as I think it is, then there is simply no need for the Supreme Court to protect the states from the national government by arrogating to itself a policymaking role in cases in which federal action is challenged on federalism grounds—a judicial role in which the Court strikes down congressional enactments in furtherance of federalism policies of the Court's own making, policies (concerning the proper division of authority between the national government and state governments) hostile to the will of the national government even if congenial to the will of some states.

In partial support of his thesis Wechsler emphasizes the fact that both houses of Congress are constituted by persons who are politically beholden to constituencies back home in their respective states and, therefore, who can be counted on to be sensitive to local as well as national interests. Wechsler quotes James Madison: "A local spirit will infallibly prevail much more in the members of Congress, than a national spirit will prevail in the legislatures of the particular states."[28]

My students, who tend to be much better political scientists than I, insist

that the political safeguards of federalism, such as they are, do not constitute an adequate protection for "the institutional interests of state governments as such," as opposed to protection for "the substantive interests of
groups influential in particular states."[29] But why suppose that the federal
character of American government should protect the interests of states
qua states—what is special about those interests?—rather than the interests of various groups within the states that would probably be unable to
count on effective representation in the national councils of a nonfederal
government? (I know that the Constitution was designed in part to protect
the interests of the states qua states—that is, the states' interests in maintaining their [limited] sovereignty and their [limited] autonomy free from
intrusions by the federal government—but that's beside the present point,
which is that the political safeguards of federalism militate against noninterpretive review. I am not arguing that they also militate against interpretive review—against, that is, judicial enforcement of the framers' value
judgments regarding what particular institutional interests of the states
merit protection.)

But even assuming that the relevant interests are "the institutional interests of state governments as such," the political safeguards of federalism
do serve to obviate any need for an activist judicial role in reviewing
congressional enactments on federalism grounds. Let me explain, briefly,
why that is so.

Recall that the present issue is not interpretive review—not, that is,
whether the Court ought to protect the states' constitutional authority and
autonomy, as (roughly) defined by the framers, from congressional trans-
gressions. Rather, the issue is noninterpretive review—whether the Court
ought to make its own policy judgments and thereby override the (implicit)
policy judgments of Congress as to the proper division of legislative authority between federal and state governments. Given existing political
safeguards of federalism, there is little if any reason to suppose that local
interests or even the interests of states qua states—which at the very least
"are brought to the attention of Congress by groups seeking to augment
their more substantive arguments for limited use of congressional
power"[30]—will be overlooked. In the course of congressional policymaking those interests will be attended to—which is not to say that they will
always, nor indeed should they always, prevail. Thus, why should the
Court undertake to resolve the competing interests anew? The Court is not
more competent to deal with such questions, which concern, after all, the
highly pragmatic political problem of which level of government ought to
govern with respect to a given matter; to the contrary, prima facie the
national legislators themselves, a majority of whom have also been state
legislators,[31] are more competent. Nor is there any reason to suppose that
the political processes are incapable of dealing with such questions in a

deliberate and impartial manner, especially given the political safeguards of federalism built into those processes.[32]

Wechsler is therefore on safe ground in concluding as he does:

> This is not to say that the Court can decline to measure national enactments by the Constitution when it is called upon to face the question in the course of ordinary litigation; the supremacy clause governs there as well. It is rather to say that the Court is on weakest ground when it opposes its interpretation of the Constitution to that of Congress in the interest of the states, whose Representatives control the legislative process and, by hypothesis, have broadly acquiesced in sanctioning the challenged Act of Congress. Federal intervention against the states is thus primarily a matter for congressional determination in our system as it stands.[33]

In terms of the distinction, on which contemporary constitutional theory insists, between interpretive and noninterpretive judicial review, Wechsler's analysis points clearly to the conclusion that there is no functional justification for noninterpretive review of congressional legislation on federalism grounds.* Once again, therefore, interpretivism remains intact.

Recently Jesse Choper has taken Wechsler's thesis a step further by arguing that the political safeguards of federalism justify abandonment of *any* judicial review of congressional legislation on federalism grounds—which necessarily means that the Court ought to abandon even interpretive review. Choper proposes that:

> The federal judiciary should not decide constitutional questions respecting the ultimate power of the national vis-à-vis the states; rather, the constitutional issue of whether federal action is beyond the authority of the central govern-

---

*Which is not to say that Wechsler himself reached that conclusion. He, after all, was not thinking in terms of the distinction between interpretive and noninterpretive judicial review.

It is fanciful to suppose that a compelling functional justification for noninterpretive review of congressional legislation on federalism grounds can be predicated on the claim that (many) federalism issues are, at bottom, human rights issues of one sort or another. For a discussion and refutation of such a claim, see J. CHOPER, supra prologue, note 9, 244–58; see also id. at 201–03.

For an argument—not at all persuasive, in my view—that a somewhat activist judicial role *is* proper in cases in which congressional legislation is challenged on federalism grounds, see Kaden, supra note 28.

With respect to action of the executive branch of the federal government, the principal political safeguards of federalism—safeguards inherent in the way *Congress* goes about its business—are inoperative. Therefore, is there any functional justification for noninterpretive review, on federalism grounds, of federal executive action? The question is largely academic, since threats to the institutional interests of state governments virtually always emanate from Congress.

ment and thus violates "states' rights" should be treated as nonjusticiable, final resolution being relegated to the political branches—i.e., Congress and the President.[34]

There are at least two serious problems with Choper's extreme thesis. First: It is at odds with the compelling functional justification for interpretive review of federal action. The framers intended that the norms they constitutionalized be the "supreme law," and their intention in that regard requires—even if the framers did not themselves specifically authorize—judicial enforcement of constitutional norms, including the power-granting provisions of Article I.[35] Hamilton recognized as much in *Federalist #78*. And Wechsler recognizes it too; he acknowledges that "the Court can[not] decline to measure constitutional enactments by the Constitution . . . ; the supremacy clause governs there as well."[36]

Second: Although the political safeguards of federalism help to assure that relevant local and state interests will not be overlooked, they do not guarantee a resolution congenial to those interests. And if the relevant interests are of concern only to a small minority of states, the resolution is likely to be uncongenial.[37] That fact of political life is not particularly important where the federalism question is merely one of policy, as it is, by hypothesis, when the Court is called upon to exercise what amounts to noninterpretive review of congressional legislation. There is no "correct" answer to the policy question; all that really matters is that the various competing interests be aired. But the fact *is* crucial where the question is the content of a norm—here, a power-granting provision—constitutionalized by the framers, as it is, again by hypothesis, when the Court is called upon to exercise interpretive review of congressional legislation. There is, in principle at least, a correct answer to that essentially historical question; and, in principle, even one small state has a right to the correct answer.

In the end, however, the difference between Choper's and Wechsler's respective positions is more academic than real. It is exceedingly difficult to imagine enactment of congressional legislation so far afield that it could be invalidated on federalism grounds in the exercise of interpretive review.[38] But precisely because Choper's proposal is not practically different from Wechsler's, and also because serious theoretical difficulties attend it, it will not, I suspect, influence the Supreme Court. But be that as it may, note that Choper's thesis serves to *reinforce* rather than undermine my claim that there is no functional justification for noninterpretive review of congressional legislation on federalism grounds.

For nearly four decades after 1937, it seemed that the Supreme Court had largely adopted Wechsler's thesis—in practice if not always in rhetoric: the Court declined to invalidate any congressional legislation on federalism grounds.[39] Then, in 1976, in *National League of Cities v. Usery*,[40] a bare majority of the Court struck down the 1974 amendments to the Fair Labor Standards Act.[41] If the result in *National League of Cities* can only be explained as a product of noninterpretive review on federalism grounds, then, given the lack of any functional or other justification for such review, the conclusion is inescapable that the Court's decision in *National League of Cities* was illegitimate.

Justice Rehnquist, who wrote the opinion for the five-man majority in *National League of Cities*[42] described the challenged statutory scheme in the following terms:

> [The Fair Labor Standards Act, enacted by Congress in 1938,] required employers covered by the Act to pay their employees a minimum hourly wage and to pay them at one and one-half times their regular rate of pay for hours worked in excess of 40 hours during a work week. . . . [The Act] specifically excluded the States and their political subdivisions from its coverage. . . . By its 1974 amendments, Congress has now entirely removed the exemption previously afforded States and their political subdivisions. . . . The Act thus imposes upon almost all public employment the minimum wage and maximum hour requirements previously restricted to employees engaged in interstate commerce.[43]

The majority did not contend—indeed the parties challenging the 1974 amendments did not claim—that the challenged provisions exceeded the inherently limited scope of Congress's power "to regulate commerce . . . among the several states."[44] Rather, the majority concluded that the amendments, although within the commerce power, exceeded an affirmative limitation on congressional legislative authority[45] Implicit in the federal structure of American government[46] and, in the majority's view, explicit in the text of the tenth amendment.[47]

However, the majority was far from clear as to the precise content of this limitation or as to how the 1974 amendments violated it. Here is the crux of what the majority had to say:

> [T]he amendments . . . will . . . significantly alter or displace the States' abilities to structure employer-employee relationships in such areas as fire prevention, police protection, sanitation, public health, and parks and recreation. . . . [I]t is functions such as these which governments are created to provide, services such as these which the States have traditionally afforded their citizens. If Congress may withdraw from the States the authority to make those fundamental employment decisions upon which their systems for performance of these functions must rest, . . . there would be little left of the States' "separate and independent existence." . . . [T]he dispositive factor is that Congress has attempted to exercise its Commerce Clause authority to prescribe

minimum wages and maximum hours to be paid by the States in their capacities as sovereign governments. In so doing, Congress has sought to wield its power in a fashion that would impair the States' "ability to function effectively within a federal system.". . .[48]

Then the majority stated its holding: "[I]nsofar as the challenged amendments operate to directly displace the States' freedom to structure integral operations in areas of traditional governmental functions," they are unconstitutional.[49]

Even if the reader does not find the majority's reasoning as amorphous as I do,[50] and, indeed, even if the reader is inclined to agree on *policy* grounds with the majority's critique of the 1974 amendments, a fundamental problem remains. Unless the majority's decision striking down the amendments can be explained as a product of interpretive review, it is illegitimate. The crucial question, then, is whether *National League of Cities* can be explained in terms of interpretive review. The answer to that question is clear. No value judgment constitutionalized by the framers even plausibly required the result in *National League of Cities*. True, the framers obviously intended the states to exist as separate political entities within the federal system, governing and making policy within their own spheres to the extent not inconsistent with the governing and policymaking activities of the national government acting within the scope of its delegated powers.[51] But, again, not even the majority claimed that in adopting the 1974 amendments Congress had acted outside the scope of the commerce power delegated to it. And the majority's claim that the amendments threatened the existence of the states as separate political entities in the federal system was nothing short of fanciful, especially when one considers the extent of the federal monies Congress pours into the states to permit them to comply with federal programs as well as to implement programs of their own.[52]

Whether the majority's position was sound as a policy matter—whether as a policy matter Congress should have enacted the 1974 amendments—is wholly beside the point. The majority's position was manifestly unsound as an institutional matter—as a matter of the Court's proper role in federalism cases. There is no excuse for the noninterpretive review exercised by the majority in *National League of Cities*, which alone explains the result reached there. Justice Brennan, writing in dissent for himself and for Justices White and Marshall, was right that "[i]t is unacceptable that the judicial process should be thought superior to the political process in *this area.*"[53] Citing Wechsler's political-safeguards essay, Brennan continued: "Judicial restraint in this area merely recognizes that the political branches of our Goverment are structured to protect the interests of the States, as well as the Nation as a whole, and that the States are fully able to protect their own interests in the premises."[54] Ironically, the noninterpretivist result in *National League of Cities* was announced in an opinion written by the staunchest and most articulate defender of interpretivism presently sitting on the Supreme Court, William Rehnquist[55]—which suggests that there might be some distance between Rehnquist's constitutional theory and his judicial practice.[56]

Our brief consideration of the Court's proper roles in the two basic types of federalism cases has not turned up any reason to question the soundness of the interpretivist claim that there is no justification for noninterpretive review. Let us now test interpretivism by inquiring into the possibility of justifying yet another sort of noninterpretive review—noninterpretive review with respect to separation-of-powers issues. The basic issue in a separation-of-powers case is whether challenged action by one branch of the federal government—legislative, executive, or judicial—unjustifiably invades the authority (or autonomy) of a coordinate branch. In one sense, this entire book is about a key problem in separation-of-powers theory: whether constitutional policymaking by the judiciary—noninterpretive review—unjustifiably invades the policymaking authority of electorally accountable institutions of government. But in general the separation-of-powers cases that come before the Supreme Court involve a claim either that executive action has invaded congressional prerogatives[57] or that congressional action has invaded executive prerogatives.[58]

As indicated in the previous chapter, only equivocal support for *interpretive* review of federal action can be derived from the text of the Constitution or the intentions of the framers. And this is no less true of interpretive review with respect to separation-of-powers issues than of interpretive review generally. Commenting on the constitutions of the states, James Madison, in *Federalist #47*, observed that "in no instance has a competent provision been made for maintaining in practice the separation [of powers] delineated on paper."[59]

Well, what "competent provision" did the framers of the United States Constitution make? Judicial review? Apparently not. In *Federalist #51*, Madison wrote:

> To what expedient, then, shall we finally resort, for maintaining in practice the necessary partition of power among the several departments as laid down in the Constitution?
> . . . [T]he great security against a gradual concentration of the several powers in the same department consists of giving to those who administer each department the necessary constitutional means and personal motives to resist encroachments of the others. . . . Ambition must be made to counteract ambition. The interests of the man must be connected with the constitutional rights of the place.[60]

Thus, as one contemporary commentator on the separation-of-powers has observed, "[i]n the design of the framers, the checks and balances system of the separation-of-powers was articulated with far greater clarity than the specific institution of judicial review."[61] No matter, though, for, again, there is a compelling functional justification for interpretive review of federal action,[62] and therefore for interpretive review with respect to separation-of-powers issues.

But is there any justification for *noninterpretive* review with respect to separation-of-powers issues? Certainly there is no textual or historical justification. A functional justification, then? What functional considerations, if any, justify judicial invalidation of challenged federal action on separation-of-powers grounds, when it cannot be said that the action is inconsistent with any value judgment constitutionalized by the framers? The issue is hardly academic: often it cannot be said that the challenged action contravenes any of the framers' judgments regarding the separation-of-powers. The framers' judgments regarding separation, after all, like their judgments regarding the federal character of American government, and for much the same reason, are somewhat indeterminate. They did not mean to establish, and thus the text of the Constitution does not ordain, a precise, airtight separation of federal powers.[63] "The accommodations among the three branches of the government are not automatic. They are undefined, and in the very nature of things could not have been defined, by the Constitution. To speak of *lines* of demarcation is to use an inapt figure. There are vast stretches of ambiguous territory."[64]

Consider the famous concurring opinion by Justice Jackson in *The Steel Seizure Case*,[65] in which the Supreme Court ruled that President Truman's order seizing the nation's steel mills invaded the legislative prerogatives of Congress, which earlier had considered but decided against enacting a provision that would have authorized such seizure under certain conditions.[66] Jackson acknowledged the virtual impossibility of resolving many separation-of-powers problems by reference to value judgments constitutionalized by the framers:

> A judge . . . may be surprised at the poverty of really useful unambiguous authority applicable to concrete problems of executive power as they actually present themselves. Just what our forefathers did envision, or would have envisioned had they foreseen modern conditions, must be divined from materials almost as enigmatic as the dreams Joseph was called upon to interpret for Pharaoh. A century and a half of partisan debate and scholarly speculation yields no net result but only supplies more or less apt quotations from respected sources on each side of any question. They largely cancel each other.[67]

Thus, in many separation-of-powers cases the Court must decide whether to defer as a matter of course to the challenged federal action or, instead, to exercise noninterpretive review and resolve the challenge on the basis of its own judgment, not the framers', as to the proper allocation of power between the legislative and executive branches of the federal government.*

Jackson's concurring opinion is suggestive of a framework for deciding when deference is appropriate and when, on the other hand, what we are calling noninterpretive review is in order. According to Jackson, the Court ought to assume a deferential stance when the legislative and executive branches agree that the challenged federal action is within the jurisdiction of the branch that took it. (Jackson articulated this and his other points as befits a case in which executive action, not legislative, was under review.)

> When the President acts pursuant to an express or implied authorization of Congress, his authority is at its maximum, for it includes all that he possesses in his own right plus all that Congress can delegate. In these circumstances, and in these only, may he be said . . . to personify the federal sovereignty. If his act is held unconstitutional under these circumstances, it usually means that the Federal Government as an undivided whole lacks power. A seizure executed by the President pursuant to an Act of Congress would be supported by the strongest of presumption, and the widest latitude of judicial interpretation, and the burden of persuasion would rest heavily upon any who might attack it.[68]

Even if the Court would not necessarily be saying that "the Federal Government as an undivided whole lacks power,"[69] there is a fundamental reason for a deferential stance—for not exercising noninterpretive review—in a case in which there is legislative and executive concord: the utter absence of any reason, of any *need*, for the Court to substitute its own policy judgment as to the proper allocation of power for the *joint* judgment of Congress and the President. Certainly the Court is not more competent than Congress and the President to make such policy judgments, which concern the highly pragmatic political problem of which of the two branches of government is better positioned to take the action in question. And certainly too there is little reason to suspect that Congress and the President lack the political motivation to arrive at their agreement in a forthright, reasonable manner.

In his concurring opinion in *The Steel Seizure Case*, Justice Jackson identified a second sort of separation-of-powers case—one in which there is neither agreement nor disagreement between the legislative and execu-

---

*The reader might wonder whether it must always be either/or. Cannot the Court be guided by the "broad conceptions" of the framers? But presumably the challenged governmental action is also guided, if implicitly, by those same broad conceptions. In rendering the framers' broad conceptions more concrete, the Court ultimately relies on its own particular judgment, not the framers', as to the proper allocation of power—in the circumstances of the case —between the legislative and executive branches.

tive branches as to whether the challenged federal action is within the jurisdiction of the branch that took it.[70] As a practical matter, such a case is likely to be one in which executive action is challenged. Congress does not always have occasion to express agreement or disagreement with executive action. On the other hand, the President usually expresses agreement or disagreement with legislation enacted by Congress—by either signing or vetoing it. In any event, Jackson suggested no functional considerations, and I can conceive of none, that would justify noninterpretive review in separation-of-powers cases in which there is neither agreement nor disagreement between the legislative and executive branches.

Consider, in that regard, Justice Powell's concurring opinion in a recent case, *Goldwater v. Carter*,[71] in which President Carter's termination of the treaty with Taiwan was challenged on separation-of-powers grounds. The case was one in which there was neither agreement nor disagreement between Congress and the President, and Powell's sensitive opinion recognized that not only was there no need for judicial resolution of the issue on the merits, but that such a resolution might have sinister consequences:

> Prudential considerations persuade me that a dispute between Congress and the President is not ready for judicial review unless and until each branch has taken action asserting its constitutional authority. Differences between the President and the Congress are commonplace under our system. The differences should, and almost inevitably do, turn on political rather than legal considerations. The Judicial Branch should not decide issues affecting the allocation of power between the President and Congress until the political branches reach a constitutional impasse. Otherwise, we would encourage small groups or even individual Members of Congress to seek judicial resolution of issues before the normal political process has the opportunity to resolve the conflict.
>
> In this case, a few Members of Congress claim that the President's action in terminating the treaty with Taiwan has deprived them of their constitutional role with respect to a change in the supreme law of the land. Congress has taken no official action. In the present posture of this case, we do not know whether there ever will be an actual confrontation between the Legislative and Executive Branches. Although the Senate has considered a resolution declaring that Senate approval is necessary for the termination of any mutual defense treaty, . . . no final vote has been taken on the resolution. Moreover, it is unclear whether the resolution would have retroactive effect. . . . It cannot be said that either the Senate or the House has rejected the President's claim. If the Congress chooses not to confront the President, it is not our task to do so.[72]

Occasionally my students argue that the separation-of-powers implicates "human rights" to a greater extent than does the federal character of American government, and that if noninterpretive review can be justified in cases involving issues of human rights, it can be justified in separation-of-powers cases too, including those in which there is legislative-executive concord. They suggest that whereas the principal beneficiaries of federalism are the states "as states," the principal beneficiaries of the separation-of-powers are individual persons. Then they cite, for example, Montesquieu, who claimed that the dispersal of governmental power among legislative, executive, and judicial branches prevented the tyranny that would ensue if too much power, much less the whole power of government, were located in one branch,[73] or *Federalist #47*, in which Madison, echoing Montesquieu, wrote that "[t]he accumulation of all powers legislative, executive, and judiciary in the same hands, whether of one, a few, or many, and whether hereditary, self-appointed, or elective, may justly be pronounced the very definition of tyranny."[74]

It is not necessary to question whether or to what extent the separation-of-powers really serves to prevent "tyranny." (If I did raise that question, my students would likely respond that the framers apparently thought the extent was great, and that the Court must abide the framers' judgment in that regard.) For even accepting that the separation-of-powers somehow and to some extent serves to prevent tyranny, my students' argument still will not work. In a separation-of-powers case in which the legislative and executive branches agree—or at least do not disagree—that the challenged federal action is within the jurisdiction of the branch that took it, *and in which no value judgment constitutionalized by the framers is to the contrary,* it is most unlikely that the Court would be able to specify with anything approaching determinacy how a resolution of the challenge one way or another would affect the state of individual persons' political freedom. Thus, the Court would be hard put to justify policymaking in such cases in terms of protecting political liberty and forestalling political tyranny.

By contrast with a separation-of-powers case in which there is legislative-executive concord or at least, as in *Goldwater v. Carter,* an absence of legislative-executive discord, the Court ought to assume an activist stance—ought, that is, to exercise noninterpretive review—when the legislative and executive branches disagree as to whether the challenged federal action is within the jurisdiction of the branch that took it. Listen again to Jackson:

> When the President takes measures incompatible with the express or implied will of Congress, his power is at its lowest ebb, for then he can rely only upon his own constitutional powers minus any constitutional powers of Congress over the matter. Courts can sustain exclusive Presidential control in such a case only by disabling the Congress from acting upon the subject. Presidential claim to a power at once so conclusive and preclusive must be scrutinized with caution, for what is at stake is the equilibrium established by our constitutional system.[75]

In a case in which there is legislative and executive discord, as Jackson's comment makes clear, there is a genuine need for the Court to resolve the conflict, and that need constitutes the justification for the Court's intervening, as a (presumably) disinterested arbiter, and resolving the conflict on the basis of its own judgment as to the proper allocation of power. In his Holmes Lectures, Learned Hand made much the same point. He contended that, although most judicial review cannot be justified (in his view) in terms consistent with the principle of electorally accountable policymaking, there is a compelling functional justification for judicial review in separation-of-powers cases in which there is a conflict between the legislative and executive branches of the federal government:

> [I]t was probable, if indeed it was not certain, that without some arbiter whose decision should be final the whole system would have collapsed, for it was extremely unlikely that the Executive or the Legislature, having once decided, would yield to the contrary holding of another "Department." . . . The courts were undoubtedly the best "Department" in which to vest such a power, since by the independence of their tenure they were least likely to be influenced by diverting pressure. It was not a lawless act to import into the Constitution such a grant of power. On the contrary, in construing written documents it has always been thought proper to engraft upon the text such provisions as are necessary to prevent the failure of the undertaking. That is no doubt a dangerous liberty, not lightly to be resorted to; but it was justified in this instance, for the need was compelling.[76]

The reader might be tempted to think that, given a conflict between the legislative and executive branches and a constitutional text and history silent as to the proper resolution of the conflict, the Court cannot avoid functioning as a policymaker; it must decide the case one way or another—in a way congenial to either the legislative or the executive branch; and that given this unavoidability, the question of justification, of legitimacy, is beside the point. Not so. The Court does *not* have to decide, if by deciding one means throwing the weight of its authority behind one branch or the other, saying that one branch or the other is in the right. It is open to the Court to dismiss a case in which there is legislative-executive conflict by saying that the Constitution is silent and that the branches will therefore have to resolve their conflict—"fight it out"—as best they can. But I can think of nothing to say in defense of that noninterventionist judicial stance. It is true, of course, that Congress and the President must each assume a very large measure of responsibility for protecting its own prerogatives against incursions by the other; that the so-called system of checks and balances was designed to permit them to do just that; and that, in particular, the judiciary can do precious little to protect a Congress unwilling to act to protect itself from the encroachments of an "imperial" presidency.[77]

Just as there are, in Wechsler's phrase, political safeguards of federalism, there are political safeguards of the separation-of-powers, and they are crucial. But none of that is to say that the Court ought to decline the role of arbiter in cases in which there is conflict, not concord, between the legislative and executive branches of the federal government. To the contrary, as the considerations articulated by Justice Jackson and Judge Hand strongly indicate, the Court should readily assume the role of arbiter in such cases.

Consider, in that regard, a recent case decided by the United States Court of Appeals for the District of Columbia Circuit. A subcommittee of the House of Representatives was authorized to investigate "the nature and extent of warrantless wiretapping in the United States for asserted national security purposes, and to determine whether legislation was required to curb possible abuse of that power."[78] In the course of its investigation, the subcommittee issued a subpoena to the American Telephone and Telegraph Co. (AT&T), ordering it to turn over all documents pertaining to the Attorney General's request for permission to use AT&T facilities to carry tapped communications to FBI monitoring stations. After informal negotiations between the subcommittee and the Justice Department broke down, the latter

> sued to enjoin AT&T from complying with the subpoena, on the ground that compliance might lead to public disclosure of the documents, with adverse effect on national security. [The chairman of the subcommittee] intervened on behalf of the House, as the real party in interest. The [federal trial court] issued the injunction and [the chairman] appealed.[79]

At first the federal appellate court declined to speak to the merits, preferring instead to remand the case to the trial court "for further proceedings during which the parties and counsel were requested to attempt to negotiate a settlement."[80] When the case later returned to the appellate court, the court noted that "[n]egotiation has narrowed but not bridged the gap between the parties"[81] and proceeded to address the merits. It is not necessary to detail the appellate court's resolution of the case,[82] but I do want to quote an introductory portion of the court's opinion that serves to illustrate the utility of sensitive judicial arbitration of interbranch conflict:

> Taking full account of the negotiating positions, we have chartered the course that we think is most likely to accommodate the substantial needs of the parties. Doubtless, neither will be satisfied. But in our view there is good reason to believe that the procedure set forth in this opinion will prove feasible in practice, with such adjustments and refinements as may be evolved by the parties and the [trial] court. What we decide is only that, so long as this procedure gives promise of satisfying the substantial needs of both parties, this court may appropriately continue to refrain from a decision upholding either of the claims of absolute authority. Should the parties test our approach and

encounter difficulties, we may have to determine whether further relief is warranted.[83]

If at some point in its history the Supreme Court had decided that the federal judiciary ought not to assume the role of arbiter in cases of inter-branch conflict, the subcommittee (on behalf of the House of Representatives) and the Justice Department (on behalf of the President), which could come only to very limited agreement either in the informal negotiations that preceded the Justice Department's suit for injunctive relief or in those supervised by the trial court, would each have been left to its own devices. Perhaps in the end AT&T would have turned over the subpoenaed documents. Or perhaps the Justice Department would have prevailed upon AT&T not to comply. In neither case would the federal government have come to a halt. Nonetheless, it is difficult to understand why the federal judiciary, simply because, as the appellate court put it, "the Constitution is largely silent on the question of allocation of powers associated with foreign affairs and national security,"[84] should have declined the role of arbiter. On the other hand, it is easy to see why the court did what it did: the conflict was resolved by an impartial arbiter, the federal judiciary, with a minimum of political bloodletting on both sides, and the subcommittee and the Justice Department were then able to turn their energies to other, presumably pressing business.[85]

There are other, doubtless more dramatic illustrations of the utility of judicial arbitration of interbranch conflict. Perhaps none more dramatic, though, than the case of *United States v. Nixon*:[86] The Supreme Court's resolution of the conflict that ensued when President Nixon challenged the Special Prosecutor's subpoena likely spared the nation the political trauma and instability of impeachment proceedings.[87]

Professor Choper has recently argued that the Supreme Court should forsake all judicial review of separation-of-powers claims that the legislative branch of the federal government has invaded the prerogatives of the executive branch, or vice versa. Choper proposes that:

> The federal judiciary should not decide constitutional questions concerning the respective powers of Congress and the President vis-à-vis one another; rather, the ultimate constitutional issues of whether executive action (or inaction) violates the prerogatives of Congress or whether legislative action (or inaction) transgresses the realm of the President should be held to be nonjusticiable, their final resolution to be remitted to the interplay of the national political process.[88]

There are, in my view, rather serious problems with Choper's proposal. To the extent the proposal calls for abandonment even of interpretive review, what I said earlier with respect to another of Choper's proposals is applicable here—that it "is at odds with the compelling functional justification for interpretive review of federal action. The framers intended that the norms they constitutionalized be the 'supreme law,' and their intention in that regard requires—even if the framers themselves did not specifically authorize—judicial enforcement of constitutional norms," including norms that allocate power among the different branches of the federal government. (A recent example of a case in which challenged congressional action plainly violated a very determinate power-allocating norm is *Buckley v. Valeo*,[89] discussed later in this chapter.)

To the extent Choper's proposal counsels abandonment of noninterpretive review in cases in which there is legislative-executive conflict, the proposal seems to me to underestimate the utility of judicial arbitration of interbranch conflict. True, such arbitration is not literally indispensable, since in most, perhaps all situations, the contending branches, armed as they are with a multitude of political weapons (such as Congress's "power of the purse" or its power to impeach[90]), can "fight it out" without destroying the federal government or the country. But why should the Court adopt a strategy that would force Congress and the President to fight it out, no matter how time-consuming and destabilizing the battle might be?[91] Choper's answer is that the Court would thereby conserve its scarce political capital for human rights cases.[92] But it is farfetched to think that the Court jeopardizes its scarce political capital—even assuming that its capital is all that scarce, which there is excellent reason to doubt[93]—by exercising judicial review in resolving issues concerning the allocation of power between Congress and the President.[94] (In truth, it is not such issues that provoke truly deep, widespread, persistent controversy, but human rights issues.)

It is much more plausible to think that Archibald Cox is correct in suggesting that historically the Supreme Court has amassed a great deal of the political capital it now enjoys—a capital that the Court today spends mainly in human rights cases, when it spends it at all—precisely by resolving problems arising under the doctrines of federalism and of the separation-of-powers.[95]

Note, however, that Choper's thesis, if sound, in no way undermines the crucial claim I make and defend at the end of this chapter, namely, that notwithstanding what I have said up to now, no consideration presented by separation-of-powers issues, even those growing out of legislative-executive conflict, serves to rebut the interpretivist position that all noninterpretive judicial review is illegitimate. (Indeed, if sound, Choper's thesis—that functional considerations do not warrant *any* judicial review in this context—serves to buttress my claim.)

But before I elaborate on that matter, let us briefly consider *Buckley v. Valeo*, in which the contemporary Supreme Court stands unanimously against the notion that it should forsake judicial review of issues concerning the allocation of power between Congress and the President. One of the issues resolved in *Buckley* was whether the manner of appointing persons to the Federal Election Commission invaded presidential authority. The Federal Election Campaign Act provided that the President *pro tempore* of the Senate and the Speaker of the House were each to appoint two persons to the eight-member Commission. Various parties challenging this provision argued that it violated the appointments clause of the Constitution, which says:

> [The President] shall nominate and by and with the advice and consent of the Senate, shall appoint . . . all other officers of the United States, whose appointments are not herein otherwise provided for, and which shall be established by law: but the Congress may by law vest the appointment of such inferior officers, as they think proper, in the President alone, in the courts of law, or in the heads of departments.[96]

The Court sustained the challenge and ruled that the commission, due to the manner in which some of its members were appointed, could not exercise the rulemaking and enforcement powers granted to it by the act. But there was no legislative-executive conflict. Neither the President nor any of his officers were among the parties challenging the act in *Buckley*. Indeed, the President had signed the act, and without expressing any reservations about the constitutionality of the manner in which persons would be appointed to the commission. Should we then conclude that, given the thesis I am advancing—in separation-of-powers cases in which there is legislative-executive conflict, *but not in those in which there is legislative-executive concord*,[97] functional considerations justify the Court assuming a policymaking stance—the Court in *Buckley* acted illegitimately in striking down the provision under discussion?

Plainly not, because in so doing, the Court was exercising interpretive, not noninterpretive, review. As the Court's opinion makes clear—and as the fact that the opinion on the appointments clause issue was unanimous underscores—there was a manifest, indissoluble inconsistency between the challenged provision and the appointments clause of the Constitution. Thus, *Buckley* is one of the rare constitutional cases in which the Court's invalidation of challenged governmental action can be explained in terms of interpretive review. (Thus, it is a mistake to point to *Buckley*, as Professor Choper has done, as an example of "Burger Court" activism.[98])

In that regard, think back to our discussion of the *National League of Cities* case. Justice Rehnquist responded to Justice Brennan's "political safeguards of federalism" argument partly in the following terms:

> The dissent . . . reasons that "Congress is constituted of representatives in both the Senate and House *elected from the states.* . . . Decisions upon the extent of federal intervention under the Commerce Clause into the affairs of

the States are in that sense decisions of the States themselves." . . . [T]he intimation which this reasoning is used to support is incorrect. . . . Just as the dissent contends that "the States are fully able to protect their own interests . . . ," . . . it could have been contended [in Buckley] that the President, [who signed that challenged provision into law], armed with the mandate of a national constituency and with the veto power, was able to protect his own interests. Nonetheless, in [Buckley] the [challenged provision was] held unconstitutional, because [it] trenched on the authority of the Executive Branch.[99]

Justice Rehnquist's rebuttal is fundamentally confused. Buckley involved interpretive review of federal action, and such review is always justified—because of compelling functional considerations set forth in the preceding chapter—regardless of the political safeguards either of federalism or of the separation-of-powers. National League of Cities, by contrast, involved noninterpretive review, and such review, even if it can be justified in some contexts, cannot be justified in cases in which congressional action is challenged on federalism grounds.

We have inquired into the possibility of justifying noninterpretive review in separation-of-powers cases in order to test interpretivism. Does the fact that functional considerations arguably justify at least one sort of noninterpretive review—noninterpretive review in cases of legislative-executive conflict—undermine interpretivist constitutional theory, with the consequence that now the issue is not whether noninterpretive review is legitimate, but what other sorts, if any, are legitimate too?

The answer, perhaps somewhat surprisingly, is no. By hypothesis, a case of legislative-executive conflict involves two conflicting policy choices, each one made by an electorally accountable branch of the federal government. Therefore, when the Supreme Court (or another federal court) resolves, on separation-of-powers grounds, an interbranch conflict as to which the Constitution is silent, necessarily the Court defers to the policy choice of one electorally accountable branch. If, as in the AT&T case discussed above, each branch gets some but not all of what it wants, the Court defers to aspects of the policy choices of both branches. In either event, the Court's policymaking is not truly countermajoritarian and thus does not pose the problem of legitimacy.* Consequently, although in cases

---

*I suppose it is true that in deferring to aspects of the policy choices of both branches, the Court might end up devising and imposing a compromise solution with which neither branch is entirely happy—a solution that cannot be said to represent, overall, a policy choice attributable to either branch. Nonetheless, such a compromise decision by the Court is fundamentally different, with respect to the problem of legitimacy, from one in which the Court simply opposes its electorally unaccountable will to the electorally accountable will of an agency or branch of government. In devising and imposing a compromise solution in a separation case of conflict, the Court is really opposing one electorally accountable will to another; to the extent the Court does not defer, in its solution, to one branch, it is deferring to the other branch, and vice versa.

of legislative-executive conflict, unlike, for example, in cases in which state action is challenged on federalism grounds, the Court does engage in *constitutional* policymaking;[100] and, further, although substantial functional considerations justify that sort of noninterpretive review, what has been justified is a unique sort of noninterpretive review, a species of constitutional policymaking by the judiciary that is not counter-majoritarian—at least, not countermajoritarian in anything remotely like the conventional sense—and so does not pose the problem of legitimacy to which interpretivist constitutional theory is addressed.

*   *   *   *   *   *   *

In this chapter we have tested interpretivism—in particular its essential argument that all noninterpretive judicial review is illegitimate—by inquiring into the possibility of justifying any of the sorts of policymaking the Supreme Court exercises in either federalism or separation-of-powers cases. We have discovered that

(1) the review the Court exercises in cases in which state action is challenged on federalism grounds, although justified, is not judicial (constitutional) review at all, and so not noninterpretive judicial review;

(2) there is no functional (or other) justification for noninterpretive review of congressional action on federalism grounds;

(3) there is no functional (or other) justification for noninterpretive review in separation-of-powers cases in which there is no conflict between the legislative and executive branches of the federal government; and

(4) the noninterpretive review the Court appropriately exercises in separation-of-powers cases in which there *is* a conflict between the legislative and executive branches is not problematic, since in resolving such conflicts the Court necessarily defers to the political judgment of at least one electorally accountable branch of the national government, with the consequence that such review does not pose "the countermajoritarian difficulty" that gives rise to the problem of legitimacy in the first place.

In short, no consideration presented by either federalism or separation-of-powers issues undermines the interpretivist claim that all noninterpretive review—that is, all "countermajoritarian" noninterpretive review—is illegitimate. Thus far, at least, interpretivism remains intact.

CHAPTER THREE

Interpretivism, Freedom of Expression, and Equal Protection

Now we come to the heart of the matter: noninterpretive review with respect to issues of human rights—issues concerning the nature and extent of the (fundamental) rights of individuals vis-à-vis government. In this and the next chapter, we consider the problem of the legitimacy of the noninterpretive review the Supreme Court exercises as it formulates and protects human rights. I want to begin by examining the implications of interpretivism—of the claim that all noninterpretive review is illegitimate—for two of the most important areas of constitutional doctrine: freedom of expression and equal protection. I also want to examine a prominent and, in my view, unsuccessful attempt to defend against interpretivism, the noninterpretive review the Supreme Court has exercised in formulating the bulk of constitutional doctrine regarding both freedom of expression and equal protection.

The first amendment to the Constitution provides that "Congress shall make no law . . . abridging the freedom of speech, or of the press; or the right of the people peaceably to assemble, and to petition the Government for a redress of grievances."[1] It was intended as a limitation only on action of the federal government,[2] but since 1925,[3] the Supreme Court has reviewed action of state governments under the first amendment on the theory that first amendment norms were made applicable to the states by the fourteenth amendment, which was intended as a constraint on state action.[4] That theory, however, is wrong. The history of the fourteenth amendment is not something from which we can escape—although some constitutional theorists, in the spirit of Joyce's Stephen Dedalus, persist in trying.[5] The framers of the fourteenth amendment apparently did not intend it to make applicable to the states the first amendment or any other provision of the Bill of Rights. Recent, exhaustive research confirms that proposition, which was already firmly established by Charles Fairman and others.[6]

To understand the text of the fourteenth amendment, a document drafted (and ratified) more than a century ago, it is necessary to understand the period in which it was written. Garry Wills, in a different context, has put the general point well:

To understand any text remote from us in time, we must reassemble a world around that text. The preconceptions of the original audience, its taste, its range of reference, must be recovered, so far as that is possible. We must forget what we learned, or what occurred, in the interval between our time and the text's. We must resurrect beliefs now discarded. Most people remember this when approaching a culture radically different from ours—that of Sophocles, or Dante, or Chaucer. They keep it in mind, but not enough, when reading Shakespeare or Milton. Yet eighteenth-century English is still read as "our" language; and anything written in America is part of the modern world, of our "young" nation's brief history. So we are tempted to read Jefferson as our contemporary.[7]

There is, of course, an even greater temptation to read the language of the fourteenth amendment, written only slightly over a century ago, as "our" language, pregnant with our sensibilities. Raoul Berger has admirably resisted that temptation.

In his inquiry into the original understanding of the fourteenth amendment,[8] Berger presents a substantially compelling reconstruction of what the amendment meant to its framers. He rightly insists that we not lose sight of the unsentimental fact that during the post–Civil War period in which the amendment was drafted and ratified, "the North was shot through with Negro-phobia, . . . the Republicans, except for a minority of extremists, were swayed by the racism that gripped their constituents rather than by abolitionist ideology."[9] Consequently, the framers did not intend the fourteenth amendment to serve as a charter for the political and social equality of the freed race. Rather, concludes Berger, section 1 of the amendment[10] was intended only to constitutionalize—and thereby place "beyond the power of a later Congress to repeal"[11]—the protections of the Civil Rights Act of 1866. The Civil Rights Act had been designed to protect freedmen in the South from discrimination with respect to certain enumerated rights without which the abolition of slavery was thought largely meaningless.[12] Even if a comparison of the general language of section 1 of the amendment to the rather specific language of the Civil Rights Act leads one to insist that section 1 must have been intended to do more than merely constitutionalize the protections of the act,[13] the fact remains that there is no historical warrant for the proposition that it was intended to do more than protect certain sorts of rights—perhaps not only those rights enumerated in the act, but only rights of the sort enumerated in the act.

As originally understood, the privileges or immunities clause—"the central provision of the Amendment's § 1"[14]—forbade any state to deny to any of its residents[15] on the basis of race any "fundamental" right the state granted to its residents generally.[16] The sorts of rights—"fundamental" rights—to which the clause, following the 1866 act, referred were rights pertaining to the physical security of one's person, freedom of movement, and capacity to make contracts and to acquire, hold, and transfer chattels and land—"life, liberty, and property" in the narrow original sense.[17] The equal protection clause forbade enactment or enforcement of laws denying on the basis of race any fundamental right granted residents generally;[18] the due process clause forbade denial on the basis of race of any judicial protections afforded residents generally for the security of their fundamental rights.[19] Given the import of the privileges or immunities clause, the equal protection and due process clauses were, in a strict sense, superfluous.[20] But then, as Kenneth Karst has noted, the framers made "no serious effort to differentiate the functions of the various clauses."[21] The framers of the fourteenth amendment simply assumed what anyone in their place would have assumed: that every state granted to its residents generally certain fundamental rights—"life, liberty, and property"—and certain judicial procedures for the protection of those rights—"due process." Under the amendment, every state was obligated to extend those same, but only those same, rights and protections to all residents without regard to race.[22]

Raoul Berger's conclusions concerning the original understanding of section 1 of the fourteenth amendment are generally sound.[23] In particular his finding that the fourteenth amendment was not intended to make the Bill of Rights, *including the first amendment,*[24] applicable to the states—which is confirmatory of earlier findings to the same effect by such eminent historians as Charles Fairman[25] and, more recently, Leonard Levy[26]—is amply documented[27] and widely accepted.[28] Given the fact that the framers of the fourteenth amendment did not intend to make the limitations on federal action specified by the Bill of Rights also applicable to state action, enforcement of the first amendment by the Court against the states is not interpretive review and is legitimate only if noninterpretive review of state action under first amendment norms can be justified.

Put aside for the moment the fact that the framers of the fourteenth amendment did not intend to make the first amendment applicable to the states; assume, for the sake of argument, that they did indeed intend the first amendment to constrain state action in the same way it was intended to constrain federal action and that consequently there is no need to distinguish between state and federal action for purposes of the first amendment. Even so, very little constitutional doctrine regarding freedom of expression fashioned in this century[29] could be understood as the product of interpretive review, *because very little of that doctrine reflects any value judgment concerning freedom of expression constitutionalized by the framers of the first amendment.* Although we cannot say with certainty precisely what effect the framers of the Bill of Rights intended the first amendment to have with respect to freedom of expression, we can say that *at most* they intended it to prohibit any system of prior restraint[30] and to modify the common law of seditious libel[31] by making truth a defense and by permitting the case to be tried to a jury.[32] In his masterful study of the original understanding of the first amendment, Leonard Levy has written that "the generation which adopted the Constitution and Bill of Rights did not believe in a broad scope for freedom of expression, particularly in the realm of politics. . . . [L]ibertarian theory from the time of Milton to the ratification of the First Amendment substantially accepted the right of the state to suppress seditious libel."[33]

Given the narrowness of the original understanding, we must conclude that even if the first amendment was intended (by the framers of the fourteenth amendment) to constrain state and federal action in the same way, very little if any modern constitutional doctrine regarding freedom of expression—for example, the protection extended subversive advocacy,[34] defamatory utterances,[35] vulgar[36] and pornographic expression,[37] commercial speech,[38] and campaign expenditures[39]—could be defended as the product of interpretive review. Such doctrine goes far beyond any value judgment constitutionalized by the framers of the first amendment. Hence, most constitutional doctrine regarding freedom of expression is not legitimate unless noninterpretive review of state and federal action under free-speech and free-press norms—which alone explains most such doctrine—can be justified. That proposition is true with respect to *state* action even if the first amendment was intended to constrain state and federal action in the same way; it is doubly true when we retrieve the fact, put aside a moment ago, that the framers of the fourteenth amendment plainly did not intend to make the first amendment applicable to the states at all. (I could make similar claims about constitutional doctrine regarding freedom of religion.[40])

Therefore, one cannot be an interpretivist—a consistent interpretivist, at any rate—and at the same time approve the Court imposing *any* first amendment limitations on state action (or imposing most of the limitations it has applied to federal action). Raoul Berger is a consistent interpretivist. Opposing judicial review of state action under free-speech and free-press norms, he writes:

> One may agree with Justice Cardozo that free speech is "the matrix, the indispensable condition, of nearly every other form of freedom," but the fact remains that the one time the American people had the opportunity to express themselves on whether free speech was "so rooted in the tradition and conscience of our people as to be ranked as fundamental" was in the First Congress, which drafted the Bill of Rights in response to popular demand. There they voted down interference with State control.[41]

William Rehnquist, on the other hand, is not a consistent interpretivist to the extent that he supports judicial review of state action under free-speech and free-press norms. But then, perhaps it is too much to expect a sitting

Supreme Court Justice to tilt quixotically at such a firmly established and, as a practical matter, invulnerable practice.[42]

What about our exemplary interpretivist, Robert Bork? Bork explains his support for judicial review of state action under free-speech and free-press norms—and for judicial review of federal action under free-speech and free-press norms not constitutionalized by the framers[43]—in the following fashion:

> [T]he entire structure of the Constitution creates a representative democracy, a form of government that would be meaningless without freedom to discuss government and its policies. Freedom for political speech could and should be inferred even if there were no first amendment. . . . [The framers] wrote a Constitution providing for representative democracy, a form of government that is meaningless without open and vigorous debate about officials and their policies.[44]

Whatever the merits of his claim that "representative democracy" requires "open and vigorous debate about officials and their policies"—a claim I am not inclined to dispute—Bork's explanation does not mitigate the inconsistency between his interpretivist constitutional theory and his support for judicial review of state and federal action under free-speech and free-press norms never constitutionalized by the framers. Recall the essential argument of interpretivism—that all noninterpretive review is illegitimate; that the Court may enforce against electorally accountable policymakers only norms constitutionalized by the framers. Bork tries to avoid inconsistency by asserting that the framers, in the Constitution, established a certain form of government and that that form of government requires constitutional protection for political speech beyond the limited protection against federal action specifically authorized by the framers of the first amendment. He asserts, in effect, that freedom of political speech is a value judgment *implicitly* constitutionalized by the framers, in that it is a value judgment implicit in the form of government they established.

The fatal problem with Bork's explanation is that the framers did not establish a government in the abstract, called "representative democracy," that requires constitutional, and therefore judicial, protection for political speech beyond the protection they specifically authorized. Rather, they adopted a Constitution that provided, in the first amendment, for *limited* protection against *federal* action abridging freedom of expression; moreover, *they specifically rejected a proposal under which state action abridging freedom of expression would have been subject to federal constitutional limitations.*[45] Consequently, the Constitution the framers adopted (the value judgments they constitutionalized) is far from congenial to Bork's abstract notion of "representative democracy"; the framers did *not* establish a representative democracy in anything like Bork's sense.[46] Recall, in that regard, Levy's documented conclusion, which Bork has accepted, that "the generation which adopted the Constitution and Bill of Rights did not believe in a broad scope of freedom of expression, *particularly in the realm of politics.*"[47]

In extending constitutional protection for political speech (or speech of any other sort) beyond the limited protection, against federal action, authorized by the framers, the Supreme Court is not engaging in interpretive review; it is not simply enforcing a value judgment constitutionalized, implicitly or otherwise, by the framers. Instead, it is making and enforcing value judgments of its own—judgments about what sorts of speech *ought* to be protected, and, at least inferentially, about what sort of government we *ought* to have. In short, the Court is engaging in noninterpretive review,[48] albeit noninterpretive review aimed more at defining the processes of governmental policymaking than at evaluating particular policy choices generated by those processes.

I can readily understand why Professor Bork is anxious to support constitutional protection for political speech beyond the exceedingly limited protection established by the framers. But the notion that the Supreme Court—in addition to the representatives of the people acting through the processes of constitutional amendment—may provide that protection is fundamentally at odds with his constitutional theory. It is possible, I believe, to justify noninterpretive review of governmental action under free-speech and free-press norms,[49] but Bork, given his commitment to interpretivism and, so, his rejection of all noninterpretive judicial review, does not have that "out." Bork cannot have his theory and ignore it too—ignore its implications. Indeed, one reason for rejecting interpretivist constitutional theory and trying to develop an alternative theory that accepts at least some noninterpretive review is precisely that the implications of interpretivism are so severe. Interpretivism necessitates the conclusion, given the original understandings of the first and fourteenth amendments, that most "first amendment" doctrine—much of which is revered[50] even by those quick to criticize most other constitutional doctrines wrought by the modern Court—is the tainted fruit of noninterpretive review and thus is illegitimate.

Even more painfully perhaps, interpretivism requires the conclusion, as we are about to see, that *Brown v. Board of Education,* the 1954 case in which a unanimous Supreme Court ruled that racially segregated public schooling contravenes the fourteenth amendment guarantee of the equal protection of the laws—the case that, in Charles Black's words, "opened our era of judicial activity"[51]—is illegitimate too. Let us turn to the matter of interpretivism and equal protection.

With respect to the seminal case of *Brown* and its progeny, the legislative history of the fourteenth amendment clearly discloses that the framers did not mean for the amendment to have any effect on segregated public schooling or on segregation generally.[52] One cannot avoid the problem of legitimacy, although many have tried,[53] by suggesting that the ruling in *Brown* represents merely an interpretation or application of the equal protection clause. To argue, as I have elsewhere,[54] that the equal protection clause can fairly be taken to radiate the principle of the equality of races is not to deny that to take it so is to read into the fourteenth amendment a principle that, for whatever reasons, the framers did not constitutionalize. In reading that principle into the amendment the Court does not enforce a value judgment the framers made but, instead, makes and enforces a value judgment of its own. Consider Paul Brest's recent comments to that effect:

> Consider the relationship between the original understanding of the four-teenth amendment and current doctrine [ ] prohibiting gender-based classifications. . . . [T]o what extent have [the text or original understanding of the equal protection clause] *guided* the evolution of [that] doctrine [ ]? The text is wholly open-ended; and if the [framers] had any intentions at all about [the] issue [ ], their resolution was probably contrary to the Court's. At most, the Court can claim guidance from the general notion of equal treatment reflected in [the equal protection clause]. I use the word "reflected" advisedly, however, for the equal protection clause does not establish a principle of equality. . . . Indeed, because of its indeterminacy, the clause does not offer much guidance even in resolving particular issues of discrimination based on race.[55]

The modern Court, in equal protection cases, has been an active, per-sistent policymaker. One cannot be a logically consistent interpretivist and accept equal protection doctrine banning, for example, racial segregation.[56] Raoul Berger is a consistent interpretivist to the extent he contends that the Court's seminal decision in *Brown v. Board of Education* was illegitimate. The Court's decision in *Brown* was unwarranted, says Berger, because segregated public schooling does not offend equal protec-tion as originally understood, which, for Berger, is the determinative norm. For Berger, the Court's policymaking under equal protection is illegitimate no matter how persuasive the substance of the policymaking might be,[57] because in the hands of the judiciary the policymaking constitutes a usur-pation of the legislative function of determining what value judgments, beyond those constitutionalized by the framers, shall inform the activities of the political community.[58]

But Berger stops short of contending that *Brown* should be overruled:

> It would be utterly unrealistic and probably impossible to undo the past in the face of the expectation that the segregation decisions . . . have aroused in our black citizenry—expectations confirmed by every decent instinct. That is more than the courts should undertake and more, I believe, than the American people would desire.[59]

Apparently even Berger cannot bring himself to accept all the implications, some of them obviously quite enormous, of interpretivist constitutional theory. Berger has sought to defend his failure to call for the overruling of *Brown*, by asserting that "[i]t is not a failure of analysis to acknowledge that eggs cannot be unscrambled."[60] But judicial precedent *can* be unscrambled—overruled—as indeed Berger himself emphasizes in his book:

> Why should "adherence to precedent" rise above effectuation of the framers' clearly expressed intention, which expresses the value choices of the sovereign people, not merely of judicial predecessors?
>   . . . .
> I assert the right to look at the Constitution itself, stripped of judicial encrustations, as the index of the constitutional law and to affirm that the Supreme Court has no authority to substitute an "unwritten Constitution" for the written Constitution the Founders gave us and the people ratified.[61]

To the extent the implications of a political theory count as a reason for accepting or rejecting the theory, Berger's seeming failure of nerve with respect to a basic implication of interpretivism—that *Brown* and its progeny ought to be overruled—is instructive.

Robert Bork has suggested that the result in *Brown* can be salvaged in terms consistent with his interpretivist premises. We do not know, says Bork, just what sorts of racial inequality the framers of the fourteenth amendment meant to attack. Yet, we cannot permit the Court to function like a policymaker and simply pick and choose what sorts of racial inequality shall be deemed improper and what sorts shall not. Rather, we must constrain the Court, which cannot be allowed to exercise the discretion of a policymaker, by insisting that it strike down *all* racial inequalities, *including* segregated public schooling.[62]

The fatal problem with Bork's convenient argument—convenient in that it spares Bork the embarrassment of acknowledging that his constitutional theory, interpretivism, and the Court's decision in *Brown* are fundamentally at odds—is that, as Berger insists, we *do* know that the framers did not intend to prohibit segregated public schooling. If one accepts interpretivist constitutional theory, as Bork, like Berger, does, it follows, given the fact that the framers did not mean to prohibit segregated schooling, that *Brown* must be deemed illegitimate. Berger's logic is quite sound in that respect. As Bork himself emphasizes:

> The words of [the equal protection clause] are general but surely that would not permit us to escape the framers' intent if it were clear. If the legislative history revealed a consensus about segregation in schooling . . . , I do not see how the Court could escape the choice [ ] revealed and substitute its own, even though the words are general and conditions have changed.[63]

The unavoidable problem for Bork and other interpretivists understandably anxious to avoid condemning *Brown* and its progeny as illegitimate is
that the legislative history of the fourteenth amendment *does* reveal a
consensus—a tragic, morally indefensible consensus—about segregation
in schooling (and, indeed, about segregation generally). And so Bork's
convenient argument simply will not work.

It is doubtless true that our reading of the original understandings of
constitutional provisions such as the free speech and free press clauses of
the first amendment and the equal protection clause is not perfectly accurate. After all, it is impossible to uncover the intentions of each of the many
framers of a provision—those who drafted the provision and then those in
the state conventions or legislatures who ratified it.[64] Moreover, historical
inquiry is inevitably subjective: to some extent our vision of the past is
irremediably colored—distorted—by our vision in the present.[65] But if not
perfectly accurate, our reading is sufficiently accurate—accurate enough
to justify the conclusion that the Court's decisions regarding human rights
in most modern constitutional cases of note, and particularly in most
freedom of expression and equal protection cases, cannot plausibly be
explained as "interpretations" or "applications" of any value judgments
constitutionalized by the framers, whatever the precise character of those
various value judgments might be. They can only be explained as products
of noninterpretive review.

In the same vein, the fact that Berger's reading of the original understanding of the fourteenth amendment is not free from doubt in every
particular has a very limited significance for present purposes. For it is
nonetheless true that very little fourteenth amendment doctrine—including the notion that various provisions of the Bill of Rights, like the
first amendment, constrain state action by virtue of the fourteenth
amendment—can be explained by reference to the original understanding
of the fourteenth amendment, *even if the original understanding is somewhat broader than Berger acknowledges.* Henry Monaghan's sound observations about the contemporary debate over the original understanding of
the fourteenth amendment are relevant here:

> Even if its architects intended § 1 [of the fourteenth amendment] to transcend
> the [Civil Rights Act of 1866], the question persists of how sweeping a change
> in the governmental structure § 1 authorized. Those who attack [Raoul] Berger
> frequently slip into a comfortable *non sequitur* at this point: they assume that if
> Berger is in error, § 1 perforce has a dynamic content. Logically, however, their
> demonstration that Berger's list of § 1 rights is too narrow is not proof that it is
> proper to measure the content of the fourteenth amendment by other than *some*
> closed set of rights as they were understood in 1868. In other words, their attack
> does not dispose of a limited conception of the fourteenth amendment, with the
> judge's function being essentially historical—to enter a time machine, return to
> the year 1868, and scrutinize "contemporary" sources to determine the extent

to which the assertedly expansive language of § 1 would prohibit only what fell within those objectives, however conceptualized, and "their twentieth century counterparts."[66]

In chapter 1, we considered—and dismissed—a number of anti-interpretivist claims. This is an appropriate point at which to consider another one, which, like the claims discussed earlier, is fundamentally flawed. In the preceding several pages, I have sought to explain why an interpretivist cannot accept most modern constitutional doctrine regarding freedom of expression and equal protection. The reason, in brief, is that the framers' intentions with respect to the first and fourteenth amendments—which intentions, for the interpretivist, are determinative—were extremely limited.

Some commentators contend that interpretivists conceive of the original understanding of many important constitutional provisions too narrowly. For example, Ronald Dworkin has argued that the framers of the equal protection clause did not mean to constitutionalize their particular "conception" of equality, which happened to be quite narrow, but rather the "concept" of equality, which is quite broad,[67] and that they intended posterity to honor the concept of equality by abiding its own conception of equality, which might be broader than the framers'.[68] The sort of claim Dworkin makes is really quite common.

> [Dworkin employs] a strategy that, in one or another form, is common to all efforts to derive from the Constitution principles relevant to a world that could not have been anticipated when the document was adopted. He reads the language of the Constitution at a very high level of abstraction, in effect as a license to interpret its provisions as the embodiment of the evolving moral conceptions of succeeding generations.[69]

There is a fatal problem with this sort of claim.[70] Evidence supporting the proposition that the framers of constitutional provisions such as the free-speech, free-press, equal protection clauses intended to constitutionalize broad "concepts" rather than particular "conceptions" is wholly lacking. Significantly, Dworkin offers absolutely no evidence whatsoever in support of the proposition.[71] Moreover, the proposition is implausible. As Henry Monaghan has written:

> Excessive generalization as to "intent" seems at war with any belief that a constitutional amendment is a *conscious* alteration of the frame of government whose major import should be reasonably apparent to those who gave it life. . . . I am unable to believe that in light of the then prevailing concepts of representative democracy, the framers . . . of § 1 [of the fourteenth amendment] intended the *courts* . . . to weave the tapestry of federally protected rights against state government.[72]

On the other side, the evidence is compelling that the framers of the first and fourteenth amendments thought they were constitutionalizing —and therefore *were* constitutionalizing—particular and, by contemporary lights, narrow value judgments about certain (sorts of) political practices.*

In claiming, inaccurately, that interpretivists conceive of the original understanding of many provisions too narrowly, proponents of the concept-conception claim and of similar claims concede, implicitly if not explicitly, the interpretivist's premise that the original understanding of a constitutional provision is, or ought to be, the alpha and omega of constitutional adjudication. Such claims serve as little more than a device for avoiding the truly difficult question, which is *whether* the original understandings of important power-limiting provisions like the first and fourteenth amendments—the plainly *narrow* original understandings—ought, as a matter of constitutional theory, to be deemed the only legitimate source of norms for constitutional adjudication.[13] Constitutional theorists would stay closer to that crucial question, which, after all, is the very heart of the matter, if they would bear in mind that power-limiting constitutional provisions—as opposed to power-granting ones—typically represent and embody, as Monaghan's comments suggest, discrete, determinate value judgments about what particular sorts of political practices government ought to forswear.

I want to take a moment at this point to set forth the various possible relationships between the original understanding of any power-limiting constitutional provision and any present-day political practice claimed to violate the provision. By doing so I hope to make clear that, contrary to the sort of anti-interpretivist claim Dworkin and others have made, a judicial decision striking down in the name of a particular constitutional provision (1) a political practice that (a) was not present to the minds of the framers of the provision and (b) is not analogous to any practice that was present to their minds, or (2) a political practice that was present to their minds but that they did not mean to ban, cannot plausibly be understood as a mere "interpretation" or "application" of the provision in question. (Dworkin's concept-conception claim, of course, is simply a variation on the interpretation-application theme.)

Let the equal protection clause be the power-limiting provision, and let P stand for the present-day political practice. If the framers of the equal

---

*More recently, Dworkin has asserted that the framers of the fourteenth amendment (Dworkin's example) intended not merely "to prohibit acts that treat people differently in what [the framers] considered their fundamental interests"; in Dworkin's view, they also "intended to prohibit acts that treat people differently in what in fact are their fundamental interests." Dworkin, *The Forum of Principle*, 56 N.Y.U. L. REV. 469, 490 (1981). *See also id.* at 497. That, too, is an historical claim, of course; and once again Dworkin has failed to supply any evidence to support it.

protection clause did not have occasion to contemplate P—that is, if P was not present to their minds, as it could not have been if P did not exist at all or in anything like its present form[74]—they could not have intended that the clause prohibit P. They might have intended that the clause serve as an open-ended provision, leaving for resolution in the future the issue of whether the clause should be deemed to prohibit any given political practice not forbidden or even foreseen by them. But it is as clear as such things can be that the important power-limiting provisions, and in particular the equal protection clause, were not intended to serve as open-ended norms.[75]

If the framers did contemplate P—and note that if P was not foreseen by the framers but is simply a modern analogue of a practice they did contemplate, different in no constitutionally significant respect from the contemplated practice, it is *as if* they contemplated P[76]—either they intended that the clause prohibit P or they did not. If they did not, either they left for resolution in the future the issue of whether the clause should be deemed to prohibit P or they intended that the clause not prohibit P. But, again, there is no evidence that the framers of important power-limiting provisions intended them to serve as open-ended norms.

Consider, for example, the Court's ruling in *Brown*, which, as I have said, cannot plausibly be taken to represent merely an interpretation or application of a value judgment constitutionalized by the framers. Either the framers of the fourteenth amendment contemplated segregated public schooling, which existed at the time, or they did not. If they did not, obviously the framers did not intend that equal protection prohibit segregated public schooling. (If segregated public schooling were simply an analogue of a practice the framers did contemplate and mean to ban, we could say that the framers did intend equal protection to ban segregated public schooling. But I am assuming that segregated public schooling is not simply an analogue of a banned practice. If that assumption seems controversial, then think about segregated golf courses, which the Court has prohibited in the name of equal protection.[77] Surely segregated golf courses are not simply an analogue of a banned practice.)

If the framers did contemplate segregated public schooling, the framers intended that the clause not prohibit the practice: they did not intend that the clause prohibit segregated public schooling, and no historical evidence suggests that they meant to leave open the question of whether the clause should be deemed to prohibit the practice.[78] (If the framers contemplated segregated public schooling, but if at the time public schooling lacked anything like the significance it has today, perhaps we should say that the framers did not contemplate it, that is, in anything like its present form.)*

*Ronald Dworkin has taken issue with my analysis by imagining a framer of the fourteenth amendment who spoke to himself in the following vein:

"I wonder what the Supreme Court will do about segregated schools when the case comes up, as one day it must. There are, I suppose, the following possibilities. The justices may think that since we intend to forbid discrimination in matters touching fundamental interests, they are required to decide whether education is, in fact, a matter of fundamental interest. Or they may think that they should be guided by our more specific intentions about segregated schools, in which case they may try to decide whether the majority of us actively thought that the clause we were enacting would forbid segregation. Or they may think that the effect of what we did was to delegate the question to them as a fresh question of political morality, so that they have the power to decide for themselves whether, all things considered, it would be better to permit or forbid segregation. I hope they won't make the last of these choices, because I think the courts should decide what we've done, not what they want. But I don't know what the right answer is to the question of what we've done. That depends on the correct conception of constitutional intention to use, and, not being a constitutional lawyer, I haven't ever thought much about that. Nor do I, as it happens, have any particular preferences myself, either way, about segregated schools. I haven't thought much about that either."

This is a realistic description of the attitude of particular legislators about a great many issues. But the three-valued scheme proposed by Perry and assumed by many other commentators is simply inadequate in the face of that attitude. The legislator I describe has none of the intentions (using that work in any familiar sense) that Perry takes to be exhaustive.

Continuing his comment on my analysis, Dworkin writes:

But of course Perry is free to construct a conception of constitutional intention that does permit the inference he describes. He can introduce a kind of closure into his conception by making it a regulative principle that if some participant in the constitutional process did not intend to limit federal or state legislative power in some way, or intend to delegate this decision to others, then he will be taken as having intended not to limit that power. This closure insures that there are no "gaps" in any one person's scheme of intention about legislation. It is no objection that this departs from ordinary usage of "intention." We are, after all, constructing a conception for a particular use. But once again the choice needs a justification.

Dworkin, *The Forum of Principle,* 56 N.Y.U. L. REV. 469, 486–87 (1981).

My justification is simply that it is implausible to suppose that the framers did not know what they were doing. To put the matter concretely, it is implausible to suppose that the framers did not know whether what they were doing jeopardized, say, state laws banning miscegenation. Surely they knew that what they were doing did *not* jeopardize antimiscegenation laws—or laws segregating public schools or public parks. We must not romanticize the framers' political-moral consciousness.

Dworkin's hypothetical legislator says that he does not "know what the right answer is to the question of what we've done." I assume, however, that the framers of the fourteenth amendment, and of power-limiting constitutional provisions generally, *did* know what they had done. They knew that they had constitutionalized a prohibition on certain contemplated political practices and on uncontemplated analogues to those practices. Now, perhaps my assumption is unsound. But Dworkin has offered no historical evidence to suggest that it is unsound. With Henry Monaghan (see text accompanying note 72 *supra*), I think that the assumption is much more plausible than Dworkin's assumption that the framers did not know (the right answer to the question of) what they were doing.

None of this, however, is to say that in *Brown* the Court's decision invalidating segregated public schooling was contraconstitutional.[79] A contraconstitutional decision would be one that decreed a result contrary to a state of affairs that is constitutionally required—or a result reached in the exercise of a mode of judicial review the framers intended to foreclose. No one suggests that the framers meant to require segregated public schooling. Nor did the framers—whether of the original Constitution and Bill of Rights or of the fourteenth amendment—intend that the Supreme Court invalidate only political practices inconsistent with value judgments attributable to the framers; *no historical materials suggest that any group of framers ever constitutionalized any theory of the proper scope of judicial review, whether narrow, like interpretivism, or broad.*[80]

Of course, to say that the Court's decision in *Brown* or in any other constitutional case was not contraconstitutional is not to justify the decision. Any effort to justify a decision that, like *Brown*, cannot be explained as an application of a value judgment the framers constitutionalized must rely on a theory that holds it proper, at least under some circumstances, for the Court to engage in noninterpretive review—to invalidate political practices on the basis of value judgments not constitutionalized by the framers. Claims that decisions such as *Brown* involve merely interpretation of the Constitution and therefore pose no problem of legitimacy must be rejected. Such decisions are predicated on value judgments not constitutionalized by the framers and that is precisely what gives rise to the problem of legitimacy, and what interpretivists, who contend that electorally accountable policymaking should not be constrained by any value judgments save those the framers constitutionalized, condemn.

In both chapter 1 and the preceding discussion I make reference to present-day political practices not foreseen by the framers but different in no constitutionally significant respect from practices they did contemplate and mean to ban—practices that are simply modern analogues of banned practices. A fair question, therefore, is: When is a present-day political practice no more than a modern analogue of a past, constitutionally banned practice? The answer, I think, is fairly straightforward: A present-day political practice, P', is simply an analogue of a past, constitutionally banned practice, P, when a person—one who aspires to logical consistency and moral coherence—who would endorse the political-moral proposition that P ought to be banned, could point to no difference between P and P' that could count as a principled reason for failing to endorse the distinct proposition that P' ought to be banned. Obviously there will be occasional differences of opinion as to whether a given political practice is simply the analogue of another political practice.[81] But that fact—which simply illustrates what no one denies: that even an interpretivist approach to constitutional adjudication can generate debatable answers—is largely irrelevant, since, again, most political practices banned by the Supreme Court in human rights cases, including freedom of expression and equal protection cases, cannot *plausibly* be characterized as simply modern analogues of past, constitutionally banned practices.

Relatedly, some constitutional theorists argue that by constitutionalizing value judgment V, the framers *necessarily* constitutionalized V', the most attractive general normative principle that explains V, and that V' justifies, even requires, invalidation of present-day political practices that are *not* simply analogues of past, constitutionally banned practices.[82] But it is rarely if ever the case that a single general normative principle is required to explain a value judgment constitutionalized by the framers. Any of several different, competing political-moral visions might dispose one to subscribe to a given value judgment the framers constitutionalized.[83] And constitutional theorists who contend to the contrary are in truth importing into the Constitution's power-limiting provisions whatever political-moral philosophy *they* find most congenial.[84]

Let me distill the foregoing discussion. Some theorists, in particular Ronald Dworkin, seem to argue that the power exercised by the Supreme Court in modern constitutional cases, involving human rights, is exercised in most instances in conformity with what the framers intended. For example, Dworkin suggests that the Supreme Court generally makes "substantive decisions of political morality not in place of judgments made by the 'Framers' but rather in service of those judgments."[85] I cannot agree. In most modern constitutional cases of consequence, involving human rights, questions are adjudicated as to which no value judgment plausibly attributable to the framers is determinative.[86]

Dworkin has written that "[t]he important question for constitutional theory is not whether the intention of those who made the Constitution should count, but rather what should count as that intention."[87] Dworkin is flatly wrong, in my view. The central question of contemporary constitutional theory is—as it should be—whether it is legitimate for the Supreme Court to oppose itself to the other branches and agencies of government on the basis of value judgments *beyond* those constitutionalized by the framers. I think it is legitimate, and this book, in particular the next chapter, is an effort to explain, and to begin to defend, my answer. Dworkin apparently prefers to persist in his effort to conscript the framers to do service in defense of judicial activism. I prefer to let the framers sleep. Just as the framers, in their day, judged by their lights, so must we, in our day, judge by ours. This is not to deny that the framers have anything to say to us, only to insist that in the end the answers the Court gives are (most often) its own, and not the framers'. And that is as it should be: the framers, after all, were not gods, but, like us, merely human beings.*

*Dean Sandalow's graceful discussion of the issue that divides Dworkin and me is quite relevant here:

In the remainder of this chapter, I will examine a recent, very prominent attempt, in my view quite unsuccessful, to defend noninterpretive review in both first amendment and equal protection cases against the challenge of interpretivism. Many constitutional theorists sympathetic to both first amendment and equal protection doctrine recognize what I have sought in this chapter to demonstrate—the impossibility of defending either of those two areas of constitutional doctrine without resort to a noninterpretivist theory of constitutional adjudication. But several of those theorists are loath to go too far, or what they think is too far, in accepting noninterpretivism, for then they would be hard put to reject constitutional policymaking with respect to norms other than freedom of expression or equal protection—in particular they feel they would be hard put to reject modern "substantive due process," a doctrine with which they are most uncomfortable.[88] They therefore attempt to articulate a *limited* noninterpretivist constitutional theory, one that justifies the particular species of constitutional policymaking they want to salvage from an interpretivist attack—usually policymaking with respect to the norms of freedom

---

The view that constitutional interpretation involves primarily an elucidation of the general intentions of the framers is understandably attractive, perhaps not only because it seems to support the institutional arrangements we have established for giving contemporary meaning to the Constitution, but also because it is so comforting. The uneasiness, often the agony, and always the responsibility that accompany a difficult choice are softened by the belief that real choice does not exist. In law, the search for repose leads us to attribute responsibility for decisions to those who have gone before and, in constitutional law, to wise men we call "the framers." They may not have foreseen the world in which we live nor the problems we now face, but the words they wrote nonetheless provide "sufficient guidance" if only we have the wisdom to understand them properly. And so the social Darwinism of Herbert Spencer and the libertarianism of John Stuart Mill, though not in the minds of those who wrote the Constitution, have at different times each been found there by men who, no doubt sincerely, believed that the "broad, majestic language" of the Constitution was intended to guarantee that "general *sort* of relationship between the government and its citizens." Nor does it pass belief that one day soon (perhaps its dawn has already broken) the egalitarianism of John Rawls will also be found there.

. . .

[I]t must be recognized that the more general the statement of the framers' intentions, the weaker is the claim that those intentions circumscribe present judgment. To begin with, our understanding of the framers' intentions is necessarily distorted if we focus solely upon their larger purposes, ignoring the particular judgments they made in expressing those purposes. Intentions do not exist in the abstract; they are forged in response to particular circumstances and in the collision of multiple purposes which impose bounds upon one another. "[T]o make a general principle worth anything," as Holmes wrote,

you must give it a body; you must show in what way and how far it would be applied actually in an actual system; you must show how it has gradually emerged as the felt reconciliation of concrete instances . . . Finally, you must show its historic relations to other principles, often of very different date and origin, and thus set it in the perspective without which its proportions will never truly be judged.

of expression, equal protection, and procedural fairness[89]—and, at the same time, that condemns species of policymaking for which they have no sympathy—in particular policymaking with respect to modern substantive due process norms.*

John Ely's *Democracy and Distrust*[90] represents the principal contemporary effort in that regard. In the next chapter, I will show how the only constitutional theory that succeeds in justifying noninterpretive review in either first amendment or equal protection cases is one that also serves to justify what many consider to be noninterpretive review *in extremis*— the noninterpretive review exercised by the Court in substantive due process cases. Here, I want to explain why Ely's particular constitutional theory—his limited noninterpretivist theory—which purports to justify noninterpretive review in both first amendment (that is, freedom of expression) and equal protection cases but not in substantive due process cases,[91] does not succeed in justifying noninterpretive review in either first amendment or equal protection cases.

The sort of noninterpretive review Ely seeks to justify he labels

---

So, too, in understanding the intentions of the framers. By wrenching the framers' "larger purposes" from the particular judgments that reveal them, we incur a loss of perspective, a perspective that might better enable us to see that the particular judgments they made were not imperfect expressions of a larger purpose but a particular accommodation of competing purposes. In freeing ourselves from those judgments we are not serving larger ends determined by the framers but making room for the introduction of contemporary values.

. . .

The reality of our [constitutional] tradition, to paraphrase Karl Llewellyn's prescription for the interpretation of aging statutes, has not been to determine the meaning of the Constitution by reference to the sense originally intended to be put into it, but rather for the sense which can be quarried out of it. The "quest does not run primarily in terms of historical intent. It runs in terms of what the words can be made to bear, in making sense in the new light of what was originally unforeseen."

Sandalow, *Constitutional Interpretation*, 79 MICH H. REV. 1033, 1038–39, 1046, 1060 (1981) (quoting Holmes, *The Use of Law Schools*, in THE OCCASIONAL SPEECHES OF JUSTICE OLIVER WENDELL HOLMES 34, 41 (M. Howe ed. 1062); K. LLEWELLYN, THE COMMON LAW TRADITION 374 (1960)).

*Of course, to accept constitutional policymaking by the judiciary with respect to a given norm, like freedom of expression, is not necessarily to accept every decision and doctrinal development fashioned by the judiciary in the course of that policymaking. On the other hand, to reject constitutional policymaking with respect to a given norm is necessarily to reject every decision and doctrinal development fashioned by the judiciary in the course of that policymaking. *See* p. 5, n. †. Therefore, one who wants to accept even one decision handed down by the judiciary in the course of policymaking with respect to a given norm must accept judicial policymaking with respect to that norm. For example, to salvage the Supreme Court's decision in *Brown v. Board of Education* from an interpretivist attack, one must salvage the judicial policymaking—with respect to equal protection—that generated the decision.

participational, as opposed to the *substantive* review he decries.[92] Participational review, according to Ely, is aimed at serving the norm of political participation—participation by persons in the political processes—and it does this by "clearing the channels of political change on the one hand, and [by] correcting certain kinds of discrimination against minorities on the other."[93] Those two endeavors are predicated, in Ely's view, on "a coherent theory of representative government."[94] Ely's "general theory is one that bounds [noninterpretive review] by insisting that it can appropriately concern itself only with questions of participation, and not with the substantive merits of the political choice under attack."[95] We can best explore Ely's meaning by considering his efforts to justify constitutional policymaking with respect to freedom of expression and equal protection.

Let us first consider Ely's effort to justify noninterpretive review in first amendment cases. According to Ely, there is a radical difference between noninterpretive review in first amendment cases and that in substantive due process cases: the former consists of judicial policymaking aimed at maintaining the processes of democratic government, whereas the latter consists of judicial policymaking aimed at revising policy choices generated by those processes.[96] The latter sort of noninterpretive review is illegitimate, says Ely, because it is undemocratic for the judiciary, in constitutional cases, to revise policy choices generated by the democratic processes (except on the basis of value judgments constitutionalized by the framers*). But the former sort is not illegitimate; first amendment rights, whether or not constitutionalized by the framers, "must nonetheless be protected [by the judiciary], strenuously so, because they are critical to the functioning of an open and effective democratic process."[97] "[I]mpediments to free speech, publication, and political association"[98] impair operation of the democratic process,[99] and, according to Ely, "unblocking stoppages in the democratic process is what judicial review ought preeminently to be about."[100] The judiciary, rather than an electorally accountable institution of government, should make the ultimate, critical choices in defining rights of speech and press, says Ely, because "we cannot trust elected officials to do so: ins have a way of wanting to make sure the outs stay out."[101] Policymaking that determines the character of rights of speech and press "cannot safely be left to our elected representatives, who have an obvious vested interest in the status quo."[102]

Ely's argument should not be confused with Robert Bork's argument, discussed earlier. Bork's effort was to persuade us that judicial enforcement of a certain norm—freedom of *political* speech—not specifically constitutionalized by the framers, in particular enforcement of that norm

*Or except to the extent authorized by Ely's limited noninterpretivist theory.

against the states, can be explained in terms of interpretive review—that such enforcement does not involve judicial policymaking, but only judicial application of a value judgment implicit in yet another value judgment, as to the nature of American government, specifically constitutionalized by the framers. Ely, by contrast, acknowledges that judicial enforcement of free-speech and free-press norms not constitutionalized by the framers can be explained only in terms of constitutional policymaking—that such enforcement involves much more than application of value judgments attributable, even indirectly, to the framers. Bork rejects all noninterpretive review; Ely seeks to justify noninterpretive review of a certain sort—that in first amendment cases.

Whereas Bork attempts to root judicial enforcement of his freedom-of-political-speech norm in a value judgment attributable (in Bork's view) to the framers, Ely's effort—or so it seems to me[103]—is to root judicial policymaking with respect to first amendment norms[104] in a consensus—specifically, a consensus in America as to something called the democratic process. Ely's argument seems to be that, given this consensus, some institution of government should be charged with primary responsibility for maintaining the process, and that the judiciary is the institution best adapted to such an enterprise.[105]

A principal reason Ely rejects substantive due process, as I indicate in the next chapter, is that there is no consensus—certainly no ascertainable consensus—as to the various values the judiciary enforces in substantive due process cases. But—and this is a critical problem with Ely's argument in defense of noninterpretive review in first amendment cases—neither is there any consensus as to the sort of democratic process that ought to prevail in America.[106] The sort of democratic process that prevails at any given point is a function mainly of two factors: first, the number of groups to whom the franchise is extended; second, the nature of rights regarding speech, publication, and political association that individuals have against government.[107] If there were a consensus as to the nature of speech, publication, and associational rights individuals ought to have, there would be, at least to that extent, a consensus as to the sort of democratic process that ought to prevail. But of course there is no consensus as to the nature of such rights and so, to that extent, no consensus as to "the democratic process."[108]

Indeed, if there were anything approaching a consensus as to what speech, publication, and associational rights individuals ought to have, the judiciary would likely have a severely diminished role in defining, and in striking down governmental action in the name of such rights, because the consensus, if authentic, would presumably be reflected in most if not all legislative and executive action. What Ely overlooks is that the very same social and political fragmentation that prevents any consensus as to the various values the judiciary enforces in substantive due process cases also prevents consensus as to process. Mark Tushnet's comments to that effect are applicable here:

> The realist synthesis . . . failed to answer the Holmesian challenge; it simply shifted the locus of the difficulty. Holmes had said that law could not be seen as the product or embodiment of neutral principles of justice because the fragmentation of society precluded agreement. The realist synthesis responded by propounding that process was all [that mattered]. But the absence of the social conditions for agreement on substance was simultaneously an absence of the conditions for agreement on process.[109]

To forestall possible confusion, I want to emphasize what I am and am not claiming. My point is that in America—*even* in America—there is no authentic consensus as to the nature of the speech, publication, and associational rights individuals ought to have against government, and therefore, in *that* respect, no consensus as to process. But this is not to claim that there is no consensus as to process in *any* respect. Certainly there is a consensus, in part reflected in the Constitution, that the franchise ought to exist, even if there is some residual disagreement as to how broadly it ought to be extended.[110] There is also a consensus—at least I am willing to concede to interpretivism the claim of a rough consensus—as to the principle of electorally accountable policymaking. All I mean to say at this point is that the particular consensus on which Ely seems to rely—consensus as to a certain sort of democratic process, one constituted in part by a particular conception of freedom of expression—is nonexistent. Ely's argument therefore fails.

But perhaps there is another way of understanding Ely's argument. Perhaps the argument Ely deploys does not rely, even implicitly, on any such consensus. Ely's argument would fail nonetheless, for in that case it would be seriously incomplete. If there is no such consensus, by what right does the judiciary impose its particular conception of the ideally functioning democratic process on the political community—that is, by what right does the judiciary substitute its particular conception for the conception of the people's electorally accountable representatives? That is the essential question posed by interpretivism, and the question has very considerable force in light of the fact that *in most first amendment cases of consequence, the proper resolution of the dispute is debatable.*

I do not deny that even a minimalist conception of democracy entails some notion of freedom of expression; at least I am not inclined to claim otherwise.[111] But that concession does not help Ely, because the representatives of the people are not out to banish the ideal of freedom of expression from the land, after all; the disagreement is about what the ideal ought to mean, what content it ought to have, how it ought to be interpreted. As modern, seminal first amendment cases illustrate, there is not just one reasonable conception of how the ideal of freedom of expression ought to operate, of precisely what content it ought to have. There are competing reasonable conceptions (and so Ely must explain why the electorally unaccountable judiciary's particular conception ought to prevail in a society committed to electorally accountable policymaking). The philosopher Thomas Scanlon puts the point well:

> Most of us believe that freedom of expression is a right. . . . There is less agreement as to exactly how this right is to be understood—what limits and requirements on decision making authority are necessary and feasible as ways of protecting central participant and audience interests and insuring the required equity in the access to means of expression. . . . This disagreement is partly empirical—a disagreement about what is likely to happen if certain powers are or are not granted to governments. It is also in part a disagreement at the foundational level over the nature and importance of audience and participant interests and, especially, over what constitutes a sufficiently equal distribution of the means to their satisfaction.[112]

The only thing Ely says that could count as an answer to the "by what right" question is his claim that the "ins"—the incumbents—cannot be trusted to resolve first amendment issues impartially. They will, says Ely, resolve such issues in a manner designed to protect their incumbency. There are two problems with that claim. First, the resolution of many first amendment issues one way or another can have no real effect on any incumbent's chances for reelection.[113] Thus, the fact that the political vision of a typical incumbent is often distorted by considerations of incumbency[114] is simply irrelevant to the resolution of many first amendment issues and certainly does not count as a reason for trusting the judiciary rather than incumbents with respect to such issues.

Second, even with respect to first amendment issues that do implicate an incumbent's reelection chances, it is fanciful to suppose that incumbents would often protect their incumbency by conspiring to deny to the electorate access to that basic store of information and ideas essential to the evaluation of the main features of public policy and performance. It is difficult to imagine such a conspiracy in contemporary American political culture—and among incumbents who have, after all, mutually antagonistic interests.[115] At any rate, the supposition that such a conspiracy is lurking in the dark underside of American politics and would erupt, but for a vigilant judiciary, is simply too thin a predicate for a constitutional theory that seeks to justify noninterpretive review in first amendment cases.[116]

The fact of the matter—and it is a crucial fact—is that incumbents generally will, and do, resolve issues concerning freedom of expression the way their constituencies—and in sum electoral majorities—want them resolved. (Or at least they generally do not resolve them in a way their constituencies do not want them resolved.) Now, concededly that is a strategy designed to protect incumbency. But one searches in vain through Ely's argument for a single reason why the people should not be able to choose, through their representatives,[117] their own conception of the ideally functioning democratic process—in particular their own reasonable conception, among competing reasonable conceptions, of freedom of expression—however opposed to the judiciary's conception—or to Ely's, or to mine—that conception might be.

> The difficulty with the argument that courts should undertake to repair the defects of the democratic processes is that the demonstration of a defect usually consists in pointing to a law that the scholar in question would have vetoed had he been the governor. The process is not really shown to be defective; the result is simply disliked.[118]

One might try to argue that if the people, through their electorally accountable representatives, are permitted to choose their own conception of the democratic process—or, more narrowly, of freedom of expression—they (in spite of what I said a moment ago) *might* end up emasculating the process, and they simply cannot be permitted to do that.[119] The first problem with that argument is that in most first amendment cases, the stricken governmental action cannot plausibly be described as even a step toward emasculation of the democratic process. A more fundamental problem is that the argument—even *if* the deep skepticism on which it is predicated is not altogether unfounded—proves too much. The people have a legal right to choose their own conception by adopting a constitutional amendment embodying it. They even have a legal right to abolish the first amendment by adopting a superceding amendment to that effect. Why, then, cannot the electorally accountable representatives of the people choose their own conception in the ordinary course of governmental policymaking—so long as they do not contravene any value judgment constitutionalized by the framers?

I hope I am not misunderstood. It is not that I think there is no answer to the interpretivist's "by what right" question. (To the contrary, I think there *is* an answer, and I set it forth, in a general way, in the next chapter.) Rather, my point is simply that nothing Ely says amounts to an adequate answer, perhaps because he does not face the question. Instead he seems to rely on a (nonexistent) consensus that permits him to avoid the question; that is, he seems to take for granted that the particular conception of the democratic process the judiciary imposes on the political community—in the form of a particular conception of freedom of expression, which conception is a principal constituent of the judiciary's vision of the democratic process— is shared by that community. Thus, Ely writes that noninterpretive review in first amendment cases "is not inconsistent with, but on the contrary is entirely supportive of the American system of representative democracy."[120] Such a statement implies that there is no real dispute as to what the precise character of "the American system of representative democracy" should be, in particular as to how the ideal of freedom of expression should be developed. Ely also writes that "it is an appropriate function of the Court to keep the machinery of democratic government running as it should. . . ."[121] That he does not pause to ponder the fact, or the significance of the fact for his theory, that there is no consensus as to how that machinery "should" run is likely because he does not acknowledge the fact; indeed, he seems to posit a contrary fact—that there is a consensus.

If Ely were right, if there were a consensus, there would be no problem of judicial "imposition"; the judiciary would simply be enforcing the people's own conception of the democratic process. But there is no such consensus. And so—*whether or not* Ely does in fact rely or instead disclaims reliance on any such supposed consensus—the interpretivist's "by what right" question cannot be avoided:

> The suggestion . . . that because First Amendment freedoms are indispensable to effective participation in the political process they therefore deserve special judicial protection, even beyond their clear constitutional scope, likewise begs the question why the Court should exercise independent judgment to enlarge First Amendment freedoms in accordance with the Court's determination of the desired relationship between those freedoms and the political process. After all, to the extent that First Amendment freedoms, or any other freedoms, *are* clearly protected constitutionally [that is, to the extent they are constitutionalized by the framers], their judicial enforcement does not depend on the political process argument. . . . [T]o the extent that such freedoms are *not* clearly protected constitutionally [not constitutionalized by the framers], the justification for judicial expansion, or contraction, of their scope depends on whether the Court is empowered to rewrite the Constitution in the service of judicially desired constitutional change.[122]

Either because it relies on a consensus that is nonexistent or because it fails to deal adequately with the very question that, in the absence of that consensus, must be addressed, Ely's argument does not justify noninterpretive review in first amendment cases. As I demonstrate in the next chapter, the theory that does succeed (in my view) in justifying noninterpretive review in first amendment cases also serves to justify a sort of noninterpretive review—in substantive due process cases—that many, including Ely, claim is illegitimate.

Let us now consider Ely's effort to justify constitutional policymaking by the judiciary with respect to the norm of equal protection. Just as Ely thinks there is a fundamental difference between noninterpretive review in substantive due process cases, which Ely claims is illegitimate, and noninterpretive review in first amendment cases, he also thinks there is a fundamental difference—indeed, largely the same difference—between noninterpretive review in substantive due process cases and that in equal protection cases. According to Ely, noninterpretive review in equal protection cases, like that in first amendment cases, consists of judicial policymaking aimed at maintaining the process of democratic government. In first amendment cases the judiciary maintains the democratic process, in Ely's view, by defining and protecting speech, publication, and associational rights and thereby assuring persons "the opportunity to participate . . . in the political processes by which values are appropriately identified and accommodated."[123] In equal protection cases the judiciary maintains the democratic process by acting to ensure that persons belonging to certain minorities—in particular racial minorities—are not denied "the opportunity to participate in the accommodation those processes have reached"[124]—not denied, that is, "access to the . . . bounty of representative government," where bounty refers to "exemptions or immunities from hurts (punishments, taxes, regulations, and so forth) along with benefits . . .patterns of distribution generally."[125]

Ely recognizes the anomaly—in Ely's view, only an apparent anomaly—of claiming that the judiciary is merely acting with the intention to maintain the democratic process when it compels the majority to grant to a minority some benefit which the majority has chosen to deny to that minority (or when it compels the majority to refrain from imposing on a minority some burden which the majority has chosen to impose only on that minority). "[A] system of equal participation in the processes of government is by no means self-evidently linked to a system of presumptively equal participation in the benefits and costs that process generates."[126]

But Ely proposes "to suggest a way in which what are sometimes characterized as two conflicting American ideals—the protection of popular government on the one hand, and the protection of minorities from denials of equal concern and respect on the other—in fact can be understood as arising from a common duty of representation."[127] He proposes to show, that is, how the judicial enterprises of, first, "clearing the channels of political change" and, second, "correcting certain kinds of discrimination against minorities" are predicated on "a coherent theory of representative government"[128]—how, in other words, "these two sorts of participation [in the processes of government and in the benefits and costs those processes generate] join together in a coherent political theory."[129]

Ely's way around the conflict is what he calls "the . . . concept of 'virtual representation'."[130] Governmental officials can get by without representing the interests of persons belonging to minorities that chronically have little if any political power—minorities, that is, unable to form effective political alliances with other groups and therefore unable to become part of those shifting majorities that wield power in a pluralist democracy —because as a *practical* matter those officials are not electorally accountable to such persons. Ely's concept of virtual representation is designed to overcome this perceived defect in political reality by requiring officials to grant benefits, which are granted to other persons, to persons with little political power, and to refrain from imposing burdens, which are not imposed on other persons, on persons with little political power, unless there is a constitutionally sufficient reason—that is, a reason the judiciary is willing to credit as legitimate and adequately weighty—for doing otherwise.[131] "[A]t least in some situations," says Ely, "judicial intervention becomes appropriate when the existing processes of representation seem inadequately fitted to the protection of minority interests, even minority interests that are not voteless."[132]

I am not interested, for present purposes, in Ely's problematic efforts to articulate criteria for determining which minorities today chronically lack sufficient political power to justify, under his theory, judicial protection of their interests against the insensitivity or animus of electorally accountable policymakers.[133] I am interested in whether the concept of virtual representation Ely posits succeeds in justifying noninterpretive review in equal protection cases.

The concept of virtual representation—or, looked at from the other side, the presumptive right to equal participation in the payoffs generated by the democratic process—may make good sense on political-moral grounds. But clearly it is not a concept the framers constitutionalized.[134] Nor, of course, is there any societal consensus as to the concept.[135] By what right, then, does the judiciary constitutionalize the concept? That, again, is the interpretivist's essential question and challenge. Ely seems at points to claim that the concept is simply an aspect of the larger concept of "representation" implicit in the notion of "the democratic process." For example, Ely writes that judicial enforcement of virtual representation—what he calls "a representation-reinforcing approach to judicial review"—"is not inconsistent with, but on the contrary . . . entirely supportive of, the underlying premises of the American system of representative democracy."[136] He also suggests that the concept has "been at the core of our Constitution from the beginning," that it "has informed our constitutional thinking from the beginning,"[137] that it "lies at the core of our system [of government]."[138]

If in fact that, or something like it, is Ely's claim, it fails on two grounds. First, even if the concept of virtual representation is somehow implicit in *Ely's* particular vision of the democratic process, that alone would hardly justify judicial enforcement of the concept in constitutional cases, for Ely's particular vision of the democratic process is not one the framers constitutionalized, nor one as to which there is any consensus. Second, and more fundamentally, far from being implicit in the notion—or at least in any conventional notion—of the democratic process, the concept of virtual representation is plainly in tension with it.

In rejecting Ely's various efforts to justify "representation-reinforcement as a value that courts are entitled to press beyond that representation provided by the written Constitution and statutes,"[139] Robert Bork, our exemplary interpretivist, has written:

> It would not do to derive the legitimacy of representation-reinforcement from such materials as, for example, the one-man-one-vote cases because those cases themselves require justification and cannot be taken to support the principle advanced to support them. Nor would it do to rest the concept of representation-reinforcement on the American history of steadily expanding suffrage. That expansion was accomplished politically, and the existence of a political trend cannot of itself give the Court a warrant to carry the trend beyond its own limits. How far the people decide not to go is as important as how far they do go.
>
> The idea of representation-reinforcement, therefore, is internally contradictory. As a concept it tends to devour itself. It calls upon the judiciary to deny representation to those who have voted in a particular way to enhance the representation of others. Thus, what is reinforced is less democratic representation than judicial power and the trend toward redistribution of goods.[140]

Of course, it is possible to define "the democratic process" prescriptively—which is precisely what Ely has done—so as to encompass the concept of virtual representation. But to do that is to try to win the argument by an act of definition—a vain strategy when the definition is one to which there is nothing approaching a consensus.[141]

A less loaded definition of the democratic process—one that tends to be more descriptive than prescriptive—will include as one of its key elements the feature that policymaking, which may or may not be constrained by a constitution,* is subject to control by officials accountable, directly or indirectly, to the electorate. (Granted, this element calls into question whether the American political system is wholly democratic, given the prevalence of constitutional policymaking by the judiciary. I address that issue in the next chapter.)

Consequently, the concept of virtual representation, because it was not constitutionalized by the framers, is in tension with the notion of the democratic process. Under the concept, as Ely elaborates it, the Supreme Court has authority to require governmental officials to grant benefits to

---

*Constrained, that is, by a set of value judgments deemed for whatever reasons to have the status of "supreme law."

persons to whom they do not want to grant them, and to refrain from imposing burdens on persons on whom they want to impose them, unless the officials can persuade the Court to let them do otherwise. In short, policymaking is partly in the hands of an institution of government that by design is not electorally accountable.

The tension has been highlighted by Robert Cover in his discussion of judicial protection of minorities in the period from 1938 to 1965.[142] "[D]evelopments after 1938," says Cover, "were surely informed by the tension between respect for the structures of [American] politics and protection for minorities."[143] The duty of virtual representation is a strategem for protecting minorities from the vagaries of a "majoritarian" political process, but protecting racial minorities (Cover's particular focus) "can hardly be understood purely as a neutral regulation of the political processes when the processes are mainly about the maintenance of Apartheid."[144]

Again, I am not saying that the concept of virtual representation is a bad thing, or that the judiciary ought never to engage in constitutional policymaking. The whole point of this book is to justify some constitutional policymaking by the judiciary (noninterpretive review), including that in equal protection cases| I mean only to say that the concept of virtual representation is in tension with the notion of the democratic process—in particular with the principle of electorally accountable policymaking—and thus the interpretivist's question cannot be ignored: By what right does the judiciary impose the concept of virtual representation—the presumptive right to equal participation in the payoffs generated by the democratic political process—on electorally accountable officials? |

Here, as in his discussion of noninterpretive review in first amendment cases, Ely points to the fact that "[a]ppointed judges . . . are comparative outsiders in our governmental system," and need worry about continuance in office only very obliquely. This, says Ely, puts them in a better position than electorally accountable officials, in particular legislators, "objectively to assess claims . . . that . . . by acting as accessories to simple majority tyranny, our elected representatives in fact are not representing the interests of those whom the system presupposes they are."[145]

I wonder what marvelous "system" it is that "presupposes" that elected officials attend to the interests of all persons, and not merely to the interests of the persons whose support they need to continue in office. If there were an actual consensus—as opposed to a rhetorical tradition (which, like most such traditions, reflects not a consensus but the rhetoric of political "elites")—supporting the proposition that the American political system ought to be such a system, judicial enforcement of the concept of virtual representation could be defended as enforcement of that consensus. But Ely does not claim, much less offer evidence to the effect that there is any such consensus, and in fact there is none. Again, if there were such a consensus, there would likely be little need for the judiciary to enforce it.

The fundamental problem with Ely's contention that elected representatives cannot be trusted to resolve impartially equal protection claims—claims that a benefit or a burden ought to be extended more widely or not at all—is that generally they will, and do, resolve such claims the way their constituencies want them resolved. And except for pointing to the possibility of "majority tyranny," Ely says nothing in response to the interpretivist's contention that those constituencies should be able, and under democratic principles are entitled, to resolve such claims the way they want—Ely concedes that the proper resolution of such claims will "be full of judgment calls"[146]—constrained only by value judgments constitutionalized by the framers. Constrained, that is, by interpretive review—judicial enforcement of the framers' value judgments—not by noninterpretive review, which, as Ely acknowledges, is what judicial enforcement of virtual representation amounts to.

Let Robert Bork make the point.

> Majority tyranny occurs if legislation invades the areas properly left to individual freedom. Minority tyranny occurs if the majority is prevented from ruling where its power is legitimate. Yet, quite obviously, neither the majority nor the minority can be trusted to define the freedom of the other. This dilemma is resolved in constitutional theory, and in popular understanding, by the Supreme Court's power to resolve both majority and minority freedom through the interpretation of the Constitution. Society consents to be ruled undemocratically within defined areas by certain enduring principles believed to be stated in, and placed beyond the reach of majorities by, the Constitution.[147]

"But," continues Bork, "this resolution of the dilemma imposes severe requirements upon the Court. For it follows that the Court's power is legitimate only if it" enforces the framers' value judgments as to the proper "spheres of majority and minority freedom. If [the Court] . . . merely imposes its own value choices, . . . [i]t then necessarily abets the tyranny either of the majority or of the minority."[148]

But what about the ugly possibility to which Ely points—indeed, if the past really is prologue, the probability—that, occasionally at least, majorities will victimize chronically powerless minorities? There is, after all, much that majorities can do to minorities that is not offensive to any value judgment the framers constitutionalized. The Constitution established by the framers does not ordain a perfectly just political order. (Recall, for example, that the 1789 Constitution accommodated slavery. And the institution of racial segregation, as we have seen, is not offensive to any value judgment the framers of the fourteenth amendment constitutionalized.) Ely's basic argument—the only thing he has to say that can serve as a response to the "by what right" question—is that it is somehow *fairer* to have politically disinterested judges resolve equal protection claims of majority tyranny than to have legislators—in effect the majority itself—resolve them. Thus, the subtitle of the chapter in which Ely elaborates the concept of virtual representation is "The Court as Referee."[149] He writes: "A referee analogy is . . . not far off: the referee is to intervene . . . when one team is gaining unfair advantage."[150]

But this elementary notion of "fairness," of impartial, disinterested conflict resolution, is not adequate to the justificatory task Ely and others assign it. Consider Terrance Sandalow's argument to that effect:

> Prevailing ideas of fairness . . . do not call for impartial decisions when rules are to be legislated. . . . No one supposes, for example, that fairness requires courts to substitute their judgments for those of legislatures with respect to tax rates for the wealthy, the level of welfare payments for the poor, or the content of regulations imposed upon milk producers in the interest of consumers. Such issues, it is commonly understood, are to be resolved through the political process, and that is so even though there is a risk that the majority will not fully appreciate the costs that are imposed upon the minority. . . . As a nation, we are committed to the idea that government, to be ethically defensible, requires the consent of the governed. . . . Since pre-Revolutionary times, the active and continuous participation of the governed in their government, either directly or by representation, government "of" and "by" the people, has been understood to be central to the democratic ideal. Courts not only are unable to draw upon this source of legitimacy, but in setting their judgment against that of the legislature, they oppose the very agency of government that is most clearly entitled to do so.[151]

Ely does not adequately grapple with the sort of argument Professors Bork and Sandalow develop, and therefore Ely's effort to justify noninterpretive review in equal protection cases is seriously incomplete and, on that score alone, unsuccessful.[152]

Ely's effort to justify the species of noninterpretive review he finds congenial, "participational" review—his effort to establish that constitutional policymaking in both freedom of expression and equal protection cases is not inconsistent with our societal commitment to democratic government—is not persuasive. And it is not persuasive mainly because it relies on a sleight of hand: Ely conceptualizes "the democratic process," with which (he argues) participational review is consistent, in a self-serving way. He builds into his conception of the democratic process those features that will permit him to conclude that participational review "is not inconsistent with, but on the contrary is entirely supportive of, the American system of representative democracy."[153] In that crucial respect, Ely's constitutional theory—his limited noninterpretivist theory—is quite circular. More generally—and here I quote Larry Alexander's artful paraphrase of my critique of Ely—"Ely fails to justify the imposition of his implied-from-the-Constitution conception of democracy against the will of the branches that are constituted according to an expressed-in-the-Constitution conception of democracy."[154] I cannot see how to avoid concluding that Ely has failed to defend, against the claims of interpretivism, what he set out to defend.[155]

In the next chapter I expect to show that Ely, moreover, has failed to justify a distinction critical to his entire enterprise—the distinction between participational review on the one hand, and substantive review on the other. The distinction, though seductive, is illusory. Or perhaps I should say (if it makes a difference) that the distinction is not consequential. For, as I contend in the next chapter, the constitutional theory that justifies—if indeed any constitutional theory finally justifies—noninterpretive review under "participational" norms like freedom of expression and equal protection, also serves to justify noninterpretive review under the "nonparticipational" political-moral norms that inform, for example, modern constitutional doctrine regarding substantive due process. A corollary, of the you-can't-have-your-cake-and-eat-it-too variety, is that one cannot do what Ely has tried to do—praise the judiciary's constitutional policymaking with respect to participational norms while at the same time condemn it with respect to all other, nonparticipational norms.

CHAPTER FOUR

Noninterpretive Review in Human Rights Cases: A Functional Justification

In chapter 1, I sketched the basic features of interpretivism, which holds that all noninterpretive review is illegitimate. In chapter 2, I concluded that noninterpretive review—that is, countermajoritarian noninterpretive review—is illegitimate in both federalism and separation-of-powers cases. In chapter 3, I argued that one prominent attempt to justify noninterpretive review in both first amendment and equal protection cases—what John Ely has called "participational" review—is unsuccessful. Thus far, it would seem, interpretivism is sound in its claim that all noninterpretive review is illegitimate. In this chapter, I propose to develop a justification for noninterpretive review in human rights cases—including, but certainly not limited to, freedom of expression and equal protection cases.

If my justification for constitutional policymaking by the judiciary in human rights cases is persuasive, I will have succeeded in defeating the interpretivist claim that all noninterpretive review is illegitimate. But I hasten to add—in the spirit of Sanford Levinson's observation that "[i]t is unlikely . . . that any of the participants in the debates about constitutional theory are going to have their minds changed by reading a polemic by a person of another sect, any more than Baptist theologians are likely to convert to Catholicism or vice versa when presented with a 'refutation' of the other's position"[1]—that my aim is less to convert than to establish that my justification is a reasonable one and that, therefore, interpretivism represents only one reasonable constitutional theory and, contrary to what its proponents sometimes claim, not the only one.

Let me remind you what the stakes are. Unless there is a justification—a *functional* justification, since, as we have seen in chapter 1, there is neither a textual nor a historical justification—for noninterpretive review in human rights cases, virtually all of constitutional doctrine regarding human rights fashioned by the Supreme Court in this century must be adjudged illegitimate, because virtually none of that doctrine can be explained, or defended, as the product of interpretive review. In the previous chapter, we saw that most constitutional doctrine regarding two fundamental political-moral norms, freedom of expression and equal protection, is the product of noninterpretive review. But so is most constitutional doctrine regarding the right to vote, freedom of religion, the procedural rights of criminal defendants and other procedural rights, the right of access to judicial process, and so on.[2]

As a historical matter, such constitutional doctrine, certainly the greater and most important part of it, cannot plausibly be explained or defended in terms of the value judgments embodied by the framers in the various constitutional provisions the Court has invoked in defining and enforcing the rights in question. (Nor can it be explained or defended in terms of any judgment by the framers that the Court, in constitutional cases, should assume a policymaking role with respect to human rights. There is no historical justification for *any* noninterpretive review, including that exercised by the Court in human rights cases.) The framers of the fourteenth amendment did not intend to ban state-ordered racial segregation, and yet the Supreme Court has done so. Neither did they intend to subject any state to the constraints of the first amendment or to any constraints on the ways in which the state administers its criminal processes.[3] And yet most of the important constitutional decisions regarding freedom of expression, freedom of religion, and the rights of criminal defendants have been ones in which the Court has struck down *state* action.[4] This is not a historical essay, and in any event there is no point in belaboring what today few if any constitutional scholars would deny: that precious few twentieth-century constitutional decisions striking down governmental action in the name of the rights of individuals—the decisions featured in the "individual rights" section of any contemporary constitutional law casebook—are the product of interpretive review.[5] The stakes are very high indeed.

The reader might think that though the stakes are uncomfortably high, we are not playing an all-or-nothing game; that perhaps there is a justification for noninterpretive review with respect to certain sorts of human rights issues—those concerning freedom of expression, for example, or equal protection—even if there is no satisfactory justification for noninterpretive review with respect to other sorts of human rights issues. But, in crucial respects, it *is* an all-or-nothing game. That, at least, is my claim, the soundness of which I shall demonstrate later in this chapter.

Recall that there is no plausible textual or historical justification for noninterpretive review. But recall also that there is no airtight textual or historical justification for most *interpretive* review either. There is, however, a compelling functional justification for interpretive review—a justification based on the function the practice serves in our system of government.[6] Similarly, as I suggested in chapter 1, if there is any justification for noninterpretive review, it must be functional in character: If noninterpretive review serves a crucial governmental function, perhaps even an indispensable one, that no other practice can realistically be expected to serve—and serves it in a manner that accommodates the principle of electorally accountable policymaking—that function constitutes the justification for the practice. |

What is the function of noninterpretive review in human rights cases? Recall, again, that noninterpretive review entails the definition, elaboration, and enforcement of values beyond merely those constitutionalized by the framers. The function of noninterpretive review in human rights cases, then, is the elaboration and enforcement by the Court of values, pertaining to human rights, not constitutionalized by the framers; it is the function of deciding what rights, beyond those specified by the framers, individuals should and shall have against government. But that does not tell us very much. Before we can fully understand that function, and before we can evaluate it as a justification for noninterpretive review, we need to know more.

Let us begin with this question: What source of values, if any, other than the set constitutionalized by the framers, can serve as a reservoir of decisional norms for human rights cases? A not uncommon answer is tradition and/or consensus. Consider, for example, this famous passage by Justice Harlan:

> Due process has not been reduced to any formula; its content cannot be determined by reference to any code. The best that can be said is that through the course of this Court's decisions it has represented the balance which our Nation, built upon postulates of respect for the liberty of the individual, has struck between that liberty and the demands of organized society. . . . The balance of which I speak is the balance struck by this country, having regard to what history teaches are the traditions from which it developed as well as the traditions from which it broke.[7]

Is "tradition"—the tradition of the American people—a plausible source of norms for constitutional adjudication? There is no single, predominant American tradition—none so determinate, at any rate, as to be of much help in resolving the particular human rights conflicts that have come before the Court in the modern period and that are likely to come before it in the foreseeable future. As one commentator has observed, "even such central American values as 'the dignity of the individual' and 'freedom' are highly ambiguous since they mean such different things, even opposite things, depending on the theoretical context in which they are interpreted."[8] The fact of the matter, our idealized Fourth of July oratory to the contrary notwithstanding, is that the so-called American tradition, to the extent it is determinate or concrete at all, is severely fragmented;[9] there are *several* American traditions, and they include denial of freedom of expression,[10] racial intolerance, and religious bigotry. A skeptical observation by Robert

Bork, concerning tradition in the sense of "the fundamental presuppositions of our society," is relevant here:

> One may doubt that there are "fundamental presuppositions of our society" that are not already located in the Constitution but must be placed there by the Court. The presuppositions are likely, in practice, to turn out to be the highly debatable political positions of the intellectual classes. What kind of "fundamental presupposition of our society" is it that cannot command a legislative majority?[11]

Is contemporary "consensus," in the sense of "basic shared national values"[12] or "conventional morality,"[13] a plausible source of norms? In my early writings I portrayed the function of noninterpretive review as that of enforcing, against government, those values as to which there is a consensus among the American people.[14] But John Ely's critique of that notion, it seems to me, is compelling.[15] Just as there is no singular American tradition sufficiently determinate to be of help to the Court in resolving particular human rights conflicts, and just as the concrete traditions that do exist are fragmented and point every which way, so too there are no consensual values sufficiently determinate to be of help to the Court, and the values that do enjoy significant support are, in our pluralist culture, fragmented and point in many different directions.[16]

Indeed, if there really were consensual values of a determinate, helpful sort, there would probably be little need for the Court frequently to enforce them against electorally accountable officials, whose policy choices presumably would usually reflect any truly authentic consensus.[17] Similarly, consensual values would probably be of little help to the main body of persons who press human rights claims in the Court—persons whose skin is not white or whose politics or lifestyle is heterodox, who participate in no consensus and, in fact, challenge whatever consensus might exist.

Recent efforts to rehabilitate the notion that tradition and consensus can serve as sources of decisional norms for human rights cases are simply not successful. One commentator has characterized the Court's function in exercising noninterpretive review as that of searching out and enforcing "values deeply embedded in the society, values treasured by both past and present, values behind which the society and its legal system have unmistakably thrown their weight."[18] Underlying that characterization is a serious failure to face the unsentimental truth about the severely fragmented character of concrete American traditions and values. What Mark Tushnet has written in criticism of G. Edward White's *Patterns of American Legal Thought* (1978) is applicable to the romantic notion that "tradition," somehow allied with "consensus,"[19] can serve as a source of decisional norms:

The fundamental Realist perception of social fragmentation—what Professor White mistakenly calls a "disintegration of common values or goals" as if there had been a time of integration in the recent past—was abandoned precisely because it threatened both the immediate political program of liberal America and the long-term premise of liberal society: that governmental coordination can somehow overcome the individualistic fragmentation that defines liberal society. Since the Realists were right, however, post-Realism failed too. Professor White, continuing the tradition that has weakened the intellectual stature of academic law, suggests a "new" course for the Court: "[A] Justice should reach for arguments which make use of reasons that appeal to deeply embedded cultural values," and then should balance individual against state interests. If he thinks that answers the Realists, he should think again.[20]

If tradition allied with consensus will not work, then perhaps adding another element to the stew—"principled interpretation"—will do the trick:

Once a traditional value has been accepted as an aspect of constitutional liberty, the Court must give that value *a consistent and principled interpretation*. Otherwise, the actual contours tradition supplies may reflect the same prejudice and insensitivity that necessitate judicial protection of unenumerated rights in the first place. While tradition offers guidance as to the identity of fundamental liberties, due process is not merely a mandate for the perpetuation of tradition with all its fortuitous historical attributes. Once it has been found that a particular right is an element of constitutional liberty, the Court no longer looks exclusively to tradition to ascertain its contours. Instead, it must develop *a reasoned exposition* of that value.

. . . .

A court which extends the right of procreative autonomy from a marital to a nonmarital context [, for example,] is not contending that the procreative rights of the ùnmarried are traditional. It is merely claiming that, given a longstanding cultural consensus that procreative activities comprise an area of human endeavor that should be regarded as within the realm of liberty, there must be *some principled basis* for treating the unmarried and married differently.[21]

The fundamental problem with the quoted passage is its assumption that there are "traditional" values (of a determinate, helpful sort) to be found. But let us put that problem aside. Let us assume that some such values—when articulated at a sufficiently high level of abstraction (and therefore in a not very determinate, controversial, *or helpful way*)—can be found. Still, a basic problem remains. For once the Court starts down the recommended path—once it starts posing and answering questions like, "What is 'a consistent and principled interpretation' of the value in question?", or "What is 'a reasoned exposition' of the value?", or "What is 'a principled basis' for extending (or refusing to extend) the scope of the value?"—the Court is no longer really enforcing, in the value-neutral way the term suggests, tradition or consensus. Rather, the Court is fabricating, by defining, tradition and consensus. And in that enterprise tradition and consensus—or rather what is taken for tradition and consensus—serve as little more than rhetorical points of departure, and quite malleable points at that, as the Court moves toward results doubtless preferred chiefly for reasons independent of their supposed rootedness in tradition and consensus. No, adding "principled interpretation" to the stew will not work either.[22]

Owen Fiss has recently suggested a view of constitutional adjudication[23] that is, in my estimate, beset by a serious ambiguity. Fiss's view could be understood as relying on the notion that there are, in America, certain traditional or consensual values which it is the Court's function, in constitutional cases, to elaborate and enforce. Fiss writes that constitutional "[a]djudication is the social process by which judges give meaning to our public values." He refers to "the constitutional character of our public values" and then goes on to say that in constitutional cases "[t]he judge tries to give meaning to our constitutional values."[24] Fiss continues:

> The task of the judge is to give meaning to constitutional values, and he does that by working with the constitutional text, history, and social ideals. . . . The function of a judge is to give concrete meaning and application to our constitutional values. . . . The task of a judge . . . should be seen as giving meaning to our public values and adjudication as the process through which that meaning is revealed or elaborated. . . . I doubt whether dispute resolution is an adequate description of the social function of courts. To my mind courts exist to give meaning to our public values, not to resolve disputes. Constitutional adjudication is the most vivid manifestation of this function. . . .[25]

If by "public values" and "social ideals" Fiss means those norms as to which there is a tradition or a consensus in American society, his view is subject to the same fatal criticism directed at others who have suggested that the function of noninterpretive review is to enforce, against government, values derived from tradition or consensus. The essential problem with such a view is that it begs the crucial question whether, *beyond rhetoric*, there even are any traditional or consensual values—"public values"—sufficiently determinate to be of use to the Court in resolving particular human rights conflicts—a question that, increasingly, is answered in the negative.[26]

But, again, Fiss's position is ambiguous. He need not be understood —and in my view should not be—as relying on an imagined tradition or consensus in America as to the public values to which he refers. In fact, Fiss's view is better understood, I think, in terms that render it quite close to the vision of constitutional adjudication I set forth later in this chapter. I will explain in due course.

We have yet to locate a source of values (other than the set constitutionalized by the framers) that can serve as a reservoir of decisional norms for human rights cases. I now want to isolate a fundamental dimension of our collective American self-understanding that is essential to our comprehension, and therefore to our evaluation, of the function of noninterpretive review in human rights cases. There are, again, no particular political-moral values supported by either "tradition" or "consensus" sufficiently determinate to be of significant use in resolving the sorts of human rights conflicts that have come and foreseeably will come before the Court. There is, however, a particular conception of the American polity that seems to constitute a basic, irreducible feature of the American people's understanding of themselves. The conception can be described, for want of a better word, as religious.

Before I indicate what that conception is, I should comment on my use of the word *religious*, which doubtless risks serious misunderstanding. Etymologically, *religion* derives from the Latin *religare*, which means "to bind together that which was once bound but has since been broken asunder." I want to emphasize, as strenuously as I can, that in the following discussion I use the word *religious* in its etymological sense, to refer to a binding vision—a vision that serves as a source of unalienated self-understanding, of "meaning" in the sense of existential orientation or rootedness. *I do not use the word in any sectarian, theistic, or otherwise metaphysical sense.*[27]

What, then, is this "religious" conception to which I refer? The American people—not each and every one of them, to be sure, but certainly the great bulk of those who have been responsible for establishing, developing, and maintaining the principal institutional constituents of the American political community—have understood themselves to be "chosen" in the biblical sense of that word; that is, they have understood themselves to be charged with a special responsibility, *an obligation*, among the nations of the world.[28] That responsibility is to realize, as best they can, which is to say only "partially and fragmentally . . . , a 'higher law'."[29] According to this self-understanding, "the will of the people is not the criterion of right and wrong. There is a higher criterion in terms of which this will can be judged; it is possible that the people may be wrong."[30] "The obligation, both collective and individual, to carry out God's will on earth," writes Robert Bellah, is "a theme that lies very deep in the American tradition."[31]

Behind [what Bellah calls American civil religion[32]] at every point lie Biblical archetypes: Exodus [from other countries to this, the "new" country], Chosen

People, Promised Land, New Jerusalem, Sacrificial Death and Rebirth.[33] But it is also genuinely American and genuinely new. It has its own prophets and its own martyrs, its own sacred events and sacred places, its own solemn rituals and symbols. It is concerned that America be a society as perfectly in accord with the will of God as men can make it, and a light to all the nations.[34]

An integral component of the American people's religious understanding of themselves is the notion of prophecy. Invariably a people, even a chosen people, fail in their responsibility and need to be called to judgment—provisional judgment—in the here and now. That is the task of prophecy:

In the beginning, and to some extent ever since, Americans have interpreted their history as having religious meaning. They saw themselves as being a "people" in the classical and biblical sense of the word. They hoped they were a people of God. They often found themselves to be a people of the devil. American history, like the history of any people, has within it archetypal patterns that reflect the general condition of human beings as pilgrims and wanderers on this earth. Founded in an experience of transcendent order, the new settlements habitually slipped away from their high calling and fell into idolatry, as the children of Israel had done before them. Time and again there have arisen prophets to recall this people to its original task, its errand into the wilderness. Significant accomplishments in building a just society have alternated with corruption and despair in America, as in other lands, because the struggle to institutionalize humane values is endless on this earth.[35]

Today the biblical imagery doubtless seems strange, or merely rhetorical, to some. Whereas in less secular times the religious conception I am discussing was expressed in openly and conventionally religious terms,[36] now the expression is more likely than not to take a secular form.[37] But the cultural cast of the metaphors matters far less than the essential vision those metaphors disclose, and that vision seems not to have changed much over the course of our history, but instead has endured. The American people still see themselves as a nation standing under transcendent judgment: They understand—even if from time to time some members of the intellectual elite have not—that morality is not arbitrary, that justice cannot be reduced to the sum of the preferences of the collectivity. They persist in seeing themselves as a beacon to the world, an American Israel,[38] especially in regard to human rights ("with liberty and justice for all"). And they still value, even as they resist, prophecy—although now it might be called, for example, "moral leadership."[39]

The significance of this religious American self-understanding for our purposes is that it supplies the crucial context in which the function of noninterpretive review in human rights cases is finally clarified. Such judicial review represents the institutionalization of prophecy. The function of noninterpretive review in human rights cases is prophetic; it is to call the American people—actually the government, the representatives of the people—to provisional judgment. My point is not that judges in general or members of the Supreme Court in particular are divinely inspired; it is not that the Supreme Court is an American Chair of Peter, such that when a majority of the justices speak *ex cathedra* on matters of political faith and morals, they speak infallibly. My point is in no sense a metaphysical or supernaturalistic one. In portraying the function of noninterpretive review in human rights cases as prophetic, I invoke no assumptions about any deity or any divinely ordained "natural law." Nor do I suppose that the members of the Supreme Court and of the judiciary generally are Learned Hand's "bevy of Platonic Guardians."[40] (As Owen Fiss has written recently, "[j]udges are most assuredly people. They are lawyers, but in terms of personal characteristics they are no different from successful businessmen or politicians. Their capacity to make a special contribution to our social life derives not from any personal traits or knowledge, but," he continues, introducing an issue to which I will turn shortly, "from the definition of the office in which they find themselves and through which they exercise power."[41]) If I am not suggesting any of that, what, then, am I suggesting? Let me elaborate.

Our religious self-understanding has generally involved a commitment—though not necessarily a fully conscious commitment—to the notion of moral evolution,[42] because in the main we have avoided the pretense that our current understanding of the moral universe—of ourselves, others, and the world we inhabit, and most fundamentally of the proper relationship among ourselves, others, and our world—was perfect and complete. Rather, we know that we are fallible and that we must struggle incessantly to achieve a better—a broader and deeper—understanding.* We also know that we are frail and that our frailty necessitates an ongoing struggle to bring our collective (political) practice into ever closer harmony with our evolving, deepening moral understanding.

To avoid misunderstanding, let me emphasize that I am *not* arguing that our religious self-understanding and attendant openness to moral evolution justify noninterpretive review in human rights cases, only that they help explain its existence and clarify its character. Moreover, the justification for noninterpretive review that I am about to develop is inde-

---

*Or, to use metaphors that have less currency today but that capture the same essential point, we know that our human fallibility necessitates an ongoing struggle to "discover God's own true will." Not even mainstream theistic theology—as opposed to fundamentalist ideology, which happily is a peripheral feature of the religious landscape—has supposed that the discovery of God's will is a closed or irreformable chapter. Hence, even a theistic understanding of the moral universe generally entails commitment to the notion of moral *evolution* rather than *stasis*.

pendent of my foregoing claims about the nature of American self-understanding. Skepticism about those claims is not reason for, and certainly ought not to be confused with, skepticism about my justification for noninterpretive review. That my claims about the nature of American self-understanding might be unsound—which of course I deny—does not mean that my justification for noninterpretive review is unsound too.

What *is* my justification for noninterpretive review in human rights cases? I begin with some observations—not very controversial observations, I think—about comparative institutional competence. In any recent generation, certain political issues have been widely perceived to be fundamental moral issues as well—issues that challenge and unsettle conventional ways of understanding the moral universe and that serve as occasions for forging alternative ways of understanding.

In twentieth-century America, there have been several such issues: for example, distributive justice and the role of government, freedom of political dissent, racism and sexism, the death penalty, human sexuality. Our electorally accountable policymaking institutions are not well suited to deal with such issues in a way that is faithful to the notion of moral evolution or, therefore, to our religious understanding of ourselves. Those institutions, when finally they confront such issues at all, tend simply to rely on established moral conventions and to refuse to see in such issues occasions for moral reevaluation and possible moral growth. That is not invariably the case, but sometimes, not infrequently, it is.

Executive and especially legislative officials *tend* to deal with fundamental political-moral problems, at least highly controversial ones, by reflexive reference to the established moral conventions of the greater part of their particular constituencies. They function that way principally because for many of them few if any values rank as high as incumbency.[43] "[L]eaders in both houses [of Congress] have a habit of counseling members to 'vote their constituencies.' "[44] Listen, in that regard, to Robert Dahl:

> [Congressional leaders] rely mainly on persuasion, party loyalty, expectations of reciprocal treatment, and, occasionally, special inducements such as patronage or public works. But none of these is likely to be adequate if a member is persuaded that a vote to support his party will cost him votes among his constituents. Fortunately, for him, the mores of Congress, accepted by the leaders themselves, are perfectly clear on this point: His own election comes first.[45]

Not that a concern for remaining (or getting) in office is always inappropriate; that concern, of course, is what makes electoral accountability work as well as it does to keep our representatives at least somewhat in tune with the polity. But a concern for remaining in office is not a particularly good way to keep faith with the notion of moral evolution, which requires ongoing, vigorous reevaluation of established moral conventions. "Legis-latures . . . see their primary function in terms of registering the actual, occurrent preferences of the people—what they want and what they be-lieve should be done."[46] "Legislators have become astute at turning a deaf ear to highly visible issues on which they do not want to gamble their political lives."[47] Over time, the practice of noninterpretive review has evolved as a way of remedying what would otherwise be a serious defect in American government—the absence of any policymaking institution that *regularly* deals with fundamental political-moral problems other than by mechanical reference to established moral conventions.

The emergence, principally though certainly not exclusively in the last twenty-five years, of the institutional practice under consideration here—noninterpretive judicial review in human rights cases—should be understood as an organic political development in response to the problem identified in the preceding paragraph. The basic function of that practice is to deal with those political issues that are also fundamental moral prob-lems in a way that *is* faithful to the notion of moral evolution (and, therefore, to our collective religious self-understanding)—not simply by invoking established moral conventions but by seizing such issues as opportunities for moral reevaluation and possible moral growth. That is the sense in which I mean that noninterpretive review in human rights cases represents the institutionalization of prophecy. Such review is an enterprise designed to enable the American polity to live out its commit-ment to an ever-deepening moral understanding and to political practices that harmonize with that understanding.

Recall the various political-moral issues the Supreme Court has ad-dressed in the modern period, in particular freedom of expression and racial and other sorts of discrimination. In dealing with those issues, the Court has not relied—that is, when acting at what is now widely regarded as its best, the Court has not relied—on established conventions. To the contrary, the Court has used such issues as occasions for moral reevalua-tion of established conventions and for possible moral development, perhaps leading, however gradually and sometimes painfully, to the estab-lishment of morally sounder conventions.[48]

Recall that the justification for noninterpretive review in human rights cases, if any, is functional. Noninterpretive review has served an im-portant, even indispensable, function. It has enabled us, as a people, to keep faith with two of the most basic aspects of our collective self-understanding: our democratic understanding of ourselves as a people committed to policymaking that is subject to control by electorally ac-countable persons, and our religious understanding of ourselves as a peo-ple committed to struggle incessantly to see beyond, and then to live beyond, the imperfections of whatever happens at the moment to be the established moral conventions. Or perhaps I should say that noninterpretive review has enabled us to maintain a tolerable accommodation between the two, sometimes seemingly irreconcilable commitments.

Earlier I said that my justification for noninterpretive review is independent of my claims about the religious aspect of American self-understanding. And yet I have just now portrayed the function of noninterpretive review in human rights cases—the function that in my view constitutes the justification for the practice—as that of helping us to keep faith with the religious aspect of our self-understanding. For the reader who suspects that in fact there is no religious aspect of American self-understanding—or that if there is, I have romanticized it beyond recognition—I can easily, and will readily, recast my essential claim. Noninterpretive review in human rights cases has enabled us to maintain a tolerable accommodation between, first, our democratic commitment and, second, the possibility that there may indeed be right answers—*discoverable* right answers—to fundamental political-moral problems.

Whether or not there is a religious aspect of American self-understanding, as a society we seem to be open to the possibility that there are right answers to political-moral problems. But even if evidence were slight that we are open to that possibility, we *should be* open to it. I shall have more to say about the matter of right answers in a moment. But I shall not defend the proposition that we should take seriously the possibility that there are right answers: this is not a metaethical treatise. Here I want merely to emphasize that the proposition, if sound, is altogether adequate for purposes of the functional justification I develop in this chapter: Noninterpretive review enables us to keep faith with a possibility to which I think we are open, and to which in any event we should be open. And, as I shall explain later, it enables us to keep faith with that possibility in a manner that accommodates our democratic commitment.

My essential claim, then, is that noninterpretive review in human rights cases enables us to take seriously—indeed is a way of taking seriously—the possibility that there are right answers to political-moral problems. As a matter of comparative institutional competence, the politically insulated federal judiciary is more likely, when the human rights issue is a deeply controversial one, to move us in the direction of a right answer (assuming there is such a thing) than is the political process left to its own devices, which tends to resolve such issues by reflexive, mechanical reference to established moral conventions. None of this, of course, is to suggest that the Supreme Court, or any other court, necessarily gives right answers. I shall have more to say about that problem later in this chapter.

I now want to amplify and defend my argument by responding to the principal contentions directed against noninterpretive review by its severest critics, interpretivists like Robert Bork and William Rehnquist.

Probably the most fundamental such contention is rooted in a deep moral skepticism. There are two ways of understanding the contention. According to the first, the contention, consisting of what philosophers call "metaethical relativism,"[49] holds that there are no right answers to the various political-moral questions presented to the Court in human rights cases—no right answers, that is, when no value judgment constitutionalized by the framers is determinative—and that any answer the Court gives, short of simply resolving (which virtually always would mean dismissing) the constitutional claim on interpretivist grounds, is ultimately nothing more than a matter of taste.[50]

Alternatively, the contention is somewhat less radical; it holds that "no one can ever say with any justification that something is good or bad, right or wrong. Some actions may be right and others wrong, but there is no way of knowing which is which."[51] The philosopher Kai Neilsen terms that position "ethical skepticism." It is, he says, the "cousin" of metaethical relativism. "The skeptic leaves open the possibility that some actions or principles are right or wrong, but he claims that we can never be in a position to know that this is so."[52]

The position Bork and Rehnquist espouse holds at least that there is no demonstrably right answer—whether or not there is some unknowable right answer—and, in that sense, no right answer. Bork writes:

> Where constitutional materials do not clearly specify the value to be preferred, there is no principled way to prefer any claimed human value to any other.
>
>   . . . .
>
> There is no way of deciding [human rights questions] other than by reference to some system of moral or ethical values that has no objective or intrinsic validity of its own and about which men can and do differ.[53]

Justice Rehnquist makes essentially the same point:

> Beyond the Constitution and the laws in our society, there simply is no basis other than the individual conscience of the citizen that may serve as a platform for the launching of moral judgments. There is no conceivable way in which I can logically demonstrate to you that the judgments of my conscience are superior to the judgments of your conscience, and vice versa. Many of us necessarily feel strongly and deeply about our own moral judgments, but they remain only personal moral judgments until in some way given the sanction of law.[54]

I said that Bork and Rehnquist hold that there is no right answer. Perhaps I should say instead that in their view the only right answer is one given by electorally accountable policymakers (unless, of course, it is inconsistent with a value judgment constitutionalized by the framers). For Bork and

Rehnquist, an answer is right not because it comports with some substantive standard of rightness, but because it was generated in the procedurally correct manner. Thus, Rehnquist writes that if a democratic society

> adopts a constitution and incorporates in that constitution safeguards for individual liberty, these safeguards do indeed take on a generalized moral rightness or goodness. They assume a general social acceptance neither because of any intrinsic worth nor because of any unique origins in anyone's idea of natural justice but instead simply because they have been incorporated in a constitution by the people. Within the limits of our Constitution, the representatives of the people in the executive [sic] branches of the state and national government enact laws. The laws that emerge after a typical political struggle in which various individual value judgments are debated likewise take on a form of moral goodness because they have been enacted into positive law. *It is the fact of their enactment that gives them whatever moral claim they have upon us as a society, however, and not any independent virtue they may have in any particular citizen's own scale of values.*[55]

Reasoning similarly, Bork concludes: "Courts must accept any value choice the legislature makes unless it clearly runs contrary to a choice made in the framing of the Constitution."[56]

At this point one might be tempted to fault Bork and Rehnquist by contending that if they *really* adhered to ethical skepticism, they would not be able to justify their interpretivism; they would not be able to supply a moral justification for their position that all policy choices should be subject to control by persons who are electorally accountable. The point of the criticism would be to say that since Bork and Rehnquist apparently intend a moral justification for interpretivism, they are reasoning inconsistently in trotting out ethical skepticism to do battle against noninterpretive review. But such criticism misconceives Bork's and Rehnquist's argument. They do not claim that it is possible to supply a moral justification for the principle of electorally accountable policymaking. Rather, they treat that principle as a given—as axiomatic—in our political-legal culture (and conclude that noninterpretive review is inconsistent with it). Certainly they are entitled to do just that: Ethical skepticism does not commit one to rejecting all moral positions—in this case, the principle of electorally accountable policymaking. It merely commits one to rejecting the proposition that any given moral position is demonstrably correct.[57]*

---

*Thomas Nagel has claimed that "no one, whatever his views about the proper role of the Court, is a complete skeptic about ethics." He explains: "Even a theory of the Court's function that assigns the Court the limited role of safeguarding the procedures of democratic majority rule and of preventing the exclusion of any citizen from the democratic process must depend on a political philosophy that is taken to be true." Nagel, *The Supreme Court and Political Philosophy*, 56 N.Y.U. L. REV. 519, 519, 520 (1981). Nagel is wrong. Robert Bork is the perfect

If Bork's and Rehnquist's moral skepticism were widely shared, it would be extremely difficult, perhaps impossible, to elaborate a justification for noninterpretive review that would have much currency. For the moral skeptic *who is committed to the principle of electorally accountable policymaking*, there is no principled reason to prefer an answer given by the Court to one given by an institution that, unlike the Court, is electorally accountable. No answer is demonstrably correct, and, therefore, better an answer by an electorally accountable institution than by an electorally unaccountable one. But moral skepticism is by no means the only respectable metaethical position. Many philosophers—including adherents to the two principal contemporary schools of moral philosophy, utilitarianism[58] and social contractarianism[59]—reject it.[60] For the person who does not subscribe to it, that skepticism cannot count as a reason for rejecting noninterpretive review in human rights cases.

Consider, for a moment, the implications of the moral skepticism to which Bork and Rehnquist subscribe. Recall that no value judgment constitutionalized by the framers enjoins laws establishing racial segregation or state laws abolishing freedom of expression or of religion. Bork says that "[w]here constitutional materials do not clearly specify the value to be preferred, there is no principled way to prefer any claimed human value to any other." Rehnquist says that unless they are enacted into law, particular value judgments have no claim on us as a society.

The necessary implication of their moral skepticism is that there is no "principled" ground on which the Court *or indeed anyone else*[61] can oppose duly enacted laws establishing segregation or abolishing freedom of expression or of religion. The value judgment that segregation is morally evil, or that freedom of expression or of religion is morally good, has no claim on us as a society (except and only to the extent that such judgments have been enacted into positive law). Indeed, according to moral skepticism, there is no "principled"—morally nonarbitrary—ground for objecting to laws authorizing torture, establishing slavery, or even instituting another Holocaust. Yes, these *are* extreme examples—at least I hope they are. But there is nothing inappropriate in using extreme examples to make the point, which is that moral skepticism is a terribly difficult position to take seriously in this post-Holocaustal age. Moreover, it is, happily, a position not widely shared in the United States today, nor has it ever been.

---

counterexample. Bork's theory of judicial review does not depend on a political philosophy that is taken to be true. Rather, it depends on a political philosophy that is taken to be a given in—an axiom of—American political-legal culture. One can treat a particular political philosophy as a given, one can even be committed to a particular political philosophy, without abandoning one's robust moral skepticism—that is, without supposing that the philosophy can be demonstrated to be true, even without supposing that truth can be predicated of political philosophy.

We have taken it for granted, as the Pledge of Allegiance with its aspiration of "liberty and justice for all" indicates, that the language of justice—the search for justice—is not morally arbitrary (even as we have disagreed about the constituents of justice).

In particular, it is a position fundamentally at odds with our understanding of ourselves as a people committed to ongoing moral reevaluation and moral growth. For the moral skeptic, moral growth is an illusion; moral positions change, but there is no principled ("objective") way to prefer any given moral position to any other. Although the abolition of slavery throughout the world in the last one hundred years—at least, the abolition of slavery in its most conspicuous forms—seems to some to be moral growth, to the moral skeptic it is not. Although the abolition of torture,[62] or of hunger, throughout the world in the next one hundred years would seem to some to be moral growth, to the moral skeptic it would not be. Such developments represent change, not growth.[63]

The reasons why moral skepticism is not a widely shared position vary. Some persons reject that skepticism on philosophical grounds (and among such persons, the philosophical grounds vary). Others reject it on religious grounds (which also vary). But the rich variety of grounds and metaphors in terms of which persons explain their rejection of moral skepticism to themselves or to others should not obscure the underlying commonality: a deep, abiding sense, which resists all reductionist attempts to explain it away, that morality—justice—is not simply a matter of taste, of willful preference.* The narrow point I want to emphasize here, however, is

---

*Moral skepticism is predicated on a problematic distinction—between factual (nonnormative) judgments, which many persons believe can in some sense be verified by "objective" criteria, and value (normative) judgments, which, according to the moral skeptic, cannot be tested because no objective criteria exist. The distinction is unsound if, as some philosophers ("naturalists") insist, there is in principle no radical difference between a factual judgment and a value judgment—if every value judgment is ultimately translatable in part into a judgment as to the nature of reality and in that sense into a factual judgment. The distinction on which moral skepticism is predicated may be largely a figment of the post-Enlightenment imagination. See generally R. UNGER, KNOWLEDGE AND POLITICS (1975); A. MACINTYRE, BEYOND VIRTUE (1981). If so, unless factual judgments can in no meaningful sense be tested, it is difficult to understand how value judgments can in no meaningful sense be tested.

Art Leff has written that "there is today no way of 'proving' that napalming babies is bad except by asserting it (in a louder and louder voice), or by defining it as so, early in one's game, and then later slipping it through, in a whisper, as a conclusion." Leff, Economic Analysis of Law: Some Realism About Nominalism, 60 VA. L. REV. 451, 454 (1974). That depends, of course, on what one means by "bad" (or "wrong"). See Brandt, Ethical Relativism, in 3 ENCYCLOPEDIA OF PHILOSOPHY (P. Edwards ed. 1967), at 75:

The metaethical relativist . . . denies that there is always one correct moral evaluation. The metaethical relativist thesis is tenable only if certain views about meaning are rejected. For instance, if "A is right" means "Doing A will contribute at least as much to

simply this: If a person rejects moral skepticism—on whatever grounds and with whatever metaphors—obviously that metaethical position cannot count for him, as it does for both Bork and Rehnquist, as a reason for rejecting noninterpretive review in human rights cases.

Obviously I reject Bork's and Rehnquist's moral skepticism. I argue that as a society we should take seriously the possibility that there are right answers to political-moral problems. My assumption that there might be right answers is not at all idiosyncratic. Frank Michelman speaks of "politics" as, in part at least, "a joint or mutual search for good or right answers to the question of directions for our evolving selves."[64] Similarly, William Bennett writes that "the spirit of constitutionalism requires, perhaps primarily, a commitment to the possibility of . . . reaching sound conclusions about right and wrong through the deliverances of judgment and sound principle. . . ."[65] Recently Owen Fiss argued that

[o]nly once we reassert our belief . . . that values such as equality, liberty, due process, no cruel and unusual punishment, security of the person, or free speech can have a true and important meaning, that must be articulated and implemented—yes, discovered—will the role of courts in our political system become meaningful, or for that matter even intelligible.[66]

If there are right answers, does it follow that there is a single authoritative moral system, whether philosophical or religious, that, properly applied, generates right answers? Perhaps there is some such system, already discovered or waiting to be discovered. Some defenders of noninterpretive review think there is such a system. Recently a number of constitutional theorists have argued contractarian moral and political philosophy[67] is an appropriate, indeed *the* appropriate source of decisional norms for human

---

the happiness of sentient creatures as anything else one might do," it is obvious that one and only one of the two opinions, "A is right" and "A is wrong" is correct. Thus, the metaethical relativist is restricted to a certain range of theories about the meaning of ethical statements.

I assume Vietnamese Buddhists claimed that napalming Vietnamese babies was "bad"; but I know that for them such a claim could not have been intended as a value judgment as opposed to a factual one, because in Buddhism there is no such distinction. For the Buddhist, the proposition that Leff says cannot be proved is a statement about reality—about the way the world hangs together—and "proving" it to another person consists of trying to open his eyes to that way of "seeing." True, the attempt might not succeed. Personal vision might be irremediably tied to personal history. But even among physical scientists, who deal mainly in facts and not values, there are often conflicting visions of the reality that underlies, and is fragmentarily disclosed by, available data. *See also* H. PUTNAM, MEANING AND THE MORAL SCIENCES 83–94 (1978); Fried, *The Laws of Change: The Cunning of Reason in Moral and Legal History,* 9 J. LEG. STUD. 335, 341–45 (1980).

rights cases.[68] The historical version of the argument holds that the framers of the 1789 Constitution and the Bill of Rights adhered to contractarian philosophy and that such philosophy therefore constitutes the political-moral foundation of the Constitution. In effect, the claim is that the framers constitutionalized, at least implicitly, contractarian philosophy, leaving it up to future generations to work out the implications of that philosophy for whatever problems might arise.[69]

The fatal problem with that historical claim is that it utterly lacks persuasive evidentiary support. In fact, the principal proponent of the claim, David Richards, has never attempted to adduce evidentiary support, beyond noticing that contractarian philosophy had its adherents during the preconstitutional period. I am willing to assume that during the 1787–91 period some, perhaps many of the framers, were adherents of contractarian philosophy, or of something like it. But there is no reason to believe that the framers of the fourteenth amendment—which, after all, is the principal constitutional basis for judicial intervention against the states—were similarly adherents of that philosophy. And in any event it is extravagant to suggest that contractarian philosophy—least of all in anything like its contemporary Rawlsian form, which is the principal form in which such philosophy is typically urged on the Court[70]—was constitutionalized by the framers of the 1789 Constitution and thus constitutes the exclusive, authoritative political-moral canon for American government (with respect to human rights).

"The social contract theory in which the framers believed [was not anything like Rawls's or Richards's theory]. The Lockean natural rights in which they believed are indeed in severe tension with [the Rawls-Richards sort of theory]. Even if Rawls's and Richards's theory is the best social contract theory, it is not part of the theory of our Constitution."[71] To be taken at all seriously, Richards's historical claim must be proved, and thus far neither he nor anyone else has even tried. Moreover, such evidence as does exist strongly suggests that any effort to prove the claim would be quixotic.[72]

The philosophical version of the argument holds that contractarian philosophy, whether or not consitutionalized by the framers, is compelling philosophy and ought for that reason to constitute the basis of whatever political-moral judgments the Court is called upon to make in human rights cases.[73] In one sense this version of the claim is more modest than the other, for it invokes no implausible historical premises. But in another sense it is more extravagant, for it apotheosizes a particular school of moral philosophy. There is so much disagreement among philosophers and theologians over basic moral principles that I, as an outsider to the debate, am exceedingly reluctant to assume that some existing moral system—

some existing moral vision—has an exclusive claim on the mind of man.*

Moreover, I am reluctant to assume that a single moral system will ever have an exclusive claim on the mind of man. The assumption that there are right answers does not seem to me to require the distinct assumption that there is a single authoritative moral system. Is there another possibility? Perhaps the correctness of a given answer to a human rights problem inheres in something other than the particular set of reasons—the particular rationalization or explanation—offered in support of the answer. The human rights problems that are presented to the Court are problems about how the collectivity *qua* government ought to act (or refrain from acting) toward individual human beings. An answer to such a problem—that government ought or ought not to act in a particular fashion—may be right not because the specific reasons adduced in its support are correct when measured against some assertedly orthodox political-moral criterion, such as social contractarianism. Rather, a right answer—that is, that racial segregation, apartheid, is wrong; or that state governments ought not to impose civil disabilities on non-Christians—frequently represents, in the United States, a point at which *a variety* of philosophical and religious systems of moral thought and belief converge.

Indeed, the "rightness" of the axiom that gives rise to the problem of the legitimacy of noninterpretive review—the principle of electorally accountable policymaking—is evidenced in just that way. As one political theorist recently noted, "a wide variety of ethical and metaethical theories all lend support to the democratic ideal."[74] Moreover, the "rightness" of the various human rights now recognized in international law is evidenced in the same way; "[i]nternational human rights . . . were designed to be acceptable in political systems that differ from ours in important respects. . . . [I]nternational human rights are as consistent with varieties of capitalism as with various socialisms."[75]

Note that I do not say that rationalization (explanation) is unimportant or dispensable, any more than myth—that is, world views, whether ancient ("magical") or modern ("scientific"), which, after all, are cultural artifacts—is unimportant or dispensable. Man—at least in his ordinary, me-

---

*A serious problem with the argument that contractarian philosophy ought to be deemed authoritative for purposes of constitutional policymaking in human rights cases is the implicit suggestion that contractarian philosophy, once accepted as authoritative, would generate noncontroversial answers. Which particular principles ought to be understood as fundamental in contractarian philosophy, after all, is a matter of controversy even among contractarians, unless the principles are expressed in a highly indeterminate and therefore uselessly vague fashion. Moreover, the correct application of those principles is a matter of controversy. Why should the Court—indeed may the Court—undertake to impose its particular resolution of any given contractarian controversy?

diated, self-conscious moments—seems to require rationalization, just as he seems to require myth. (Indeed rationalization is an aspect, or perhaps the matrix, of myth.) My point is simply that the correctness of a given answer may not depend on any particular rationalization that may be offered in its support, but may transcend particular rationalizations.

"Well, then," one might ask, "on what *does* it depend? That is, in what does the correctness of a given answer inhere if not the particular rationalization that is offered, or at least *some* particular rationalization that can be offered, in its support? How can we know whether a given answer is or is not correct except in terms of the (actual or possible) reasons adduced in its support?" Particular rationalizations—particular philosophical or theological systems of morality—are, unlike our common humanity, "relative to linguistic and theoretical schemes which are historically and culturally conditioned and therefore reformable."[76] Wallace Stevens wrote that "we live in the description of a place and not in the place itself."[77]

Perhaps what is essential is not orthodoxy, in the sense of a particular idea- or belief-system, which, again, is profoundly a function of place and time. Perhaps what is essential is orthopraxis: "right" action—here, right governmental action toward individual human beings—rather than any particular "right" philosophical or theological rationalization offered in support of that action.[78] In that crucial sense, then, correctness may be a matter of orthopraxis, and the correctness of a given answer—an answer in the form of a proposition that government must act or refrain from acting toward individual human beings in a certain way—is evidenced, in part at least, by its location at a point of convergence among a variety of moral systems.

Now, I am not a philosopher, and perhaps I am simply mistaken in suggesting that there is a critical distinction between a right answer and any particular rationalization that may be offered in its support.[79] Suffice it to say that my assumption that there are right answers ought not to be confused with the distinct assumption that there is—or will be—a single authoritative moral system that should inform the exercise of noninterpretive review in human rights cases. Perhaps there is such a system, or perhaps one will be discovered. But my justification for noninterpretive review is not predicated on any such assumption.

How shall a justice of the Supreme Court or other judge proceed in adjudicating a constitutional human rights case (when the written Constitution is silent)? I have expressed skepticism that any one school of political-moral philosophy should be deemed authoritative for purposes of noninterpretive review in human rights cases—that is, authoritative for all justices, such that a justice who declined to be led by that philosophical school would be in error.

But that is a far cry from saying that individual justices should refrain from consulting what they personally regard to be the most relevant and fruitful moral thought. To the contrary. It would be absurd to insist that "the literature of moral philosophy is irrelevant to the proper performance of the judge's task."[80] How, after all, could a justice submit established moral conventions to a sensitive, critical reevaluation without reference to (among other things) past and present moral thinking?[81] For that matter, how could a legislator proceed, who takes seriously the possibility that there are right answers, without reference to past and present moral thinking? The problem of how to proceed, when dealing with a difficult human rights issue, is not different for the justice than it is for the legislator. As Cardozo wrote: "If you ask me how [the judge] is to know when one interest outweighs another, I can only answer that he must get his knowledge just as the legislator gets it, from experience and study and reflection; in brief, from life itself."[82] And the justice, like the legislator, will inevitably conclude that some particular political-moral principles (perhaps even a particular political-moral system) are better than others. Inevitably each justice will deal with human rights problems in terms of the particular political-moral criteria that are, in that justice's view, authoritative. I do not see how it could possibly be otherwise.*

The notion of moral evolution—of ongoing moral reevaluation and moral growth—may not justify application, by the Court, of a single moral system in resolving moral problems. But what the notion of moral evolution *can* help explain and justify is a policymaking institution (the Court) whose members, not every one of which has the same criteria of moral rightness, deal with moral problems, not passively, by bowing to established moral conventions, but actively, creatively, by subjecting those conventions to critical reevaluation. It can explain and justify a policymaking institution whose morality is "open," not "closed"—an institution that resolves moral problems not simply by looking backward to the sediment of old moralities, but ahead to emergent principles in terms of which fragments of a new moral order can be forged.[83]

An implication of my argument is that answers to human rights questions are right (or not) independently of what a majority of Americans happen to believe, either in the short-term or in the long-term. But what the majority comes to believe in the long-term, after having been rebuffed by the electorally unaccountable Supreme Court in the short-term, is more likely to be morally correct than are established but untested, unreflective moral conventions.

Let me explain. In adjudicating a person's claim that government has

---

*See Gibbons, Keynote Address, *Symposium: Constitutional Adjudication and Democratic Theory*, 56 N.Y.U. L. Rev. 260, 274 (1981): "Academics may dispute which school of ethics, or moral theology, or political philosophy is best, but they will agree, I think, that when called upon to legitimate the imposition of sanctions arguably at war with human rights, judges do, and should, make a personal selection among competing values on the basis of individual conscience."

violated (or is violating) his human rights—which is really a claim about what human rights he ought to be deemed to have—the Court, when no value judgment constitutionalized by the framers is determinative, in effect submits the challenged governmental action to a moral critique, and in striking down such action, the Court assumes a prophetic stance, opposing itself to established conventions. But that is not the end of the matter. The relationship between noninterpretive review and electorally accountable policymaking is dialectical. The electorally accountable political processes generate a policy choice,[84] which typically reflects some fairly well established moral conventions; at least typically the policy choice does not challenge those conventions. In exercising noninterpretive review, the Court evaluates that choice on political-moral grounds, in the end either accepting or rejecting it. If the Court rejects a given policy choice, the political processes must respond, whether by embracing the Court's decision, by tolerating it, or, if the decision is not accepted, or accepted fully, by moderating or even by undoing it. (The matter of how the political processes can undo a decision is addressed later in this chapter.)

The constitutional literature of the modern period—especially that part of it sympathetic to constitutional policymaking by the judiciary in human rights cases—is replete with language that tries to capture the dialectical relationship between noninterpretive review and electorally accountable policymaking.[85] Eugene Rostow wrote:

> The process of forming opinion in the United States is a continuous one with many participants—Congress, the President, the press, political parties, scholars, pressure groups, and so on. The discussion of problems and the declaration of broad principles by the Court is a vital element in the community experience through which American policy is made. The Supreme Court is, among other things, an educational body, and the Justices are inevitable teachers in a vital national seminar.[86]

Rostow then spoke of the Court entering into a "reciprocal relation" with "the community in the formation of policy."[87] "[T]he judicial opinion," said Rostow, "is a piece of rhetoric and of literature, intended to educate and persuade."[88] "Popular sovereignty," Rostow insisted, "is a more subtle idea than the phrase 'majority rule' sometimes implies."[89] Justice Robert Jackson wrote that "[n]o sound assessment of the Supreme Court can treat it as an isolated, self-sustaining, or self-sufficient institution. It is a unit of a complex, interdependent scheme of government from which it cannot be severed."[90] Robert McCloskey noted that "what people will when they have thought only of immediate interests may be quite different from what they will when they have been reminded that cherished long-term values are involved." Thus, McCloskey concluded, "the Court can be regarded, not as an adversary, but as an auxiliary to democracy."[91] In a similar vein,

Alexander Bickel wrote that "[t]he society also values the capacity of judges to draw its attention to issues of the largest principles that may have gone unheeded in the welter of its pragmatic doings."[92] With particular reference to the dialectical nature of the relationship, Bickel observed:

> Virtually all important decisions of the Supreme Court are the beginnings of conversations between the Court and the people and their representatives. They are never, at the start, conversations between equals. The Court has an edge, because it initiates things with some immediate action, even if limited. But conversations they are, and to say that the Supreme Court lays down the law of the land is to state the ultimate result, following upon a complex series of events, in some cases, and in others it is a form of speech only. The effectiveness of the judgment universalized depends on consent and administration.[93]

I want to emphasize that I am *not* claiming that the Court always gives right answers. Of course it does not, and I explore the implications of that fact later in this chapter. My basic point is simply this: In the constitutional dialogue between the Court and the other agencies of government—a subtle, dialectical interplay between Court and polity—what emerges is a far more self-critical political morality than would otherwise appear, and therefore likely a more mature political morality as well—a morality that is moving (inching?) toward, even though it has not always and everywhere arrived at, right answers, rather than a stagnant or even regressive morality.* This dialectical relationship represents "an idealized conception of how societal change should be structured, reaching beyond a sim-

---

*I say "likely," not "necessarily." *See, e.g.,* J. CHOPER, *supra* prologue, note 12, at 168: "[T]he *Plessy* edict led to the expansion of segregation; the *Japanese Exclusion Cases* were relied on to support McCarran Act's detention camps; the *Gobitis* decision stimulated flag salute programs . . ."

Ronald Dworkin's vision of constitutional adjudication seems very close to mine. *See* Dworkin, *The Forum of Principle,* 56 N.Y.U. L. REV. 469, 517, 518 (1981):

> Judicial review insures that the most fundamental issues of political morality will finally be set out and debated as issues of principle and not simply as issues of political power, a transformation that cannot succeed, in any case not fully, within the legislature itself. That is important beyond the importance of the actual decisions reached in courts so charged.
>   . . . .
> [Judicial review] called some issues from the battleground of power politics to the forum of principle. It holds out the promise that the deepest, most fundamental conflicts between individual and society will once, someplace, finally, become questions of justice.

(Dworkin, however, persists in the mistaken belief that in the exercise of judicial review, "judges . . . make substantive decisions of political morality not in place of judgments made

plistic majoritarian deference . . . to provide us with alternative means for moral growth.''[94]

To be sure, the framers of the Constitution certainly did not anticipate, much less authorize, noninterpretive review in its modern sense; they did not themselves ordain the dialectic to which political evolution has since given rise. In that sense, noninterpretive review is extraconstitutional —beyond any value judgment the framers constitutionalized.

But the fact that the practice of noninterpretive review is extraconstitutional is hardly a reason to reject it. Many of our contemporary political practices and institutions—that is, the ''imperial'' presidency[95]—go far beyond anything the framers likely contemplated.[96] But they are not illegitimate on *that* account (even if they are suspect for some other reasons). The argument that the framers did not themselves authorize constitutional policymaking by the judiciary ''simply begs the question. Unless we conclude that the Constitution allows for no institutional growth beyond the original understanding—the very point to be proved—the belief of the framers in a weak judiciary is only as persuasive as the arguments supporting that belief.''[97]

John Ely has criticized those who would explain the function of noninterpretive review as ''predicting progress.'' He notes that Alexander Bickel claimed that

> [t]he Warren Court . . . had tried to prefigure the future, to shape its constitutional principles in accord with its best estimate of what tomorrow's observers would be prepared to credit as progress. . . . Bickel was somewhat elusive about whether he himself was prepared to credit ''tomorrow's values'' as a source of constitutional judgment: his formal claim was that that had been the criterion of the Warren Court and that by its own criterion that Court had to be judged a failure. Though the point is arguable, I believe there was a good deal of prescription folded into Bickel's description. In any event others, before and after, have endorsed the method, even if Bickel did not mean to.[98]

Ely is quite critical of such a ''method.'' ''Prediction is a risky business for anyone,'' he says, and there is no warrant for an appointed judge's supposing that he is so much better at it than the legislature that he is going to declare their efforts unconstitutional on the basis of his predictions.''[99] Moreover, argues Ely, ''the reference [to ''tomorrow's values''] is antidemocratic on its face. Controlling today's generation by the values of its grandchildren is no more acceptable than controlling it by the generation

---

by the 'Framers' but rather in service of those judgments.'' *Id.* at 490. For my criticism of that view, see pp. 70–76 *supra*. I wonder: Would Dworkin really think judicial review—the forum of principle—illegitimate if there were no written constitution and therefore no framers? Or would he then look for a justification not tied to the framers?

of its grandparents: a 'liberal accelerator' is neither less nor more consistent with democratic theory than a 'conservative brake'."[100]

Without evaluating Ely's critique of the "predicting progress" conception of noninterpretive review—a morally skeptical conception as Ely portrays it, in which tomorrow's values are assumed to be merely different from today's ("change, not growth")—I want to emphasize that the conception I have proffered—noninterpretive review as an agency of moral reevaluation and moral growth—is a very different one. As I took care to emphasize a few pages ago, answers are morally correct *independently of what a majority of the American people comes to believe in the future.* My point is not that noninterpretive review is (or should be) aimed at predicting what tomorrow's majority might come to credit as progress, but that the dialectical relationship between noninterpretive review and the processes of electorally accountable policymaking leads to a far more self-critical morality, and likely, therefore, to a more mature political morality as well. It is not a question of "controlling today's generation by the [predicted] values of its grandchildren," but of *aspiring* to give, in any generation, right answers to the fundamental political-moral problems that exercise that generation.

The relationship between self-criticism and maturity is not a necessary one, however. Certainly it is possible that noninterpretive review will retard rather than advance the polity's political morality. And that possibility brings us to the interpretivist's second basic criticism of noninterpretive review, which takes as its point of departure a proposition that is indisputably true: The Court is a fallible institution. It is capable of giving false prophecy. If the Court can serve as an instrument of moral growth, it can also serve as an instrument of moral retardation. Justice Rehnquist reminds us that it was in the exercise of noninterpretive review, after all, that the Court handed down its decisions in Dred Scott v. Sanford[101] and Lochner v. New York[102]—decisions now virtually universally rejected on sound political-moral grounds.[103] Raoul Berger's book abounds with cautions that those who are euphoric over what the Court has done in recent times, in particular during the tenure of Chief Justice Earl Warren, should recall the abominations the Court wrought in earlier periods of its history, especially during the first third or so of this century, when the Court acted to frustrate the emergence of the welfare state.[104] Rehnquist's and Berger's point is not merely that the Court is quite capable of handing down fundamentally unsound decisions, but that because such decisions are constitutional in character, they (and their unfortunate consequences) cannot be undone in the comparatively swift and simple way improvident legislation can be undone—by electorally accountable officials acting through ordinary policymaking processes.

Is the Court's fallibility sufficient reason to reject the whole enterprise of noninterpretive review? Surely a prudent answer will reflect a sense of proportion: If in the foreseeable future the Court is likely to hand down only few (if any) decisions destined for the widespread condemnation now visited on cases such as *Lochner*, and if the function of noninterpretive review is *generally* salutary, on the whole helping us in our struggle to keep faith with our commitment to moral reevaluation and moral growth, then why count the fact of the Court's fallibility as a conclusive reason to reject noninterpretive review (especially given the political control over such review discussed later in this chapter)?

Few if any political institutions or practices work perfectly; the proper test is whether, on balance, they work tolerably well. A good case can be made that during any particular historical period the Court is likely to hand down comparatively few decisions striking down governmental action on idiosyncratic moral grounds. If anything, it is far more likely that the Court will hand down many decisions sustaining morally suspect governmental action. The justices of the Court, after all, are creatures of the larger, pluralistic moral culture, especially the larger moral culture of other governmental officials;[105] indeed, "judges tend generally to be drawn from roughly the same rank as legislators."[106] Certainly they are not alien to the larger culture in any important respect.[107]

Nonetheless, the specters of *Dred Scott* and especially of *Lochner* and its two-hundred-case progeny[108] loom. We should not discount, and in any event interpretivists will not let us discount, what cases like those signify. But at the same time, we must resist specious historical generalizations about the performance of the Supreme Court. Constitutional theory, like political theory generally, must be rooted in present as well as in past experience, lest the theory's relevance be confined primarily to the past. The issue for the present generation of constitutional theorists is not—not principally, at any rate—how noninterpretive review worked in the last half of the nineteenth century or even in the first half of the twentieth century, but whether noninterpretive review has served a salutary, perhaps crucial governmental (policymaking) function during the modern period. What Alexander Bickel said of judicial review generally we may say of noninterpretive review in particular—that it "is a *present* instrument of government. It represents a choice men have made, and ultimately we must justify it as a choice *in our own time*."[109]

Of course, it would be both foolish and dangerous to ignore the relevant lessons of the past. When Justice Rehnquist buttresses his theoretical critique of noninterpretive review by reminding us of *Dred Scott* and *Lochner*, we should not take lightly his historical point—the absence of any guarantee that noninterpretive review will in fact serve, during any given period, as an instrument of moral growth.[110] But neither should we fail to appreciate that examples drawn from one historical context can have a rather diminished significance in a different context.[111] Our evaluation of noninterpretive review in human rights cases must be contextual, which is to say that it must proceed principally by reference to how such review has worked, can work, and is likely to work in the modern period—"in our own time."[112]

In the human rights cases that have come before the Court in the modern period, has noninterpretive review served, on balance, as an instrument of moral growth or as an impediment? Of the three substantive areas of constitutional doctrine that are serving as the principal points of reference for our discussion—freedom of expression, equal protection, and substantive due process—only one, substantive due process, is the focus of significant controversy. Inevitably *details* of the Court's policymaking regarding freedom of expression and equal protection are seen as problematic.[113] But likely only few persons—few members of the American polity, at any rate—upon surveying the broad features of the Court's workproduct and judging with the benefits of hindsight and reflection, would today take issue with much of what the Court has done in the name of either freedom of expression or equal protection. Certainly not many would take issue with what is most consequential—the Court's establishment of freedom of expression as a constraint on *state* action and its disestablishment of laws and other official practices aimed at maintaining racial segregation. (Recall that our exemplary interpretivist, Robert Bork, sought to justify those two basic features of the Court's modern human rights activities, although, as I have indicated, his constitutional theory is fundamentally inconsistent with his justificatory efforts.[114]

But what about constitutional theory's perennial hobgoblin, "substantive due process?"* Constitutional policymaking in substantive due process cases in the modern period has been aimed at according the individual's interests in sexual, reproductive, and associational autonomy a constitutional status.[115] That is, it has been concerned with developing what Kenneth Karst has aptly named "the freedom of intimate association."[116] For example, the Supreme Court has invalidated various state policies directed against the distribution and/or use of "artificial"

---

*The referent of the term *substantive due process* is a particular area of constitutional doctrine; the term serves to demarcate this area from, say, first amendment or equal protection doctrine. In that sense, substantive due process comprises whatever norms the Supreme Court has invoked, formally in the name of the due process clauses, to limit the sorts of policy choices governmental officials, in particular legislators, may make. *Procedural due process*, by contrast, comprises the norms the Court has invoked, in the name of due process, to limit the ways in which, the procedures through which, officials, in particular those charged with administering law, may enforce policy choices once made. During the early, "Lochner" period of substantive due process, the principal norm was "liberty of contract." During the contemporary period, the principal norm has been what the Court persists in calling a "right of privacy," but which might be better termed a principle of sexual or at least procreative autonomy. For a good historical overview of the career of substantive due process, See L. TRIBE, AMERICAN CONSTITUTIONAL LAW 427–55, 886–990 (1978).

contraceptives;[117] a zoning provision prohibiting a grandchild from living with his grandmother;[118] and a statute preventing an indigent person from getting a marriage license.[119] Some lower federal courts and certain state courts have opposed governmental policies directed against nonmarital sexual activity, including homosexual activity, and cohabitation.[120] I suspect that these judicial efforts to establish the freedom of intimate association will not long be the occasion of widespread controversy. The Supreme Court's decision in the Abortion Cases,[121] which involved much more than an issue of associational freedom, presents a much more troubling matter, and I want to address it separately, at the end of this chapter.

My own view is that noninterpretive review in most substantive due process cases, specifically those in which the judiciary has sought to establish freedom of intimate association as a human right, consists, in the main, of right answers to the questions the courts have addressed— answers approaching or perhaps even reaching an emergent point of convergence among a variety of systematic moral theories. (This is not necessarily to say that the judiciary has given answers to which there is a "consensus" among the American people. The moral sensibilities of the pluralistic American polity typically lag behind, and are more fragmented than, the developing insights of moral philosophy and theology. A point of convergence among a variety of systematic moral theories, even if one exists or is emergent, does not necessarily consist of an answer as to which there is a present consensus among the people.)

If I am right—surely my view is not implausible—it follows that in the modern period, in cases involving issues of freedom of intimate association as well as in those involving issues of freedom of expression and of equal protection, noninterpretive review has functioned, on balance, as an instrument of deepening moral insight and of moral growth. And there is no reason to think that in the modern period noninterpretive review has functioned any differently, in the main, in human rights cases involving other matters—for example, freedom of religion or administration of the criminal process. (Again, inevitably some details of the Court's policymaking are seen as problematic.)

Robert Bork has written: "What can [a defender of noninterpretive review] say of a Court that does not share his politics or his morality? I can think of nothing except the assertion that he will ignore the Court whenever he can get away with it and overthrow it if he can."[122] I am a defender of noninterpretive review. May I help? Here is what I can and do say "of a Court that does not share my politics or my morality": Noninterpretive review is a policymaking process; it is one among many policymaking processes in American government. Noninterpretive review, like any of the other policymaking processes, might generate particular policies I oppose, and I might even conclude that a certain policy is morally illegitimate. (Note that my conclusion in that regard would be predicated on the content of the policy, not on the character of the policymaker. The question of the legitimacy, *as a matter of political theory,* of a policymaking process ought not to be confused with the distinct question of the legitimacy, *as a matter of one's own morality,* of a particular policy choice.) If so, I can oppose those policies without opposing the policymaking process.

How, as a practical political matter, can one oppose constitutional policies one vigorously rejects? I address that question later in this chapter, by considering the nature and extent of political control over noninterpretive review. (None of this is to deny that a defender of noninterpretive review, faced with a Court that persistently generates policy choices he believes to be morally infirm, has the option of becoming, with Bork, a defender of interpretivism instead. As I have emphasized, constitutional theory must not be propounded in a historical vacuum; it must be sensitive to context—the context of our own time.)

In the previous chapter, I noted that some constitutional theorists, most prominently John Ely,[123] praise noninterpretive review in both first amendment and equal protection cases even as they condemn it in substantive due process cases. But that is not a consistent theoretical position, because, as I claimed at the end of the last chapter, the only constitutional theory that succeeds in justifying (if any succeeds in justifying) noninterpretive review in either first amendment or equal protection cases is one that also serves to justify noninterpretive review in substantive due process cases. I now want to defend that claim.

Methodologically, noninterpretive review in all three sorts of cases—or, more precisely, with respect to all three sorts of issues—is the same animal: The determinative decisional norms are not value judgments constitutionalized by the framers. Rather, the determinative norms are the value judgments of the individual justices', judgments reached in their search for right answers—albeit, as a descriptive matter, judgment inevitably rooted in the larger, pluralistic moral culture that has been formative for each of the justices. Therefore, methodology of adjudication cannot explain the asserted difference between Ely's "participational" review—noninterpretive review in either first amendment or equal protection cases—and "nonparticipational" review—in particular noninterpretive review in substantive due process cases.

What can? Ely's answer is that the values the Court elaborates and enforces in both first amendment and equal protection cases are of a special sort, and that that explains the asserted difference:

[T]he "values" the Court should pursue are "participational values" of the sort I have mentioned,*since those are the "values" (1) with which our Constitution has preeminently and most successfully concerned itself, (2) whose "imposition" is not incompatible with, but on the contrary supports, the American system of representative democracy, and (3) that courts set apart from the political process are uniquely situated to "impose."[124]

Ely's first point will not work. Ely means to say—and elsewhere, in amplifying his point, does say[125]—that in the main the value judgments the framers constitutionalized were judgments about how American government ought to be structured. And that is true enough. But in the exercise of *noninterpretive* review in both first amendment and equal protection cases, the Court does not enforce any of those judgments. Rather, the Court enforces judgments *of its own* about precisely how the processes of American government ought to operate. Why is that legitimate?[126] Ely's second point—that the imposition of the Court's own judgments as to how the processes of American government ought to operate "is not incompatible with, but on the contrary supportive of, the American system of representative democracy"—is an inadequate response, for reasons detailed in the preceding chapter.

All this is left, then, is Ely's third point, that institutionally the Court is comparatively competent to elaborate and enforce participational values. Why? Because the Court, unlike a legislature, is not biased. As Ely puts it elsewhere, the Court ought to limit "its intervention to disputes with respect to which there exist special reasons for supposing elected officials cannot be trusted—those involving the constriction of the political process or the victimization of politically defenseless minorities."[127] What Ely is saying, of course, is that where the dispute involves the legitimate reach of governmental power to intrude on a "nonparticipational" value, there is no particular reason to suppose that elected officials cannot be trusted. Trusted to do what? Resolve the dispute in an impartial, politically disinterested fashion. But that is simply not true.

The typical human rights dispute arises when a person who is one of a minority of persons interested in enjoying some value, including a nonparticipational value like sexual autonomy, challenges the majority's right to intrude on that value. (If a majority of persons were interested in enjoying the value in question, and were prevented from doing so, the dispute would not likely arise in a judicial, as opposed to political, forum in the first place.) Unlike Ely, I can see no special reason for supposing elected officials can be trusted to resolve such disputes in an impartial, politically disinterested fashion. To the contrary, the high premium elected officials place on remaining in office virtually assures that most of them will resolve

*Ely refers here to norms—chiefly freedom of expression and equal protection—that enable persons to participate as equals in the processes of governmental policymaking and in the enjoyment of the benefits of such policymaking.

such disputes in whatever fashion they think best serves their interest in reelection, which is to say in the fashion the majority, not the minority, wants the disputes resolved. At least, I can see no reason for supposing elected officials can be trusted to any significantly greater extent to resolve in a politically selfless fashion disputes involving nonparticipational values than they can disputes involving participational ones. (Recall here a point I made in the preceding chapter, that the outcome of very few "participational" disputes one way or another—I am thinking mainly of disputes involving "freedom of expression"—will have any consequential effect on an incumbent's reelection chances.)

My point is not that one who supports (the general features of) what the Court has done—the policy choices it has made—in either first amendment or equal protection cases is somehow committed to supporting what the Court has done in substantive due process cases too. That would be an absurd claim. My argument, rather, is that there is no good reason—Ely has given none, and I can think of none—for concluding that judicial policymaking with respect to what Ely calls "participational" values is legitimate but that judicial policymaking with respect to all other, "nonparticipational" values is not. If the function served by noninterpretive review in human rights cases can justify judicial policymaking with respect to the values of freedom of expression and of equal protection, it can also justify judicial policymaking with respect to at least some nonparticipational values. Can, that is, unless it is exclusively in terms of the participational values of freedom of expression and of equal protection that a polity achieves moral growth—or unless judicial elaboration and enforcement of nonparticipational values (that is, freedom of intimate association) is either irrelevant to or even an impediment to moral growth—implausible a priori suppositions, and ones Ely nowhere makes.

The distinction between "participational" and "nonparticipational" values Ely deploys in his constitutional theory is consequential only if participational values are elevated to a position of dominance in our society. I join G. Edward White in saying that "[w]hile I am not opposed to those values, . . . [w]e cannot adequately protect rights against the state unless we are prepared, in suffering [noninterpretive review], also to suffer the use by the judiciary of [noninterpretivist] reasoning that goes beyond an emphasis on structure, process and participation."[128]

The functional considerations that justify noninterpretive review in both freedom of expression and equal protection cases also justify it in substantive due process cases—cases in which the determinative norms are, in Ely's terms, "nonparticipational."* (I should mention, although it probably goes without saying, that none of this is to suggest that the noninter-

---

I trust that by now it is clear why I said, in the prologue (p. 2, n.) that "the constitutional theory that succeeds in justifying the judicial activism underlying the Court's decision in Brown [v. Board of Education] also serves to justify the activism underlying its decision in Roe [v. Wade]."

pretivist is committed to accepting each and every decision the Court renders in the course of nonparticipational policymaking, any more than he need accept every decision rendered in the course of participational policymaking.) Ely's valiant effort to construct a constitutional theory in terms of the unavailing participational-nonparticipational distinction calls to mind George Braden's observation about Justice Felix Frankfurter:

> [I]t can be argued that [Frankfurter's conception of the proper scope of judicial review] is a way of expressing two things: his own set of values for his society and his own conception of the safe limits of his function. Some things he believes in strongly enough to use his power to protect them. Others he may believe in but not strongly enough to risk the charge of abuse of office.[129]

At the close of a key chapter of his book, Ely writes:

> Before embarking on his career-long quest for a satisfactory approach to constitutional adjudication, Alexander Bickel described the challenge thus:
>
> > The search must be for a function . . . which is peculiarly suited to the capabilities of the courts; which will not likely be performed elsewhere if the courts do not assume it; which can be so exercised as to be acceptable in a society that generally shares Judge Hand's satisfaction in a "sense of common venture"; which will be effective when needed; and whose discharge by the courts will not lower the quality of the other departments' performance by denuding them of the dignity and burden of their own responsibility.
>
> As quoted, it's a remarkably appropriate set of specifications, one that fits the orientation suggested here precisely. Unfortunately, by adding one more specification (where I have put the ellipsis) and thereby committing himself to a value orientation—"which might (indeed must) involve the making of policy, yet which differs from the legislative and executive functions"—he built in an inescapable contradiction and thereby ensured the failure of his enterprise.[130]

As it turns out, it was Bickel, not Ely, who was right: the judicial function, for the noninterpretivist, must indeed involve the making of policy, in the sense of elaborating and enforcing nonparticipational values as well as participational ones. Ely built on an inadequate distinction —between participational and nonparticipational review—and thereby ensured the failure of his enterprise.

Earlier in this chapter, I suggested that Owen Fiss's ambiguous conception of the function of constitutional adjudication is best understood as harmonious with the view I have developed thus far in this chapter. When

Fiss writes that "[t]he task of the judge is to give meaning to constitutional values, and he does that by working with . . . social ideals,"[131] Fiss does not mean ideals (supposedly) rooted in (imagined) consensus or tradition, for he goes on to say that the judge "searches for what is true, right, or just."[132] The judge must "constantly . . . strive for the true meaning of the constitutional value."[133] "[H]e among all the agencies of government is in the best position to discover the true meaning of our constitutional values."[134] It seems, then, that Fiss too assumes that there are right—"true"—answers to the human rights problems that confront the judiciary. He is plainly impatient with the skeptical notion that there are no (demonstrably) right answers:

> We have lost our confidence in the existence of the values that underlie the litigation of the 1960s, or, for that matter, in the existence of any public values. All is preference . . . . Only once we reassert our belief in the existence of public values, that values such as equality, liberty, due process, no cruel and unusual punishment, security of the person, or free speech can have a true and important meaning, that must be articulated and implemented—yes, discovered —will the role of the courts in our political system become meaningful, or for that matter even intelligible.[135]

But Fiss's view remains incomplete. He writes that in striving for the "true meaning" of constitutional values, the judge may "not . . . express his . . . personal beliefs . . . as to what is right or just."[136] I can readily understand why Fiss and others are hesitant to push the logic of their positions to the point of acknowledging that, once the judge resolves to move beyond specific value judgments constitutionalized by the framers, the ultimate source of decisional norms is the judge's own values (albeit, values ideally arrived at through, and tested in the crucible of, a very deliberate search for right answers). After all, it is a radical thing to say, and hence a thing not often said, that the source of judgment is the judge's own values. As Ely has noted, "[t]he view that the judge, in enforcing the Constitution, should use his or her *own values* to measure the judgment of the political branches is a methodology that is seldom endorsed in so many words."[137] But I cannot see any way to avoid concluding that, in the exercise of noninterpretive review—*including noninterpretive review in freedom of expression and equal protection cases*—the determinative norms derive—again, not in an unself-critical way—from the judge's own moral vision.

That raises an interesting, if somewhat academic, question. Suppose that a judge firmly believes that porpoises are so intelligent that they should be treated as persons,[138] or that all imprisonment is terribly immoral.[139] Surely there are *practical* limits to what a judge should say is constitutionally required or forbidden, his own values notwithstanding. For one thing, courts, including the Supreme Court, do not have a literally inexhaustible supply of political capital to spend on controversial causes[140] (although that supply is probably much greater than we sometimes imagine, if the modern period of constitutional law is any indication[141]). For another, the development of constitutional doctrine should proceed somewhat cautiously and incrementally if the dialectical relationship between noninterpretive review and the processes of electorally accountable policymaking is to be a stable, productive one, working as well as it can and not precipitating spiraling crises and conflict.[142]

Perhaps we should say, with Kent Greenawalt, that in their constitutional policymaking, courts should give weight—which is not to say *conclusive* weight—"to the stable underlying moral sentiments of the community."[143] Perhaps we should say, with Alexander Bickel, that "the Court should declare as law only such principles as will—in time, but in a rather immediate foreseeable future—gain general assent."[144] The problem is one of line drawing—only here, unlike in the rest of constitutional law, line drawing not so much with respect to the contours of substantive doctrine as to the limits of judicial innovation.[145]

I must confess that the present issue seems somewhat academic to me, precisely because Supreme Court justices, and judges generally, as I noted earlier, tend to be more or less conventional members of the class that comprises legislators and other policymaking officials.* But what if there is an occasional member of the federal judiciary whose moral views are, by most conventional measures, eccentric, even outrageous, and who refuses to abide the sort of caution urged by Greenawalt and Bickel? There is no reason to believe that such an individual will not be constrained by his or her peers: "[L]ower court decisions are subject to review, and the higher the court the more judges must approve the decision. . . . [O]n many issues a judge might assume that if his values are far wide of community standards, he will be outvoted by his brethren or reversed by a higher court."[146]

---

*Samuel Estreicher has written that "[p]erhaps only Michael Perry . . . can be said to be articulating a process of constitutional value formation that is without the slightest tether to the constitutional text or the usual sources or modes of interpretation." Estreicher, Book Review, 56 N.Y.U. L. REV. 547, 549 n. 7 (1981). By way of response to Professor Estreicher, I quote Dean Sandalow:

> To stress the element of choice in constitutional interpretation is not to argue that contemporary discretion is unlimited, but only that the limits are not those imposed by the language and pre-adoption history of the Constitution. The limits, so far as they exist, are those that have developed over time in the ongoing process of valuation that occurs in the name of the Constitution. So understood, the limits upon permissible constitutional interpretation are not external constraints upon our ability to read the Constitution as the embodiment of current values; they are, rather, the elements of reason that are intrinsic to the process of determining whether a proposed interpretation truly reflects those values.

Sandalow, *Constitutional Interpretation*, 79 MICH. L. REV. 1033, 1054–55 (1981).

Still, mindful of *Dred Scott, Lochner,* and certain other cases, we cannot deny the possibility of serious judicial misadventure. (This is not to suggest that the Court's decisions in *Lochner* and even *Dred Scott* were, by conventional measures of the time, eccentric. They were not, and to think otherwise is to indulge sentimental assumptions about the past.) I have said that the function of noninterpretive review in human rights cases can be understood as prophetic. But the usefulness of the biblical analogy is limited, for, unlike prophecy, noninterpretive review is coercive, and there is a radical difference between prophecy and coercion. "Having highlighted an issue of principle," wrote Bickel, "the Court proceeds with the attempt to make society live up to its resolution of it, which is another sort of function altogether."[147]

How can noninterpretive review, given its coercive aspect—the fact that the Court supplants value judgments of electorally accountable officials with value judgments of its own—be reconciled with the principle of electorally accountable policymaking? Moreover, as I have said, we must not take lightly the interpretivist's historical point—that on occasion noninterpretive review has served, and can again, as an impediment to moral growth. How does the American polity deal with a Court decision or, worse, series of decisions that, even with the benefits of hindsight and thoughtful deliberation, it rejects—perhaps wrongly, perhaps rightly, but in any event rejects? The tension between noninterpretive review and the principle of electorally accountable policymaking seems especially acute in light of the fact that the decisional norms the Court elaborates and enforces in the exercise of such review are derived not from some authoritative source of value, external to the Court, to which "the people" subscribe, but from the justices' own values. "Thus the recurring embarrassment of the noninterpretivists: majoritarian democracy is, they know, the core of our entire system, and they hear in the charge that there is in their philosophy a fundamental inconsistency therewith something they are not sure they can deny."[148]

Up to this point in this chapter, I have sought to portray noninterpretive review in human rights cases as a salutary feature of American government. If the practice were not salutary, there would be no point in proceeding to the question of whether the practice can somehow be reconciled with the principle of electorally accountable policymaking. But because in my estimate noninterpretive review *is* salutary, I must now turn to just that question. Earlier in this chapter I indicated that the answer to the principal question before us—whether the function served by noninterpretive review in human rights cases constitutes a persuasive justification for such review—depends ultimately on whether noninterpretive review enables us to keep faith (or try to) with our commitment to moral growth—or, if you prefer, with the possibility that there are right answers—but *in a* manner that tolerably accommodates our other basic, constitutive commitment—our commitment to the principle of electorally accountable policymaking. Noninterpretive review does indeed accommodate the latter commitment, and I now want to explain how.

My effort will be to establish that the Court's exercise of noninterpretive review is subject to significant political control—that constitutional policymaking by the judiciary is subject to important control at the hands of electorally accountable officials—and that, consequently, noninterpretive review operates in a manner—that is, subject to that control—that accommodates the principle of electorally accountable policymaking. Recall that the principle requires that governmental policymaking be subject to control by persons accountable to the electorate, not that such persons invariably be the actual policymakers. If the principle required that, not even nonconstitutional policymaking by an electorally unaccountable judge—"common law" policymaking, or policymaking under a vague statute—would be legitimate.[149] The Supreme Court (and the federal judiciary generally) is by design an electorally unaccountable institution. Supreme Court justices (and other federal judges) are electorally unaccountable policymakers. But that is not to say that their constitutional policymaking necessarily contravenes the principle of electorally accountable policymaking.

Let me begin by rejecting several ineffective claims with which others have sought to prove an accommodation between constitutional policymaking by the judiciary and the principle of electorally accountable policymaking. The familiar claim that in the long run—"ultimately"—the polity will prevail over a Court not in harmony with it,[150] even if sometimes true,[151] is rather beside the point. Clifton McCleskey's reply is apt:

> It seems fair to say that in late-nineteenth-century Britain the House of Lords was unable to stop effectively "the people" from eventually winning certain highly desired goals, although they were often able to delay them. Are we to conclude that the Lords then—or now, with their present attenuated power to delay legislation—should therefore be reckoned as a democratic institution?[152]

The claim that over time the polity has consented to and thereby legitimated noninterpretive review[153] is both doubtful and beside the point. How could the polity as a whole have consented to a mode of judicial review with which many of its members were not even familiar? And has the problem of the legitimacy of noninterpretive review ("judicial activism") not been a matter of deep controversy among those who were aware? Moreover, what one person interprets as consent, especially when that consent is silent, another may see as forbearance or simply lethargy.[154] Most fundamentally, popular consent to a practice does not render the

practice consistent with the principle of electorally accountable policymaking. There could be popular consent, after all, to the abolition of
elections and the establishment of a dictatorship.[155]

The claim that the possibility of amending the Constitution dissolves the
tension between noninterpretive review and the principle of electorally
accountable policymaking[156] is simply not true. Both proposal and
ratification of a constitutional amendment require supermajorities;[157] a
minority of electorally accountable officials can block proposal or
ratification. The principle of electorally accountable policymaking, at least
by most accounts, subsumes the notion that a majority of electorally accountable officials—and, through them, of the polity—should be empowered to have its way[158] (albeit, only after successfully hurdling difficult
practical obstacles and thereby overcoming the burden of inertia[159]).

The claim that the joint power of the President and Congress to make
appointments to the Court[160] dissolves the tension[161] is also unsound. Ely
has identified some of the reasons:

> [I]t generally takes several successive terms, and the concurrence of several
> successive Senates, to replace a majority of the justices. It has also proved hard
> to predict how someone in another line of work will function as a justice and
> one sometimes wonders whether the appointee who turns out differently from
> the way the President who appointed him expected is not the rule rather than
> the exception. . . . Nor is it the least bit unusual for a justice to sit for decades
> during which the issues are likely to have shifted markedly from those the
> President had in mind when the appointment was made.[162]

Furthermore, by tradition the appointments power is exercised with
reference to a range of factors, including party, general judicial philosophy, region, sometimes religion, and now even race and gender. To
suggest that the power be exercised with single-minded reference to how a
person is inclined or committed to vote on a particular issue is to urge, in
effect, a practical reorientation of the power—in my view, an irresponsibly
narrow reorientation. Finally, and perhaps most important as a theoretical
matter, the appointments power does not give the President and Congress
the ability to *themselves* revise policy choices made by the Court in the
course of its constitutional policymaking. It merely empowers them to
appoint persons whom the President (and perhaps Congress) hopes will,
by voting a certain way, revise those policy choices, but who, once appointed, are not legally obligated to vote in the hoped-for way, nor are they
electorally accountable. And so the requirement of the principle of electorally accountable policymaking—that governmental policymaking be subject to control by *persons accountable to the electorate*—is not met. (For
much the same reasons, the power to increase the number of justices on the
Court does not dissolve the tension either. The exercise of that power, after

all, merely creates the occasion for the exercise of the appointments power.)

Finally, for reasons adequately surveyed elsewhere, neither Congress's power to impeach federal judges nor its power to control the budget of the federal judiciary is a source of significant political control over noninterpretive review.[163]

Well, then, what is the source of significant political control to which, I have said, the Court's exercise of noninterpretive review is subject? It is, I submit, the legislative power of Congress (and the President, who may sign or veto legislation passed by Congress) to define, and therefore to limit, the appellate jurisdiction of the Supreme Court and the original and appellate jurisdiction of the lower federal courts.

Under Article III of the Constitution, the Supreme Court "shall have appellate jurisdiction, both as to law and fact, *with such exceptions, and under such regulations, as the Congress shall make.*" The Supreme Court exercises appellate jurisdication at the discretion of Congress. Congress may specify the classes of cases, even the classes of questions, over which the Court may exercise jurisdiction.[164] Also under Article III, Congress has discretion to establish lower federal courts, but it is not obligated to do so. Congress may abolish the lower federal judiciary altogether,[165] or, maintaining a system of lower federal courts, it may specify the classes of cases over which those courts may exercise jurisdiction.[166]

John Ely has suggested that "Congress'[s] theoretical power to withdraw the Court's jurisdiction over certain classes of cases is . . . fraught with constitutional doubt."[167] Of course, Congress's power to control jurisdiction, like its other legislative powers, is limited by the value judgments the framers constitutionalized. Therefore, Congress could not, for example, deny to the federal judiciary jurisdiction over cases "brought by a Roman Catholic."[168] But no value judgment constitutionalized by the framers forbids Congress to use its jurisdiction-limiting power as a means of exerting control over the constitutional-policymaking activities of the federal judiciary, and therefore the Supreme Court could not strike down jurisdiction-limiting legislation designed to exert such control unless it were to do so on the basis of a value judgment of its own. However, the national legislative power over the jurisdiction of the federal judiciary is, in Charles Black's apt phrase, "the rock on which rests the legitimacy of the judicial work in a democracy,"[169] and so the Court must not subject jurisdiction-limiting legislation to noninterpretive review; that is, it must not measure such legislation by its own value judgments. A passage in Charles Black's recent Holmes Lectures, which I can do no better than to quote, amplifies the reason why:

> If Congress does not have wide power over [the federal judiciary's] jurisdiction, but is limited, as many now say, by an implicit constitutional

reservation—roughly to the effect that all constitutional claims against the states must have a federal judicial forum for their assertion—the contradiction to democratic assumptions is maximized. Consider the case in which a dominant majority of the state legislatures, charged with the general responsibility for order and justice, think that federal judicial intervention in a certain field is of proven catastrophic consequence. Being obviously not empowered themselves to take any action, they memorialize Congress. Congress, by large majorities, and the President, agree with their judgment. If some modern ideas are right, then even in such a case there would be no power on earth that could do anything but continue to submit to the federal judicial jurisdiction as the judges defined it—except by constitutional amendment, which can be thwarted by thirty-four senators out of a hundred, or by states containing as few as nine million people. I confess I am staggered by the implied assertion, or assumption, that such a position can be consonant with the root-ideas and greater sayings of democracy.

If, on the other hand, Congress has just about the power that it seems to be given in the Constitution, with no broad implied limits on that power, then it is possible to say, to those states passionately objecting to the activity of the federal courts in respect of, let us say, the racial composition of school populations: "You are wrong in imagining an arrogation of power by the courts. Look, it says in the United States Code that the federal courts are to take these cases and decide them according to law as those courts see the law. If you think we are misconstruing the Code, try to get Congress to pass a clarifying amendment. If you think this congressional empowerment of the federal judiciary to be very unwise, then go to Congress and try to get them to change it. If Congress won't do either of these things, stop talking about usurpation, bootstraps, and especially about contradiction to democracy, because the national democracy, through its only voice, will have decided against you."

What we believe on this question of Congressional power over jurisdiction makes a difference, above all, in the kind of law and legal method that is *tolerable,* as a basis for striking down actions of the states. In the farther ranges of legal indeterminacy, the range of as yet unestablished constitutional values, you are in one situation when you can say that Congress—not merely guessing, in the late eighteenth century, on the basis of eighteenth-century legal philosophy, what the work would be like, but from time to time fully able to observe it, fully able to take into account all modern thought on the intellectual processes of legal decision—keeps in force the direction that this work be done by the courts. You are in quite another situation when you have to say that the concept in the phrase "keeps in force" rests on a misapprehension which honesty requires be corrected, because Congress has no choice—and consequently the democracy has no choice. *For how many centuries do you think the existence of this uncheckable and self-defining judicial power would be consonant with democratic ideas?*[170]

I want to emphasize the limited scope of my argument (without suggesting that Professor Black's argument is similarly limited). My position is not that Congress may use its jurisdiction-limiting power as a means of preventing the federal judiciary from enforcing value judgments constitutionalized by the framers—that Congress may exert political control over interpretive as well as noninterpretive review. My argument does not and need not go that far. No interpretivist disputes the legitimacy of interpretive review—of determining the constitutionality of governmental policy choices by reference to the framers' value judgments. Even for the interpretivist, the principle of electorally accountable policymaking is not absolute; the policymaking authority of electorally accountable officials is constrained by the framers' value judgments. Thus, it is unnecessary for the noninterpretivist (or anyone else) to concede to Congress power to control interpretive review.

Some readers might object that in constitutional adjudication the line between interpretive and noninterpretive review is not always as hard and fast as my argument about Congress's jurisdiction-limiting power implies. There might be classes of cases in which the Court truly thinks it is simply enforcing one of the framers' value judgments while Congress thinks the Court is really enforcing one of the Court's own value judgments, with the consequence that the Court disagrees with Congress's position that legislation withdrawing jurisdiction over some such class of cases is aimed at controlling only noninterpretive review.[171]

While it is possible to conjure up imaginary cases like that, those imaginary cases will not cause any trouble—at least, not a significant amount of trouble—in actuality. Recall that in very few consequential human rights cases of the modern period can the Court's decisions *even plausibly* be explained as products of interpretive review. The decisions in most such cases

> are not in any significant sense derived from the Constitution, viewed as an historical document. The justification . . . for the great bulk of our constitutional law of individual rights [ ] depends rather upon an evolving constitutional tradition that owes far more to the values of the twentieth century than to those of the late eighteenth.[172]

While no one denies the existence of national legislative power over the jurisdiction of the federal judiciary, including the appellate jurisdiction of the Supreme Court,[173] some commentators have not thought that power to be a source of *effective* political control over noninterpretive review. First, jurisdiction-limiting legislation cannot undo the decision by the Court that provoked the legislation in the first place; by the time such legislation is considered, much less enacted, the decision is a fait accompli. However, while it may be a fait accompli, as a single decision it is binding only as between the parties and therefore has extremely limited force.

As Herbert Wechsler has written, "[u]nder *Marbury*, the Court decides a case; it does not pass a statute calling for obedience by all within the purview of the rule that is declared."[174] Wechsler quotes Lincoln's *First Inaugural* (where Lincoln was speaking of the Court's decision in *Dred Scott*) in support of that position:

> I do not forget the position assumed by some that constitutional questions are to be decided by the Supreme Court, nor do I deny that such decisions must be binding in any case upon the parties to a suit as to the object of that suit, while they are also entitled to very high respect and consideration in all parallel cases by all other departments of the Government. And while it is obviously possible that such decision may be erroneous in any given case, still the evil effect following it, being limited to that particular case, with the chance that it may be overruled and never become a precedent for other cases, can better be borne than could the evils of a different practice. At the same time, the candid citizen must confess that if the policy of the Government upon vital questions affecting the whole people is to be irrevocably fixed by decisions of the Supreme Court, the instant they are made in ordinary litigation between parties in personal actions the people will have ceased to be their own rulers, having to that extent practically resigned their Government into the hands of that eminent tribunal. Nor is there in this view any assault upon the court or the judges. It is a duty from which they may not shrink to decide cases properly brought before them, and it is no fault of theirs if others seek to turn their decisions to political purposes.[175]

Of course, there is good practical reason for acting *as if* a single decision were binding generally, like "a statute calling for obedience by all within the purview of the rule declared,"[176] but *only where the Court retains jurisdiction to decide future, similar cases in the same way* (and gives indication it intends to decide them in that way).

Second, Congress's power over jurisdiction does not extend to state courts; Congress cannot exert political control over noninterpretive review by state courts. But if a state court strikes down action in the exercise of noninterpretive review, there is no problem of legitimacy if in the state in question the judges are electorally accountable, as in many states they are.[177] And even if they are not electorally accountable, presumably the state legislature has power over the jurisdiction of the state judiciary analogous to Congress's power over the jurisdiction of the federal judiciary.

What about the other possibility—a state court striking down *federal* action in the exercise of noninterpretive review? *Assuming* that a state court would have jurisdiction to review the federal action,[178] I can think of no reason why, as a matter of political-constitutional theory, least of all as a matter of the theory of federalism, a decision by a *state* court opposing its own value judgment to the value judgment of a branch of the *national* government should be deemed binding on the national government (or, therefore, on litigants relying on the authority—and if necessary the power—of the national government) *unless the state court's decision is subject to appellate review by the Supreme Court (or by some other federal court)*. If such a decision is subject to review by the Supreme Court, as all such decisions now are,[179] and if it is not reversed there, the decision is ultimately attributable to the Supreme Court, itself a branch of the national government.*

Expressing a more generalized objection to the notion that the national legislative power over the jurisdiction of the federal judiciary is a source of significant political control, Clifton McCleskey has written that "[w]hat Congress can do theoretically may not in fact be practicable. Resort to [jurisdiction-limiting legislation] with sufficient frequency to approximate effective popular control would demoralize and upset the judicial process. . . ."[180]

First, there is no need for Congress to resort to jurisdiction-limiting legislation with frequency; a majority of Congress rarely disagrees with the federal judiciary's constitutional policymaking to the point where it sees a need to seriously contemplate exercising its jurisdiction-limiting power. Second, where it does see the need, the whole point of exercising the power is to "upset" the judicial process—to overrule it, as it were.[181]†

Jesse Choper has proposed that "the Supreme Court should pass final constitutional judgment on questions concerning the permissible reach

*One might try to impugn my reliance on Congress's jurisdiction-limiting power by arguing that under the tenth amendment—which reserves to the states all power not delegated to the national government (*see* chap. 2, note 2 *supra*)—Congress lacks power to authorize, directly *or otherwise*, constitutional policymaking (with respect to human rights) against the states by the national judiciary. (Presumably the argument is predicated on the prior claim that under the tenth amendment Congress lacks power to itself engage in constitutional policymaking—with respect to human rights—against the states. "At least," the argument would run, "whatever power Congress enjoys in that regard—such as the 'power to enforce, by appropriate legislation, the provisions of' the fourteenth amendment [U.S. CONST. amend. XIV, § 5]—is limited to implementing the [narrow, determinate] value judgments constitutionalized by the framers.") But that argument questions the legitimacy of constitutional policymaking (by the federal judiciary against the states, *even by Congress itself*) not as a matter of democratic theory, which is the concern of this book, but as a matter of the theory of federalism. (As an argument sounding in federalism, it is dated. Today—when, unlike two hundred years ago, human rights are a principal concern of international covenants [*see* Henkin, *Rights: American and Human*, 79 COLUM. L. REV. 405 (1979)]—human rights are widely regarded as a proper concern of the national government.)

†The argument that Congress, by exercising its jurisdiction-limiting power in the manner I suggest it may, would be shamelessly bypassing the amendment process, which process requires supermajorities, seems to me altogether specious. The amendment process is the proper vehicle—the vehicle designed by past framers—for present and future framers to constitutionalize value judgments. The jurisdiction-limiting power, on the other hand, is a proper vehicle for electorally accountable policymakers to control the value judgments, not of past framers, but of electorally unaccountable judges.

and circumscription of 'the judicial power.' "[182] Without evaluating Choper's proposal, I want to note that nothing I have said up to this point is necessarily inconsistent with the proposal. I am not claiming, in contradistinction to Choper's proposal, that it is improper for the Court to review particular congressional efforts to limit its appellate jurisdiction (which of course the Court may do, since its Article III grant of appellate jurisdiction is self-executing).[183] My claim, rather, is that Congress's efforts to control noninterpretive review by means of its jurisdiction-limiting power ought not, as a matter of constitutional theory, to be deemed illegitimate—by the Court or anyone else. Put another way, if the Court reviews congressional legislation aimed at undoing particular constitutional policies established by the federal judiciary, the review should be interpretive in nature, not noninterpretive. The Court should not measure such legislation by its own value judgments.

Lest I be accused of performing *Hamlet* without the Prince, let me address Henry Hart's famous *Dialogue* on Congress's jurisdiction-limiting power.[184] Hart suggests this basic limitation on Congress's power to curtail the jurisdiction of the Supreme Court: "[T]he exceptions [to the Court's jurisdiction] must not be such as will destroy the essential role of the Supreme Court in the constitutional plan. McCardle,[185] you will remember, meets that test. The circuit courts of the United States were still open in habeas corpus. And the Supreme Court itself could still entertain petitions for the writ which were filed with it in the first instance."[186] My position is not necessarily inconsistent with Hart's, for it seems to me self-serving in the extreme to suppose that "the *essential* role of the Supreme Court in the constitutional plan" is anything more than to enforce the value judgments constitutionalized by the framers, and I am not suggesting that Congress may exercise its jurisdiction-limiting power to interfere with interpretive judicial review—that is, with the Court's enforcement of the framers' value judgments.* My claim is merely that it may exercise its power to control noninterpretive judicial review.

Why has Congress not relied on a jurisdiction-limiting proposal in over a hundred years as a way of dealing with an unpopular Supreme Court decision?[187] Many such proposals have been offered.[188] Indeed, many are

---

*Lawrence Sager's version of the "essential role" argument is, in part, that "[t]he Court must be available to superintend state compliance with federal law unless Congress provides effective review elsewhere within the federal judiciary." Sager, *Foreward: Constitutional Limitations on Congress' Authority to Regulate the Jurisdiction of the Federal Courts,* 95 HARV. L. REV. 17, 57 (1981). If by "federal [constitutional] law" we understand "the value judgments constitutionalized by the framers," I quite agree with Sager's claim. If Sager means more than that, however—if he means "the value judgments attributable, not to the framers, but only to the Court itself"—I cannot agree with him.

pending in Congress even as I write.[189] Why has Congress not adopted any of the proposals offered? I do not pretend that doubts as to the extent of Congress's jurisdiction-limiting power have played no role. But I am arguing that as an issue in constitutional theory, the doubts are unfounded —that as a normative matter Congress must be deemed to have the power in question. It is beside the normative point that, as a descriptive matter, some doubts exist—even some congressional self-doubt—about how the Court might eventually react to an exercise of the power by Congress.

A deeper reason for Congress's reticence about jurisdiction-limiting proposals, it seems to me, has been the fact that many members of Congress approve of the Court's policymaking with respect to human rights, even those aspects of its policymaking that have borne the brunt of widespread criticism, though their approval is often strategically covert. The following observation by Jesse Choper is instructive in that regard:

> Congress has recognized that political expediency often renders it impotent to uphold the constitutional rights of vulnerable minorities and that it would not be displeased to have the Court set the record straight. Thus, when it seemed imminent that popular pressure would finally overcome the long-held congressional impression that aid to parochial schools violated religious freedom, the path of least resistance for many legislators lay in formally authorizing the Court to review the constitutionality of such appropriations. And when Congress could not itself muster the strength to abolish poll taxes, its way out was to direct the Attorney General to request the judiciary to do so.[190]

One can begin to understand why many members of Congress may have a vested interest in turning a deaf ear to jurisdiction-limiting proposals, *even to the extent of acting as if there are serious doubts as to the extent of its jurisdiction-limiting power.*

Another possible reason for Congress's failure to adopt any jurisdiction-limiting proposals (of the sort under discussion) in the last one hundred years is simply that the burden of legislative inertia, so ably discussed by Jesse Choper,[191] is carried by those who would have such proposals become law. And so the opposition of even a significant minority of the Senate or House can, as a practical matter, doom such proposals. It will not do, however, to argue that the burden of legislative inertia prevents Congress's jurisdiction-limiting power from serving as a source of significant political control over noninterpretive review. The burden of legislative inertia operates throughout our governmental system to give legislative minorities more (negative) power than they would otherwise enjoy. (That state of affairs is certainly not inconsistent with the principle of electorally accountable policymaking—unless we are now to pronounce policymaking by the United States Congress electorally unaccountable!) If the burden of legislative inertia does not count as a reason for concluding that Congress's power to regulate interstate commerce, say, is ineffective, I certainly cannot see why it suddenly counts as a reason for concluding that Congress's power to limit the jurisdiction of the federal judiciary is ineffective.

Moreover, the burden of legislative inertia is a very important constituent of the dialectical process of constitutional growth. If it were relatively easy to enact a jurisdiction-limiting proposal, the temptation to do so frequently and unreflectively would likely prove irresistible to legislators willing, indeed eager, to bend to prevailing if momentary passions in order to preserve their incumbency. And that state of affairs quickly would dissipate the inter-institutional tension—the tension between the Court and the other agencies of government, in particular Congress—necessary to preserve the dialectical character of constitutional development in America. That tension is an important matrix of the dialogue between Court and polity, and frequent, unreflective resort to the jurisdiction-limiting power would reduce to little more than a transient whisper the now powerful, not easily ignored voice of the Court in that ongoing dialectic. The burden of legislative inertia serves to enhance the Court's voice by enhancing the allied voice of those in Congress, likely only a minority, who are prepared to defend—or at least to take very seriously, to the point of not disturbing—the Court's position on a given, deeply controversial political-moral issue.

A fair question, at this point, is whether there is any reason why someone who, like myself, feels constrained by the principle of electorally accountable policymaking to concede to Congress such a broad jurisdiction-limiting power, should not go a step further and concede to Congress the power legislatively to reverse Court decisions (*noninterpretive* decisions) Congress determines are substantively—morally—incorrect. Is there any reason for refusing to concede to Congress the power to rule, for example, that even in the previability period of pregnancy a woman's interest in having an abortion is *not* constitutionally weightier than government's interest in protecting fetal life (thus reversing *Roe v. Wade*)? (As I write, Congress is considering legislation—the so-called Human Life statute—to just that effect.[192])

First: The Constitution, in Article III, gives Congress the jurisdiction-limiting power, but not the power legislatively to reverse. Second: Were Congress to be conceded the power to reverse, we would come to view the Court, in its noninterpretive role, as a sort of delegate of Congress, much as a court in its common-law role is a delegate of the legislature, which may revise the common law. Such a change in the relationship between Congress and the Court would tend to undermine the very inter-institutional tension—the dialectical interplay between Court and Congress—that is the

reason to value noninterpretive review in the first place. The moral authority of the Court's voice would be diminished; its opinions would be essentially only advisory.

One might object that Congress's jurisdiction-limiting power has much
the same consequence. However, there *is* a difference between reversing
the Court on a particular issue, and merely silencing the Court. The power
to silence (the jurisdiction-limiting power) has never been thought to
reduce the Court to Congress's delegate. The power to reverse, however,
would tend to do just that.*

---

*Lawrence Sager has argued that "it makes no sense to single out one rather bizarre form of
legislation [that is, jurisdiction-limiting legislation] . . . and make it the last democratic
hurrah." Sager, *Foreward: Constitutional Limitations on Congress' Authority to Regulate the
Jurisdiction of the Federal Courts,* 95 HARV. L. REV. 17, 39–40 (1981). Why does it make no
sense? "Special costs . . . attach to jurisdictional surgery . . . [N]o rational legal system would
routinely exact these costs as the price for legislative supremacy." *Id.* at 40. And what are
these special costs? Sager identifies several. First: "Congress can limit federal jurisdiction in
an effort to override the Supreme Court's constitutional decisions concerning federal conduct only at the cost of forgoing the assistance of the federal judiciary in administering federal
programs." *Id.* Here Sager is relying on an insight of Herbert Wechsler, who has suggested that
a major difficulty might prevent, as a practical matter, the use of the jurisdiction-limiting
power to curtail review of *federal* law: "[G]overnment cannot be run without the use of courts
for the enforcement of coercive sanctions and within large areas it will be thought that federal
tribunals are essential to administer federal law. Within that area, the opportunity for litigating constitutional defenses is built in and cannot be foreclosed." *The Courts and the
Constitution,* 65 COLUM. L. REV. 1001, 1006 (1965).

Unlike Wechsler, I am not prepared to concede to Congress any jurisdiction-limiting power
to control *all* judicial review, including interpretive review. But were I, like Wechsler,
prepared to make that concession, then I too would insist that under the supremacy clause
Congress may not authorize a federal court to hear a case while at the same time denying to the
court the power to enforce a norm constitutionalized by the framers. The supremacy clause
obligates any federal court hearing any case to enforce any relevant norm constitutionalized
by the framers. But there is no reason to think that the clause obligates a federal court to
enforce a norm *not* constitutionalized by the framers. Thus, in my view the supremacy clause
does not prevent Congress from authorizing a federal court to hear a case while at the same
time denying to the court the power to enforce a norm not constitutionalized by the framers.

Note, moreover, that the practical difficulty Wechsler and, following him, Sager have
identified has no affect on Congress's power to withdraw from the federal courts jurisdiction
over cases involving constitutional challenges to *state* laws. And yet it is precisely those
cases—cases in which federal courts have stricken state laws (for example, laws segregating
schools, authorizing prayer in the classroom, restricting access to abortion) on constitutional
grounds—that are at the very center of the controversy over the legitimacy of noninterpretive
review. "[S]ome of the Court's gravest difficulties, not only with state officials but with the
national political branches as well, have come in response to judicial review of state and local
programs." J. CHOPER, JUDICIAL REVIEW AND THE NATIONAL POLITICAL PROCESS: A FUNCTIONAL
RECONSIDERATION OF THE ROLE OF THE SUPREME COURT 131 (1980).

Another of Sager's "special costs" concerns the need for uniformity:

With the courts of fifty states ruling independently on the constitutionality of challenged federal programs, the frequent result would be chaos of a magnitude that we have

Perhaps I attach too much significance to the difference between reversing and silencing. Perhaps in the end there is not an adequate reason for refusing to go further and concede to Congress the power to reverse. I confess I remain reluctant to make that concession. If my position in that regard proves indefensible, it is nontheless true that, *whether or not Congress is conceded the power to reverse*, its power to limit the jurisdiction of the federal judiciary is, as Herbert Wechsler, Charles Black, and others have recognized, a source of significant political control over judicial review—in particular, of state action—by the federal courts. Thus, the principle of electorally accountable policymaking is, to that extent, satisfied.

I am not happy conceding such a broad jurisdiction-limiting power to Congress. (I would be most unhappy were any of the jurisdiction-limiting bills now pending in Congress to become law.) One opposed to noninterpretive review, and so not interested in justifying it, has the option of refusing to make that concession. Some interpretivists, like Robert Bork, have refused. But I do not see how anyone who is interested in justifying noninterpretive review, *and who takes seriously the principle of electorally accountable policymaking*, can avoid making that concession.

Perhaps I have overlooked something. Perhaps it is possible to justify noninterpretive review in a way that takes seriously the principle of electorally accountable policymaking but that does not concede a broad jurisdiction-limiting power to Congress. I invite anyone interested in elaborating such a justification to try to do so.

Perhaps I am mistaken in taking seriously the principle of electorally

---

thus far been unable to produce in our legal system. From Congress' vantage, it will rarely be useful to extricate federal programs from federal judicial scrutiny and thus allow their implementation to take grossly different form from state to state."

Sager, *supra* this note, at 40.

The problem Sager has identified simply does not arise with respect to a congressional withdrawal of federal jurisdiction over cases involving challenges to *state* laws, which, again, are the cases at the center of the present controversy.

Sager finally observes that a congressional withdrawal of federal jurisdiction over cases involving challenges to federal laws might do no more than "take Congress out of the grip of the federal courts and put it into the grip of state judiciaries." *Id.* at 41. I have already suggested, in the text, why a decision by a *state* court opposing its own value judgment to the value judgment of a branch of the *national* government should not be deemed binding on the national government. But in any event this problem too simply does not arise with respect to a congressional withdrawal of federal jurisdiction over cases involving challenges to *state* laws.

So, with respect to the actual as opposed to some imaginary possible controversy—that is, with respect to the jurisdiction-limiting bills now pending in Congress, bills designed to withdraw federal jurisdiction over certain classes of cases involving challenges to *state* laws—Professor Sager's list of "special costs" is simply irrelevant.

accountable policymaking. As I indicated at the outset of this book, I think that any constitutional theory that does not take the principle seriously is destined to have little currency—at least, less currency than a theory that does take the principle seriously. But whether or not that is so, perhaps there is a better principle—a sounder axiom of democratic political morality—that should ground our inquiry into legitimacy, and perhaps that better principle does not eventuate in any concession to Congress of a broad jurisdiction-limiting power. I eagerly await the elaboration of such a principle, and I invite others who, like myself, are interested in justifying (a fierce) judicial activism to try to elaborate such a principle.

Pending such attempts to avoid a concession to Congress of a broad jurisdiction-limiting power, I must look upon all arguments to the effect that Congress lacks such a (broad) power as attacks—albeit, often unwitting attacks, by those enthusiastic about the modern Court's activist workproduct—on noninterpretive review. Because if in fact Congress did lack such a power, I would not know how to defend noninterpretive review in terms consistent with the principle of electorally accountable policymaking:

> [T]hose people are very badly mistaken who think they strengthen the position of the Court by arguing that its jurisdiction is outside congressional control. The root objection to the Court's power of constitutional review is that it is undemocratic. . . . It seems to me that the most effective answer to this objection is and always has been that the Court could have been and still can be curbed by Congress, . . . and that Congress, with this power to curb, has not only refrained almost entirely from using it, but has in several crucial Acts accepted this judicial function. I am not sure that I could defend, as consistent with the postulates of democracy, a system which really did put nine men, with life tenure, in an absolutely invulnerable position of final power [save, of course, for constitutional amendment, which requires supermajorities]. I am very sure that the designation of such a government as one of "checks and balances" would be quite absurd.[193]

Of course, Congress's jurisdiction-limiting power is not a source of perfect control over noninterpretive review, in the way, for example, that the presidential veto power is a source of perfect control over much congressional policymaking. For some, that fact is sufficient reason to reject the functional justification I have developed here. However, it seems to me deeply unrealistic to insist on perfect control. Yes, the American polity is committed to the principle of electorally accountable policymaking. But that commitment is neither absolute nor exclusive. The polity is also committed to ongoing moral reevaluation and moral growth. At times those two basic commitments, which together are constitutive of our collective self-understanding, tug in different directions.[194] When they do, the American polity is committed, in effect, to a paradox.

Robert McCloskey observed in that regard:

Popular sovereignty suggests *will*; fundamental law suggests *limit*. The one idea conjures up the vision of an active, positive state; the other idea emphasizes the negative, restrictive side of the political problem. It may be possible to harmonize these seeming opposites by logical sleight of hand, by arguing that the doctrines of popular sovereignty and fundamental law were fused in the Constitution, which was a popularly willed limitation. But it seems unlikely that Americans in general achieved such a synthesis and far more probable, considering our later political history, that most of them retained the two ideas side by side. This propensity to hold contradictory ideas simultaneously is one of the most significant qualities of the American political mind at all states of national history, and it helps substantially in explaining the rise to power of the United States Supreme Court.[195]

So, the most we can realistically hope for is some governmental institution or practice that enables us to keep a rough faith with both commitments, that permits us to maintain a tolerable accommodation between commitments that sometimes—not always, but sometimes—pull in opposite directions. In the past quarter of a century, noninterpretive review in human rights cases has been such a practice. And there is no reason to think that, in the foreseeable future, it will not continue to be (unless, of course, a President packs the Court with interpretivist justices!). Obviously my position in that regard is not susceptible to empirical demonstration. But then, what Alexander Bickel said of judicial review generally we may say of noninterpretive review in particular: that "it will not be possible fully to meet all that is said against it." Bickel continued:

Such is not the way with questions of government. We can only fill the other side of the scales with countervailing judgments on the real needs and the actual workings of our society and, of course, with our own portions of faith and hope. Then we may estimate how far the needle has moved.[196]

The final issue I want to address before turning to the *Abortion Cases* is what we may call the problem of candor. Robert Bork has written:

The Supreme Court regularly insists that its results, and most particularly its controversial results, do not spring from the mere will of the Justices in the majority but are supported, indeed compelled, by a proper understanding of the Constitution of the United States. Value choices are attributed to the Founding Fathers, not to the Court. The way an institution advertises tells you what it thinks its customers demand.[197]

Bork's observation is not entirely accurate. Value choices are *not* invariably attributed to the framers. Nonetheless, Bork has a point. Commenting on "the tendency of our courts . . . to resort to bad legislative history and strained reading of constitutional language to support results" that cannot plausibly be supported in those terms, Thomas Grey has said:

> [T]his tendency . . . in no way helps to establish the legitimacy of noninterpretive judicial review. Indeed, standing alone it tends to establish the opposite; for if judges resort to bad interpretation in preference to honest exposition of deeply held but unwritten ideals, it must be because they perceive the latter mode of decisionmaking to be of suspect legitimacy.[198]

And of course the Court *does* perceive noninterpretive review to be of suspect legitimacy. That should come as no surprise, given the duration and vigor of the controversy over the legitimacy of "judicial activism." My effort has been, in this chapter, to dissipate the suspicion, to establish a justification for noninterpretive review in human rights cases. The question now arises of whether there is any justification for the Court's lack of candor.

In my view, the Court's lack of candor is not justifiable.* But if it is, I leave it to others so inclined to articulate the justification. It would be rather incongruous, to say the least, were I, while insisting that noninterpretive review in human rights cases is a legitimate mode of judicial review, to support any effort to conceal the fact that the Court exercises such review. There is no excuse, so far as I can see, for trying to deny to the members of the American polity, and to their governmental representatives, the opportunity of deciding for themselves whether noninterpretive review is legitimate. If they are to make that decision, they must not be deceived as to the nature of the sort of judicial review the Court exercises.[199]

Raoul Berger insists that if the people only knew what the Court really does in constitutional cases—policymaking rather than enforcement of the framers' value judgments—they would not stand for it. The court's policymaking powers, says Berger, "are self-conferred and survive only because the American people are unaware that there is a yawning gulf between judicial profession and practice."[200] He writes:

> [A] prime task of scholarship . . . is to heighten public awareness that the Court has been overleaping its bounds. "[S]cholarly exposure of the Court's abuse of its powers," Frankfurter considered, would "bring about a shift in the Court's viewpoint." Such awareness is a necessary preliminary for, as Mason observed, "only that power which is recognized can be effectively limited."[201]

Berger's point seems to me far more rhetorical than real. To which people—unaware of what is "really" going on in constitutional

---

*Nor, since I think noninterpretive review is legitimate and would be accepted by the polity as such, do I think the Court's lack of candor is necessary as a matter of strategy.

cases—does Berger refer? The people best positioned to make a fuss are aware: political representatives (many of whom are lawyers), lawyers, journalists, and any educated citizen who takes half a minute to look.[202] The conservative columnist James Kilpatrick has written:

> Somewhere in this broad land, perhaps, one or two innocents still truly believe in Santa Claus. And somewhere one or two simpletons still cling to the vacuous notion that "ours is a government of laws, not of men." But the image of the Supreme Court as a body of nine gods roosting on a marble Olympus, breathing the rarefied air of pure air of pure law and pure justice, is an image most Americans abandoned in their cradles.[203]

Articles appearing in the popular press tend to confirm Kilpatrick's position, by emphasizing again and again that the emperor has no clothes.[204] Woodward and Armstrong's *The Brethren*, a strong bestseller, has perhaps been useful in that regard as well.[205]

Moreover, the Court does not always conceal what is really going on. For example, in a recent substantive due process case, *Moore v. City of East Cleveland*,[206] every member of the Court who spoke to the constitutional issue[207] *openly* acknowledged that neither the text of the Constitution nor some original understanding of the framers explained the result.[208] I am not suggesting that the American polity fully understands the issues surrounding the debate about the legitimacy of noninterpretive review. But I am suggesting that significant segments of the polity are probably well aware that the Court's most controversial constitutional decisions—the decisions that engage the polity's attention in the first place—are compelled by neither constitutional text nor original understanding. Certainly the crucial segments are well aware: Bear in mind that in terms of the principle of electorally accountable policymaking, the important issue is less whether "the people" support or reject noninterpretive review than whether the political representatives of the people—electorally accountable officials—support or reject it. They—specifically members of Congress—are the ones empowered to curtail noninterpretive review, if they resolve to do so.

Furthermore, if the members of the American polity fully understood the issues—*and the stakes*—doubtless many of them would, just as many constitutional theorists and lawyers now do, reject the interpretivism of Bork, Berger, and Rehnquist and accept as a salutary feature of American government noninterpretive review in human rights cases. Noninterpretive review is a creature of political evolution; over time it has emerged, as I have said, to remedy what would otherwise be a serious defect in the overall policymaking processes of American government. If interpretivism were accepted and noninterpretive review rejected, what new political practice would fill the void?

> In a world of abstractions, one might argue that this historic division [between legislative policymaking on the one hand and constitutional policymaking by the judiciary on the other], since it defies good sense, ought to be obliterated. But in the world that history has given us, the almost certain result would be that pure calculation of interest-group pressures defined the course of government in the United States. It is too much to ask that a legislative process as interest-dominated as ours abjure its traditions at this late date and take on the functions of a high court as well.[209]

The American political system is much like an organism whose various parts function in delicate balance. To excise one interdependent part of the organism is to run the risk of upsetting the careful balance evolution—here, political evolution—has achieved, even to run the risk of creating a new, less sympathetic organism.[210]

Raoul Berger, forthrightly facing the harsh implications of his interpretivist constitutional theory, has asked: "Can it be . . . that in a civilized society there exists no means of ridding ourselves of such a blight as segregation?"[211] Berger's interpretivist thesis, of course, will not tolerate judicial action ridding us of blight.[212] In the [real world] of the United States, however, the world that history has given us, the "means of ridding ourselves of such a blight as segregation" has been precisely the dialectical processes of governmental policymaking, of which noninterpretive judicial review is an essential component.

Donald Woods, a self-exiled South African journalist, has written:

> The obscene laws which constitute apartheid are not crazed edicts issued by a dictator, or the whims of a megalomaniac monster, or the one-man decisions of a fanatical ideologue. They are the result of polite caucus discussions by hundreds of delegates in sober suits, after full debate in party congresses. They are passed after three solemn readings in a parliament which opens every day's proceedings with a prayer to Jesus Christ. There is a special horror in that fact.[213]

Against the background of South Africa's parliamentary apartheid, and against the background of so much else in the political experience of this century, the American polity would, I think, be hesitant to forsake our dialectical processes of governmental policymaking for Berger's—for the interpretivist's—simplistic version of the democratic ideal. Interpretivists are dogmatists for whom there are clear orthodoxies and heresies. The American polity, by contrast, is not dogmatic but pragmatic. The American people, by and large, are pragmatists who are keenly aware of the necessarily *provisional* character of discourse about the State. For them *experience*—the political experience of their own time, primarily; their experience of what works, of what enables them to keep faith with their diverse commitments—and not the text of the Constitution or some original understanding, is the ultimate criterion of the propriety, the legitimacy, of any governmental practice or function, including any judicial function. So I am not terribly concerned that more candor on the Court's part would signal the beginning of the end of noninterpretive review.[214]

Moreover, candor in acknowledging the reality and the extent of noninterpretive review is important for a very practical reason. Recently Justice Rehnquist wrote:

> The Framers intended to create an independent judiciary, and once a judge became a member of that judiciary he was to be independent of public or political pressure. But to become a member of that judiciary, whether of the Supreme Court of the United States or one of the other federal courts, one had to receive the imprimatur of representatives of the two popularly chosen branches of the federal government.[215]

To that extent, concludes Rehnquist, "the Framers provided [for] popular control . . . over the Supreme Court of the United States."[216] I have already indicated why the appointments power does not serve to render noninterpretive review consistent with the principle of electorally accountable policymaking, but it does, as Rehnquist suggests, provide an important measure of popular control. And candor with respect to the reality and extent of noninterpretive review can help ensure that the appointments power, and the popular control it represents, is exercised to full effect.

Those who oppose noninterpretive review can seek the appointment of justices who, like Rehnquist, oppose it too.[217] And those who support noninterpretive review can seek the appointment of justices who, though they are not Learned Hand's "Platonic Guardians,"[218] are nonetheless capable of exercising noninterpretive review well. Noninterpretive review cannot serve the function I have attributed to it unless the Court is staffed by persons capable of subjecting established moral conventions to critical reevaluation—thoughtful, deliberate individuals not wedded to a closed morality, but committed to the notion of moral evolution and are themselves open to the possibility of moral growth.[219] At the same time, the appointments power can help ensure that the individuals who comprise the Court are not so monolithic in their political-moral philosophies as to encourage institutional arrogance and impede institutional caution and self-criticism. Moreover, the appointments power can serve to prevent the appointment to the Court of individuals who are so idiosyncratic or exotic in their own moral values and sensibilities as to be hopelessly (and dangerously) out of touch with the larger moral culture, which must function to some (indeterminate) extent as a constraint on the outer reaches of judicial innovation.[220] Candor, then, is not only obligatory as an ethical matter; as a practical matter it can serve as the handmaiden of effective but prudent noninterpretive review.*

---

*What words does a candid noninterpretivist justice use in striking down governmental action? Should the justice say that it violates the Constitution—the equal protection clause,

In the prologue I noted that more than any other constitutional decision of recent times, the *Abortion Cases—Roe v. Wade*[221] and *Doe v. Bolton*[222]—rekindled the debate about the legitimacy of what I am now calling noninterpretive review. The Court's decision in the *Abortion Cases* was, and remains, problematic in part—in major part, I think—because the Court failed to articulate anything like a rigorous argument in support of its bare assertion that, in the previability period of pregnancy, a woman's interest in terminating her pregnancy is weightier than government's interest in preventing the taking of fetal life. The *Abortion Cases* thus suggest an interesting and important question: When the Court is called upon to resolve a fundamental political-moral problem of unusual complexity—the problem of abortion, for example, as opposed to, say, the problem of racial segregation—ought the Court to resolve the benefit of any doubt in government's favor and simply sustain the challenged governmental action? Perhaps in such a case the morally and practically prudent judicial strategy is to leave the electorally accountable policymaking processes to their own devices.*

But then, perhaps a majority of the justices concludes that the question at issue is not really one of unusual complexity and so resolves it against government, which is precisely what the Court did in the *Abortion Cases*. And perhaps in doing so the Court gives a very problematic answer—at least, an answer a majority of the polity, after deliberation, resolves to reject. In such a situation, what recourse does the polity have? To par-

---

say—even though the stricken action offends no value judgment fairly attributable to the framers? Surely there is no harm in maintaining the linguistic convention of saying that the action violates the Constitution, so long as the justice is candidly clear that by that he or she means not that the action offends the original understanding of the clause, but that it contravenes the Court's developing equal protection doctrine, which is itself not explicable in terms of any value judgment constitutionalized by the framers.

*See, in that regard, Nagel, *The Supreme Court and Political Philosophy*, 56 N.Y.U. L. REV. 519, 523–24 (1981):

When the issue is one of individual right, rather than of collective satisfaction of individual preferences, the justification for leaving it to the majority to decide is not clear. On the other hand, [abortion] also seems to be a case of basic moral uncertainty—or so at least one might reasonably hold given the present radical division of opinion. This raises the question of the correct method of decision for the Court when it must act under moral uncertainty. If, as may be possible in some cases if not in this one, the Court cannot decide who is right on the purely moral issue, should it allow its decision to be dominated by the aim of protecting other rights that are more certain? If so, which should be counted as more important: the right to equal democratic representation—*even with respect to the determination of what rights everyone has*—or the right to individual liberty? This is a matter for further constitutional reflection and therefore for political theory.

ticularize: If in the *Abortion Cases* the Court gave an answer that in the end the polity cannot accept as right, what recourse, beyond amending the Constitution, does the polity have?

Again, noninterpretive review is subject to political control in the form of Congress's power to define and limit the jurisdiction of the federal courts. Congress may, if it chooses, enact legislation denying to the lower federal courts and to the Supreme Court jurisdiction over any case in which a state law restricting access to abortion is challenged on constitutional grounds. It is interesting to note, in that regard, that at this writing 69 percent of American Protestants and 64 percent of American Catholics agree with the proposition that "the right of a woman to have an abortion should be left entirely to the woman and her doctor."[223] This data, if accurate, makes it unlikely that Congress could now be moved to enact jurisdiction-limiting legislation, much less to propose a constitutional amendment restoring the status quo ante or, more radically, banning state laws liberalizing access to abortion. Indeed, it is arguable that the shift in moral sensibilities these and other data[224] reflect makes it unlikely that in the *Abortion Cases* the Court gave an answer that the polity in general—as distinct, for example, from the so-called Moral Majority—even wants to reject.

I want to repeat, by way of emphasis and conclusion, two points bearing on the controversy surrounding the Court's decision in the *Abortion Cases*. First, the legitimacy of that decision on the merits, as an answer to a difficult political-moral question, is an issue distinct from the legitimacy of noninterpretive review. If that particular decision is illegitimate on the merits, it does not follow that noninterpretive review in human rights cases—including substantive due process cases, of which the *Abortion Cases* are an example—is illegitimate too. Second, the Court's decision, like all noninterpretive review, is subject to political control, and so to say that in the *Abortion Cases* the Court acted "undemocratically"[225] is an oversimplification, indeed a distortion, of a rather complex reality. Everything should be made as simple as possible, but not simpler.[226]

Judicial Protection of "Marginal" Persons: Some Notes on a Central Contemporary Task of Noninterpretive Review

Those who neither exploit nor are exploited are ready to fight when their own interests are harmed; they will not be involved when not personally affected. Who shall plead for the helpless? . . . In a sense, the calling of the prophet may be described as that of an advocate or champion, speaking for those who are too weak to plead their own cause. Indeed, the major activity of the prophets was *interference*, remonstrating about wrongs inflicted on other people, meddling in affairs which were seemingly neither their concern nor their responsibility. A prudent man is he who minds his own business, staying away from questions which do not involve his own interests, particularly when not authorized to step in—and prophets were given no mandate by the widows and orphans to plead their cause. The prophet is a person who is not tolerant of wrongs done to others, who resents other people's injuries. He even calls upon others to be the champions of the poor.

Abraham Heschel, *The Prophets*

In the preceding chapter, I articulated a functional justification for noninterpretive review in human rights cases; I defended the modern Supreme Court's activism (which is not to say that I applaud every decision rendered by the Court in the course of that activism). Now, I want to take issue with those who denounce the recent activism of the lower federal courts in upholding, against government, claims brought by inmates of prisons and of mental health facilities. The Supreme Court, which has yet to become significantly involved in such litigation, should underwrite that activism. This chapter is certainly less theoretical than the previous four. My reason for including it is simply that institutional reform litigation (as it is called) represents one of the most important recent developments in constitutional law, and the issue of the legitimacy of noninterpretive review in the institutional reform context is one no constitutional theorist should ignore.

In the modern period of American constitutional law, as we have seen, the Supreme Court has been engaged in the elaboration and protection of certain basic political-moral principles of general concern, among them freedom of expression, freedom from racial and analogous sorts of discrimination, and, more recently and therefore more tentatively, freedom of intimate association. I say "of general concern," because while those principles probably do not at any given time implicate the immediate personal interests of a majority of Americans, they do implicate the interests of many Americans—upper-middle class as well as poor—who are by no realistic standard on the margin of society. For example, the powerful, influential "fourth estate"—the press—has a personal stake in freedom of expression; blacks and women from every socioeconomic strata have a personal stake in freedom from racial and sexual discrimination; and certainly society's well-to-do care as much about freedom of intimate association as society's underclasses.

A central contemporary task of noninterpretive review in human rights cases should be the protection of interests that are not of general concern in any similar sense: the vital interests of the poor,[1] especially the nonwhite poor,[2] and of other persons who exist on the bare margin of society, such as prisoners and the mentally disabled. Contemporary noninterpretive review—noninterpretive review in this emergent age of scarcity—must be informed and guided by a developing sensitivity to the moral and political plight of society's "marginal" persons.

In American society, few persons are more marginal—the material condition of few persons is more desperate, the political voice of few persons is more mute—than the inmates of those two most "total" of all institutions:[3] prisons and institutions for the mentally disabled (the mentally retarded and the mentally ill). If the reader has any doubt at all about the accuracy of that claim, he or she need only consider the depraved and brutal conditions in which many prisoners and mentally disabled persons have been, and are, forced to exist. As a society, we are more solicitous of the welfare of even the poorest poor than of that of prisoners and the mentally disabled. If noninterpretive review should be exercised for the protection of any group of marginal persons, certainly it should be exercised for the protection of persons confined to prisons and institutions for the mentally disabled.[4] Many federal judges have acknowledged as much. In the 1970s, several lower federal courts, haltingly at first and then more confidently, began to supervise aspects of the operation of state prisons and mental health facilities for the purpose of safeguarding the basic human dignity of the persons confined there.[5]

A term has been coined to describe the cases to which I am referring: institutional reform litigation.[6] Such litigation constitutes a genuinely novel development in constitutional adjudication,[7] resulting in judicial decrees that, as one prominent critic of such litigation describes them, "involve fairly elaborate provisions for administration, [decrees that] tell agents of government just how they are to operate, in specific detail, and [that] almost inevitably involve some provisions for continued [judicial] oversight for an indeterminate period of time and some mechanism whereby special agents of the court assist it in this oversight."[8] Institutional reform litigation, in the words of one of its most articulate defenders, "is in large part distinguished by the effort to give meaning to constitutional values in the operation of large-scale organizations."[9]

The Supreme Court has not yet become significantly involved with institutional reform litigation.[10] Given the controversial character of the litigation—in particular the insistent claim that the lower federal courts simply have no business interfering with the administration of prisons and mental health facilities[11]—there is a danger that the Court, when it does become involved, will in effect order the lower federal courts to back off. That would be a tragic development, in my view, and so I want to say a few words here—against the background of the functional justification offered in chapter 4—in defense of the lower federal courts' activism in institutional reform cases.

Consider the horrible state of affairs disclosed by the evidentiary records in institutional reform cases. One critic of institutional reform litigation has described prison conditions in the these terms:

> Federal judicial review of prison conditions in dozens of cities and states has clearly demonstrated "[t]he sad and shameful history of penology in this country." The same problems recur again and again: dilapidated, unsanitary, and understaffed physical facilities, serious overcrowding, medical and psychiatric services insufficient to provide even minimally adequate care, food lacking in proper nutrition and prepared in unsanitary conditions, and the almost total absence of conditions that might serve to rehabilitate, or at least retard the dehabilitation of, prisoners, such as recreation, vocational training, or visits with friends and relatives.[12]

If that account is too abstract and sanitized, read what *Newsweek* reported about the specific conditions disclosed in one prison reform case:

> Euris Francis was serving fifteen years for robbery and assault when supervisors at a Texas prison farm told him to feed silage into a threshing machine by hand. The order violated normal safety procedures, and Francis, 26, lost both his arms below the elbow. An ambulance was called from the prison hospital at Huntsville, but it broke down on the way—and Francis went without medical care until another ambulance arrived from a town 20 miles away.
>
> Another inmate, Oscar Turner, was at the hospital when Francis was admitted. Later, he saw the defenseless Francis being raped by a patient. "The man without arms was crying," Turner recalled.
>
> Francis and Turner are only two of a procession of witnesses who already have testified in *Ruiz v. Estelle*, a class-action civil suit brought by inmates against the country's largest state penal system—the Texas Department of

Corrections. The suit argues that prisons are severely overcrowded and that prisoners are frequently denied adequate medical care and access to the courts. Prisoners also say that they are brutalized by guards and other inmates and exposed to unsafe working conditions.

. . . .

Hellish is an apt description of the testimony thus far. In his original plea to Judge Justice, David Ruiz told of a stint in solitary confinement, sleeping naked on a concrete floor and subsisting for days on bread and water. Ronald Goforth, who worked as a registered nurse at the hospital in Huntsville, said that he was once told by an administrator to suture the arms of an inmate relying on the same anesthetic that the patient had used to mutilate himself—that is, none. An expert witness named John Henry Albach, a Dallas attorney, told the court that he had walked into an operating room at a TDC hospital and found an inmate—a former truck driver—performing surgery.[13]

The situation with respect to conditions in institutions for the mentally disabled is no less gruesome. Confinement in such a place

typically means incarceration in a massive, antiquated, and geographically remote mental institution. Most of these institutions are hopeless places dedicated to custodial care; long term warehousing rather than effective treatment is the norm. The institutions usually are grossly underfunded. Abuse and neglect of residents are common, and deterioration of their physical and mental condition often occurs. Such institutions persist despite occasional scandal and a gradual change in professional philosophy from the institutional model of treatment to community-based alternatives. Movements for reform in human services have had beneficial effects in some areas, but much misery persists.[14]

Wyatt v. Stickney,[15] the most widely discussed of the institution cases, involved two district court orders, one for state mental institutions and one for an institution for the mentally retarded. The conditions in those institutions presented classic examples of conditions that "would shock the conscience of any citizen who knew of them": dangerous physical facilities, severe overcrowding, inadequate staffing, denial of the basic necessities of life to residents, and even brutality in the treatment of those confined for care.[16]

The overall factual picture that emerges from the institutional reform cases is deeply disturbing. Surely very few persons would dispute the moral claim that rests at the foundation of those cases—the claim that the basic respect owing to any human being is grievously violated by the depraved and brutal conditions under which many prisoners and inmates of mental institutions are required to live.[17] That claim—unlike, for example, the claim that a woman's interest in terminating her pregnancy is weightier than the countervailing interest in protecting fetal life—is simply not controversial. At least, it is not controverted by those who otherwise take issue with institutional reform litigation, and certainly it will not be controverted by a majority of the Supreme Court justices. As one critic of institutional reform cases readily acknowledges:

> Whatever the Supreme Court eventually decides about the existence of a constitutional right to treatment for the mentally ill, or habilitation for the mentally retarded, or of rehabilitation for prisoners, the Court is likely to find that involuntary confinement in conditions which are so degrading and deplorable that they fail to meet certain minimum standards of decency constitutes a deprivation of liberty without due process of law. Given the records in a number of the institution cases, the requisite level of degradation, whatever it may be, exists in a number of state institutions.[18]

What, then, is the controversy over institutional reform litigation about? There are two categories of objections to the federal courts' activism in institutional reform cases. The first category comprises claims that the judiciary lacks the competence necessary for the sound resolution of the difficult issues raised in institutional reform cases. The second category involves the claim that it is illegitimate for the electorally unaccountable federal judiciary to interfere with the states' administration of their prisons and mental health facilities on the basis of no value judgment constitutionalized by the framers. The issue of competence and the issue of legitimacy are not unrelated. If the judiciary utterly lacked competence—the institutional wherewithal—to perform a task, it would be difficult to imagine any functional justification for the judiciary's even attempting to perform it. A functional justification, as we have seen, is the only one available, if indeed any is available, and how can the function of performing a particular task possibly be salutary if the judiciary utterly lacks competence to perform it? In that sense, some degree of competence is a prerequisite to legitimacy. (Note, however, that to say that the judiciary is competent to perform a task is not necessarily to say that the judiciary may legitimately perform it.) But, while not unrelated, the issues of competence and of legitimacy raise distinct problems.

I will comment on the issue of competence only briefly. The allegation that the judiciary is institutionally unsuited to many of the tasks it has assumed in constitutional cases, typically proffered by critics of noninterpretive review, is a familiar one. Frequently the passage of time disproves the allegation. But in the context of institutional reform litigation the allegation is thought by some to have particular force,[19] principally because few tasks are as demanding as supervising the administration of a large bureaucracy, such as a prison or a mental health facility. The legal literature speaking to the issue of the judiciary's competence (or lack thereof) to perform the tasks engendered by institutional reform litigation is now voluminous.[20] In the main, that literature speaks loudly and clearly against any claim that the judiciary is substantially without competence to resolve the issues involved in institutional reform cases.[21] Indeed, one eminent authority has concluded that, in certain respects, the judiciary has "some important institutional advantages for the tasks it is assuming."[22]

When the judiciary is at an institutional disadvantage, modifications can be made, and are being made, in the conventional adjudicatory processes to remedy the problems.[23] Although the judiciary's competence may never be as great as the tasks demand, it is useful to remember that neither is the competence of the legislative or the executive branch of government that great.[24] To the extent the legislative and executive branches possess superior competence, at least with respect to certain of the tasks required, in many instances they have effectively abdicated, ignoring the desperate, shameful situation of many prisoners and mentally disabled persons. "In such circumstances," the judiciary's supposed inferior competence "must be weighed against the [legislature's and the] executive's refusal to protect constitutional rights."[25] Finally, although the judiciary may be better suited to certain less demanding tasks it faces in more conventional forms of litigation, that hardly counts as a reason for the judiciary to forswear involvement with institutional reform litigation. "[I]t is not clear," Owen Fiss has rightly observed, "why any social institution should be devoted to one and only one task, even the one it does best."[26]

Kent Greenawalt has reduced what is perhaps the most prominent and vigorous allegation of judicial incompetence in the institutional reform context—that pressed by Nathan Glazer[27]—to the following, appropriately bland terms:

> [A]lthough judges must sometimes involve themselves in administration [of large, bureaucratic institutions], a court, in deciding whether to declare doubtful rights and in deciding what sorts of remedies to give, should take account of its own inadequate knowledge and of the significantly harmful effects of what it may do on the administration of social services. When expenditures of money are involved, a court should remember that if money is going to be used for one thing, it may not be used for other things that are even more important.[28]

If that is what Glazer's argument boils down to, and I think Greenawalt is right in suggesting that it is, then the argument is not merely bland but trite. Greenawalt concludes: "In particular cases we might disagree about how much weight should be given to these considerations, but I would be surprised if anybody would disagree that they are relevant and ought to be given some weight."[29]

On the assumption, which seems to me not merely plausible but accurate, that the problems of judicial competence raised by institutional reform litigation are neither inherent nor insurmountable, let us turn to the issue of legitimacy.[30] Of course, the judicial review exercised by the courts in institutional reform cases is noninterpretive in character; the courts' decrees in those cases do not rest on value judgments constitutionalized by the framers. So, the arguments leveled against noninterpretive review generally—in particular Bork's interpretivist critique—are applicable to noninterpretive review in institutional reform cases. But at the same time, the functional justification for noninterpretive review in human rights cases developed in the preceding chapter is also applicable to noninterpretive review in institutional reform cases. If the debate over the legitimacy of institutional reform adjudication is to be waged in terms of noninterpretive review (in human rights cases) generally, I stand by what I had to say in chapter 4. On the assumption, however, that it is to be waged with particular reference to the institutional reform context, I now want to show that my functional justification for noninterpretive review in human rights cases has special force with respect to the noninterpretive review that animates institutional reform adjudication.

In most constitutional cases, the challenged governmental action represents a deliberate policy choice, whether by a legislature, administrative official, or whomever. In institutional reform cases, however, the challenged state of affairs rarely reflects deliberate policy choices in any comparable sense. The degrading, brutal conditions that exist in too many prisons and mental health facilities are not part of some institutional master plan, ratified by a legislature. Rather, such conditions—conditions, it must be emphasized, no one is prepared to defend on their merits—are in significant measure the consequence of legislative and bureaucratic inertia[31] and, of course, of budgetary priorities.[32] That fact leads to two points; each one supports my claim that the functional justification for noninterpretive review in human rights cases has especial force with respect to institutional reform adjudication.

First. Because they are a product of inertia and budgetary priorities, the conditions at issue in institutional reform litigation are dramatic evidence of a fundamental defect in the processes of electorally accountable policymaking. The human beings grievously affected by those conditions—prisoners, the mentally ill, the mentally retarded—exist on the bare margin of society; they lack ability to take effective political action to remedy their pitiful, desperate plight. And, left to its own devices, the legislative process is not likely to take meaningful action, because the cardinal legislative value—incumbency[33]—would not be appreciably served thereby. Surely it is more accurate than cynical to suggest that many a legislature would rather spend money for highways than for serious institutional reform of prisons or mental health facilities.[34]

The following passages put the point well, and although particular reference is made to prisons, the situation is certainly no different with respect to institutions for the mentally disabled:

Funding the penal system is rarely, if ever, a high-priority item in the budget. It has few political advantages and is not one of the more glamorous expenditures with which legislators like to be associated. The more visible public programs usually receive a legislative priority, and money for badly needed penal system maintenance and reform too often comes as a last resort or when compelled by external sources.[35]

[T]he improvement of prison living conditions is not an issue likely to engender widespread political support. States have limited financial resources, the public is increasingly alarmed about crime, and a disproportionate number of convicted criminals come from socioeconomic groups which themselves lack political power. Legislative and executive officials therefore have few but humanitarian incentives to finance improvements in prison conditions.[36]

In this emergent age of scarcity—the post-Proposition 13 era—there is every reason to expect that the cause of institutional reform of prisons and mental health facilities would remain, but for the federal courts' activism in institutional reform cases, a low-priority item on the legislative agenda. There is *at least* as great a need for noninterpretive review to remedy the defects of the political processes in the institutional reform context as in other, more familiar constitutional contexts.[37]

Second. Again, the degrading, brutal conditions challenged in institutional reform cases do not represent deliberate policy choices but are the product instead of legislative and bureaucratic inertia and default. No one is so wanting in compassion as to defend those conditions, or most of them, on the merits. To the contrary, most persons would doubtless agree that the persistence of such conditions bespeaks a callous, shocking, shameful disregard for the basic dignity of human beings. With respect to the fundamental question of what human rights a person ought to be deemed to have,[38] noninterpretive review likely generates morally sound answers in the institutional reform context *at least* as often as it does in other, more familiar constitutional contexts. Far fewer persons would controvert the moral claim that rests at the foundation of institutional reform litigation—the claim that the basic respect owing to any human being is grievously violated by the depraved and brutal conditions under which many prisoners and mentally disabled persons are required to live—than would controvert the claim, for example, that Nazis ought to enjoy freedom of expression, or that gender is a morally irrelevant trait, or that every woman ought to be able to terminate her pregnancy at will.

The values enforced by courts in totality of [institutional reform] cases are "communally shared" in that they reflect basic societal notions of decency. While the public is generally apathetic about prisons, studies indicate that most people are horrified by prison living conditions if and when they learn what those conditions are like. Virtually no one favors the savage conditions which exist in the worst American prisons; when a court orders those conditions improved, it is acting to enforce a communally shared sense of justice.[39]

Recall, in that regard, what one critic of institutional reform litigation has readily acknowledged—that when the Supreme Court eventually becomes significantly involved in institutional reform cases, it ["is likely to find that involuntary confinement in conditions which are so degrading and deplorable that they fail to meet certain minimum standards of decency constitutes a deprivation of liberty without due process of law."[40]]

In the preceding chapter, I portrayed the function of noninterpretive review in human rights cases as that of assisting us, as a polity, to deal with basic political-moral problems in a way that is faithful to our commitment to moral growth (and that accommodates our commitment to the principle of electorally accountable policymaking). That function, I argued, constitutes the justification for such review. Noninterpretive review in institutional reform cases serves as an exemplary illustration of my thesis. Again, the shameful conditions existing at many prisons and institutions for the mentally disabled have very low political visibility.

Although the immediate object of litigants who press for institutional reform is, of course, to remedy conditions at particular institutions, certainly that is not the only function of such litigation. The widespread publicity attending institutional reform litigation dramatically heightens the political visibility of the degradation and brutality that characterize life in many prisons and mental health facilities. The salutary effect of that greater visibility should come as no surprise. Frank Johnson, the federal judge who spearheaded institutional reform litigation in the 1970s, reported that "[a] not-altogether-unexpected benefit resulting from the public exposure given the problem [that is, conditions at Alabama mental health facilities] has been a substantial increase in legislative approriations for the state's mental health system."[41] In much the same vein, one commentator has noted: "The fact that general cooperation with the thrust of the court orders in the institution cases has occurred to date stems . . . from the use of the courts' principal enforcement tool: their power publicly to make illegitimate the maintenance of intolerable conditions in the institutions."[42]

The sunshine effect is not coincidental. From the very outset a prime function of institutional reform litigation has been "to bring forcefully to the attention of legislators, executives, bureaucrats, and other public and private decisionmakers and to the attention of the citizenry at large, certain facts . . . which have not had great visibility . . . before."[43] It is impossible for us, as a polity, to deal with a basic political-moral problem in any very deliberate way, much less in a way that is faithful to our commitment to moral growth, unless we are aware—fully, painfully aware—of the problem in all its concreteness. And sometimes it is necessary for us to have our faces rubbed in the problem before it dawns on us that the problem really *does* exist. Noninterpretive review in institutional reform cases makes us aware of the problem in a way and to an extent that we—the polity as a whole—were not aware of it before, thereby freeing us from our collective ignorance and making it possible for us to begin to deal with the problem in a fashion that keeps faith with our moral commitments.[44]

And how have we, as a polity, begun to deal with the problem of the degradation and brutality that characterize life in too many total institutions? It is too early for a definitive answer, but already there are significant developments. For example, Judge Frank Johnson's landmark decision in *Wyatt v. Stickney*[45]

> had an impact going far beyond the state of Alabama. The Department of Health, Education, and Welfare drew on *Wyatt*'s standards in establishing requirements for medicaid eligibility of psychiatric facilities, . . . and several states have adopted *Wyatt*-type standards without having been sued. . . .[46]

In 1975, Congress, in its turn, enacted the Developmentally Disabled Assistance and Bill of Rights Act,[47] which expressly provides that "persons with developmental disabilities have a right to appropriate treatment, services, and habilitation for such disabilities . . . in the setting that is least restrictive of the person's liberty."[48]

In the preceding chapter, I said that

> [t]he relationship between noninterpretive review and electorally accountable policymaking is dialectical.
>
> . . . .
>
> In the constitutional dialogue between the [judiciary] and the other agencies of government—a subtle, dialectical interplay between [judiciary] and polity—what emerges is a far more self-critical political morality than would otherwise appear, and therefore likely a more mature political morality as well . . .[49]

Institutional reform adjudication strongly supports my characterization of the overall process as dialectical: Noninterpretive review in institutional reform cases has served as an important catalyst to legislative and other actions.[50] And certainly one outcome of the dialectical process in the institutional reform context fulfills the hope of a more mature political morality: the commitment of the national government, evidenced in part by the Developmentally Disabled Assistance and Bill of Rights Act, to safeguarding the vital interests of mentally ill and mentally retarded persons.* (Another piece of relevant congressional legislation is the "Civil

---

*Further evidence is the participation of the United States (through the Department of Justice) as a "litigating amicus" in support of the plaintiffs' side in several institutional reform cases.

Rights of Institutionalized Persons Act,"[51] enacted into law in 1980, about which I will have something to say shortly.)

A prominent critic of institutional reform litigation, Nathan Glazer, has contended that such litigation "contribute[s] to the . . . weakening of democracy[,] . . . because it encourages that very refusal to deal with great issues directly or indirectly, among legislatures and executives, that many argue is the cause and justification of judicial intervention."[52] Glazer's indictment paints the world upside down. Institutional reform adjudication, as we have just seen, has not encouraged a refusal to deal with "great issues." To the contrary, it has greatly enhanced the political visibility of the issue of our shameful neglect of prisoners and the mentally disabled, and has thereby helped make it possible for the political processes to begin to resolve that problem. The Developmentally Disabled Assistance and Bill of Rights Act points up the infirmity of Glazer's claim.

But there is more. Consider the fact, for example, that after many years of pass-the-buck noncompliance by the Alabama Board of Corrections with Judge Johnson's directives in several prison reform cases, the Governor of Alabama, Forrest H. James, Jr.—who took office in January 1979, nine years after the first of the cases commenced—petitioned the court

> that he be designated temporary receiver [in the cases], for a period of not less than one year, and that this Court order that defendant members of the Board of Corrections of the State of Alabama (hereinafter "Board") to transfer to Petitioner, as such receiver, all of its functions, duties, powers and authority to manage, supervise and control all penal and correctional institutions in the State of Alabama and all other duties and functions imposed upon the said Board under the laws of Alabama, including without limitation, the power to hire, discharge, suspend and supervise the Commissioner of Corrections, deputy commissioners, and any other personnel employed by the Board. Petitioner further moves that the Court enjoin all members of the Board, and all other defendants in these actions, their agents, servants, employees, and all persons in active concert or participation with them, from interfering in any manner, either directly or indirectly, with the performance of his functions and duties as such receiver.[53]

In support of his petition, Governor James stated:

> Of intense concern to Petitioner in the performance of his duties as Governor, and in seeing to it that the laws are faithfully executed, are the establishment, maintenance and proper operation of a corrections system in the State of Alabama in accord with, and not in contravention of, the guaranties of the Constitution of the United States and of the State of Alabama. Indeed, an effective corrections system, legally and constitutionally operated, directly involves the safety and welfare of the citizens of the State of Alabama.
>
> Petitioner knows that in its orders of January 12, 1976 (hereinafter the "Court

Order"), after an extensive trial, this Court found—*and indeed the state through its attorney general conceded*—indefensible conditions involving overcrowding; segregation and isolation; inadequate classification; physical and mental health care; protection from violence; inmate living conditions; unsanitary food service; unmeaningful work, recreation and education opportunities; and physical facilities and staff.

. . . .

Petitioner is informed and believes that the Alabama prison system is in a distress situation and that compliance with the standards and requirements of the Court's Order, and the achievement as well as the goal of an effective prison system maintained and operated in the interest of the safety and welfare of the citizens of this state, require the assertion of the extraordinary equitable powers of this Court. The more usual remedies heretofore pursued by this Court have not produced these desired results, but instead have invited confrontation and delay. A receivership is essential to get the job done.

. . . .

Petitioner considers that the prompt achievement of these goals, of the standards set in the Court Order, and the establishment, maintenance and operation of an effective corrections system are among the paramount duties of his office, and directly involve the constitutional performance of his duty to see to it that the laws are faithfully executed. But as the Court of Appeals concluded in this litigation (*Newman v. Alabama*, 559 F.2d 283, 292 (1977)), the Governor of Alabama "has no hand in the operations of the Alabama penal system beyond the customary budget recommendations to the legislature and the appointment of the Alabama Board of Corrections. The statute vests all power and control in the Board."

Accordingly, if Petitioner is to be able to perform this important task for the citizens of Alabama as their governor, it is imperative that this Court appoint Petitioner temporary receiver.[54]

Governor James's petition, which the court quickly granted, is eloquent refutation of Professor Glazer's simplistic cant about how institutional reform litigation weakens democracy by encouraging a refusal on the part of responsible officials to deal with great issues.[55]

Glazer concluded his critique by saying that "[i]f the judges didn't do it [that is, reform prisons and institutions for the mentally disabled], . . . the executives and the legislatures would have to. . . ."[56] (Critics of the Supreme Court's activism in deciding *Brown v. Board of Education* the way it did said much the same thing.) I am deeply skeptical of Glazer's easy claim. Perhaps in time the political processes would have responded on their own, unassisted by federal judicial intervention. (In time too, perhaps, the political processes would have put an end to segregated public schooling, though I seriously doubt it would have happened anytime soon.) But consider the price of judicial nonintervention and of the consequent delay: the continuing degradation and brutalization of many prisoners and mentally disabled persons. Some critics of institutional reform litigation seem willing to pay that cost—a cost that, happily for them, would be paid out in someone else's suffering. Frank Johnson and certain other federal judges are not willing to pay. And it is difficult to find fault in that: in the institutional reform cases over which they have presided, they—unlike their critics—have come face to face with that degradation and brutalization.*

There is an important problem we have not yet addressed. Compliance with a judicial directive in an institutional reform case can cost state government a great deal of money.

Estimates of the cost of compliance with the federal court orders in the institution cases are rare, but the few hints available indicate that the sum will be substantial. Louisiana, for example, appropriated more than 106 million dollars for capital improvements following a court decree concerning the Angola state penitentiary, compared with approximately 1 million dollars annual total capital outlay previously made for all state correctional facilities. The state also added more than 18 million dollars of supplementary operating funds to the prison budget, an amount almost equal to the total operating budget of the entire state prison system at that time. These additional expenditures did not purport to cover all the additional costs involved in complying with the court order concerning the Angola facility, let alone the costs required to meet other federal court decrees concerning other Louisiana prisons. Compliance with one Alabama prison order has been estimated at more than 28 million dollars compared to the total state corrections budget of roughly 22 million dollars, and this estimate specifically does not include the costs of improving medical care in the Alabama prison system mandated by another federal court order. Whether these figures are representative of the magnitude of increase in state expenditures necessary to comply with the orders in the institution cases cannot be accurately determined because of the lack of data

---

*Critics like Glazer, willing to pay the price of delay with the suffering of others, remind me of the chaplain in Shaw's *Saint Joan*, who insists that Joan be put to death by fire. Later, in seeing Joan's flesh incinerate, the chaplain comes face to face with the terrible cruelty of what he had demanded:

I meant no harm. I did not know what it would be like. . . .I did not know what I was doing. . . .I let them do it. If I had known, I would have torn her from [the executioners'] hands. You don't know: you haven't seen: it is so easy to talk when you don't know. You madden yourself with words: you damn yourself because it feels grand to throw oil on the flaming hell of your own temper. But when it is brought home to you; when you see the thing you have done; when it is blinding your eyes, stifling your nostrils, tearing your heart, then—then—[*Falling on his knees*] O God, take away this sight from me! O Christ, deliver me from this fire that is consuming me! She cried to Thee in the midst of it: Jesus! Jesus! Jesus! She is in Thy Bosom; and I am in hell for evermore.

G. B. Shaw, SAINT JOAN, scene 6 (1923).

available; however, even a cursory examination of the extensive changes involved, both in terms of capital construction and annual operating costs, suggests that a major reallocation of resources to the institutions for the mentally ill or mentally retarded, prisons and juvenile detention centers will be required.[57]

The significantly greater cost involved in the institutional reform context constitutes a problem for anyone contending for the legitimacy of noninterpretive review in institutional reform cases. As one critic has put it, because they entail such great compliance costs, "the court orders in the institution cases . . . are a greater intrusion into democratic decisionmaking than the normal invalidation of a law on constitutional grounds. . . . [T]he court orders involve a subject matter that is the very foundation of the discretion lodged in the other branches: the raising, allocation, and spending of government funds."[58] Although in certain important respects, the problem of legitimacy has diminished force in the institutional reform context—that is, the functional justification for noninterpretive review has special force in that context—with respect to compliance costs the problem of legitimacy has greater force.[59]

Nonetheless, in the end the solution to the problem of the legitimacy of noninterpretive review in institutional reform cases is the same as the solution to the problem of the legitimacy of noninterpretive review in human rights cases generally. Noninterpretive review in institutional reform cases is subject to significant control at the hands of electorally accountable officials—it is subject to the legislative power of Congress to limit the classes of cases the federal judiciary may adjudicate.[60] If the Congress of the United States—which, after all, is the principal electorally accountable policymaking institution in the United States—believes that the federal judiciary's policymaking in the area of institutional reform has been improvident—if it believes, for example, that compliance costs are simply too high, that the game is not worth the candle—Congress can simply enact legislation withdrawing from the federal courts jurisdiction over cases in which state prisons and mental health facilities are challenged on constitutional grounds.

It is not a bit surprising, in my view, that not only has Congress not contemplated legislation curtailing the jurisdiction of the federal courts in institutional reform cases, but, to the contrary, it has enacted legislation indirectly supportive of what the federal courts have been trying to accomplish in those cases. Moreover, during the drafting of this book, Congress passed and the President signed into law the Civil Rights of Institutionalized Persons Act, which authorizes the Attorney General of the United States to initiate (or to intervene in) institutional reform actions against state governments.[61]

It is difficult to imagine a clearer statement of congressional and presidential support for the lower federal courts' activism in institutional reform cases—or a clearer refutation of the claim, made by Glazer and others, that that activism exemplifies judicial imperialism. One critic of institutional reform litigation conceded that "[m]ost complaints about unwarranted judicial interference with democratic decisionmaking would not survive an explicit congressional decision to authorize the judicial action in question."[62] Well, that "explicit congressional decision" now exists. Congress and the President, through the Civil Rights of Institutionalized Persons Act, have in effect authorized the federal judiciary to serve as their agent for the vindication, in the context of total institutions, of "rights, privileges, or immunities secured or protected by the Constitution or laws of the United States."[63]

The Civil Rights of Institutionalized Persons Act is further support for, and illustration of, my claim about the dialectical nature of constitutional policymaking by the judiciary in human rights cases, particularly in institutional reform cases. The act represents a response by Congress and the President to the fact that the conditions prevailing at many state prisons, mental health facilities, and similar institutions, such as juvenile detention facilities,[64] are manifestly intolerable by any civilized standard. But it took the lower federal courts to give that fact dramatic political visibility—the visibility that is prerequisite to effective legislative action. And it will take the federal courts, as the act recognizes, to maintain a persistent vigilance in eradicating those shameful conditions and the human rights violations they represent. I hope the Supreme Court will come to share Congress's and the President's implicit view—implicit in the act—that the federal judiciary's role in institutional reform litigation is to be praised and encouraged and assisted, not curtailed.

A problem remains. It has been suggested that judicial directives in institutional reform cases, at least if not suitably limited in scope, are not enforceable by the courts themselves.

> Only the legislature can provide the necessary money, and only the executive can administer the spending of that money. The courts cannot imprison the legislature for contempt unless it raises or reallocates the necessary money, nor jail an executive official to ensure implementation of a government program. Courts ultimately lack the power to force state governments to act.[65]

I hesitate to call the problem one of competence, since it concerns not a court's ability to fashion a sound resolution of a dispute, but its ability to secure compliance with that resolution. I also hesitate to call it a problem of legitimacy, since it concerns not the legitimacy of the court's undertaking to resolve the dispute in the first place, but, again, its ability to secure compliance. But however it is characterized, the limited ability of federal courts to secure compliance with their directives in institutional reform cases is a potential problem. I am not interested in denying—nor, here, in exploring possible judicial strategies for sidestepping—the problem. Rather, I want to consider the significance courts ought (and ought not) to attach to the problem.

In the reality of institutional reform litigation, a federal court's limited ability to secure compliance with its directives will inevitably lead most courts to exercise caution in formulating their remedial orders. But more than that, it will lead them to exercise caution in defining the underlying right the remedial orders are designed to vindicate. Owen Fiss's discussion of the matter is illuminating:

> [N]o judge is likely to decree more than he thinks he has the power to accomplish. The remedy will be limited, and even more importantly it will be viewed in adaptive terms. The judge will seek to anticipate the response of others, and though he may try to transcend the limits imposed by that response, he is likely to accept the reality of those limits and compromise his original objective in order to obtain as much relief as possible. He will bargain against the people's preferences. . . . [E]ven if the remedy were all that were affected, all that were compromised, there would be reason to be concerned. But the truth of the matter is that the stakes are likely to be higher— the distortion will be felt in the realm of rights, too. Just as it is reasonable to assume that a judge wishes to be efficacious, it is also reasonable to assume that no judge is anxious to proclaim his impotence. He will strive to lessen the gap between declaration and actualization. He will tailor the right to fit the remedy.[66]

That the judge, in a spirit of realpolitik, will limit the remedy or tailor the right is not altogether troublesome. There is virtue, after all, in being efficacious.[67] The real problem, of course, is that the judge will attach too much significance to his limited ability to secure compliance and so attempt to accomplish too little. Federal courts ought not lightly to assume that key state officials will be recalcitrant. Recall, for example, the performance of Alabama Governor James. In *Nixon v. Sirica*,[68] the famous Watergate tapes case, the United States Court of Appeals for the District of Columbia Circuit said that "the courts in this country always assume that their orders will be obeyed, especially when addressed to responsible government officials."[69] If there is virtue in that assumption, perhaps not the least of the reasons why is that the assumption doubtless functions to some extent as a self-fulfilling prophecy. At any rate, typically the courts' orders *are* obeyed.[70] Moreover, the problem of the courts' limited ability to secure compliance may be a passing one. As institutional reform litigation becomes a more familiar and accepted feature of the legal landscape, bureaucratic and legislative resistance to the courts' orders may wane. And in any event in cases brought by, or joined by, the Attorney General of the

United States, courts will have little difficulty securing compliance: The federal executive branch will stand immediately behind the courts' directives.[71]

But for the moment assume the worst: a case in which state bureaucratic and legislative recalcitrance is unrelenting and at a time when neither Congress nor the President is particularly sympathetic to the federal judiciary's institutional reform efforts. In our political-legal culture, such a situation is not likely to develop, certainly not with enough frequency to be significant. After all, the court's

> power to declare conditions unconstitutional is a potent weapon, as demonstrated not only by the institution cases but by cases involving Presidents and Congress as well. Indifference to the institutional conditions is made impossible by the judicial order, publicly stated, that the outrageous conditions must be ended; its order that action be taken arms the reform movement to achieve the desired political result.[72]

Nonetheless, in such a situation, how much significance ought the federal court to attach to its limited ability to secure compliance? The court's paramount duty, within limits,[73] is to declare the human rights at issue as it sees them. Of course the court must try to enforce those rights as well. But even if in the end it cannot fully enforce them, the court must declare them to exist. If the political processes were to persist in transgressing the human rights declared by the court rather than comply with the court's directives, that would be less of a problem* for the federal judiciary than for the American polity as a whole. In this day and age when we make so much of human rights violations elsewhere in the world,[74] as of course we should, it would be an especial problem, raising grave questions about the extent to which our own house is in order.

We must not minimize the judiciary's role in focusing our collective attention on the worst features of the desperate plight of our society's most marginal persons, prisoners and the institutionalized mentally disabled. The importance of that role is perhaps diminished but certainly not belied by the fact that, occasionally, a court might lack the capacity to compel the other branches of government to respond to that plight immediately and in a manner the court deems fully acceptable. The judiciary must not forsake its prophetic function simply because its ability to secure compliance is sometimes weak,[75] for that function is virtually indispensable when the vital, vulnerable intersts of our society's marginal persons are imperiled. We may resist the courts' prophecy in the short run—as sometimes, of course, we will, and as sometimes, no doubt, we should—and yet, in time, we may be deeply nourished by it.

---

*If a problem at all in any particular instance: I do not mean to foreclose the possibility that a given court's vision of the human rights at issue might be fundamentally unsound.

EPILOGUE

I have articulated a functional justification for noninterpretive review in human rights cases. I have argued, among other things, that in the modern period of American constitutional law such review—constitutional policymaking by the judiciary—has served the American polity as an agency of ongoing, insistent moral reevaluation and ultimately of moral growth. It is not the sole such agency, of course (although it might sometimes sound as if we defenders of noninterpretive review think otherwise). To some extent political dissent serves that function, as do congressional deliberations from time to time. My claim is not that noninterpretive review serves as the only agency of moral evaluation and growth. To the contrary, an aspect of my argument has been that noninterpretive review serves its function in part by interacting, in a dialectical way, with other agencies of moral reevaluation and growth.[1]

But, while it is not the sole agency of political-moral maturation, noninterpretive review is nonetheless a crucial agency—sometimes, perhaps, a virtually indispensable one. Similarly, the political-moral issues with which the judiciary, in particular the Supreme Court, deals in exercising noninterpretive review are not always the most important or urgent ones facing the country, but they are important nonetheless.[2] And since, as I have demonstrated, constitutional policymaking by the judiciary proceeds in a manner that accommodates our commitment to the principle of electorally accountable policymaking,[3] I can think of no good reason why we should join with Robert Bork, Raoul Berger, William Rehnquist, and other interpretivists in their efforts to curtail it. If one wants, like John Ely, not to curtail noninterpretive review but to confine it to narrower limits than those in which it has operated in recent years, one must supply a firm theoretical foundation for the particular limits proposed. That is something Ely has failed to do.

* * * * * * *

The human rights of which noninterpretive review has served as a principal matrix, in the modern period, have generally been political and civil in character rather than social and economic. By social and economic rights I mean rights of the sort recognized by the Universal Declaration of Human Rights[4] and the International Covenant on Economic, Social, and Cultural Rights:[5] "a right to food, clothing, housing, and education; rights to work, leisure, fair wages, decent working conditions, and social security; rights to physical and mental health, protection for the family, and for mothers and children; a right to participate in cultural life."[6] One of the great open questions in constitutional law is whether, and to what extent, the Supreme Court and the judiciary generally have the institutional capacity to formulate and to implement socioeconomic rights.[7] Implementation of socioeconomic rights costs money[8]—an obvious fact, and one the International Covenant recognizes and accommodates.[9] Would the judiciary press its institutional capacity, even its legitimate authority, to and perhaps past the breaking point were it to undertake to resolve complex issues of social and economic welfare and, hence, to reallocate scarce and perhaps diminishing fiscal resources?

Our collective commitment to human rights of the socioeconomic sort is doubtless thought by many, here and abroad, to be suspect—and perhaps with good reason. But surely the situation in America with respect to human rights of the political and civil sort is exemplary. Other societies committed to improving their own human rights situations[10]—as many are, now that the issue of human rights is ascendant throughout the world[11]—must not overlook, or discount, this crucial feature of the American experience: The existence and content of human rights in America is in significant measure, as this book has demonstrated, a function of policymaking—constitutional policymaking—not by an electorally accountable institution, but by one that is electorally unaccountable and otherwise politically independent:* the federal judiciary, in particular the Supreme Court. There is an important lesson in that fact for other societies, and learning it can help them deal more effectively with the challenge of elaborating and protecting human rights among their own members.[12] Surely one must wonder what the American situation with respect to human rights would be like today were it not for noninterpretive judicial review—a practice that for so long has been of suspect legitimacy.

There is an important lesson in that fact for our society too. Human rights, again, are rights the individual has—or, if one is making a normative claim, ought to have—against government. The function of human rights is to protect the individual from the leviathan of the state. As government increases in size and power, government's capacity to harm individuals—whether deliberately or unthinkingly—increases too, and so the matter of human rights becomes even more important. "[T]he importance of the welfare state is twofold: it provides a wide range of benefits to be made available by the state to the citizen as of right, but at the same time it enhances the power of the bureaucrat, since the benefits thus provided are inevitably administered by government departments or their agents."[13] The welfare state did not emerge fullblown in America in the 1930s. In the

---

*To say that the Court is politically independent is to say that the justices cannot be retired on the basis of their policymaking, not that their policymaking is not subject to significant political control. (It *is* subject to such control. *See* chap. 4.)

years ahead—with their unhappy promise of increased governmental regulation owing to serious shortages of cheap energy, worldwide economic distress, and God knows what—doubtless the welfare state will continue to grow. (Hopefully that worldwide economic distress will lead to a more just distribution of the world's resources—a development that would be the occasion for greater, not lesser, governmental regulation here at home, at least in the painful transitional period.) No President, no matter how conservative, can do very much about that eventuality, which is dependent, after all, on factors largely beyond our national control and which therefore seems inexorable. The choices we face are not between dismantling the welfare, or regulatory, state and maintaining it, or even between maintaining a static welfare state and accepting a growing one. The choices, rather, go to how efficient the growing welfare state will be, *and how respectful of basic human rights.*[14]

The lesson for us, then, is this: If in the past constitutional policymaking by the judiciary has been an essential matrix of human rights, in the future, as government's regulatory powers extend even more widely and deeply into the fabric of our society, it will certainly be no less essential. Noninterpretive review will surely be a crucial safeguard for the individual caught in the grip of the bureaucratic state—the individual intent on maintaining, or regaining, his or her autonomy. One has only to contemplate the apparent regimentation of life in what is perhaps the bureaucratic state, the Soviet Union, to appreciate the dangers.[15]

NOTES

PROLOGUE

1. 347 U.S. 483 (1954).
2. In *Brown* the Court held that the equal protection clause of the fourteenth amendment (*see* U.S. CONST. amend. XIV, § 1: "No state shall . . . deny to any person within its jurisdiction the equal protection of the laws") forbids state officials to take action designed to segregate public schools on the basis of race. *See also* Bolling v. Sharpe, 347 U.S. 497 (1954) (due process clause of fifth amendment (*see* U.S. CONST. amend. V: "No person shall . . . be deprived of life, liberty, or property, without due process of law") forbids District of Columbia officials to take action designed to segregate public schools on basis of race).
3. 410 U.S. 113 (1973).
4. In *Roe* the Court held that the due process clause of the fourteenth amendment (*see* U.S. CONST. amend. XIV, § 1: "No state shall . . . deprive any person of life, liberty, or property, without due process of law") denies to states authority to outlaw abortions in the previability period of pregnancy. *See also* Doe v. Bolton, 410 U.S. 179 (1973).
5. In chap. 4 I explain what I mean by the Court's "own" value judgments.
6. *See* J. ELY, DEMOCRACY AND DISTRUST: A THEORY OF JUDICIAL REVIEW 2–3 (1980) (*Roe* is "the clearest example of noninterpretivist 'reasoning' on the part of the Court in four decades"); Alschuler, *Burger's Failure: Trying Too Much to Lead*, NAT'L L. J., February 18, 1980, at 19 (*Roe* is "the [C]ourt's most remarkable adventure in activism since *Lochner v. New York* (1905)"); Howard, *Pragmatism, Compromise Marks Court, id.,* at 17, 28 ("Whatever else one may say about [*Roe*], no more activist opinion ever came from the pens of the Warren Court").
7. *See generally* Ely, *The Wages of Crying Wolf: A Comment on* Roe v. Wade, 82 YALE L. J. 920 (1973).
8. *See, e.g.,* Gunther, *Some Reflections on the Judicial Role: Distinctions, Roots, and Prospects,* 1979 WASH U. L. Q. 817, 819 ("In my view, *Brown v. Board of Education* was an entirely legitimate decision. . . . By contrast, . . . I have not yet found a satisfying rationale to justify *Roe v. Wade* . . . on the basis of modes of constitutional interpretation I consider legitimate"); Lynch, Book Review, 63 CORN. L REV. 1091, 1099 n. 32 ("to most lawyers of my generation, *Brown* is a touchstone for constitutional theory fully as powerful as *Lochner* [v. New York, 198 U.S. 45 (1905)] was for a previous generation"); Yudof, *School Desegregation: Legal Realism, Reasoned Elaboration, and Social Science Research in the Supreme Court,* 42 L. & CONT. PROB. 57, 69–70 (1978) ("I persist with many others in thinking that the decision to declare race discrimination in *Brown* unconstitutional was about as well justified a constitutional decision as any ever rendered by the Supreme Court"). *See also* Cover, *The Origins of Judicial Activism in the Protection of Minorities,* in THE ROLE OF THE JUDICIARY IN AMERICA (Moore ed., forthcoming 1982): "Each constitutional generation organizes itself about paradigmatic events. . . . For my generation it is clear that the events are *Brown v. Board of Education* and the Civil Rights Movement." There was a time, of course, when *Brown* too was at the center of controversy. *See* Bell, Brown v. Board of Education *and the Interest-Convergence Dilemma,* 93 HARV. L. REV. 518, 519 (1980).
9. *See* J. CHOPER, JUDICIAL REVIEW AND THE NATIONAL POLITICAL PROCESS: A FUNCTIONAL RECONSIDERATION OF THE SUPREME COURT 64 (1980): "[T]he overriding virtue of and justification for vesting the Court with [the] awesome power [of judicial review] is to

guard against governmental infringements of individual liberties secured by the Constitution."

10. See C. BLACK, DECISION ACCORDING TO LAW 33 (1981) (referring to Brown as "the decision that opened our era of judicial activity").

11. See J. ELY, supra note 6, at 48: "[T]he Court's power . . . probably has never been greater than it has been over the past two decades." In earlier periods, the Court played other roles. For example, under Chief Justice John Marshall, who sat on the Court from 1801 to 1835, the Court's most significant decisions served to nurture the new national government. In the first third of the 20th century, the Court sought to retard, or at least to moderate, the emergence of a centralized welfare state. For an excellent brief history of the Court's constitutional decision making from the beginning of the Republic to the late 1950s, see R. MCCLOSKEY, THE AMERICAN SUPREME COURT (1960).

12. See, e.g., J. ELY, supra note 6, at 2–3.

13. This is reflected by a spate of articles published in the popular press during 1979, the year in which most of this book was first drafted. See, e.g., Have the Judges Done Too Much?, TIME, January 22, 1979, at 91; When Judges Govern, NEWSWEEK, August 13, 1979, at 79; Hunt, The Lawyers' War against Democracy, COMMENTARY, October 1979, at 45; Miller, For Judicial Activism, N.Y. Times, Novmber 11, 1978, § 4, at E21, col. 6; Zion, The Supreme Court: A Decade of Constitutional Revision, N.Y. TIMES MAG., November 11, 1979, at 26, and November 18, 1979, at 76; Will, The Injudicial Justices, NEWSWEEK, December 10, 1979, at 140 (one of very many reviews of Bob Woodward's and Scott Armstrong's immediate bestseller, THE BRETHREN (1979)).

14. See also J. CHOPER, supra note 9, at 10: "[I]rrespective of the content of its decisions, the process of judicial review is not democratic because the Court is not a politically responsible institution."

15. For a recent example of the definitional strategem, see Bishin, Judicial Review in Democratic Theory, 50 S. CAL. L. REV. 1099 (1977). John Ely can fairly be understood as relying, at points in his book (supra note 6), on the definitional argument. See chap. 3.

16. J. PENNOCK, DEMOCRATIC POLITICAL THEORY 7 (1979). For a similar definition, see H. MAYO, AN INTRODUCTION TO DEMOCRATIC THEORY 70 (1960). See also J. PENNOCK, supra this note, at 14:

> As has been shown, it is at least arguable that the same substantive concept of democracy will fit both West and East. A formal or procedural definition of democracy that would fit our Western-style democracy, however, clearly would rule out Communist regimes and so-called peoples' democracies.

Cf. Giraudo, Judicial Review and Comparative Politics: An Explanation for the Extensiveness of American Judicial Review Offered from the Perspective of Comparative Government, 6 HAST. CONST. L. Q. 1137, 1161 n. 162 (1979).

17. Constitutional policymaking by state courts does not invariably give rise to the problem of legitimacy, or give rise to it to anything like the same extent, because state judges, unlike federal judges, are often electorally accountable. See THE BOOK OF THE STATES (published annually). Cf. Note, State Economic Substantive Due Process: A Proposed Approach, 88 YALE L. J. 1487, 1490 n. 12 (1979).

18. With respect to the meaning of the constitution of a state, the courts of that state, and ultimately the state's highest court of appeal, have the last word. See, e.g., Brennan, State Constitutions and the Protection of Individual Rights, 90 HARV. L. REV. 489 (1977). This book deals solely with policymaking, by federal and state courts, that resolves issues arising under the federal Constitution. However, some of what I say concerning the problem of the legitimacy of federal constitutional policymaking bears on the distinct problem of the legitimacy of policymaking, by the courts of a state, that resolves issues arising under the state constitution. (The latter problem does not arise in every state, since, again, state judges are often electorally accountable.)

19. Occasionally the courts of a state, in particular a state's highest court, assume a posture more activist than the Supreme Court's. Again, the courts of a state have the last word with respect to the meaning of the state constitution. Consequently, they may impose limits on their state government that exceed the limits the Supreme Court is willing to impose, so long as those limits are imposed in the name of the state, as opposed to the federal, constitution. For example, *compare* Santa Barbara v. Adamson, 48 LW 2783 (Calif. Sup. Ct. 1980) *to* Belle Terre v. Boraas, 416 U.S. 1 (1980). *See generally* Brennan, *supra* note 18; Howard, *State Courts and Constitutional Rights in the Day of the Burger Court*, 62 VA. L. REV. 873 (1976). Welsh & Collins, *Taking State Constitutions Seriously*, THE CENTER MAGAZINE, September–October 1981, at 6. *See also* Weinstein, *Equality, Liberty, and the Public Schools: The Role of the State Courts*, 1 CARD. L. REV. 343 n. 3 (1979): "[A]s the federal courts are doing less to protect constitutional rights, the state courts are doing more." (Occasionally too the courts of a state will assume a more passivist posture, evading—or, more precisely, helping their state government evade—federal constitutional limits the Supreme Court has imposed. *See, e.g.,* J. CHOPER, *supra* note 9, at 142.)
20. *See, e.g.,* Kurland, *The Irrelevance of the Constitution: The Religion Clauses of the First Amendment and the Supreme Court*, 24 VILL. L. REV. 3 (1978–79).
21. Moreover, distinctions among different categories of substantive doctrine are less important than John Ely insists if, as I claim in chap. 3, his attempt to devise a theory that would (1) justify judicial policymaking with respect to both first amendment and equal protection issues, for example, but, at the same time, (2) condemn it with a respect to substantive due process issues (*see* J. ELY, *supra* note 6), is ultimately unavailing.
22. M. SHAPIRO, LAW AND POLITICS IN THE SUPREME COURT vii (1964).
23. *See* Bork, *Neutral Principles and Some First Amendment Problems*, 47 IND. L. J. 1(1971); Bork, *The Impossibility of Finding Welfare Rights in the Constitution*, 1979 WASH. U. L. Q. 695.
24. *See* J. ELY, *supra* note 6. *Cf.* Michelman, *Welfare Rights in a Constitutional Democracy*, 1979 WASH. U. L. Q. 659, 666 (referring to Ely's as "the most conservative, restrained theory of transcontractualist constitutional interpretation I know of").
25. *See* J. ELY, *supra* note 6. Noninterpretive review with respect to both freedom of expression and equal protection issues Ely terms *participational review.* The other he terms *substantive* review. *See, e.g., id.* at 182. Ely expresses doubt as to whether his theory "is properly regarded as a form of interpretivism or instead is more comfortably described as sitting somewhere between an interpretivist and a noninterpretivist approach"—"a question," says Ely, "that seems neither answerable nor important." *Id.* at 12. (On the distinction between *interpretivism* and *noninterpretivism*, see chap. 1.) *See also id.* at 88 n. *: "I don't think this terminological question is either entirely coherent or especially important." Mindful of Ely's expressed doubt, I have chosen to label Ely's theory noninterpretivist. That is, I have chosen to label the constitutional policymaking Ely defends—*participational review*—a species of noninterpretive review, as Ely himself once did (*see* Ely, *Constitutional Interpretivism: Its Allure and Impossibility*, 53 IND. L. J. 399 (1978)). I want to emphasize however, that nothing in my critique of Ely's theory depends on the label I have affixed to it. Nonetheless, in terms of the distinction between interpretive and noninterpretive review I mark out in chap. 1, Ely's participational review seems to me clearly a species of noninterpretive review. See also Alexander, *Modern Equal Protection Theories: A Taxonomy and Critique*, 42 OHIO ST. L. J. 3, 9 (1981) (explaining why "[t]he form of noninterpretivism that is closest to pure interpretivism, a form that I label 'neo-interpretivism,' is represented by Ely"). The reader, in due course, can decide what label seems apt.
26. *See, e.g.,* Glazer, *The Judiciary and Social Policy*, in THE JUDICIARY IN A DEMOCRATIC SOCIETY 67 (L. Theberge ed. 1979).
27. W. WILSON, CONSTITUTIONAL GOVERNMENT IN THE UNITED STATES 173 (1911). *See also* Black,

Book Review, N.Y. Times Bk. Rev., February 29, 1976, at 23, col. 4 ("no exhaustion of that great question ["the ultimate relations of law and politics"] is possible, short of heavenly revelation."); White, *The Evolution of Reasoned Elaboration: Jurisprudential Criticism and Social Change*, 54 Va. L. Rev. 279, 302 (1973):

> In the final analysis no theory of jurisprudence or mode of Supreme Court criticism can survive the passing of the social milieu from which it emerges. As the Burger Court attempts to meet its obligations in the seventies, and as a court-watchers attempt to help define those obligations, recurrent questions about judicial decision-making and opinion-writing . . . will be posed again. The context of those questions, however, will have altered, and that alteration, regardless of how dimly it may be perceived, will in the long run make all the difference.

28. R. McCloskey, The Modern Supreme Court 290–91 (1972).

CHAPTER 1

1. *Cf.* Hazard, *The Supreme Court as a Legislature*, 64 Corn. L. Rev. 1, 2 (1978):

> By a "legislature," I mean a body whose chief function in government is to formulate general rules of law that primarily reflect the notions of utility and value held by its members. Such a body is to be distinguished from a trial court, which applies law received from legally superior sources; from an administrative agency, which, in its rulemaking capacity, formulates policy only within the limits of its organic statute; and from a "traditional" appellate court, which, in formulating law, is guided primarily by precedent. By "policy," I mean the specific social purposes that a legislative body seeks to fulfill through its enactments. These definitions are not watertight. . . .

2. *See* p. 3–4 and n. * *supra.* It is not uncommon for judges who are not electorally accountable to engage in policymaking by fashioning "common law" or by "interpreting" vague statutory provisions. But judges engage in such policymaking as delegates of the legislature, and whatever policy choices they make are subject to revision by the legislature. Thus, nonconstitutional policymaking by the judiciary is consistent with the principle in the text. *See* p. 28 and n * *infra.*
3. *See* J. Choper, *supra* prologue, note 9, at 29.
4. *See* R. Dahl, A Preface to Democratic Theory 106, 108, 131, 132, 133 (1956). *See also* Bishin, *supra* prologue, note 15, at 1103. In his recent book, Jesse Choper stresses the fact that policymaking by Congress—the electoral accountability of whose members is, of course, direct—does not "result in the automatic translation of the majority will into detailed legislation." J. Choper, *supra* prologue, note 9, at 12. *See also id.* at 12–25. But that state of affairs is somewhat beside the point, since the political principle to which we are philosophically committed demands only that policymaking be electorally accountable, not that it necessarily generate policies supported by a majority of the electorate—although, to be sure, one important reason we value electorally accountable policymaking is that we think it more sensitive to the sentiments of majorities than is policymaking that is not electorally accountable.
5. Nor are the lower federal courts electorally accountable. Under Article III, § 1 of the Constitution, "[t]he judges, both of the supreme and inferior courts, shall hold their offices during good behavior, and shall, at stated times, receive for their services a compensation, which shall not be diminished during their continuance in office."

   That the Supreme Court is not accountable to the electorate does not mean that the Court is altogether immune to political influence or even exempt from political control. *See* chap. 4.

6. *See* J. ELY, *supra* prologue, note 6, at 5, 7:

> We have as a society from the beginning, and now almost instinctively, accepted the notion that a representative democracy must be our form of government.
>
>   . . . .
>
> Moral absolutists and moral relativists alike have embraced and defended democracy on their own terms—the former on the ground that it is a tenet of natural law, the latter as the most natural institutional reaction to the realization that there is no moral certainty.
>
>   . . . .
>
> [W]hatever the explanation, and granting the qualifications, rule in accord with the consent of a majority of those governed is the core of the American governmental system.

   Cf. R. DAHL *supra* note 4, at 125 (quoted in text accompanying note 120 *infra*).

7. *See* A. BICKEL, THE LEAST DANGEROUS BRANCH 19 (1962):

> [N]othing can finally depreciate the central function that is assigned in democratic theory and practice to the electoral process; nor can it be denied that the policy-making power of representative institutions, born of the electoral process, is the distinguishing characteristic of the system. Judicial review works counter to this characteristic.

8. Morton Horwitz seems not to take the principle seriously, but then Horwitz is not trying to justify judicial review. *See* Horwitz, *The Jurisprudence of Brown and the Dilemmas of Liberalism,* 14 HARV. CIV. RTS.—CIV. LIB. L. REV. 599 (1979).

9. *See* Grey, *Do We Have an Unwritten Constitution?*, 27 STAN. L. REV. 703 (1975); *see also* J. ELY, *supra* prologue, note 6, at 1.

10. The so-called unwritten constitution is a different matter, consisting of value judgments not plausibly attributable to the framers but nonetheless constitutionalized by the Supreme Court. *See* Grey, *supra* note 9. The unwritten constitution is the constitution generated by noninterpretive review. Hence, if noninterpretive review is illegitimate, in whole or in part, then the unwritten constitution, as the tainted fruit of such review, is illegitimate too, in whole or in part.

11. *See* J. CHOPER, *supra* prologue, note 9, at 2 n. *: "Most other constitutional clauses concern 'housekeeping' matters. These deal with details of the federal departments (for example, the minimum ages for elected national officials) or with relations among the states (for example, the extradition clause)."

12. *See* Grey, *supra* note 9, at 706 n. 9:

> The interpretive model . . . certainly contemplates that the courts may look through the sometimes opaque text to the purposes behind it in determining constitutional norms. Normative inferences may be drawn from silences and omissions, from structures and relationships, as well as from explicit command. . . . What distinguishes the exponent of the pure interpretive model is his insistence that the only norms used in constitutional adjudication must be those inferable from the text—that the Constitution must not be seen as licensing courts to articulate and apply contemporary norms not demonstrably expressed or implied by the framers.
>
> For an influential discussion of governmental "structure" as a source of decisional norms in constitutional cases, C. BLACK, STRUCTURE AND RELATIONSHIP IN CONSTITUTIONAL LAW (1969).

13. *See* J. ELY, *supra* prologue, note 6, at 1 (defining "interpretivism" as the position "that

judges deciding constitutional issues should confine themselves to enforcing *norms that are stated or clearly implicit in the written Constitution,*" and "noninterpretivism" as "the contrary view that courts should go beyond that set of references and enforce *norms that cannot be discovered within the four corners of the document*") (emphasis added).

14. For a comment on why "the Court has always, when plausible [and, indeed, even when not plausible], tended to talk an interpretivist line" (*id.* at 3), *see id.* at 3–5. The fundamental reason, of course, is the suspect legitimacy of a noninterpretivist line.

15. For a recent example of a rare acknowledgement to that effect, *see* Moore v. City of East Cleveland, Ohio, 431 U.S. 494 (1977).

16. *See, e.g.,* J. CHOPER, *supra* prologue, note 9, at 137 (it is "virtually impossible to justify the Court's actions [in providing "vigorous protection for the constitutional rights of minorities"] on the ground that it is doing no more than 'finding' the law of the Constitution and fulfilling the intentions of its framers."); Brest, *The Misconceived Quest for the Original Understanding,* 60 B.U. L. REV. 234 (1980) ("if you consider the evolution of doctrines in just about any extensively-adjudicated area of constitutional law . . . explicit reliance on [interpretivist] sources has played a very small role compared to the elaboration of the Court's own precedents. It is rather like having a remote ancestor who came over on the Mayflower."); Sandalow, *Judicial Protection of Minorities,* 75 MICH. L. REV. 1162, 1183 (1977) ("the evolving content of constitutional law is not controlled, or even significantly guided, by the Constitution, understood as an historical document."). *See also* Lusky, *Public Trial and Public Right: The Missing Bottom Line,* 8 HOFSTRA L. REV. 273 (1980).

17. *Cf.* J. ELY, *supra* prologue, note 6, at 186 n. 10 (noting that even an interpretivist approach generates debatable decisions).

18. Which is not to say that in such cases the Court does not try to maintain that the framers constitutionalized the determinative value judgment. *See, e.g.,* Griswold v. Connecticut, 381 U.S. 479 (1965).

19. Article III, § 1 provides in relevant part that: "The judicial power of the United States, shall be vested in one supreme court, and in such inferior courts as the Congress may from time to time ordain and establish. . . . The judicial power shall extend to all cases, in law and equity, arising under this Constitution. . . ."

20. A. BICKEL, *supra* note 7, at 12–13.

21. *Id.* at 13. *See also* C. BLACK, *supra* note 12, at 74: "[I]t seems to me that Congress could have provided for [appellate review by the Supreme Court of state court review of state action] even without an Article III, simply by creating a court and endowing it with the power to perform this necessary and proper function." That, as Bickel said in the passage accompanying this note, "Congress has so provided—consistently, from the first Judiciary Act of the first Congress onward—and it has done so unambiguously," constitutes at least some evidence that the framers of the 1789 Constitution might have intended to authorize interpretive review of state action by the Supreme Court.

22. *See, e.g.,* 28 U.S.C. § 1254(1), (2).

23. True, the Court's "judgment" might be merely a refusal to review the judgment of the state court or the lower federal court. *See* 28 U.S.C. §§ 1254(1), 1257(3). The Court, after all, is much too busy to review all such judgments. Nonetheless, the Court may review any such judgment that in its view merits its consideration, and in that crucial sense the ultimate judgment is the Supreme Court's. *Cf.* C. BLACK, *supra* note 12, at 74:

> The particular ways in which the federal courts get their hands on questions of this class [the constitutionality of state action] are in every case prescribed by Congress, and those particular ways have sometimes been attacked as unconstitutional. But in the leading case on this, *Martin v. Hunter's Lessee,* [14 U.S. (1 Wheat.) 304 (1816),]

which upheld the power of Congress to direct the Supreme Court to hear writs of error to state court judgments denying federal claims under a jurisdictional statute which lumped federal constitutional claims with others, counsel conceded, and it was assumed, that cases involving such federal claims could undoubtedly be brought by Congress under the hand of the federal judiciary; it was only the particular manner of doing so that was under attack.

In the text I say that "there is no sensible reason to oppose interpretive review of state action by the lower federal courts." But is there any reason to support it? Such review, by a multitude of lower federal courts, does not further the objective of uniform consitutional interpretation that is served by having a single federal court —the Supreme Court—be the ultimate arbiter of constitutional claims against the states. A principal reason for such review has been the belief that often the better forum for the dispassionate resolution of federal constitutional claims against the states is the federal judiciary, and that the Supreme Court—both because it can handle only a limited workload and because in this context it functions as an appellate court and so is without the crucial factfinding powers of a trial court—could not adequately supervise all the state court judgments that would be brought before it if constitutional claims against the states were invariably litigated in state courts.

24. See Wechsler, *Toward Neutral Principles of Constitutional Law*, 73 HARV. L. REV. 1, 3–5 (1959).
25. See 28 U.S.C. § 1254(1).
26. Wechsler, *supra* note 24, at 4–5. Because questions concerning the constitutionality of federal action frequently arise in connection with, and depend on the outcome of, disputes as to the proper meaning of a federal statute or regulation, often the more competent forum for the resolution of such questions is the federal judiciary, which is in a better position to determine the meaning of federal statutes and regulations. Of course, the Supreme Court could not adequately supervise all the state court judgments that would be brought before it if constitutional claims against the federal government were invariably litigated in state courts. *See* note 23 *supra*.
27. *See* Van Alstyne, *A Critical Guide to* Marbury v. Madison, 1969 DUKE L. J. 1, 20–21:

> The phrase [in the supremacy clause] "in pursuance thereof" might as easily mean *"in the manner prescribed by this Constitution,"* in which case acts of Congress might be judicially reviewable as to their procedural integrity, but not as to their substance. . . . The phrase might also mean merely that only those statutes adopted by Congress *after* the reestablishment and reconstitution of Congress pursuant to the Constitution itself shall be the supreme law of the land. . . .

But see R. BERGER, CONGRESS V. THE SUPREME COURT 228–36 (1969) (arguing that to the framers "in pursuance thereof" meant "consistent with"); G. WILLS, EXPLAINING AMERICA: THE FEDERALIST 141–42 (1981) (to same effect).
28. A. BICKEL, *supra* note 7, at 11.
29. *Id.* at 11–12.
30. Indeed, one should not ignore historical materials even where a textual provision *seems* on its face to disclose what the framers' value judgment was, for appearances can deceive and, after all, the value judgment and not the language that serves as its embodiment has priority. *Cf.* chap. 3, note 7 and accompanying text *infra*.
31. C. BEARD, THE SUPREME COURT AND THE CONSTITUTION (1912).
32. R. BERGER, *supra* note 27.
33. *See also* P. BATOR, P. MISHKIN, D. SHAPIRO, & H. WECHSLER, HART & WECHSLER'S THE FEDERAL COURTS AND THE FEDERAL SYSTEM 9–11 (1973).

34. L. BOUDIN, GOVERNMENT BY JUDICIARY (1932).
35. W. W. CROSSKEY, POLITICS AND THE CONSTITUTION IN THE HISTORY OF THE UNITED STATES (1953).
36. L. HAND, THE BILL OF RIGHTS 27–29 (1958; Atheneum ed. 1963).
37. *See also* Hazard, *supra* note 1, at 3.
38. Corwin's "vacillations" are discussed in L. LEVY, JUDGMENTS: ESSAYS ON AMERICAN CONSTITUTIONAL HISTORY 26 (1972).
39. *Id.* at 28. *See also* J. CHOPER, *supra* prologue, note 9, at 62–63, 243; J. ELY, *supra* prologue, note 6, at 40, 225 n. 47.
40. *Federalist #78* was first published on June 14, 1788. Rossiter, *Introduction,* THE FEDERALIST PAPERS viii (Mentor ed. 1961).
41. *Cf.* J. CHOPER, *supra* prologue, note 9, at 66: "In introducing the Bill of Rights . . . to the First Congress, Madison declared that 'independent tribunals of justice will consider themselves in a peculiar manner the guardians of those rights; they will be an impenetrable bulwark against every assumption of power in the legislative or executive.' " (*Citing* 1 ANNALS OF CONGRESS 457 (1834).)
42. *See also* Hamilton, *Federalist #78,* THE FEDERALIST PAPERS 464 (Mentor ed. 1961).
43. *Cf.* Marbury v. Madison, 5 U.S. (1 Cranch) 137, 176–77 (1803).
44. *See, e.g.,* Marbury v. Madison, 5 U.S. (1 Cranch) 137, 177 (1803): "It is emphatically the province and duty of the judicial department to say what the law is."
45. *Cf.* A. BICKEL, *supra* note 7, at 173:

> There are crucial differences—which, of course, the opinions in *Marbury v. Madison* and *Cohens v. Virginia* [19 U.S. (6 Wheat.) 264 (1821)] seek to obscure—between the role of the Supreme Court in constitutional cases and the function of courts of general jurisdiction. The latter sit as primary agencies for the peaceful settlement of disputes and, in a more restricted sphere, as primary agencies for the vindication and evolution of the legal order. They must, indeed, resolve all controversies within the jurisdiction, because the alternative is chaos. The Supreme Court in constitutional cases sits to render an additional, principled judgment on what has already been authoritatively ordered. Its interventions are by hypothesis exceptional and limited, and they occur, not to forestall chaos, but to revise a pre-existing order that is otherwise viable and was itself arrived at by more normal processes. Fixation on an individual right to judgment by the Supreme Court is, therefore, largely question-begging.

46. The institution with final authority to enforce, and therefore interpret, the *federal* Constitution must itself be *federal. See* note 21 and accompanying text *supra.*
47. Hamilton, *Federalist #78,* THE FEDERALIST PAPERS 464, 465 (Mentor ed. 1961).
48. In this sense Bickel was right in suggesting that the framers "invited" even if they did not specifically authorize interpretive review of federal action. A. BICKEL, *supra* note 7, at 19.
49. *See* Marbury v. Madison, 5. U.S. (1 Cranch) 137 (1803).
50. L. LEVY, *supra* note 38, at 28. *See also id.* at 32:

> The idea of judicial review was, nevertheless, rapidly emerging, a fact which adds retrospective significance to the few precedents, even to the scattered judicial dicta and lawyers' arguments. Federalism hastened the emergence, supported by Section 25 of the Judiciary Act of 1789; the ratification controversy and the demand for a Bill of Rights also quickened the spread of the idea. Madison's remark about the Supreme Court as protector of the Bill of Rights . . . echoed Jefferson, Sam Adams, John Hancock, Patrick Henry, Richard Henry Lee, and others. No less important in contributing to a widespread acceptance of the idea of judicial review was the

emergence of party politics. Charles Warren's study of the records of Congress during its first decade shows that the parties . . . argued the constitutionality of bills they liked and the unconstitutionality of those they disliked, but Federalists and Republicans alike "were united in one sentiment at least, that under the Constitution it was the Judiciary which was finally to determine the validity of an Act of Congress."

(Quoting C. WARREN, CONGRESS, THE CONSTITUTION, AND THE SUPREME COURT 99 (1925).)

51. That is not to say, however, that Congress must permit every court other than the Supreme Court to exercise judicial review of federal action. For example, there may be good reasons for authorizing review in only one lower federal court. See, e.g., South Carolina v. Katzenbach, 383 U.S. 301 (1966). See also P. BATOR, et al., supra note 33, at 317–22.

52. A challenged governmental action is not inconsistent with a value judgment assertedly constitutionalized by the framers if either (1) the framers did not actually constitutionalize the value judgment in question or, if the framers did constitutionalize it, (2) the challenged action is not inconsistent with that judgment.

53. Quoted in L. LEVY, ed., JUDICIAL REVIEW AND THE SUPREME COURT 43 (1967).

54. Thayer, The Origin and Scope of the American Doctrine of Constitutional Law, 7 HARV. L. REV. 129, 143–44 (1893).

55. See note 61 infra. Thayer did not seem to argue that by asking the first question a court acts undemocratically, although of course one could argue to that effect, and certainly any modern Thayerian would want to. Cf. note 61 infra. But Thayer was writing a good quarter of a century before the issue of "the countermajoritarian difficulty" (see A. BICKEL, supra note 7, at 16–23) began to be widely debated.

56. Thayer, supra note 54, at 144, 150.

57. J. THAYER, JOHN MARSHALL 106–07 (1901).

58. But see J. THAYER, supra note 57, at 109–10:

And if it be true that the holders of legislative power are careless or evil, yet the constitutional duty of the court remains untouched; it cannot rightly attempt to protect the people by undertaking a function not its own. On the other hand, by adhering rigidly to its own duty, the court will help, as nothing else can, to fix the spot where responsibility lies, and to bring down on that precise locality the thunderbolt of popular condemnation. . . . For that course—the true course of judicial duty always—will powerfully help to bring the people and their representatives to a sense of their own responsibility.

Thayer was certainly more sanguine about the operation of the political processes, as the preceding comment by him would suggest, than I could ever be. Perhaps that is because whereas Thayer wrote against the background of disputes mainly about issues of federalism (cf. note 59 infra), I write against the background of disputes mainly about issues of human rights. See J. CHOPER, supra prologue, note 9, at 66:

[O]n the one hand, it is impossible convincingly to refute the propositions that lawmaking would be more sensitive to individual liberties if it were conducted with the knowledge that its resolutions were final, and that the ever present potential of judicial disapproval actually encourages popular irresponsibility and stultifies the people's sense of moral and constitutional obligation. On the other hand, it is equally impracticable to reject the contention that, without the threat of judicial invalidation in the background, majoritarian excesses in respect to minority rights would be all the less restrained.

59. A Thayerian deference may well be appropriate, for example, with respect to congres-

sional judgments as to the requirements of federalism, or to certain congressional and executive judgments as to the requirements of the separation of powers. See J. CHOPER, supra prologue, note 9, at 203: "[C]onstitutional questions of federalism differ from those of individual liberty both in terms of their distinctive, pragmatic quality and in the likelihood of their fair resolution within the national political chambers." See also id. at 236, 238. Cf. chap. 2.

60. Learned Hand may have been a rare exception. See L. HAND, supra note 36. For another, see S. GABIN, JUDICIAL REVIEW AND THE REASONABLE DOUBT TEST (1980). Although at times Felix Frankfurter seemed to endorse Thayer's position, see note 61 infra, Frankfurter was a confused constitutional theorist at best, and certainly not one committed solely to interpretive review. See, e.g., Adamson v. California, 332 U.S. 46, 59 (1947) (Frankfurter, J., concurring).

61. Thayer's position is sometimes confused with the different position, widely endorsed, that ordinarily a court ought to defer to a "not irrational"—that is, plausible—legislative judgment as to the nature of the facts on which a challenged policy choice is predicated. See also Bennett, "Mere" Rationality in Constitutional Law: Judicial Review and Democratic Theory, 67 CALIF. L. REV. 1049, 1051 n. 14 (1979). For an example of the confusion of Thayer's with this position, see Mendelson, The Influence of James B. Thayer upon the Work of Holmes, Brandeis, and Frankfurter, 31 VAND. L. REV. 71, 74 et seq. (1978).

It ought to be noted that Thayer—in making what was essentially a separation-of-powers argument—distinguished judicial review of the action of a coordinate branch of government from that of the action of an inferior branch. See Thayer, supra note 54, at 153–55. Thayer's point was that judicial deference is appropriate when a federal court reviews federal action, or a state court state action, but that a federal court may legitimately assume a more activist stance in reviewing state action. However, that distinction makes no sense against the background of what is the contemporary concern: legitimacy in terms not of separation-of-powers theory, but of the theory, the principle, of electorally accountable policymaking. Hence my discussion in the text ignores Thayer's distinction, but not at the cost of portraying his fundamental thesis unfairly. In fact most commentators who discuss Thayer fail even to note the distinction (see e.g., A. BICKEL, supra note 7, at 35–46; Mendelson, supra this note; but see C. BLACK, supra prologue, note 10, at 34–35), as did the judge who was perhaps Thayer's most prominent disciple. See, e.g., West Virginia State Board of Education v. Barnette, 319 U.S. 624, 661–62, 666–67 (1943) (Frankfurter, J., dissenting):

> Only if there be no doubt that any reasonable mind could entertain can we deny to the states the right to resolve doubts their way and not ours.
>
> . . . .
>
> I think I appreciate fully the objections to the law before us. But to deny that it presents a question on which men might reasonably differ appears to me to be intolerance. And since men may so reasonably differ, I deem it beyond my constitutional power to assert my view of the wisdom of this law against the view of the State.

62. R. BERGER, GOVERNMENT BY JUDICIARY 300 (1977).

63. Id. at 302.

64. See G. WILLS, supra note 27, at 153.

65. Cf. Hazard, supra note 1, at 4–5. By the same token, if the framers did not contemplate noninterpretive review thus circumscribed—and certainly they did not contemplate anything like the noninterpretive review exercised by the modern Supreme Court—it cannot be said that the framers intended that the judiciary exercise such review. The justification for the practice must be sought elsewhere.

66. J. ELY, supra prologue, note 6, at 22–30, 34–38.

67. See Barron v. Baltimore, 32 U.S. (7 Pet.) 243 (1833).

68. See J. ELY, supra prologue, note 6, at 22–30. But see R. BERGER, supra note 62, at 20–51.

69. See J. ELY, supra prologue, note 6, at 11–41. See also Michelman, Politics and Values or What's Really Wrong with Rationality Review?, 13 CREIGHTON L. REV. 487, 502 (1979).

70. See J. ELY, supra prologue, note 6, at 13:

> [I]nterpretivism runs into trouble—trouble precisely on its own terms, and so serious as to be dispositive. For the constitutional document itself, the inter-pretivists Bible, contains several provisions whose invitation to look beyond their four corners—whose invitation, if you will, to become at least to that extent a noninterpretivist—cannot be construed away.

71. Id. at 40.

72. See Berger, The Ninth Amendment, 66 CORN. L. REV. 1, 21 (1980): "[Madison explained] that the Bill of Rights would impel the judiciary 'to resist encroachments upon rights expressly stipulated for . . . by the declaration of rights,' and reinforces the conclusion that the courts were not empowered to enforce the retained and unenumerated rights." Quoting 1 ANNALS OF CONGRESS 457 (Gales & Seaton eds. 1836) (print bearing running title "History of Congress").

    In his recent Holmes Lectures, Charles Black has argued that the ninth amendment authorizes noninterpretive review of state as well as federal action. By itself the ninth amendment constrains only federal action (see note 69 and accompanying text supra). Black's claim is that section 1 of the fourteenth amendment, which constrains state action, should be taken to incorporate the ninth no less than the other amendments of the Bill of Rights that have been declared applicable against the states. C. BLACK, supra prologue, note 10, at 46–48. (For an opposed view, see R. BERGER, supra note 62, at 134–65.) However, Black's claim must be rejected. The legislative history of the four-teenth amendment simply does not support the proposition that the framers intended the fourteenth amendment to incorporate any or all of the Bill of Rights. See chap. 3.

73. For one view of what history discloses, or does not disclose, about the ninth amendment, see Berger, supra note 72.

74. "There is a difference," writes Ely, "between ignoring a provision, such as the First Amendment, because you don't like its substantive limitations and ignoring a provision, such as the Ninth Amendment, because you don't like its institutional implications. But it's hard to make it a difference that should count." J. ELY, supra prologue, note 6, at 38. It is not at all hard to make it a difference that should count. For a court to ignore a provision like the first amendment is to ignore a constraint specified by the framers and intended by them to have the status of supreme law. But for it to ignore the ninth amendment is not to ignore any constraint specified by the framers.

75. The framers of the fourteenth amendment meant also to prohibit any state from dis-criminating on the basis of race with respect to judicial protection of those fundamental rights. See chap. 3. (A careful reading of Justice Washington's opinion in Corfeld v. Coryell (6 F. Cas. 546 (C.C.E.D. Pa. 1823)), which figures in so many discussions of the original understanding of the privileges or immunities clause of the fourteenth amend-ment (see, e.g., J. ELY, supra prologue, note 6, at 28–30), discloses only one "privilege or immunity" not subsumed by the description of "fundamental" rights in the text accom-panying this note (or by judicial protection of those rights): the right to vote. And everyone agrees that Washington was in error in listing that right.) Moreover, the framers did not differentiate the functions of the three main clauses of section one of the fourteenth amendment: the privileges or immunities, due process, and equal protection clauses. See chap. 3, note 21 and accompanying text infra. Ely, discussing the original understanding of the three clauses, presupposes a functional differentiation among them (see J. ELY, supra prologue, note 6, at 14–32), and in that respect too his discussion is historically unsound.

76. Id. at 28. See also id. at 30.

77. *See* Bork, *The Impossibility of Finding Welfare Rights in the Constitution,* 1979 WASH.
    U. L. Q. 695, 697–98:

    > In the first place, not even a scintilla of evidence supports the argument that the
    > framers and the ratifiers of the various amendments intended the judiciary to
    > develop new individual rights, which correspondingly create new disabilities for
    > democratic government. Although we do not know precisely what the phrase
    > "privileges or immunities" meant to the framers, a variety of explanations exist for
    > its open-endedness other than that the framers intended to delegate to courts the
    > power to make up the privileges or immunities in the clause.
    >
    > The obvious possibility, of course, is that the people who framed the privileges-
    > or-immunities clause did have an idea of what they meant, but that their idea has
    > been irretrievably lost in the mists of history. If that is true, it is hardly a ground for
    > judicial extrapolation from the clause.
    >
    > Perhaps a more likely explanation is that the framers and ratifiers themselves
    > were not certain of their intentions. Although the judiciary must give content to
    > vague phrases, it need not go well beyond what the framers and ratifiers reasonably
    > could be supposed to have had in mind. If the framers really intended to delegate to
    > judges the function of creating new rights by the method of moral philosophy, one
    > would expect that they would have said so. They could have resolved their uncer-
    > tainty by writing a ninth amendment that declared: "The Supreme Court shall, from
    > time to time, find and enforce such additional rights as may be determined by moral
    > philosophy, or by consideration of the dominant ideas of republican government."
    > But if that was what they really intended, they were remarkably adroit in managing
    > not to say so.
    >
    > It should give theorists of the open-ended constitution pause, moreover, that not
    > even the most activist courts have ever grounded their claims for legitimacy in
    > arguments along those lines. Courts closest in time to the adoption of the Constitu-
    > tion and various amendments, who might have been expected to know what powers
    > had been delegated to them, never offered argument along the lines advanced by
    > Professor Michelman. The Supreme Court, in fact, has been attacked repeatedly
    > throughout its history for exceeding its delegated powers; yet this line of defense
    > seems never to have occurred to its members. For these reasons I remain unper-
    > suaded that the interpretivist argument can be escaped.

78. J. ELY, *supra* prologue, note 6, at 41.
79. *See id.* at 72–183.
80. *See* Greenawalt, *The Enduring Significance of Neutral Principles,* 78 COLUM. L. REV.
    982, 989 (1978).
81. In fact, the requirement of principled explanation is a necessary condition for the
    legitimacy of any sort of adjudication. *See* Wechsler, *supra* note 24, at 15 ("the main
    constituent *of the judicial process* is precisely that it must be genuinely principled, . . .";
    emphasis added); Greenawalt, *supra* note 80, at 985.
82. Wechsler, *supra* note 24, at 12 (emphasis added).
83. *Id.* at 15–16. *See also id.* at 14–15:

    > [P]rinciples are largely instrumental as they are employed in politics, instrumental
    > in relation to results that a controlling sentiment demands at any given time.
    > Politicians recognize this fact of life and are obliged to trim and shape their speech
    > and votes accordingly, unless perchance they are prepared to step aside; and the
    > example that John Quincy Adams set somehow is rarely followed.

84. *Id.* at 15, 19. For a luminous account of Wechsler's thesis, much more extensive than my
    comments on the constituents of principled explanation, see Greenawalt, *infra* note 105.

85. *Id.* at 985.
86. *Id.* at 987. *See also* L. JAFFEE, ENGLISH AND AMERICAN JUDGES 38 (1969) ("The judge must believe in the validity of the reasons given for the decision at least in the sense that he is prepared to apply them to a later case which he cannot honestly distinguish").
87. *See* Fiss, *Foreward: The Forms of Justice,* 93 HARV. L. REV. 1, 13 (1979):

> [T]he notion of justification, as opposed to explanation, implies that the reasons supporting a [judicial] decision be "good" reasons, and this in turn requires norms or rules for determining what counts as a "good" reason. . . . [A good reason] cannot consist of a preference, be it the preference of the contestants, of the body politic, or of the judge. The statement "I prefer" or "we prefer" in the context of a judicial, rather than a legislative decision, merely constitutes an explanation, not a justification.

Courts often fasten on the result they think, or feel, is best and then proceed to see if that result can be defended in terms of a principled and otherwise proper explanation. *See* Greenawalt, *supra* note 80, at 991; R. WASSERSTROM, THE JUDICIAL DECISION 25–30 (1961) (elaborating the distinction between reaching and justifying results). I do not mean to question the propriety of such a decisional strategy. *Cf.* Wechsler, *The Nature of Judicial Reasoning,* in LAW AND PHILOSOPHY 290, 297 (S. Hook ed. 1964):

> If the point is that courts may reach correct decisions by accident or intuition, I should readily agree, while noting that correctness turns on someone else's statement of the reasons that the court has sensed but has not stated in its judgment. But if it is contended that there is a measure of correctness apart from the existence of such reasons, I must say that I am forced to disagree.

88. *See generally* Greenawalt, *supra* note 80.
89. *See, e.g.,* Miller & Howell, *The Myth of Neutrality in Constitutional Adjudication,* 27 U. CHIC. L. REV. 661 (1960).
90. H. WECHSLER, PRINCIPLES, POLITICS, AND FUNDAMENTAL LAW xiii–xiv (1961). *See also* Frankel, *The Moral Environment of the Law,* 61 MINN. L. REV. 921, 944 (1977): "But these principles, as Professor Wechsler has made plain, are not morally neutral. Although they are higher principles whose significance and validity transcend the case at hand, they may well throw the weight of the political and legal system behind one set of controverted social claims as against another."
91. H. WECHSLER, *supra* note 90, at xiii–xiv.
92. *See, e.g.,* Rostow, *American Legal Realism and the Sense of the Profession,* 34 ROCKY MTN. L. REV. 123, 139–40 (1969); *cf.* Henkin, *Neutral Principles and Future Cases,* in LAW AND PHILOSOPHY 301, 304–05 (S. Hook ed. 1964).
93. Wechsler, *supra* note 87, at 297–98.
94. Kent Greenawalt raises the tantalizing question whether courts are not sometimes justified in failing to specify the actual grounds of decision. *See* Greenawalt, *supra* note 80, at 1006–13.
95. *See* Wechsler, *supra* note 87, at 299:

> [The requirement of principled explanation does not] offer[ ] a court a guide to exercising its authority, in the sense of a formula that indicates how cases ought to be decided. . . . That an adjudication be supported or at least supportable [*see* note 107, *infra*] in general and neutral terms is no more than a negative requirement. A decision is not sound unless it satisfies this minimal criterion. If it does, but only if it does, the other and harder questions of its rightness and its wisdom must be faced.

See also J. ELY, *supra* prologue, note 6, at 55: "[R]equirements of generality of principle and neutrality of application do not provide a source of substantive content."

96. Ely's characterization of the interpretivist position is flawed. He writes:

> [T]he interpretivist takes his values from the Constitution, which means, since the Constitution itself was submitted for and received popular ratification, that they ultimately come from the people. Thus the judges do not check the people, the Constitution does, which means the people are ultimately checking themselves.

Id. at 8. That argument, says Ely,

> is largely a fake. Given what it takes to amend the Constitution, it is likely that a recent amendment will represent, if not necessarily a consensus, at least the sentiment of a contemporary majority. The amendments most frequently in issue in court, however—to the extent that they ever represented "the voice of the people"—represent the voice of people who have been dead for a century or two. . . . [J]udges are [not] simply applying the people's will. Incompatibility with democratic theory is a problem that seems to confront interpretivist and noninterpretivist alike.

Id. at 11–12. But sophisticated interpretivists, like Robert Bork, do not proffer the argument Ely rejects. Rather, they argue that the (only) value judgments that legitimately constrain electorally accountable policymaking are those constitutionalized by the framers, whether or not those judgments now represent or indeed ever represented "the people." That argument creates no problems for interpretivists, however, since they are committed not merely to the principle of electorally accountable policymaking, but also to the principle that such policymaking is constrained by the value judgments the framers constitutionalized.

97. See Rehnquist, The Notion of a Living Constitution, 54 Texas L. Rev. 693 (1976).
98. See R. Berger, supra note 62.
99. See Bork, supra note 77 at 695: "I represent that school of thought which insists that the judiciary invalidate the work of the political branches only in accordance with an inference whose underlying premise is fairly discoverable in the Constitution itself."
100. Bork, Neutral Principles and Some First Amendment Problems, 47 Ind. L. J. 1, 1 (1971).
101. Id. at 3, 6, 8, 10–11, 12.
102. Id. at 6–7.
103. Bork is wrong: The Court does not invariably profess an interpretivist view. See, e.g., Moore v. City of East Cleveland, Ohio, 431 U.S. 494 (1977).
104. Bork, supra note 100, at 3–4.
105. See note 4 and accompanying text supra.
106. Hazard, supra note 1, at 9.
107. See also Holland, American Liberals and Judicial Activism: Alexander Bickel's Appeal from the Old to the New, 51 Ind. L. J. 1025, 1041 (1976). The problem, after all, is one of constitutional theory, not political science.
108. R. Dahl, supra note 4, at 125. One reason for insisting on electorally accountable policymaking is precisely the difficulty of knowing, with respect to many issues, just what the sentiments of an actual majority are.
109. Hazard, supra note 1, at 9.
110. Id.
111. See also J. Choper, supra prologue, note 9, at 29–38.
112. See, e.g., Bishin, supra prologue, note 15, at 1110.
113. See McCleskey, Judicial Review in a Democracy: A Dissenting Opinion, 3 Hous. L. Rev. 354, 361–62 (1966):

> One would do well . . . by recalling that the status of [officials of independent agencies] has not escaped criticism. . . . More significantly, . . . Congress can define their powers, limit their policy discretion, overcome their decisions and actions by

ordinary legislation, and speed their removal from office by granting dismissal authority to the President or to its own officers.

114. *Cf.* A. BICKEL, *supra* note 7, at 18: "[I]mpurities and imperfections, if such they be, in one part of the system are no argument for total departure from the desired norm in another part." *See also* R. DWORKIN, TAKING RIGHTS SERIOUSLY 141 (1977); Monaghan, *The Constitution Goes to Harvard,* 13 HARV. CIV. RTS.—CIV. LIB. L. REV. 117, 131 n. 66 (1978).

115. *See, e.g.,* Berger, *Ely's "Theory of Judicial Review,"* 42 OHIO ST. L. J. 87 (1981). *See* note 30 and accompanying text *supra.*

116. *See* note 12 *supra. See also* Brest, *supra* note 16, at 205–09.

117. The matter of analogues is discussed in chap. 3.

118. *See* J. ELY, *supra* prologue, note 6, at 13:

> [T]he job of the person interpreting [a constitutional] provision, [interpretivists would say], is to identify the *sorts of evils* against which the provision was directed and to move against their contemporary counterparts. Obviously this will be difficult, but it will remain interpretivism—a determination of "the present scope and meaning of a decision that the nation, at an earlier time, articulated and enacted into the constitutional text."

(Quoting Linde, *Judges, Critics, and the Realist Tradition,* 82 YALE L. J. 227, 254 (1972).) *See also* Brest, *supra* note 16, at 221; The Slaughter-House Cases, 83 U.S. (16 Wall.) 36, 72 (1873):

> We do not say that no one else but the negro can share in [the protection of the Civil War Amendments]. Both the language and spirit of these articles are to have their fair and just weight in any question of construction. Undoubtedly while negro slavery alone was in the mind of the Congress which proposed the thirteenth article, it forbids any other kind of slavery, now or hereafter. If Mexican peonage or the Chinese coolie labor system shall develop slavery of the Mexican or Chinese race within our territory, this amendment may safely be trusted to make it void. And so if other rights are assailed by the States which properly and necessarily fall within the protection of these articles, that protection will apply, though the party interested may not be of African descent.

119. *See, e.g.,* Katz v. United States, 389 U.S. 347 (1967). (Of course, interpretivists may disagree among themselves as to whether or not a challenged political practice is in fact an analogue of a practice the framers contemplated and meant to ban. *See, e.g., id.* at 364 (Black, J., dissenting). No one ever claimed that an interpretivist approach avoided debatable answers.) *See also* White, *Reflections on the Role of the Supreme Court: The Contemporary Debate and the "Lessons" of History,* 63 JUDICATURE 162, 168 (1979):

> Protecting a couple's right to sexual intimacy, for example, requires a different technique of judicial interpretation from protecting persons against electronic eavesdropping. In the latter, judges merely extrapolate the original meaning of "search and seizure" to a 20th century technological context; in the former, judges create a constitutional right of privacy by "discovering" an unenumerated value of privacy in the design of the Constitution.

120. *See* Brown v. Board of Education, 347 U.S. 483 (1954) (segregated public schooling); Loving v. Virginia, 388 U.S. 1 (1967) (antimiscegenation laws).

121. I develop and defend this claim in chap. 3.

122. Other lines of attack on interpretivism are considered in due course.

123. McCulloch v. Maryland, 17 U.S. (4 Wheat.) 316, 407 (1819).

124. *Id.* at 415.

125. *See, e.g.,* A. BICKEL, *supra* note 7, at 103–10.

126. *See, e.g.,* R. BERGER, *supra* note 62, at 284.
127. Marshall was referring to the necessary and proper clause, which provides that: "The Congress shall have power . . . to make all laws which shall be necessary and proper for carrying into execution the foregoing powers, and all other powers vested by this Constitution in the government of the United States, or in any department or officer thereof." U.S. CONST. art. I, § 8, cl. 18.
128. 17 U.S. at 423. *See* Marshall, *A Friend to the Constitution,* in G. Gunther, ed., JOHN MARSHALL'S DEFENSE OF McCULLOCH V. MARYLAND 185 (1969).
129. Of course, the framers also expected that posterity would, from time to time, amend the Constitution. *See* U.S. CONST. art. V.
130. Which, with a single exception, is precisely what the modern Court has done. *See* chap. 2.
131. Remarkably, the confusion is quite common. *See, e.g.,* A. BICKEL, *supra* note 7, at 103–10.
132. R. BERGER, *supra* note 62, at 315. For an example of the sort of question-begging answer Berger protests, see L. LEVY, ed., *supra* note 53, at 143: "[T]he dead hand of the past need not and should not be binding. . . ." *See also* Brest, *supra* note 16, at 229 n. 96: "[T]here is no justification for binding the present to the compromises of another age." (Paul Brest writes that "the fact that a [constitutional] provision was drafted by an unrepresentative and self-interested portion of the adopters' society weakens its moral claim on a different society one or two hundred years later." *Id.* at 230. But that fact, even if it justifies ignoring certain value judgments constitutionalized by the framers two hundred years ago, does not justify noninterpretive review; that is, it does not justify judicial action striking down challenged governmental policy choices in the name of value judgments *not* constitutionalized by the framers.)
133. 5. U.S. (1 Cranch) 137 (1803).
134. C. BLACK, *supra* note 12, at 73.
135. *Id.* at 73, 74, 75. *See also* C. BLACK, *supra* prologue, note 10, at 34 *et seq.*
136. C. BLACK, *supra* note 12, at 73.
137. A. BICKEL, *supra* note 7, at 33.
138. Black mentions Judge Learned Hand's Holmes Lectures, published as THE BILL OF RIGHTS (1958). C. BLACK, *supra* note 12, at 72–73.
139. *See* C. BLACK, *supra* prologue, note 10, at 35–36.
140. But *cf.* p. 132, n. *; p. 136, n. *. "This is not to say, however, that there will not be instances when it seems justifiable to exercise judicial review more vigorously against the states than against the federal legislature or executive, and instances calling for less vigor as well." A. BICKEL, *supra* note 7, at 33.
141. C. BLACK, *supra* note 12, at 76.
142. Bickel's position too is not entirely adequate. In the quoted passage (text accompanying note 137 *supra*), and indeed through the entire first chapter of his book (*supra* note 7), Bickel neglected the same fundamental distinction that Black overlooks. In discussing the legitimacy of judicial review, Bickel conflated the problem of the legitimacy of interpretive review with the distinct and profoundly more difficult problem of the legitimacy of noninterpretive review. There is no doubt, however, that Bickel was addressing principally the latter problem. *See* A. BICKEL, *supra* note 7, at 23–33. *See also* J. ELY, *supra* prologue, note 6, at 71–72.

CHAPTER 2

1. U.S. CONST. art. I, § 8, cl. 3.
2. The tenth amendment of the Constitution provides: "The powers not delegated 'o the United States by the Constitution, nor prohibited by it to the states, are reserved ῑo the states respectively, or to the people."

3. *See generally* Schwartz, *Commerce, the States, and the Burger Court,* 74 N.W. U. L. Rev. 409 (1979).

4. Which is not surprising, since the commerce clause was intended to serve as a power-granting provision, not a power-limiting one. *Cf.* chap. 1. That is, the clause was intended to serve as a broad grant of legislative authority, not as a narrow provision outlawing particular evils—although, to be sure, by granting the commerce power to Congress the framers sought to prevent an "evil": the balkanization of national commerce that would occur if there were not national legislative authority over such commerce. *See* Stern, *That Commerce Which Concerns More States Than One,* 47 Harv. L. Rev. 1335 (1934).

5. *See, e.g.,* Raymond Motor Transportation, Inc. v. Rice, 434 U.S. 429 (1978).

6. *See, e.g.,* Note, *Pre-emption as a Preferential Ground: A New Canon of Construction,* 12 Stan. L. Rev. 200 (1959).

7. Because Congress has constitutional authority to regulate interstate commerce, Congress may acquiesce in particular local regulations of interstate commerce in effect adopting them at its own. *See* note 12 *infra.*

8. Brown, *The Open Economy: Mr. Justice Frankfurter and the Position of the Judiciary,* 67 Yale L. J. 219, 220 (1957). *See also* J. Choper, *supra* prologue, note 9, at 208.

9. That is not to say that Congress could not devise another way of dealing with the problem. *See id.* at 210–11:

> [T]here may be merit in the establishment of some federal agency . . . to act in the Court's stead in this entire area. Unlike the courts, such an administrative agency could enact general rules and regulations governing the subject areas as well as adjudicate particular cases. An agency would presumably possess greater expertise on the variety of complex questions—frequently economic—presented by the cases and, because of the specific nature of its duties and the political control over its personnel, it should be more familiar with both the spoken and unspoken thinking of Congress.

See also Freund, *Review and Federalism,* in Supreme Court and Supreme Law 86, 100–01 (E. Cahn ed. 1954).

10. *See, e.g.,* the sources cited in note 12 *supra; see also* L. Tribe, American Constitutional Law 319 (1977); Dowling, *Interstate Commerce and State Power,* 27 Va. L. Rev. 1 (1940).

11. J. Choper, *supra* prologue, note 9, at 207–08; L. Tribe, *supra* note 10 at 321; Henkin, *Infallibility under Law: Constitutional Balancing,* 79 Colum. L. Rev. 1022, 1041 (1979).

12. Wechsler, *The Political Safeguards of Federalism,* in H. Wechsler, Principles, Politics, and Fundamental Law 49, 81 (1960) (emphasis added). *See also* L. Tribe, *supra* note 10, at 401:

> Although Congress cannot authorize a state to violate a constitutional command designed to protect private rights against government action (such as the commands of the fourteenth amendment), and cannot authorize a state to disregard an explicit constitutional prohibition (such as the article I, § 10 provision that no state may enter into any "Treaty, Alliance, or Confederation," coin money, issue bills of credit, or take certain other designated steps), congressional consent or ratification may suffice to validate otherwise unconstitutional state action in three different settings: first, where the Constitution expressly makes congressional consent a prerequisite of state action, as in the provisions of article I, § 10, with respect to import and export duties, interstate compacts, and certain other topics; second, where the existence of a constitutional ban on state action is inferred entirely from a grant of legislative power to Congress, as in the case of the commerce clause; and third, where the constitutional prohibition against state intrusion is thought to

follow from concerns of federalism that may properly be entrusted to Congress, as in the case of federal immunity from state taxation.

13. Because the commerce clause cases in which the Supreme Court reviews state action do not involve *constitutional* review, whether interpretive or noninterpretive, it is inappropriate to use those cases to frame or illustrate a theory of constitutional review, as Mark Tushnet has recently done. *See* Tushnet, *Rethinking the Dormant Commerce Clause,* 1979 WISC. L. REV. 125.

14. Professor Choper's succinct discussion of the matter I have addressed in the preceding few pages merits quotation:

> When the Court rules on a contention that state or local laws conflict with an existing federal enactment and thus violate the supremacy clause, or that they improperly impose upon domains over which the national government is empowered . . . , or that they unduly interfere with the property or activities of the central government and thus violate its implied constitutional immunity, the Court does not exercise the momentous power of judicial review. In such decisions, unlike its constitutional rulings on individual liberties and national power versus states' rights, the Court does not speak the final constitutional word. The federal political branches do. The Court's decisions on the federalism limits on state's actions may be revised by ordinary federal statutes. The judiciary acts only as an intermediate agency between the states and Congress. This is most obvious when the Court passes on state or local ordinances that allegedly conflict with an act of Congress. But it is equally true when, in the absence of pertinent federal legislation, the Court determines whether the challenged state action unduly imposes on a delegated but unexercised national power. In so doing, the Court performs an essentially legislative role, quite nakedly constructing policies for the particular case that are the product of the Court's own value-balancing of national versus state concerns. (Indeed, the Court not infrequently performs this very same task under the guise of the supremacy clause when it "interprets" a "relevant" federal statute whose message in relation to the state or local law before the Court is exceedingly indistinct.)
>
> The Court may fashion its own policy determinants in the name of fulfilling some unspoken intention of Congress . . . . Or the Court may act more openly by virtue of implicit authorization from Congress based on the long-standing practice. But the fact remains that this aspect of the Court's work—determining whether state and local laws improperly control an area of national concern even in the absence of relevant federal legislation—is akin to statutory interpretation and not to judicial review. For this reason, the traditional tension between constitutional decisionmaking by the federal judiciary and the principles of majoritarian democracy is not of any real concern.

J. CHOPER, *supra* prologue, note 9, at 207–08 (*quoting* Graves v. New York ex rel. O'Keefe, 306 U.S. 466, 479 n. 1 (1939)).

15. The controversial case is National League of Cities v. Usery, 426 U.S. 833 (1976). The other case is Oregon v. Mitchell, 400 U.S. 112 (1970), in which the Court struck down a congressional provision lowering the voting age to eighteen to the extent the provision applied to state elections. (The provision was sustained to the extent it applied to federal elections.) Subsequently, in 1971, the twenty-sixth amendment was ratified, lowering the voting age to eighteen for all elections.

16. Those four decades were the only period in which the Court invalidated congressional legislation on federalism grounds with some regularity. Thus, it was—and remains—an extremely controversial period. For a sampling of the cases, see G. GUNTHER, CASES AND MATERIALS ON CONSTITUTIONAL LAW 129–52 (10th ed. 1980); W. LOCKHART, Y. KAMISAR, & J. CHOPER, CONSTITUTIONAL LAW 113–22 (5th ed. 1980).

17. *See* G. GUNTHER, *supra* note 16, at 153–84; W. LOCKHART *et al.*, *supra* note 16, at 122–55.

18. The cases in which the Court has struck down congressional legislation on federalism grounds have generally involved statutes predicated on one of three constitutional grants of legislative authority to Congress: the power "to regulate commerce . . . among the several states" (*supra* note 1); "to lay and collect taxes" (U.S. CONST. art. I, § 8, cl. 1); or to spend money in order "to provide for the general welfare of the United States" (*id.*).

19. *See* Stern, *supra* note 4, at 1337–41. *See also* Cushman, *Social and Economic Control through Federal Taxation*, 18 MINN. L. REV. 759, 759–61 (1934).

20. Even James Madison, principal architect of American federalism, acknowledged "the impossibility of dividing powers of legislation, in such a manner, as to be free . . . even from ambiguity in the judgment of the impartial." 5 THE WRITINGS OF JAMES MADISON 26 (G. Hunt ed. 1905).

21. THE FEDERALIST PAPERS 464, 467 (Mentor ed. 1961).

22. *See id.* at 467–68:

> [T]he courts were designed to be an intermediate body between *the people* and the legislature in order, among other things, to keep the latter within the limits assigned to their authority. . . . A constitution is, in fact, and must be regarded by the judges as, a fundamental law. . . . If there should happen to be an irreconcilable variance between the two, that which has the superior obligation and validity ought, of course, to be preferred to the statute, the intention of *the people* to the intention of their agents. . . . Where the will of the legislature, declared in its statutes, stands in opposition to that of *the people*, the judges ought to be governed by the latter rather than the former. They ought to regulate their decisions by the fundamental laws rather than by those which are not fundamental. (emphasis added)

23. L. LEVY, *supra* chap. 1, note 38, at 28. *See also* L. HAND, *supra* chap. 1, note 36, at 7.

24. *See* U.S. CONST. art. I, § 8, cl. 18: "The Congress shall have power . . . to make all laws which shall be necessary and proper for carrying into execution the foregoing powers, and all other powers vested by this Constitution in the government of the United States, or in any department or officer thereof."

25. L. LEVY, *supra* chap. 1, note 38, at 28.

26. *Supra* note 12.

27. *Id.* at 78–79.

28. Madison, *Federalist #46*, quoted in Wechsler, *supra* note 12, at 55.

It has been suggested that changes in American politics since 1789 and, indeed, during the quarter of a century since Wechsler wrote—Wechsler's essay was first published in 1954, *see* 54 COLUM. L. REV. 543 (1954)—have eroded important political safeguards of federalism. *See, e.g.*, L. TRIBE, *supra* note 10, at 241–42:

> [A] number of the means state governments were formerly able to use to make their presence felt in Congress are no longer available. State legislatures, for example, no longer choose United States Senators [citing the seventeenth amendment, ratified in 1913] and no longer utilize such devices as the poll tax [citing the twenty-fourth amendment, ratified in 1964, and a Supreme Court decision, Harper v. Virginia Board of Elections, 383 U.S. 663 (1966), which held poll taxes in state elections unconstitutional] and the malapportioned election district [citing Wesberry v. Sanders, 376 U.S. 1 (1964), which was one of the first constitutional cases to establish the "one man, one vote" principle] to define the electorate of the United States Representatives.

See also Kaden, *Politics, Money, and State Sovereignty: The Judicial Role*, 79 COLUM. L. REV. 847, 860–68 (1979). But Wechsler's thesis has been thoroughly reexamined and persuasively (and enthusiastically) reaffirmed from a contemporary perspective. *See* J. CHOPER, *supra* prologue, note 9, at 171–259. Indeed, Professor Choper outdoes Wechsler in urging reliance on the political safeguards of federalism rather than on judicial safeguards. *See* this chap. *infra.*

29. *See* L. TRIBE, *supra* note 10, at 242:

> Other points of contact between the states and congressional processes, such as the definition of the Senate electorate in terms of states [*see* U.S. CONST. art. I, § 3], guarantee only that federal legislators will take heed of the substantive interests of groups influential in particular states, not that Congress will necessarily make allowance in its exercise of power for the institutional interests of state governments as such.

For a discussion of the problem of "identifying the 'viewpoint' of a 'state,' " see J. CHOPER, *supra* prologue, note 9, at 181–84.

30. L. TRIBE, *supra* note 10, at 242.
31. *See* J. CHOPER, *supra* prologue, note 9, at 178.
32. *See id.* at 236–40; *cf. id.* at 201–03.
33. Wechsler, *supra* note 12, at 80–81. *See also* Freund, *supra* note 9, at 96:

> [T]he institution of judicial review is not designed primarily to check the national power; there the inner check of representation of local interests and the clash and compromise of factions serves as an independent safeguard. The institution performs its most useful task in repressing the parochialism of local interests at the local level. . . .

Cf. Wickard v. Filburn, 317 U.S. 111, 120 (1942):

> At the beginning Chief Justice Marshall described the federal commerce power with a breadth never yet exceeded. *Gibbons v. Ogden,* 9 Wheat. 1, 194–195 [1824]. He made emphatic the embracing and penetrating nature of this power by warning that effective restraints on its exercise must proceed from political rather than from judicial processes. [9 Wheat.] at 197.

34. J. CHOPER, *supra* prologue, note 9, at 175. Choper's proposal is predicated on the view that

> [w]hen judicial review is unnecessary for the effective preservation of our constitutional scheme . . . the [Supreme] Court should decline to exercise its authority. By so abstaining, the Justices both reduce the discord between judicial review and majoritarian democracy and enhance their ability to render enforceable constitutional decisions when their participation is critically needed.

Id. at 2. Their participation is critically needed, in Choper's view, in protecting "individual rights, which are not adequately represented in the political processes." *Id.* For a comment on the predicate of Choper's proposal, see Howard, *The Supreme Court and Federalism,* in THE COURTS: THE PENDULUM OF FEDERALISM 49, 70 (J. Dailey ed. 1979):

> In defense of the position that the Court should refrain from passing on claims to limit national power in the name of federalism, it has been argued that this would "husband the Supreme Court's scarce political capital." Certainly one would recoil from returning to the days of the pre–1937 Court, when states' rights became a talisman from thwarting economic and social reform legislation. But cases like *National League of Cities v. Usery* do not in fact raise this specter.
>
> Most storms over Supreme Court cases, since 1937, have involved decisions on such issues as abortion, school prayers, and criminal justice. These decisions would not be avoided if the Court refused to consider the limits imposed on national power by federalism. Cases like *National League of Cities* may provoke critical comment, as indeed that case has done, but they do not use up "scarce political capital."

(Quoting Choper, *The Scope of National Power vis-à-vis the States: The Dispensability of Judicial Review*, 86 Yale L. J. 1552, 1577 (1977).) See also Monaghan, Book Review, 94 Harv. L. Rev. 296, 300–01 (1980); Sager, Book Review, 81 Colum. L. Rev. 707, 708–11 (1981).

35. See chap. 1. Choper defends his thesis against the claim that it is at odds with the intentions of the framers (see, e.g., Howard, *supra* note 34, at 68) by noting that it is not clear that the framers specifically authorized judicial review of congressional legislation. And he is right; it is not clear. In fact, in *Federalist #33*, Hamilton, the author of *Federalist #78*, indicated that "Congress in the first instance and the people in the last would judge" whether Congress has acted beyond the scope of its delegated powers. See note 25 and accompanying text *supra*. Madison too made different noises at different times. See Wechsler, *supra* note 12, at 79; 2 W. Crosskey, Politics and the Constitution 1044 (1953). But I do not see how Choper can defend himself against the distinct claim I am making—that his thesis is at odds with the functional justification for interpretive review of federal action.

36. See note 16 and accompanying text *supra*.

37. See Howard, *supra* note 34, at 69–70.

38. See J. Choper, *supra* prologue, note 9, at 912–93; *cf. id.* at 222–23, 258.

39. There was a single exception, not consequential for present purposes: Oregon v. Mitchell, 400 U.S. 112 (1970). See note 19 *supra*.

40. 426 U.S. 833 (1976).

41. Pub. L. No. 93–259, § 6(a)(1), (5), (6), 88 Stat. 58 (1974) (codified at 29 U.S.C. § 203(d), (s), (x)).

42. His opinion was joined by Chief Justice Burger and Justices Stewart, Blackmun, and Powell. Justice Blackmun wrote a concurring opinion (426 U.S. at 856), which sounds a somewhat different note from the majority opinion's and so leaves in doubt the precise extent of support on the Court for all that Justice Rehnquist said.

43. *Id.* at 835–36, 838–39.

44. Congress's commerce power was the articulated predicate for the Fair Labor Standards Act and the 1974 amendments to it.

45. See *id.* at 837:

> The gist of [plaintiffs'] complaint was not that the conditions of employment of such public employees were beyond the scope of the commerce power had those employees been employed in the private sector, but that the established constitutional doctrine of intergovernmental immunity . . . affirmatively prevented the exercise of this authority in the manner which Congress chose in the 1974 Amendments.

See also *id.* at 845:

> We have repeatedly recognized that there are attributes of sovereignty attaching to every state government which may not be impaired by Congress, not because Congress may lack an affirmative grant of legislative authority to reach the matter, but because the Constitution prohibits it from exercising it in that manner.

The distinction to which these passages refer is that between negative, or internal, limitations on congressional legislative authority that derive from the fact that grants of such authority are inherently limited in scope, and, on the other hand, affirmative, or external, limitations on legislative authority that derive from various prohibitory norms—for example, the rule that "Congress shall make no law . . . abridging the freedom of speech, or of the press" (U.S. Const. amend. 1).

46. See 426 U.S. at 842.

47. See *id.* at 843. The majority's reliance on the text of the tenth amendment was, strictly speaking, unnecessary, given the fact that the majority was prepared to derive the

affirmative limitation from the federal structure of government ordained by the Constitution. *Cf.* C. BLACK, *supra* chap. 1, note 12. Moreover, the majority's (formal) reliance on the tenth amendment was historically unsound, since, as Justice Brennan indicated in dissent:

> "The amendment states but a truism that all is retained which has not been surrendered. There is nothing in the history of its adoption to suggest that it was more than declaratory of the relationship between the national and state governments as it had been established by the Constitution before the amendment. . . ."

Id. at 862 (Brennan, J., joined by White & Marshall, JJ., dissenting) (emphasis deleted) (*quoting* United States v. Darby, 312 U.S. 100, 124 (1941)). *See id.* at 863 n. 5 (Brennan, J., joined by White & Marshall, JJ., dissenting) (citing historical evidence).

48. *Id.* at 851–52.
49. *Id.* at 852.
50. What constitutes "direct" as opposed to "indirect" displacement? *See id.* at 852 n. 17 ("We express no view as to whether different results might obtain if Congress seeks to affect integral operations of state governments by exercising authority granted it under other sections of the Constitution such as the Spending Power, art. 1, § 8, cl. 1 . . ."). What precisely is this "freedom to structure"? What operations are "integral"? What governmental functions are "traditional," and why protect only traditional functions? *See* Kaden, *supra* note 28, at 887–88; Tushnet, *Constitutional and Statutory Analyses in the Law of Federal Jurisdiction.* 25 UCLA L. REV. 1301, 1339–41 (1978).
51. *See, e.g.,* Lane County v. Oregon, 7 Wall. 71, 76 (1869) ("in many articles of the Constitution the necessary existence of the States and, within their proper spheres, the independent authority of the States, is distinctly recognized."); Texas v. White, 7 Wall. 700, 725 (1869) ("The Constitution, in all its provisions, looks to an indestructible Union, composed of indestructible States."); Metcalf & Eddy v. Mitchell, 269 U.S. 514, 523 (1926) ("neither government may destroy the other nor curtail in any substantial manner the exercise of its powers.").
52. *See* 462 U.S. at 878 (Brennan, J., joined by White & Marshall, JJ., dissenting):

> The largest estimate by any of the [plaintiffs] of the cost impact of the 1974 Amendments—one billion dollars—pales in comparison with the financial assistance the States receive from the Federal Government. In fiscal 1977 the President's proposed budget recommends $60.6 billion in federal assistance to the States, exclusive of loans. . . . [Plaintiffs] complain of the impact of the amended FLSA on police and fire departments, but the 1977 budget contemplates outlays for law enforcement assistance of $716 million. . . . Concern is also expressed about the diminished ability to hire students in the summer if States must pay them a minimum wage, but the Federal Government's "summer youth program" provides $400 million for 670,000 jobs.

53. *Id.* at 876 (emphasis added).
54. *Id.*
55. *See* Rehnquist, *supra* chap. 1, note 97.
56. *See also* Shapiro, *Mr. Justice Rehnquist: A Preliminary View,* 90 HARV. L. REV. 293 (1976). True, Rehnquist's opinion in *Usery* made interpretivist noises, but there are few Supreme Court opinions that do not.
57. *See, e.g.,* Youngstown Sheet & Tube Co. v. Sawyer, 343 U.S. 579 (1952).
58. *See, e.g.,* Buckley v. Valeo, 424 U.S. 1 (1976); Nixon v. Administrator of General Services, 433 U.S. 425 (1977). However, perhaps the most famous separation-of-powers

case involved a claim that congressional action invaded *judicial* prerogatives. *See* Marbury v. Madison, 5 U.S. (1 Cranch) 137 (1803). *See also* United States v. Klein, 80 U.S. (13 Wall.) 128 (1872).

For an interesting discussion of "the Court's proper adjudicative function in respect to alleged impositions by either or both of the political branches on the judicial power" (J. CHOPER, *supra* prologue, note 9, at 261), *see id.* at 380–415.

59. THE FEDERALIST PAPERS 300, 308 (Mentor ed. 1961).
60. *Id.* at 320–22.
61. Frohnmayer, *The Separation of Powers: An Essay on the Vitality of a Constitutional Idea*, 52 ORE. L. REV. 211, 214 n. 6 (1973). *See also* J. CHOPER, *supra* prologue, note 9, at 266–70.
62. *See* chap. 1.
63. *See, e.g.,* Frohnmayer, *supra* note 61, at 215–20. *See also* L. TRIBE, *supra* note 10, at 17.
64. Frankfurter & Landis, *Power of Congress over Procedure in Criminal Contempts in "Inferior" Federal Courts—A Study in Separation of Powers*, 37 HARV. L. REV. 1010, 1016 (1924). *See also* J. CHOPER, *supra* prologue, note 9, at 260:

> [B]ecause of the inherent deficiencies of the written word and because an unyielding separation-of-powers was neither contemplated nor enacted, a host of fundamental questions regarding this division of authority has arisen for which the basic charter offers only the most ambiguous guidance or, indeed, no helpful signal at all.

65. Youngstown Sheet & Tube Co. v. Sawyer, 343 U.S. 579, 634 (1952).
66. For a study of this famous case, see M. MARCUS, TRUMAN AND THE STEEL SEIZURE CASE: THE LIMITS OF PRESIDENTIAL POWER (1977).
67. 343 U.S. at 634–35.
68. *Id.* at 635–37.
69. The Court might be saying, for example, only that Congress must itself exercise the power it has attempted to delegate to the executive branch. For a contemporary discussion of the "nondelegation" doctrine, and a plea for its revival, see J. ELY, *supra* prologue, note 6, at 131–34.
70. *See* 343 U.S. at 637:

> When the President acts in absence of either a congressional grant or denial of authority, he can only rely upon his own independent powers, but there is a zone of twilight in which he and Congress may have concurrent authority, or in which its distribution is uncertain. Therefore, congressional inertia, indifference, or quiescence may sometimes, at least as a practical matter, enable, if not invite, measures on independent presidential responsibility. In this area, any actual test of power is likely to depend on the imperatives of events and contemporary imponderables rather than on abstract theories of law.

71. 444 U.S. 996 (1979).
72. *Id.* at 997–98. In Goldwater v. Carter, the Court vacated the judgment of the Court of Appeals and remanded the case to the District Court with directions to dismiss the complaint. There was, however, no majority opinion. Justice Powell concurred in the judgment and filed a separate opinion.
73. *See* Montesquieu, THE SPIRIT OF THE LAWS 151–52 (Nugent trans. 1942).
74. THE FEDERALIST PAPERS 300, 301 (Mentor ed. 1961).
75. 343 U.S. at 637–38.
76. L. HAND, *supra* chap. 1, note 36, at 29. Hand went on to say, by way of emphasizing his central argument that most judicial review is illegitimate, that

it was absolutely essential to confine the power to the need that evoked it: that is, it was and always has been necessary to distinguish between the frontiers of another "Department's" authority and the propriety of its choices within those frontiers. The doctrine presupposed that it was possible to make such a distinction, though at times it is difficult to do so.

Id. at 29–30.

77. See Frohnmayer, supra note 61. Cf. Youngstown Sheet & Tube Co. v. Sawyer, 343 U.S. 579, 654 (1952) (Jackson, J., concurring):

I have no illusion that any decision by this Court can keep power in the hands of Congress if it is not wise and timely in meeting its problems. A crisis that challenges the President equally, or perhaps primarily, challenges Congress. If not good law, there was worldly wisdom in the maxim attributed to Napoleon that "The tools belong to the man who can use them." We may say that power to legislate for emergencies belongs in the hands of Congress, but only Congress itself can prevent power from slipping through its fingers.

78. United States v. American Telephone & Telegraph Co., 567 F.2d 121, 123 (D.C. Cir. 1977).
79. Id. at 122–23.
80. Id. at 123.
81. Id.
82. The court, after negotiations by the parties had produced some limited results, devised and imposed a compromise solution. See id. at 130–34.
83. Id. at 123.
84. Id. at 128.
85. It is no answer to say that the federal judiciary lacks the competence essential to the prudent resolution of difficult interbranch conflicts. If in a particular case a court lacks, or thinks it lacks, competence, it can decline to arbitrate the dispute on the technical ground that the case is not "justiciable." See A. Cox, The Role of the Supreme Court in American Government 27–28 (1976). More frequently, however, the Court will be able to draw upon the respective competences of the two branches whose positions are in conflict before the Court. After all, in the end all the Court is doing is deferring to the policy choice made by one of the two branches.
86. 418 U.S. 683 (1947).
87. See also Monaghan, supra note 34, at 307. In Nixon, the Court rightly recognized that what was in form an intrabranch conflict—between President Nixon and his own Justice Department—was in substance an interbranch conflict—between Nixon and the Congress. See 418 U.S. at 692–97 & nn. 9 & 10. For a different view of the Nixon case, portraying the conflict as not legislative-executive in character but as wholly executive-judicial, see J. Choper, supra prologue, note 9, at 336–42. Try as I might, and notwithstanding aspects of the Court's opinion that support Choper's interpretation, I cannot discern any actual conflict between the executive and the judiciary in Nixon.
88. Id. at 263.
89. 424 U.S. 1 (1976).
90. See J. Choper, supra prologue, note 9 at 281–308.
91. See also McGowen, Book Review, 79 Mich. L. Rev. 616, 629–33 (1981).
92. See note 35 supra.
93. See J. Ely, supra prologue, note 6, at 47–48.
94. See Monaghan, supra note 34, at 303. Cf. note 43 supra.
95. See A. Cox, supra note 85, at 3–30.
96. U.S. Const. art. 2, § 2, cl. 2.

97. It ought to be noted that it is not invariably easy to determine whether the case is one of concord or conflict. *See* Nixon v. Administrator of General Services, 433 U.S. 425 (1977) (conflict between former President Nixon and Congress; concord between former President Ford, who signed challenged law, and Congress; concord between President Carter, who supported law, and Congress; arguably conflict between *Office* of the Presidency and Congress).

98. *See* Choper, *The Burger Court: Misperceptions Regarding Judicial Restraint and Insensitivity to Individual Rights,* 30 Syr. L. Rev. 767, 772 (1979).

99. National League of Cities v. Usery, 426 U.S. 833, 841–42 n. 12 (1976).

100. As I explained earlier in this chapter, in cases in which state action is challenged on federalism grounds, the Court's policymaking is legislative, not constitutional, in that it is subject to revision by the ordinary processes of electorally accountable decision making. There is a sense in which the Court's constitutional policymaking in separation-of-powers cases of legislative-executive conflict is subject to revision too, at least if my thesis is accepted: Whichever party to the legislative-executive conflict, Congress or the executive, contends that the challenged federal action is not within the jurisdiction of the branch that took it can, *even after the Court has ratified that contention,* change its mind, with the result that there is no longer any legislative-executive conflict. But surely that possibility is more hypothetical than real.

CHAPTER 3

1. The amendment also provides that Congress shall make no law "respecting an establishment of religion, or prohibiting the free exercise thereof."

2. No one disputes the fact that the first amendment and the rest of the Bill of Rights were not intended as limitations on state governments. *See* Barron v. Baltimore, 32 U.S. (7 Pet.) 243 (1833). *See generally* L. Levy, *supra* chap. 1, note 38, at 64–79.

3. *See* Gitlow v. New York, 268 U.S. 652 (1925).

4. *See, e.g.,* J. Ely, *supra* prologue, note 6, at 24–28.

5. *See* J. Joyce, Ulysses 40 (Penquin ed. 1922): "History, Stephen said, is a nightmare from which I am trying to awake."

6. *See* notes 25–28 *infra.*

7. G. Wills, Inventing America: Jefferson's Declaration of Independence 259 (1978).

8. *Supra* chap. 1, note 62.

9. *Id.* at 10.

10. For present purposes, the relevant portion of the amendment is § 1, which provides in part that:

    No state shall make or enforce any law which shall abridge the privileges or immunities of citizens of the United States; nor shall any state deprive any person of life, liberty, or property, without due process of law; nor deny to any person within its jurisdiction the equal protection of the laws.

11. R. Berger, *supra* chap. 1, note 62, at 23.

12. The Civil Rights Act of 1866 was a limited step beyond the thirteenth amendment, a step necessitated by the infamous Black Codes. Section 1 of the act provided that all persons born in the United States were "citizens of the United States" and that "such citizens, of every race and color, without regard to any previous condition of slavery . . . have the same right . . . [to] make and enforce contracts, to sue, be parties, and give evidence, to inherit, purchase, lease, sell, hold, and convey real and personal property, and to full and equal benefit of all laws [for] the security of persons and property, as enjoyed by white citizens, and shall be subject to like punishment, [and] to none other, any law,

statute, ordinance, regulation, or custom, to the contrary notwithstanding." Civil Rights Act of 1866, ch. 31, §§ 1, 2, 14 Stat. 27 (1866). The modern counterparts of § 1 are 42 U.S.C. §§ 1981 & 1982. Section 2 of the act, the modern counterpart of which is 42 U.S.C. § 242, provided criminal penalties for violations of § 1.

13. *See, e.g.,* J. ELY, *supra* prologue, note 6, at 30 & 199 n. 66.

14. R. BERGER, *supra* chap. 1, note 62, at 20.

15. Berger concludes that the distinction between "citizen" and "person" in § 1 of the fourteenth amendment "was not carefully considered." *Id.* at 215. *See also* J. ELY, *supra* prologue, note 6, at 25; Karst, *Foreward: Equal Citizenship under the Fourteenth Amendment,* 91 HARV. L. REV. 1, 44 (1977).

16. *See* R. BERGER, *supra* chap. 1, note 62, at 37–51.

17. *See id.* at 22–30.

18. *See id.* at 166–92.

19. *See id.* at 18, 209.

20. *See id.* at 19 ("The three clauses of § 1 were three facets of one and the same concern: to insure that there would be no discrimination against the freed men in respect of 'fundamental rights,' which had clearly understood and narrow compass.").

21. Karst, *supra* note 15, at 15.

22. *See* R. BERGER, *supra* chap. 1, note 62, at 176–77.

> The framers sought only to secure to blacks the same specified rights as were enjoyed by whites; if whites did not have them there was no state duty to supply them to anyone. . . . So much appears from Shellabarger's explanation that the Civil Rights Bill secures "equality of protection in these enumerated civil rights which the *States may deem proper to confer* upon any race."

(Citing Cong. Globe, 39th Cong., 1st Sess., 1868, 1293 (remarks of Rep. Shellabarger) (emphasis supplied by Berger).) *See also id.* at 150 n. 70, 178 & n. 49.

23. For examples of commentary generally accepting Berger's history—though not necessarily the constitutional theory Berger marries to that history—see Abraham, *"Equal Justice under Law" or "Justice at Any Cost"?—The Judicial Role Revisited: Reflections on Government by Judiciary: The Transformation of the Fourteenth Amendment,* 6 HAST. CONST. L. Q. 467 (1979); Alfange, *On Judicial Policymaking and Constitutional Change: Another Look at the "Original Intent" Theory of Constitutional Interpretation,* 5 HAST. CONST. L. Q. 603 (1978); Beloff, Book Review, LONDON TIMES HIGHER EDUC. SUPP., April 7, 1978, at II, col. 1; Bridwell, Book Review, 1978 DUKE L. J. 907; Gunther, Book Review, WALL ST. J., November 25, 1977, at 4, col. 4; Kay, Book Review, 10 CONN. L. REV. 801 (1978); Kommers, Book Review, REV. OF POL. 409, 413 (July, 1978); Lynch, Book Review, 63 CORN. L. REV. 1091–93 (1978); Nathanson, Book Review, 56 TEXAS L. REV. 579, 581 (1978); Perry, Book Review, 78 COLUM. L. REV. 686 (1978). *See also* Bridwell, *The Scope of Judicial Review: A Dirge for the Theorists of Majority Rule,* 31 S. CAR. L. REV. 617 (1980).

For generally effective rebuttals by Berger to criticisms of his history, *see* Berger, *"Government by Judiciary": Judge Gibbons' Argument Ad Hominem,* 59 B. U. L. REV. 783 (1979) (responding to Gibbons, Book Review, 31 RUTGERS L. REV. 839 (1978); Berger, *The Scope of Judicial Review: An Ongoing Debate,* 6 HAST. CONST. L. Q. 527 (1979) (responding to various articles in a symposium on Berger's book (*supra* chap. 1, note 62), 6 HAST. CONST. L. Q. 403 (1979)); Berger, *Government by Judiciary: John Hart Ely's "Invitation,"* 54 IND. L. J. 277 (1979) (responding to Ely, *Constitutional Interpretivism: Its Allure and Impossibility,* 53 IND. L. J. 399 (1978)); Berger, *The Scope of Judicial Review and Walter Murphy,* 1979 WIS. L. REV. 341 (1979) (responding to Murphy, Book Review, 87 YALE L. J. 1752 (1978)); Berger, *Government by Judiciary: Some Countercriticism,* 56 TEXAS L. REV. 1125, 1136–45 (1978) (responding to Clark, Book Review, 56

TEXAS L. REV. 947 (1978)). (Berger's rebuttals to criticisms of his constitutional theory are much less effective in my view.)

Aviam Soifer, in his *Protecting Civil Rights: A Critique of Raoul Berger's History*, 54 N.Y.U. L. REV. 651 (1979), claims that Berger's "*Government by Judiciary* [, *supra* chap. 1, note 62,] contains very poor history. . . . [T]he history [Berger] offers . . . is misleading and frequently internally inconsistent in the most crucial areas." *Id.* at 654, 655. However, Soifer does "not dispute Berger's assertion that the fourteenth amendment simply constitutionalized the guarantee of civil rights contained in the Civil Rights Act of 1866." *Id.* at 657. Rather, Soifer argues that, "[a]ssuming for the sake of argument that the fourteenth amendment merely constitutionalized the statutory rights guaranteed by the Civil Rights Act of 1866, Berger is simply wrong about how broad those rights were." *Id.* at 658. Yet nowhere in his entire essay does Soifer take issue with Berger's central claims that neither the 1866 act nor the fourteenth amendment were intended to affect suffrage or segregation.

> Berger is probably correct in arguing that suffrage was not deemed a civil right in 1866. After all, women were citizens but they did not have the vote. The continued separation of the races in the schools of the District of Columbia and in a few Northern states indicates that a majority of the 39th Congress, if they gave any thought to it at all might not *then* have included a right to integrated schooling in their definition of civil rights.

Id. at 705. What, then, is Soifer's critique of Berger? Soifer says essentially only this: "[T]he members of the 39th Congress did not carefully limit and specify the civil rights with which they were concerned, nor did they indicate that they hoped to set those rights in 1866, as in Devonian amber." *Id.* Soifer's "critique" of Berger's history is, in the end, not much of a critique. Moreover, nowhere does Soifer take issue with the conclusion that the fourteenth amendment was *not* intended to make the Bill of Rights applicable to the states.

24. *See* Berger, *The Fourteenth Amendment: Light from the Fifteenth*, 74 N.W.U. L. REV. 311, 346–47 (1979):

> Striking confirmation [that the fourteenth amendment did not incorporate the Bill of Rights] is furnished by an amendment proposed by James Blaine in 1875, in a Congress which included twenty-three members of the Thirty-ninth Congress, among them Blaine. Prior thereto he had written a letter published by the *New York Times* indicating that the fourteenth amendment did not forbid states from establishing official churches or maintaining sectarian schools. Consequently he proposed that "No state shall make any law respecting an establishment of religion or prohibiting the free exercise thereof."

> Not one of the several Representatives and Senators who spoke on the proposal even suggested that its provisions were implicit in the [first] amendment ratified just seven years earlier. . . . Remarks of Randolph, Christaincy, Kernan, White, Bogy, Eaton and Morton give confirmation to the belief that none of the legislators in 1875 thought the Fourteenth Amendment incorporated the religious provisions of the First.

> To cling to the Bingham-Howard remarks on which Justice Black relied for his incorporation doctrine [*see* Adamson v. California, 332 U.S. 46, 68–92 (1947) (dissenting)] is obstinately to ignore the facts showing they were not generally shared and were untenable.

(*Quoting* J. MCCLELLAN, JUSTICE STORY AND THE AMERICAN CONSTITUTION 154; F. O'BRIEN, JUSTICE REED AND THE FIRST AMENDMENT 116 (1958).)

25. See Fairman, *Does the Fourteenth Amendment Incorporate the Bill of Rights?: The Original Understanding*, 2 STAN. L. REV. 5 (1949); C. FAIRMAN, Volume VI, THE OLIVER WENDELL HOLMES DEVISE HISTORY OF THE SUPREME COURT (RECONSTRUCTION AND REUNION 1864–88: PART ONE) 1292–93 n. 275 (1971). *See also* Morrison, *Does the Fourteenth Amendment Incorporate the Bill of Rights?: The Judicial Interpretation*, 2 STAN. L. REV. 140 (1949).

26. See L. LEVY, *supra* chap. 1, note 38, at 70 (agreeing with Fairman that "there is very little evidence either that [the] framers [of the fourteenth amendment] intended [that the amendment make the Bill of Rights applicable to the states] or that the country understood that intention"). *Cf.* Perry, *supra* note 23, at 689–90:

> The historian Leonard Levy, in an assessment of the "incorporation" debate between Justice Black and Charles Fairman, argued that:
>
>> Though the palm must be awarded to Fairman as the better historian by far, . . . Fairman's findings were basically negative. He did not disprove that the Fourteenth [Amendment] incorporated the Bill of Rights; he proved, rather, that there is very little evidence either that its framers intended that result or that the country understood that intention. Fairman himself criticized Black for relying too heavily on negative evidence, yet he followed Black's example by drawing conclusions from silence or the absence of proof positive. In short, the historical record . . . is inconclusive.
>
> Berger's response to Levy's analysis is, in my view, persuasive:
>
>> The proposition that "The Fourteenth Amendment incorporated the Bill of Rights" constitutes an invasion of rights reserved to the States by the Tenth Amendment, an invasion of such magnitude as to demand proof that such was the framers' intention. Levy would shift the burden of proof and require Black's critics to prove the negative [that the framers did not intend the Fourteenth Amendment to incorporate the Bill of Rights] before he proved the intention to incorporate.

(*Quoting* L. LEVY, *supra* chap. 1, note 38, at 70; R. BERGER, *supra* chap. 1, note 62, at 137 n. 17.) Berger's response to Levy constitutes an adequate response to John Ely as well. *See* J. ELY, *supra* prologue, note 6, at 25–28 & 195 n. 56.

27. See R. BERGER, *supra* chap. 1, note 62, at 134–56. *See also* Berger, *Government by Judiciary: John Hart Ely's "Invitation,"* 54 IND. L. J. 277, 299–302 (1979); note 24 *supra*.

28. See e.g., A. BICKEL, *supra* chap. 1, note 7, at 102 (Charles Fairman "conclusively disproved [Justice] Black's contention, [in Adamson v. California, 332 U.S. 46, 68–92 (1947) (dissenting), that the fourteenth amendment was intended to make the Bill of Rights applicable to the states,] at least, such is the weight of opinion among disinterested observers"); Grey, *supra* chap. 1, note 9, at 711–12 (referring to Justice Black's "flimsy historical evidence" in *Adamson*); Alfange, *supra* note 3, at 607 ("it is all but certain that the Fourteenth Amendment was not intended to incorporate the Bill of Rights"); Kurland, *supra* prologue, note 20, at 9–10 ("nothing in the history of the fourteenth amendment suggests that [it was intended to make the religion clauses of the first amendment applicable to the states]. The transmogrification occurred solely at the whim of the Court. An attempt to pass a constitutional amendment providing for the application of the religion clauses to the states, the Blaine Amendment, failed in 1876, eight years after effectuation of the fourteenth amendment."); Brest, *supra* chap. 1, note 16, at 224 (even a "moderate" interpretivist "would have serious difficulties justifying . . . the incorporation of provisions of the Bill of Rights into the fourteenth amendment"). *See also* Duncan v. Louisiana, 391 U.S. 145, 174 n. 9 (1968) (Harlan, J., joined by Stewart, J., dissenting). *But see* Curtis, *The Bill of Rights as a Limitation on State Authority: A Reply to Professor Berger*, 16 WAKE FOREST L. REV. 45 (1980). For Berger's reply to Curtis,

see Berger, *Incorporation of the Bill of Rights in the Fourteenth Amendment: A Nine-Lived Cat,* 42 OHIO ST. L. J. 435 (1981).

29. No first amendment doctrine of consequence was fashioned before this century. *See generally* N. DORSEN, P. BENDER, & B. NEUBORNE, I EMERSON, HABER, & DORSEN'S POLITICAL AND CIVIL RIGHTS IN THE UNITED STATES 15–37 (4th ed. 1976).

30. A system of prior restraint consists of administrative censorship under which nothing can be printed until a license is first issued by the appropriate functionary. Such a system "had expired in England in 1695, and in the colonies by 1725." Z. CHAFEE, FREE SPEECH IN THE UNITED STATES 18 (1941). Apparently a system of prior restraint flourishes in the Soviet Union. *See* Lifshitz-Losev, *What It Means to Be Censored,* N.Y. REV. OF BOOKS, June 29, 1978, at 43–50.

31. *Seditious libel* has been defined as "the intentional publication, without lawful excuse or justification, of written blame of any public man, or of the law, or of any institution established by law." Z. CHAFEE, *supra* note 30, at 19. According to Chafee, "[t]here was no need to prove any intention on the part of the defendant to produce disaffection or excite an insurrection. It was enough if he intended to publish the blame, because it was unlawful of him merely to find fault with his masters and betters." *Id.*

See also L. LEVY, LEGACY OF SUPPRESSION 10 (1960):

[Seditious libel] can be defined in a quite elaborate and technical manner in order to take into account the malicious or criminal intent of the accused, the bad tendency of his remarks, and their truth or falsity. But the crime has never been satisfactorily defined, the necessary result of its inherent vagueness. Seditious libel has always been an accordion-like concept. Judged by actual prosecutions, the crime consisted of criticizing the government: its form, constitution, officers, laws, symbols, conduct, policies, and so on. In effect, any comment about the government which could be construed to have the bad tendency of lowering it in the public's esteem or of disturbing the peace was seditious libel, subjecting the speaker or writer to criminal prosecution.

32. With respect to the possibility that the first amendment was intended to prohibit any system of prior restraint—or, more accurately, to prohibit Congress from instituting any such a system—*see* Levy, *Liberty of the Press from Zenger to Jefferson,* in L. LEVY, *supra* chap. 1, note 38, at 115, 136. *But see* Z. CHAFEE, *supra* note 30, at 18:

If we apply Coke's test of statutory construction, and consider what mischief in the existing law the framers of the First Amendment wished to remedy by a new safeguard, we can be sure it was not the [system of prior restraint]. This had expired in England in 1695, and in the colonies by 1725. They knew from books that it destroyed liberty of the press; and if they ever thought of its revival as within the range of practical possibilities, they must have regarded it as clearly prohibited by the First Amendment. But there was no need to go to all the trouble of pushing through a constitutional amendment just to settle an issue that had been dead for decades, What the framers did have plenty of reason to fear was an entirely different danger to political writers and speakers [—namely, prosecution for seditious libel].

With respect to the possibility that the first amendment was intended to modify the common law of seditious libel in the respects indicated, *see* L. LEVY, *supra* note 31, at ix:

Take . . . the two major libertarian propositions of the later eighteenth century, that truth is a defense against a charge of criminal libel, and that the jury should have the power of deciding the questions that judges reserved to themselves: whether the defendant's intent was malicious and whether his words had the seditious tendency alleged. That these libertarian propositions were "in the air" is beyond doubt. But most of the scraps of evidence that can be gathered on the subject tend to show that it was not the intention in America to modify the common law by incorporating these propositions within the meaning of free-press guarantees. Yet I am certain that if the American people at any time between the Zenger case and the ratification of the First Amendment would have held a referendum, they would have overwhelmingly cast their ballots in favor of the two propositions. Working with the "evidence," however, leads to the conclusion that this certainty on my part is utterly unprovable; according to the evidence, the issue was, at best, unsettled.

It *is* provable, however—and Levy's book, *id.*, supplies the proof—that

freedom of speech and press . . . was not understood to include a right to broadcast sedition by words. The security of the state against libelous advocacy or attack was always regarded as outweighing any social interest in open expression, at least through the period of the adoption of the First Amendment. The thought and experience of a lifetime, indeed the taught traditions of law and politics extending back many generations, supplied a prior belief that freedom of political discourse, however broadly conceived, stopped short of seditious libel.

id. at 237.

In a later piece, Levy has written that the injunction of the first amendment— "Congress shall make no law . . ."—"was intended to prohibit any Congressional regulation of the press, whether by means of a licensing act, a tax act, or a sedition act. The framers meant Congress to be totally without power to enact legislation regarding the press." Levy, *supra* note 32, at 136. As Levy explains:

We have noted that a constitutional guarantee of a free press did not per se preclude a sedition act, but the prohibition on Congress did, although it left the federal courts free to try [common law] cases of seditious libel. It . . . appears that the prohibition on Congress was motivated far less by a desire to give immunity to political expression than by a solicitude for states' rights and the federal principle. The primary purpose of the First Amendment was to reserve to the states an exclusive authority, as far as legislation was concerned, in the field of speech and press.

Id. at 137–38.

But surely Levy does not mean to suggest—at any rate it beggars belief to suggest—that in the first amendment the framers constitutionalized a value judgment that would preclude Congress from outlawing, for example, any publication calling for the assassination of a federal official, or disclosing troop movements in time of war. Therefore, it seems safest to conclude that *at most* the first amendment was intended to prohibit Congress from instituting any system of prior restraint and perhaps from discriminating against the press as press (as, for example, by levying a special tax on the press), and to require Congress, if it later chose to make seditious libel a crime, to make truth a defense and to permit the case to be tried to a jury.

With respect to the latter point, the Sedition Act, 1 Stat. 596 (July 14, 1798), which is virtually contemporaneous with the first amendment, tends to bear me out. In section 3 of the act, Congress provided that:

[I]f any person shall be prosecuted under this act, for the writing or publishing any libel aforesaid, it shall be lawful for the defendant, upon the trial of the cause, to give evidence in his defense, the truth of the matter contained in the publication charged as a libel. And the jury who shall try the cause, shall have a right to determine the law and the fact, under the direction of the court, as in other cases.

(The Sedition Act expired on March 3, 1801, but prior to that time its constitutional validity "was sustained by the lower federal courts and by three Supreme Court Justices sitting on circuit." N. DORSEN et al., *supra* note 29, at 22.)

33. L. LEVY, *supra* note 31, at vii.
34. *See* Brandenburg v. Ohio, 395 U.S. 444, 447 (1969) (government may not "forbid or proscribe advocacy of the use of force or of law violation except where such advocacy is directed to inciting or producing imminent lawless action and is likely to incite or produce such action.").
35. *See, e.g.*, Gertz v. Robert Welch, Inc., 418 U.S. 323 (1974) (discussing constitutional privileges against liability for defamation of public and private figures).
36. *See, e.g.*, Cohen v. California, 403 U.S. 15 (1971) (government may not punish act of wearing, in public, jacket with "Fuck the Draft" emblazoned on back).
37. *See, e.g.*, Miller v. California, 413 U.S. 15 (1973) (discussing protection afforded pornographic expression).
38. *See, e.g.*, Virginia State Board of Pharmacy v. Virginia Citizens Consumer Council, Inc., 425 U.S. 748 (1976) (discussing protection afforded commercial speech).
39. *See, e.g.*, Buckley v. Valeo, 424 U.S. 1 (1976) (discussing protection afforded campaign expenditures).
40. *See* Kurland, *supra* prologue, note 20.
41. R. BERGER, *supra* chap. 1, note 62, at 272 (*quoting* Palko v. Connecticut, 302 U.S. 319, 325, 327 (1937) (Cardozo, J., . . .). *See* note 46 *infra*.
42. Then too, perhaps Justice Rehnquist subscribes to Robert Bork's attempt to explain away the inconsistency between interpretivism and support for judicial review of state action under free-speech and free-press norms. *See* this chap. *infra*.

    Henry Monaghan has suggested, though I am not persuaded, that a justice *ought not* to tilt at firmly established constitutional practice. "I do not think that an individual appointed to the Court could responsibly base his vote, in relevant cases, on the theory that only the national government is bound to respect free expression. . . . History has its claims, at least where settled expectations of the body politic have clustered around constitutional doctrine." Monaghan, *Taking Supreme Court Opinions Seriously*, 39 MD. L. REV. 1, 7 (1979).
43. Bork accepts Levy's "demonstration" in *Legacy of Suppression* (*supra* note 31) that at best the framers of the first amendment intended it to have an exceedingly narrow scope. Bork, *supra* chap. 1, note 100, at 22.
44. *Id.* at 23, 26.
45. *See* R. BERGER, *supra* chap. 1, note 62, at 134–35 n. 4:

    > It has been little noticed that, as Egbert Benson, speaking with reference to freedom of speech and press, said, all the Committee of Eleven to whom the amendments had been referred "meant to provide against was [their] being infringed by the [federal] Government." 1 *Annals of Congress* 732. Madison urged that "the State governments are as liable to attack these invaluable privileges as the General Government is, and therefore ought to be as cautiously guarded against." *Id.* 441. But his attempt failed. Charles Warren, "The New 'Liberty' under the Fourteenth Amendment," 39 Harv. L. Rev. 431, 433–35 (1926). . . . The view that prevailed was that of Thomas Tucker: "It will be much better, I apprehend, to leave the State Governments to themselves, and not to interfere with them more than we already do." *Id.* 755.

    See also Prudential Ins. Co. v. Cheek, 259 U.S. 530, 538 (1922) (the Constitution "imposes upon the States no obligation to confer upon those within their jurisdiction . . . the right of free speech"). *Cf.* note 24 *supra*.
46. Indeed, the framers established a government whose principal constituency were propertied white males, many of whom were slaveholders. Some "representative democracy" that! *Cf.* Brest, *supra* chap. 1, note 16, at 230.

    Note that Article IV, § 4 of the Constitution—which provides in relevant part that "[t]he United States shall guarantee to every State in this Union a Republican Form of Government"—does not lend support to Bork's argument, as indeed Bork himself would seem to acknowledge. See Bork, supra chap. 1, note 100, at 19: "[James] Madison's writing on the republican form of government specified by the guarantee clause suggests that representative democracy may properly take many forms, so long as the forms do not become 'aristocratic or monarchical.' " (Quoting Federalist #43.) (Obviously the guarantee clause cannot explain judicial review of federal action under free-speech and free-press norms never constitutionalized by the framers.)

47. L. LEVY, supra note 31 at vii (emphasis added). Note that the presence in state constitutions of provisions corresponding to the first amendment does nothing to explain judicial review of state action by federal courts under federal free-speech and free-press norms. If anything, the existence of such provisions in the late eighteenth century or the nineteenth century suggests that freedom of expression, as a constraint on state action, is properly the business of state courts enforcing state constitutions, not federal courts enforcing the federal Constitution.

48. That the Court's review is noninterpretive rather than interpretive in most freedom of expression cases should not be surprising. After all, "one can better protect . . . the integrity of democratic processes by protecting them than by guessing how other people meant to govern a different society a hundred or more years ago." Brest, supra chap. 1, note 16, at 238.

49. See chap. 4.

50. But not all of it, least of all, perhaps, that protecting pornography (see, e.g., Bork, supra chap. 1, note 100, at 28–29) and commercial speech (see, e.g., Jackson & Jeffries, Commercial Speech: Economic Due Process and the First Amendment, 65 VA. L. REV. 1 (1979)).

51. C. Black, supra prologue, note 10, at 33.

52. See R. BERGER, supra chap. 1, note 62, at 117–33. Even Berger's critics seem not to dispute this point. See, e.g., Soifer, supra note 23, at 705.

53. See, e.g., Bickel, The Original Understanding and the Segregation Decision, 69 HARV. L. REV. 1 (1955).

54. See Perry, Modern Equal Protection: A Conceptualization and Appraisal, 79 COLUM. L. REV. 1023 (1979). See also Perry, The Principle of Equal Protection, 32 HAST. L. J. 1133 (1981).

55. Brest, supra chap. 1, note 16, at 231–32. See id. at 231–34.

56. It is tempting to say that one cannot be an interpretivist and accept any equal protection constraints on federal action, because the fourteenth amendment was intended as a constraint only on state action. John Ely has argued to that effect. J. ELY, supra prologue, note 6, at 32–33. See also Brest, supra chap. 1, note 16, at 224.

But it is not implausible to think that one can be an interpretivist and at the same time accept application of section 1 of the fourteenth amendment, as originally understood, to federal action. The framers of the fourteenth amendment constitutionalized the judgment that it is wrong to discriminate on the basis of race with respect to certain sorts of rights. The distinction between action by state government and action by the federal government is irrelevant to—it makes no sense with respect to—that judgment. (I do not mean to suggest that the framers of constitutional provisions are somehow obligated to constitutionalize only "sensible"—coherent, internally consistent—value judgments. But surely we ought not to presume that a particular value judgment constitutionalized by the framers is not sensible.

True, the framers were focused on state action, in particular the infamous Black Codes (see note 12 supra). But they had no occasion to focus on federal action, since the federal government did not discriminate on the basis of race with respect to the sorts of rights that concerned the framers. (Indeed, at that time the federal government had little to do with those sorts of rights; such rights—regarding "life, liberty, and property" in the narrow original sense—were almost wholly the state's concern.) The important point is that the value judgment the framers constitutionalized—that racial discrimination regarding certain rights is wrong—was at bottom a judgment about what government in general should not do, and not simply about what state government should not do. (Of course, one cannot be an interpretivist and accept any equal protection constraints on either federal or state action beyond those established by the framers.)

57. Berger is emphatic about his moral enthusiasm for the result in *Brown*. R. BERGER, *supra* chap. 1, note 62, at 117. He opposes it on constitutional grounds.

58. *See generally id.* at 249–418.

59. *Id.* at 412–13.

60. Berger, Letter to the Editor, THE NEW REPUBLIC, February 11, 1978, at 7.

61. R. BERGER, *supra* chap. 1, note 62, at 281, 297–98. *Cf.* Monaghan, *supra* note 42, at 7 (quoted in note 42 *supra*).

62. Bork, *supra* chap. 1, note 62, at 14–15. Bork's argument is a strange one for an interpretivist to make. If in fact we did not know just what sorts of racial inequality the framers of the fourteenth amendment meant to ban, then the proper office for an interpretivist court would not be to pick and choose what sorts of racial inequality shall be banned and what sorts shall not. Nor, contrary to what Bork argues, would it be to ban all racial inequalities. Rather, its proper office would be to ban only those sorts of racial inequalities which we *did* know the framers meant to ban. In short, a court may not, consistently with interpretivism, ban any political practice unless it can say that the practice is of the sort the framers meant to ban; if it cannot say that, the court must, consistently with interpretivism, sustain the practice. Discretion of the sort Bork wants to constrain does not even enter into the matter.

63. *id.* at 13.

64. *See* Brest, *supra* chap. 1, note 16, at 209–17. *But see* Dellinger, *School Segregation and Professor Avins' History: A Defense of* Brown v. Board of Education, 38 MISS. L. J. 248, 251 n. 6 (1967): "[W]hatever the congressional debates establish should constitute a rebuttable presumption, since it is not unrealistic, in the main, to assume notice of congressional purpose in the state legislatures.' " *Quoting* Bickel, *supra* note 53, at 7.

65. *See* Brest, *supra* chap. 1, note 16, at 221–22.

66. Monaghan, *supra* chap. 1, note 114, at 126–27.

67. *See* R. DWORKIN, *supra* chap. 1, note 114, at 134:

Suppose I tell my children that I expect them not to treat others unfairly. I no doubt have in mind examples of the conduct I mean to discourage, but I would not accept that my "meaning" was limited to these examples, for two reasons. First, I would expect my children to apply my instructions to situations I had not and could not have thought about. Second, I stand ready to admit that some particular act I had thought was fair when I spoke was in fact unfair, or vice versa, if one of my children is able to convince me of that later; in that case I should want to say that my instructions covered the case he cited, not that I had changed my instructions. I might say that I meant the family to be guided by the *concept* of fairness, not by any specific *conception* of fairness that I might have had in mind. (emphasis in original)

See also Munzer & Nickel, *Does the Constitution Mean What It Always Meant?*, 77 COLUM. L. REV. 1029, 1037 (1977):

The object of the [concept-conception] distinction is to justify the claim that the core meaning of the Constitution remains unchanged even when judges diverge from the specific content that the framers would have found there. To appeal to a conception is to appeal to a specific understanding or account of what the words one is using mean. To appeal to a concept is to invite rational discussion and argument about what words used to convey some general idea mean. Concepts are not tied to the author's situation and intentions in the way that conceptions are. Broad phrases such as "cruel and unusual punishment," "freedom of speech," "due process," and "equal protection" tend to be vague and abstract. While Dworkin is apparently not committed to thinking of the concepts denoted by these phrases as utterly lacking in content, their content is not usually specific enough to decide troubling cases involving issues such as capital punishment. They are "contested" concepts; their proper content is always disputable. Even though some people may agree on some paradigm cases of what is and is not cruel and unusual punishment, the boundaries of this concept are always open to dispute.

68. *See* R. DWORKIN, *supra* chap. 1, note 114, at 134–36.
69. Sandalow, *supra* chap. 1, note 16, at 1168.
70. For a variation on the sort of claim Dworkin makes, see Bennett, *supra* chap. 1, note 61, at 1090–91.
71. Professors Munzer and Nickel are quite properly critical of Dworkin in that regard. *See* Munzer & Nickel, *supra* note 67, at 1040–41. For further criticism of reliance on the concept-conception distinction in constitutional theory, see Saphire, *Professor Richard's Unwritten Constitution of Human Rights: Some Preliminary Observations,* 4 U. DAYTON L. REV 305 (1979).
72. Monaghan, *supra* chap. 1, note 114, at 127–128. *See also* Munzer & Nickel, *supra* note 67, at 1041.
73. *See also* Munzer & Nickel, *see also id.* at 1041.
74. Or with anything like its present significance. *Cf.* Brest, *supra* chap. 1, note 16, at 220–21 (suggesting that in the pervasively Christian American society of the late eighteenth century, in which belief in an afterlife was the norm, the death penalty could not have had anything like the significance it has today).
75. *See* R. BERGER, *supra* chap. 1, note 62, at 99–116. *See also* Monaghan, *supra* chap. 1, note 114, at 127–28 (quoted in part in text accompanying note 71, *supra*); Monaghan, *Professor Jones and the Constitution,* 4 VT. L. REV. 87, 91 (1979): "[N]o satisfactory evidence exists to show that judicial development of a *lex non scripta* reflects the purpose of either the drafters or ratifiers of the eighteenth-century Constitution or of the Civil War Amendments."
76. *See* Alfange, *supra* note 23, at 620.
77. Holmes v. City of Atlanta, 350 U.S. 879 (1955).
78. *See generally* R. BERGER, *supra* chap. 1, note 62, at 99–133.
79. *See* p. 20, n. *.
80. *But see* Bennett, *supra* chap. 1, note 61, at 1092: "[T]he intent of some legislators, without whose votes the fourteenth amendment could not have been passed, may have been to erect the Supreme Court as a body with continuing authority to put content into the fourteenth amendment's general phrases." That suggestion is wholly speculative; no historical materials lend credence to it. *Cf.* Brest, *supra* chap. 1, note 16, at 220: "Perhaps [the framers of any given constitutional provision limiting governmental power] wanted to bind the future as closely as possible to their own notions. Perhaps they intended [the] provision to be interpreted with increasing breadth as time went on. *Or—more likely than not—[they] may have had no intentions at all concerning these matters."* (emphasis added)

Concededly, the proposition that the framers intended the equal protection clause not to prohibit segregated public schooling is equivalent to the proposition that they intended such schooling not be proscribed in the name of the particular, narrow value judgment they embodied in the clause. But in *Brown* the Court avoided acting contrary to *that* intent by not relying on the claim that its invalidation of segregated public schooling merely represented enforcement of the framers' intentions. Rather, the Court suggested that no one could tell whether the framers meant to prohibit segregated public schooling. 347 U.S. 483, 489 (1954).

81. *See* chap. 1, note 119 *supra*.
82. For a critique of such arguments, see Bayles, *Morality and the Constitution*, 1978 ARIZ. ST. L. REV. 561.
83. *See Id*.
84. *See* chap. 4.
85. Dworkin, *The Forum of Principle*, 56 N. Y. U. L. REV. 469, 490 (1981).
86. The reader who still has doubts on that score is invited to consult Sandalow, *Constitutional Interpretation*, 79 MICH. L. REV. 1033 (1981).
87. Dworkin, *supra* note 85, at 499–500.
88. *See, e.g.*, J. Ely, *supra* prologue, note 6, at 14–15 (the old, early-twentieth-century substantive due process cases, "conventionally referred to under the head of *Lochner v. New York*, [198 U.S. 45 (1905),] one of the earlier ones, . . . are now universally acknowledged to have been constitutionally improper—for obvious reasons by interpretivists, for somewhat less obvious ones by noninterpretivists.").
89. *See* note 152 *infra*.
90. J. ELY, *supra* prologue, note 6.
91. *See id*. at 43–72.
92. *Id*. at 182
93. *Id*. at 74.
94. *Id. See also id*. at 77 ("a coherent political theory").
95. *Id*. at 181. *See also* Freund, *The Judicial Process in Civil Liberties Cases*, 1975 U. ILL. L. F. 493.
96. *See also* T. EMERSON, THE SYSTEM OF FREEDOM OF EXPRESSION 13 (1970):

> In considering the role of the judiciary in a system of freedom of expression it is essential to narrow the issues and establish a fundamental distinction. We are not dealing here with any general function of our judicial institutions to foster the whole range of freedoms in a democratic society, nor are we dealing with any broad power to supervise or review all major actions of the legislative and executive branches. We are concerned with the specific function of the judiciary in supporting a system of freedom of expression. This involves the application of general principles of law to assure that the basic mechanisms of the democratic process will be respected. It does not involve supervision over the decisions reached or measures adopted as a consequence of employing democratic procedures. Responsibility for this is primarily that of the legislature. In other words, the judicial institutions are here dealing essentially with the methods of conducting the democratic process, not with the substantive results of that process. In this differentiation of function lies a generic distinction between the role of the judiciary and the role of the legislature.

97. J. ELY, *supra* prologue, note 6, at 105.
98. *Id*.
99. *See, e.g.*, Freund, *supra* note 95, at 495: "[I]t is by virtue of speech and assembly that the winds of doctrine blow and the freshets of change can course."
100. J. ELY, *supra* prologue, note 6, at 117.
101. *Id*. at 106.
102. *Id*. at 117. Ely makes essentially the same argument in support of noninterpretive review with respect to issues concerning access to the franchise and the ballot. *See id*. at 116–25.

103. See also Leedes, The Supreme Court Mess, 57 TEX. L. REV. 1361, 1424 (1979); Tushnet, Darkness on the Edge of Town: The Contributions of John Hart Ely to Constitutional Theory, 89 YALE L. J. 1037, 1047 (1980).

104. See J. ELY, supra prologue, note 6, at 105: "Virtually everyone agrees that the courts should be heavily involved in reviewing impediments to free speech, publication, and political association."

105. Ely's discussion is not always clear. Perhaps Ely means to proffer an argument very much like Bork's. Perhaps he means to say that the value—"the democratic process"—was implicitly constitutionalized by the framers to the extent that "the nature of the United States Constitution" (see id. at 88–101) established by the framers presupposes and even ordains "the democratic process." If that is indeed Ely's argument, then it is infirm for the same reasons that Bork's is infirm.

106. See Tushnet, supra note 103, at 1047:

> Ely thinks that the society agrees that participation is the primary value; he criticizes natural law on the basis that society does not agree about anything to a degree substantial enough to enable one to rely upon social agreement as the basis for a theory. The empirical claim implicit in Ely's critique contradicts the one implicit in his theory, and the first empirical claim is more plausible.

107. Cf. R. DAHL, supra chap. 1, note 4, at 59: "[T]he 'key prerequisites to political equality and popular sovereignty' are the right to vote, freedom of speech, freedom of assembly, and freedom of the press."

108. See, e.g., Hazard, supra chap. 1, note 1, at 26–27:

> [Most] of the people most of the time do not have a binding commitment to the open political process. I would surmise that at any given time an open political process is preferred only by a transient minority. All political parties, like all businesses, strive for monopoly; all interest groups try to drown out their opponents and very likely would seek to stifle them if not legally restrained; all branches and agencies of government seek ascendancy when confronted by opposition; and summary justice for deviants is probably favored by a clear majority.

109. Tushnet, Truth, Justice, and the American Way: An Interpretation of Public Law Scholarship in the Seventies, 57 TEX. L. REV. 1307, 1315 (1979). See also chap. 4, note 20 and accompanying text infra.

110. As Ely reminds us: "Excluding the Eighteenth and Twenty-First Amendments—the latter repealed the former—[five of our last ten constitutional amendments] have extended the franchise to persons who had previously been denied it." J. ELY, supra prologue, note 6, at 7; see also id. at 98–99.

Of course, to the extent a consensus as to a value is reflected in the Constitution, it is unnecessary to defend judicial enforcement of that value by reference to the consensus.

111. See p. 3, note *.

112. Scanlon, Freedom of Expression and Categories of Expression, 40 U. PITT. L. REV. 519, 536 (1979). See also Wellington, On Freedom of Expression, 88 YALE L. J. 1105, 1113–16 (1979).

113. Examples of such issues include the protection to be afforded speech advocating conduct unlawful under a valid statute (see, e.g., Brandenburg v. Ohio. 395 U.S. 444 (1969)); the protection to be afforded pornography (see, e.g., Miller v. California, 413 U.S. 15 (1973), or "vulgar" expression (see e.g., Cohen v. California, 403 U.S. 15 (1971)); and the protection to be afforded commercial speech (see, e.g., Virginia Pharmacy Board v. Virginia Consumer Council, 425 U.S. 748 (1976)).

114. See generally D. MAYHEW, CONGRESS: THE ELECTORAL CONNECTION (1974).

115. Recall that in the Pentagon Papers Case—New York Times Co. v. United States, 403 U.S.

713 (1971)—the Court did not order the papers released, but merely refused to enjoin their publication.

116. *See* R. DAHL, *supra* chap. 1, note 4, at 143:

> To assume that this country has remained democratic because of its Constitution seems to me an obvious reversal of the relation; it is much more plausible to suppose that the Constitution has remained because our society is essentially democratic. If the conditions necessary to polyarchy had not existed, no constitution intended to limit the power of leaders would have survived. Perhaps a variety of constitutional forms could easily have been adapted to the changing social balance of power. It is worth emphasizing . . . that the constitutional system did not work when it finally encountered, in slavery, an issue that temporarily undermined some of the main prerequisites for polyarchy.

117. Certainly the electorally accountable representatives of the people are more likely than the electorally unaccountable federal judiciary to reflect the preferences of the people. *See* J. ELY, *supra* prologue, note 7, at 68: "[T]he theory that the legislature does not truly speak for the people's values, but the [Supreme] Court does, is ludicrous."

118. Bork, *The Consequences of Judicial Imperialism,* in THE ROLE OF THE JUDICIARY IN AMERICA (Moore ed., forthcoming 1982). *See also* White, *supra* chap. 1, note 119, at 165:

> Here one confronts the central dilemma for the intraprofessionalist argument. If one assumes that the Court should be constrained in the exercise of its lawmaking power and that the constraints should be "professionally" derived, and one seeks the derivation of those constraints in the text, history, and original purposes of the Constitution, how can one justify constraints that follow from a contemporary political interpretation of those purposes? In other words, what if an equally plausible or more plausible contemporary interpretation of the purposes of the Constitution can be put forth that would not justify judicial review of legislative malapportionment? Such an interpretation is, of course, relatively easy to advance. If the framers were so fundamentally dedicated to the principle of representativeness, why did they permit so many classes of persons to be denied the right to vote?

119. *See* Auerbach, *The Communist Control Act of 1954: A Proposed Legal-Political Theory of Free Speech,* 23 U. CHIC. L. REV. 173 (1956).
120. J. ELY, *supra* prologue, note 6, at 102; *see also id.* at 88.
121. *Id.* at 76.
122. S. GABIN, JUDICIAL REVIEW AND THE REASONABLE DOUBT TEST 76–77 (1980).
123. J. ELY, *supra* prologue, note 6, at 77.
124. *Id.*
125. *Id.* at 74 & n. *.
126. *Id.* at 77. The other principal way the judiciary assures persons equal participation in the process of government—the way other than by defining and protecting first amendment rights, that is—is by defining and protecting voting rights. *See id.* at 116–25. By "equal" participation in the process of government, Ely does not mean equal political clout, of course, but equal legal rights—*i.e.,* the same legal rights others have—to speak one's mind, cast a vote, and the like.
127. *Id.* at 86–87.
128. *Id.* at 74.
129. *Id.* at 77.
130. *Id.* at 82.
131. *See id.* at 82:

> [The concept of virtual representation] cannot mean that groups that constitute

minorities of the population can never be treated less favorably than the rest, but it does preclude a refusal to represent them, the denial to minorities of what Professor Dworkin has called "equal concern and respect in the design and administration of the political institutions that govern them."

(Quoting R. DWORKIN, supra chap. 1, note 114, at 180.) Ely underscores the fact that constitutionally sufficient reasons can justify denials of equal participation in particular payoffs by terming the right to equal participation "presumptive." Id. at 77.

132. Id. at 86.
133. Compare id. at 145–70 to Alexander, supra prologue, note 25, at 44–51; Brest, The Substance of Process, 42 OHIO ST. L. J. 131 (1981).
134. I do not take issue with Ely's interesting suggestion that something like the concept of virtual representation is implicit in certain constitutional provisions, such as the privileges and immunities clause of Article IV or the commerce clause (art. I, § 8, cl. 3), which were designed, at least in part, to curtail parochial state legislation discriminating against "geographical outsiders." See J. ELY, supra prologue, note 6, at 82–84. But it is clear that the particular concept of virtual representation Ely espouses, designed to prevent unjustified discrimination by a state against certain of its voting "insiders," is not one the framers constitutionalized. And Ely does not claim otherwise. If the framers had constitutionalized the concept, judicial enforcement of it would constitute interpretive review; Ely recognizes that judicial enforcement of the concept is a species of constitutional policymaking, and he seeks to justify it as such.
135. See note 109 and accompanying text supra.
136. J. ELY, supra prologue, note 6, at 88.
137. Id. at 82.
138. Id. at 135.
139. Bork, supra chap. 1, note 77, at 698.
140. Id. at 698–99.
141. See prologue, note 15 supra.
142. Cover, The Origins of Judicial Activism in the Protection of Minorities, in THE ROLE OF THE JUDICIARY IN AMERICA (Moore ed., forthcoming 1982).
143. Id.
144. Id.
145. J. ELY, supra prologue, note 6, at 103. See id. at 88, 102–03.
146. Id. at 103.
147. Bork, supra chap. 1, note 100, at 3.
148. Id.
149. J. ELY, supra prologue, note 6, at 73.
150. Id. at 103.
151. Sandalow, supra chap. 1, note 16, at 1177–78.
152. His effort to justify noninterpretive review in procedural due process cases, in terms of "fairness" is similarly unsuccessful. Compare J. ELY, supra prologue, note 6, at 21 ("what procedures are needed fairly to make what decisions are the sorts of questions lawyers and judges are good at.") with id. at 102 ("Lawyers are experts on process writ small, the processes by which the facts are found and contending parties are allowed to present their claims. . . . And of course many legislators are lawyers themselves."). Cf. J. CHOPER, supra prologue, note 9, at 72–73: "[T]he Court's constitutional reappraisal of those popularly sponsored policies that arguably endanger one cluster of plainly articulated personal liberties, those that involve the administration of justice . . . may be independently justified as being of intrinsic and intimate concern to the functioning of the judicial department itself."
153. J. ELY, supra prologue, note 6, at 102. Cf. prologue, note 15 and accompanying text supra.

154. Alexander, *supra* prologue, note 25, at 44.
155. *See also* Estreicher, Book Review, 56 N.Y.U. L. REV. 547, 551–52 (1981).

CHAPTER 4

1. Levinson, *The Constitution in American Civil Religion*, 1979 SUP. CT. REV. 123, 150.
2. Cases and other materials setting forth constitutional doctrine regarding such matters can be found in any constitutional law casebook. *See, e.g.,* G. GUNTHER, *supra* chap. 2, note 16.
3. The framers of the fourteenth amendment *did* intend to prohibit any state from administering its criminal processes in a racially discriminatory manner. *See* chap. 3.
4. *See generally* G. GUNTHER, *supra* chap. 2, note 16, at 506–47, 1040–1531.
5. *See* chap. 1, note 16, *supra*. Recall that the formal textual basis of most such decisions is § 1 of the fourteenth amendment (or some provision thereof), and that the framers intended § 1 to have a very narrow scope. *See* chap. 3.
6. *See* chap. 1.
7. Poe v. Ullman, 367 U.S. 497, 542–43 (1961) (Harlan, J., dissenting).
8. Bellah, *Religion and Polity in America,* in ANDOVER NEWTON Q. 107, 113 (1974). *See also* Brest, *Accommodation of Majoritarianism and the Rights of Human Dignity,* 53 S. CAL. L. REV. 761 (1980) (criticizing Murphy, *An Ordering of Constitutional Values,* 53 S. CAL. L. REV. 703 (1980)).
9. *See* J. ELY, *supra* prologue, note 6, at 50–51.
10. *See* Dorsen, Bender, & Neuborne, *supra* chap. 3, note 29, at 20–37.
11. Bork, *The Legacy of Alexander M. Bickel,* YALE L. REP. 6, 9 (Fall 1979).
12. *See* Grey, *supra* chap. 1, note 9, at 709.
13. *See* Wellington, *Common Law Rules and Constitutional Double Standards: Some Notes on Adjudication,* 83 YALE L. J. 221, 266–67 (1973). *See also* Moore v. City of East Cleveland, Ohio, 431 U.S. 494, 501 (1977) (plurality op'n) (*quoting* Poe v. Ullman, 367 U.S. 497, 542–43 (1961) (Harlan, J., dissenting)) "That tradition is a living thing.").
14. *See, e.g.,* Perry, *Abortion, The Public Morals, and the Police Power: The Ethical Function of Substantive Due Process,* 23 UCLA L. REV. 689 (1976).
15. J. ELY, *supra* prologue, note 6, at 63–69.
16. *See id.*
17. I say "little need," not "no need," because people do not always work out the implications of—or, when they do, do not always act on the basis of—values they accept. In the main, however, they do.
    See J. ELY, *supra* prologue, note 6, at 219 n. 118 (commenting on the possibility that a vigorous minority might prevent repeal of existing but antiquated legislation).
18. Lupu, *Untangling the Strands of the Fourteenth Amendment,* 77 MICH. L. REV. 981, 1040 (1979) (emphasis deleted).
19. *See id.* at 1044–45, 1047:

   A difference exists . . . between a test that entails only a vague and general scrutiny of "traditions," . . . and one that demands a *continuous and continuing historical momentum* in favor of a liberty interest over any competing claims in society. I advocate the latter approach. . . .

   . . . .

   [C]onsensus is a necessary component of any theory of constitutional adjudication in support of unenumerated values.

20. Tushnet, *The Dialectics of Legal History,* 57 TEXAS L. REV. 1295, 1304 (1979). *See also* J. ELY, *supra* prologue, note 6, at 63–64, 71.
    For a different and, in my view, successful attack on Lupu's position—an attack that

implicitly concedes the existence of a relevant American tradition and consensus but that questions whether the Court is as competent as Congress to divine the character of that tradition and consensus—see Maltz, *Judicial Competence and Fundamental Rights*, 78 MICH. L. REV. 284 (1979). *See also* J. ELY, *supra* prologue, note 6, at 64, 67.

21. Note, *Developments in the Law—The Constitution and the Family*, 93 HARV. L. REV. 1156, 1180, 1182 (1980). *See also id.* at 1179:

> In its resort to tradition, the Court is attempting to determine that a value has historically been regarded as within the province of individual freedom of action where society's interference is improper. . . .
> A fundamental right must be something in which we continue to believe. That fact that a right has, in the past, been regarded as of vital importance will not suffice in and of itself to elevate it to constitutional status.

22. *See also* J. ELY, *supra* prologue, note 6, at 67 & n. * (*citing* R. DWORKIN, *supra* chap. 1, note 114, at 126, 240–58):

> [B]y viewing society's values through one's own spectacles—resolving apparent inconsistencies in popular thinking in the "appropriate" direction by favoring the "emergent over the recessive," the "general over the particular," or whatever—one can convince oneself that some invocable consensus supports almost any position a civilized person might want to see supported. . . . Ronald Dworkin [, for example,] argues that community values must be refined by the judge in a way that removes prejudice, emotional reaction, rationalization, and "parroting," and in addition should be tested for sincerity and consistency. . . . Some such . . . "laundering" device[] is plainly needed, lest one be forced to the conclusion that the law the legislature passed is likely to reflect the way contemporary community values bear on the issues in question.

23. Fiss's particular focus is institutional reform litigation—or "structural adjudication," as he calls it—which I discuss in chap. 5. *See* Fiss, *supra* chap. 1, note 87.

24. *Id.* at 2.

25. *Id.* at 9, 14, 29.

26. *See, e.g.*, J. ELY, *supra* prologue, note 6, at 63–64, 71 and sources cited there; sources cited in chap. 3, note 108; and note 20 *supra*.

27. *See also* NEW WORLD METAPHYSICS: READINGS ON THE RELIGIOUS MEANING OF THE AMERICAN EXPERIENCE xx (G. Gunn ed. 1981):

> Is not religion to be associated with specific convictions, such as belief in God or the divinity of man, specific rituals, such as prayer or confession, or specific feelings, such as adoration, awe, or absolute dependence? Such elements as these, cultural anthropologists and historians of religion have recently suggested, are merely the attributes of religion, its formal properties. The essence of religion, they generally agree, lies elsewhere, lies not in particular beliefs, rites, or feelings, but in a certain way of looking at things, a certain perspective on experience.

28. *See generally* R. BELLAH, THE BROKEN COVENANT: AMERICAN CIVIL RELIGION IN TIME OF TRIAL 36–60 (1975). Robert N. Bellah, whose work I quote in the following discussion, is Ford Professor of Sociology and Comparative Studies at the University of California at Berkeley. For his most recent work on "civil religion," see R. BELLAH & P. HAMMOND, VARIETIES OF CIVIL RELIGION (1980).

29. Bellah, *American Civil Religion in the 1970s*, ANGLICAN THEOLOGICAL REVIEW, Supp. Ser. No. 1, July 1973, at 8.

30. Bellah, *Civil Religion in America*, 96 DAEDALUS 1, 4 (1967).

31. *Id.* at 5.
32. I [use] the phrase [civil religion in America] to describe the religious dimension of American political life that has characterized our republic since its foundation, and whose most central tenet is that the nation is not an ultimate end in itself but stands under transcendent judgment and only has virtue insofar as it realizes, partially and fragmentally at best, a "higher law."

    . . . .

    [I]f there is any utility in the notion of civil religion it is as an analytic tool for the understanding of something that exists.

    Bellah, *supra* note 29, at 8, 10.

    The fact that we have no established religion does not mean that our public life has no religious dimension nor that fundamental questions of our national existence are not religious questions. I have called that tradition of religious symbolization through which Americans have interpreted their national experience, the American civil religion.

    Civil religion, a dimension more than an entity, . . . is a religious interpretation of the American experience derived mainly from biblical images and symbols.

    Bellah, *Religion and Polity in America, supra* note 8.

    By civil religion I refer to that religious dimension, found I think in the life of every people, through which it interprets its historical experience in the light of transcendent reality.

    R. BELLAH, *supra* note 28, at 3.

    [P]art of the reason this issue [of American civil religion] has been left in obscurity is due to the particularly Western concept of "religion" as denoting a single type of collectivity of which an individual can be a member of one and only one at a time. The Durkheimian notion that every group has a religious dimension, which would be seen as obvious in southern or eastern Asia, is foreign to us. This obscures the recognition of such dimensions in our society.

    Bellah, *supra* note 30, at 19 n. 1. *See also* M. MARTY, A NATION OF BELIEVERS 180–203 (1976).
33. Here Bellah refers to imagery associated with war, in particular our own Civil War. *Cf.* Bellah, *supra* note 30, at 10:

    The earlier symbolism of the civil religion had been Hebraic without being in any specific sense Jewish. The . . . symbolism [of Lincoln's Gettysburg Address] ("those who here gave their lives, that that nation might live") is Christian without having anything to do with the Christian church.
34. *Id.* at 18.
35. R. BELLAH, *supra* note 28, at 2. (There is, of course, the problem of false prophets. *See, e.g.,* Gray, *The Heavenly Deception*, N.Y. REV. OF BOOKS, Oct. 25, 1979, at 8 (a discussion of the "Moonies").)
36. *See, e.g.,* P. MILLER, ERRAND INTO THE WILDERNESS (1956); THE AMERICAN PURITAN IMAGINATION (S. Bercovitch ed. 1974); S. BERCOVITCH, THE AMERICAN JEREMIAD (1978).
37. *See* NEW WORLD METAPHYSICS: READINGS ON THE RELIGIOUS MEANING OF THE AMERICAN EXPERIENCE 89 (G. Gunn ed. 1981).
38. *See* Bellah, *supra* note 30, at 7–8:

    [T]he equation of America with [ancient] Israel in the idea of the "American Israel" is not infrequent. What was implicit in the words of Washington becomes explicit in

Jefferson's second inaugural when he said: "I shall need, too, the favor of that Being in whose hands we are, who led our fathers, as Israel of old, from their native land and planted them in a country flowing with all the necessaries and comforts of life." Europe is Egypt; America, the Promised Land. God has led his people to establish a new sort of social order that shall be a light unto all the nations.

See also id. at 9:

The phrases of Jefferson constantly echo in Lincoln's speeches. His task was, first of all, to save the Union—not for America alone but for the meaning of America to the whole world so unforgettably etched in the last phrase of the Gettysburg Address.

39. *See, e.g., Transcript of [President] Carter's Welcoming Statement [to Pope John Paul II] at White House,* N.Y. Times, Oct. 7, 1979, § 1, p. 37, col. 1.
40. See L. HAND, *supra* chap. 1, note 36, at 73–74.
41. Fiss, *supra* chap. 1, note 87, at 12. *See also* J. CHOPER, *supra* prologue, note 9, at 67–68.
42. For a profound discussion of moral evolution, see H. BERGSON, THE TWO SOURCES OF MORALITY AND RELIGION (1932; Eng. trans. 1935).
43. *See generally* D. MAYHEW, *supra* chap. 3, note 113.
44. *Id.* at 101–02.
45. R. DAHL, PLURALIST DEMOCRACY IN THE UNITED STATES: CONFLICT AND CONSENT 131 (1967). *See id.* at 135.
46. Fiss, *supra* chap. 1, note 87, at 10.
47. Traynor, *The Limits of Judicial Creativity,* 63 IOWA L. REV. 1, 8 (1977). Prophets, after all, are rarely popular, especially among their own people.
48. I should pause here to disclaim any suggestion that every time the Court exercises noninterpretive review in a human rights case, the Court is grappling with a *fundamental* political-moral problem. Not every case is *Brown v. Board of Education,* after all. In many human rights cases, the Court is simply "elaborating" a principle—working out what it understands to be the details or implications of a principle—that the Court began to establish, but only began, more or less inchoately, in an earlier case. Or the Court is devising procedures to enable it and other courts to enforce compliance with the principle. Thus, for example, the constitutional rules about "standards or review" or for testing allegations of unconstitutional motivation. *See* Perry, *supra* chap. 3, note 54, at 1033–40.
49. *See* Brandt, *Ethical Relativism,* in 3 ENCYCLOPEDIA OF PHILOSOPHY 75 (P. Edwards ed. 1967).
50. *See id.:* "The metaethical relativist . . . rejects [the] thesis [that there is always only one correct moral appraisal of a given issue] and denies that there is always one correct moral evaluation."
51. Neilsen, *Problems of Ethics,* in 3 ENCYCLOPEDIA OF PHILOSOPHY 117, 125 (P. Edwards ed. 1967).
52. *Id.*
53. Bork, *supra* chap. 1, note 100, at 8, 10.
54. Rehnquist, *supra* chap. 1, note 97, at 704.
55. *Id.* (emphasis added).
56. Bork, *supra* chap. 1, note 100, at 10–11. *Cf.* Levinson, *The Specious Morality of the Law,* HARPER'S, May 1977, at 35, 38:

Law is the outcome of a bargaining process . . . but it is altogether possible that such outcomes will include "repressive, evenoming," "unwise and even dangerous" laws. The substantive content that underlay Bracton's and Adams' concept of law has vanished, and the notion of law has decayed into pure proceduralism—the recognition of public will as mediated by the institutions authorized by the Constitution to pass laws. Without seeking to denigrate the importance of procedure, which we might well cherish and defend as necessary to any proper notion of a decent political order, one can nonetheless point to dangers in viewing them as sufficient to evoke the reverence claimed for them.

57. *See* Brandt, *supra* note 49, at 77.
58. *See, e.g.,* P. SINGER, PRACTICAL ETHICS (1980).
59. *See, e.g.,* J. RAWLS, A THEORY OF JUSTICE (1971). *See also* R. NOZICK, ANARCHY, STATE, AND UTOPIA (1974).
60. *See, e.g.,* R. UNGER, KNOWLEDGE AND POLITICS (1975).
61. *Cf.* Bork, *supra* chap. 1, note 100, at 10: "[T]he principle [that the act of preferring any given value to another be "principled"] is not applicable to legislatures. Legislation requires value choice and cannot be principled in the sense under discussion."
62. *See* Driscoll, *The Development of Human Rights in International Law,* in THE HUMAN RIGHTS READER, 41, 52 (W. Laquer & B. Rubin eds. 1971): "Even with regard to a right as basic as freedom from torture, the system-wide violation of the right is shattering." (*Citing* Amnesty International, REPORT ON TORTURE (2d ed. 1975)). *See also* Kaufman, *A Legal Remedy for International Torture?,* N.Y. TIMES MAG., November 9, 1980, at 44.
63. For a rather different view, and one to which I am very sympathetic, see R. PANIKKAR, MYTH, FAITH AND HERMENEUTICS 208 (1979):

Man is not "finished," finite. Man is open because he is not closed, he is not complete because he is itinerant, not definite, not "finished," in-complete. . . . No person considers himself as finished, as having exhausted the possibilities of becoming. The opening of which we speak is constitutive of the human being, the other side of what we call contingency. . . . Recognizing Man's openness means admitting he is . . . not (yet?) finished, absolute, definitive. It means admitting there is something in him that must evolve; it also affirms the capacity for such evolution.

64. Michelman, *supra* chap. 1, note 69, at 509.
65. Bennett, *A Comment on Cecelia Kenyon's "Constitutionalism in Revolutionary America,"* in NOMOS XX: CONSTITUTIONALISM 210, 213 (J. Pennock & J. Chapman eds. 1979). Professor Bennett adds that the spirit of constitutionalism also requires a "commitment to responsible action on [the] basis" of those "sound conclusions about right and wrong." *Id.*
66. Fiss, *supra* chap. 1, note 87, at 17.
67. For an illuminating, and critical, discussion of contractarian philosophy, see B. ACKERMAN, SOCIAL JUSTICE IN THE LIBERAL STATE 327–48 (1980).
68. *See, e.g.,* R. DWORKIN, *supra* chap. 1, note 114, at 131–49; D. RICHARDS, THE MORAL CRITICISM OF LAW 44–56 (1977); Richards, *Sexual Autonomy and the Constitutional Right to Privacy: A Case Study in Human Rights and the Unwritten Constitution,* 30 HAST. L. J. 957 (1979); Richards, *Human Rights as the Unwritten Constitution: The Problem of Change and Stability in Constitutional Interpretation,* 4 U. DAYTON L. REV. 295 (1979). *See also* O'Fallon, *Adjudication and Contested Concepts: The Case of Equal Protection,* 54 N.Y.U. L. REV. 19 (1979).
69. *See* the pieces by David Richards cited in the preceding note.
70. *See* the sources cited in note 68 *supra.*
71. Greenawalt, *supra* chap. 1, note 80, at 1019 (referring to J. RAWLS, A THEORY OF JUSTICE (1971) and D. RICHARDS, A THEORY OF REASONS FOR ACTION (1971)). *See also* Gerety, *Pornography and Violence,* 40 U. PITT. L. REV. 627, 643: "[M]oral premises surely lie behind [constitutional constraints like the first amendment]. Nonetheless we mistake them when we identify them altogether with [John Stuart] Mill or Rawls, or whatever we take for the best presently-available moral philosophy."

72. See Henkin, *Rights: American and Human*, 79 COLUM. L. REV. 405, 406–07 (1979). *See also* Gerety, *supra* note 71, at 643 ("The Constitution was and is a collective and applied moral effort, likely to escape the confines of any one [moral] theory.").

73. *See* the sources cited in note 68 *supra*.

74. J. PENNOCK, *supra* prologue, note 16, at xxi.

75. Henkin, *supra* note 72, at 415, 418.

    Mark Tushnet has recently asked "whether society should accept the notion of objectively valid moral principles." He then dismisses the question by saying that "our purposes . . . [do not] require that this issue be resolved." Why not? "The focus of constitutional theory is defining and justifying a role for the Supreme Court in society as we find it, not in an Ideal Society. It is enough, then, to establish the empirical claim that we do not believe that there are objective values." Tushnet, *Darkness at the Edge of Town: The Contributions of John Hart Ely to Constitutional Theory*, 89 YALE L. J. 1037, 1044 (1980). I wonder who "we" is. Metaethical relativists? The intelligentsia? Members of the Conference on Critical Legal Studies? Inhabitants of the secular city?

76. *See* Sheehan, *The Struggle within the Church: An Exchange*, N. Y. REV. OF BOOKS, August 14, 1980, 52, 53: "All articles of faith, whether taken in their Gospel expression or in the utterances of Councils and Popes, are theory-laden articulations of the act and habit of communal Christian faith. As such they are relative to linguistic and theoretical schemes which are historically and culturally conditioned and therefore reformable." *Cf.* O. W. HOLMES, JR., COLLECTED LEGAL PAPERS 139 (1920): "The past gives us our vocabulary and fixes the limits of our imagination; we cannot get away from it."

77. *Quoted in* Bellah, *supra* note 29, at 9.

78. *See* R. PANIKKAR, *supra* note 63, at 195–203.

79. I am painfully aware that my distinction between a right answer and particular rationalizations that may be offered in its support calls for greater elaboration than I have undertaken here. But that elaboration will require much more study on my part. On the distinction between "orthodoxy" and "orthopraxis," see *id.* at 195–203. *See also* R. PANIKKAR, THE INTRARELIGIOUS DIALOGUE 1–23 (1978) (on the distinction between "faith," an existential condition, and "belief," a particular rationalization of that condition); T. MERTON, ZEN AND THE BIRDS OF APPETITE 1–14 (1968) (discussing similar distinction).

    Were I intent on conscripting the ninth amendment to do service in my effort to defend noninterpretive review in human rights cases, I would argue (for the argument seems to me quite plausible) that the framers of the ninth amendment, given the language they employed, seem to have believed that there are indeed right answers to questions concerning human rights, answers beyond those which they themselves proffered in the other provisions of the Bill of Rights.

80. *See* the passage by Frank Michelman quoted in note 81 *infra*.

81. Thus, I largely agree with David Richards's argument in *Moral Philosophy and the Search for Fundamental Values in Constitutional Law*, 42 OHIO ST. L. J. 319 (1981), although I think Richards is mistaken in supposing that his argument is responsive to John Ely's position with respect to "philosophy." Ely seems to me to reject not "the method of philosophy" as much as the notion that any one philosophical school should be deemed authoritative for constitutional purposes. *Cf.* Michelman, *supra* prologue, note 24, at 669:

    That a judge cannot proceed by simply choosing among competing philosophical theories or systems must, of course, be accepted; but not (if, indeed, Professor Ely means to go this far) that the literature of moral philosophy is irrelevant to proper performance of the judge's task. As we shall see, Ely himself believes that judges must begin a process of normative reasoning from a premise emergent from, if not exactly in, the historical Constitution. There is no reason why judges may not call upon the methods and contents of the philosophical literature to inform and clarify that reasoning process once its constitutionally connected premise is in place.

82. B. CARDOZO, THE NATURE OF THE JUDICIAL PROCESS 113 (1921).
83. *See* H. BERGSON, *supra* note 42.
84. Or refuse to generate one. Inaction too can be constitutionally problematic. *See, e.g.,* Griffin v. Illinois, 351 U.S. 12 (1956).
85. For a recent example, *see* White, *supra* prologue, note 27, at 296–98.
86. Rostow, *The Democratic Character of Judicial Review,* 66 HARV. L. REV. 193, 208 (1952).
87. *Id.* at 209.
88. Rostow, *The Court and Its Critics,* 4 SO. TEX. L. J. 160, 163 (1959).
89. Rostow, *The Supreme Court and the People's Will,* 33 NOTRE DAME LAW. 573, 576 (1958).
90. R. JACKSON, THE SUPREME COURT IN THE AMERICAN SYSTEM OF GOVERNMENT 2 (1955).
91. McCloskey, Introduction to R. MCCLOSKEY, ESSAYS IN CONSTITUTIONAL LAW 18 (1957). (McCloskey's reference to "cherished long-term values" seems to me much too backward-looking.) *See also* Kluger, *quoted in Race against Time: School Desegregation,* OPTIONS IN EDUCATION (a coproduction of National Public Radio and the Institute for Educational Leadership at George Washington University), program no. 252, transcript at 4 (1980):

> I think the whole issue of segregation came to the courts because the other parts of government, and certainly our private society, were unwilling to face it. We left it to the courts to settle, and they couldn't—all they could do was serve as a moral exemplar, which they did. We listened to that, and then we'd squawk and we'd get angry and we'd say, "Don't make us do that." But we know they're right, they're telling us something; most of us know they're right when we hear a thing like that. . . . So for me, it made me feel [judicial review] works. It's hard and it's bumpy . . . and the machinery is squeaky, but it works.

(Richard Kluger is the author of SIMPLE JUSTICE (1975).)
92. A. BICKEL, THE SUPREME COURT AND THE IDEA OF PROGRESS 177 (1970). *See also* Hart, Foreword: *The Time Chart of the Justices,* 73 HARV. L. REV. 84, 99 (1959) (referring to the Court's "creative function of discerning afresh and of articulating and developing impersonal and durable principles"); A. BICKEL, *supra* this note, at 96 ("[t]he process of the coherent, analytically warranted, principled declaration of general norms alone justifies the Court's function").
93. *Id.* at 91. *See also* Wechsler, *The Courts and the Constitution,* 65 COLUM. L. REV. 1001, 1002–03 (1965):

> A Court which . . . regards the continuing vitality of a decision as dependent "altogether on the force of the reasoning by which it supported" necessarily initiates a dialogue when it pronounces an opinion.
>   To say that it initiates a dialogue, is not, of course, to say that it is necessarily attentive to its critics. Yet it is hard to think that the erosion of the laissez-faire position [of the *Lochner*-era Court; *see* pp. 115–17] was uninfluenced by the sustained and vigorous attack that had been mounted for so many years in Congress, in the schools and in important organs of opinion, not to speak of the continuous dissent within the Court itself.

(Quoting Chief Justice Taney in the Passenger Cases, 48 U.S. (7 How.) 283, 470 (1849).)
94. Gale, Book Review of L. LEVY, AGAINST THE LAW: THE NIXON COURT AND CRIMINAL JUSTICE (1975), N.Y. Times, April 27, 1975, § 7 at 7, col. 4. *Cf.* Deutsch, *Harvard's View of the Supreme Court: A Response,* 57 TEXAS L. REV. 1445, 1448–49 (1979):

> [T]he searching dialogues forced upon judges by the institutions of the judicial

opinion and conference render judicial entities such as the Supreme Court more likely than other political bodies to arrive at trustworthy choices. . . It is, however, the aspect of the Supreme Court's work embodied in these dialogues, rather than Professor Ely's dichotomy between process and substantive choices, that legitimates the imposition of the Court's political choices upon the society at large.

95. *Cf.* Youngstown Sheet & Tube Co. v. Sawyer, 343 U.S. 579, 653 (1952) (Jackson, J., concurring in the judgment and opinion of the Court):

> As to whether there is imperative necessity for such powers, it is relevant to note the gap that exists between the President's paper powers and his real powers. The Constitution does not disclose the measure of the actual controls wielded by the modern presidential office. That instrument must be understood as an Eighteenth-Century sketch of a government hoped for, not as a blueprint of the Government that is. Vast accretions of federal power, eroded from that reserved by the States, have magnified the scope of presidential activity. Subtle shifts take place in the centers of real power that do not show on the face of the Constitution.

96. *See* R. DAHL, *supra* chap. 1, note 4, at 141–42:

> [The framers] did not know what they were doing. They thought the popular House would be dynamic, populistic, egalitarian, levelling, and therefore a dangerous center of power that needed restraint; they thought the President would represent the wellborn and the few and that he would use his veto against popular majorities lodged in the House. They were wrong; for the dynamic center of power has proved to be the presidency, and after Jackson the President could claim, and frequently did claim, to be the only representative of a national majority in the whole constitutional system. Meanwhile, the House has scarcely revealed itself as the instrument of those impassioned majorities that the men at the Convention so desperately feared. Today the relationship they envisaged is, by and large, reversed. It is the President who is the policymaker, the creator of legislation, the self-appointed spokesman for the national majority, whereas the power of Congress is more and more that of veto—a veto exercised, as often as not, on behalf of groups whose privileges are threatened by presidential policy.
>
> Whether the men at the Convention anticipated judicial review is an issue that will probably never be settled; but there is not a single word in the records of the Convention or in the "Federalist Papers" to suggest that they foresaw the central role the Court would from time to time assume as a policymaker and legislator in its own right.

97. Lynch, *supra* prologue, note 8, at 1095. It might be a different matter if noninterpretive review were contraconstitutional—contrary to a value judgment the framers constitutionalized. *See* p. 20, n. *

98. J. ELY, *supra* prologue, note 6, at 69 (*discussing* A. BICKEL, *supra* chap. 1, note 7).

99. *Id.* at 70.

100. *Id.*

101. 60 U.S. (90 How.) 393 (1857).

102. 198 U.S. 45 (1905).

103. For a discussion of the *Dred Scott* and *Lochner* cases, see Rehnquist, *supra* chap. 1, note 97, at 700–03.

104. *See* Berger, *supra* chap. 1, note 62, at 249–69.

105. "[T]he great tides and currents which engulf the rest of men do not turn aside in their course and pass the judges by." Benjamin Cardozo, *quoted in* Desmond, *The Federal Courts and the Nature and Quality of State Law,* in THE FUTURE OF FEDERALISM 87, 89 (S. Shuman ed. 1968).

106. J. ELY, *supra* prologue, note 6, at 57.
107. The problem of significant disharmony between a justice's own values and the values of the larger moral culture is discussed later in this chapter.
108. *See* P. BREST, PROCESSES OF CONSTITUTIONAL DECISIONMAKING 738 (1975).
109. A. BICKEL, *supra* chap. 1, note 7, at 16 (emphasis added).
110. *But cf.* Porter, *That Commerce Shall Be Free: A New Look at the Old Laissez-Faire Court,* 1976 SUP. CT. REV. 135; Deutsch, *Neutrality, Legitimacy, and the Supreme Court: Some Intersections between Law and Political Science,* 20 STAN. L. REV. 169, 231–32 (1968):

> It might be argued that, if the function of the Court is truly to afford our society an opportunity for "sober second thought" concerning measures that challenge, in some significant way, either cherished ideals or deep-rooted social beliefs, then the actions of the thirties [the end of the *Lochner* era] were thoroughly in accord with that function. The fact is that the impropriety of government intervention in the economy did represent such a belief; and the effect of the Court's decisions was precisely to impress upon society the magnitude of the departure from received tradition entailed by acceptance of the view that there exist no principled checks on governmental economic actions. . . . [T]he public consensus on the economic legislation of the 1930's was ultimately strengthened, not weakened, as a result of the Court's intervention.

111. Consider in that regard how dated Henry Steele Commager's critique of judicial review, first published in 1943, now appears. Commager, *Judicial Review and Democracy,* 19 VA. Q. 417 (1943), *reprinted in* L. LEVY, *supra* chap. 1, note 53, at 74.
112. *See* prologue, note 27 and accompanying text *supra*. *See also* Lynch, *supra* prologue, note 8, at 1099 n. 32 ("to most lawyers of my generation, *Brown* is a touchstone for constitutional theory fully as powerful as *Lochner* was for a previous generation."); Tribe, *Seven Pluralist Fallacies: In Defense of the Adversary Process—A Reply to Justice Rehnquist,* 33 MIAMI L. REV. 43, 54–55 (1978).
113. While the justice of "affirmative action"—preferential treatment for nonwhites, blacks in particular—is the subject of significant controversy, recall that the Supreme Court's present general position is one that any interpretivist with a clear-eyed view of the original understanding of the fourteenth amendment could accept, namely, that government may (not must) establish programs of affirmative action. That is, the Court's general position is one of (guarded) defense to electorally accountable policymaking, not one of opposition to it. *See, e.g.,* Fullilove v. Klutznick, 448 U.S. 448 (1980). In that sense, it would be something of a misconception to refer to a case like *Fullilove* as an example of a deeply controversial aspect of the Court's *policymaking* regarding equal protection.
114. *See* chap. 3.
115. *See* Note, *Fornication, Cohabitation, and the Constitution,* 77 MICH. L. REV. 252 (1978); Richards, *Sexual Autonomy and the Constitutional Right to Privacy: A Case Study in Human Rights and the Unwritten Constitution,* 30 HAST. L. J. 957 (1979).
116. *See* Karst, *The Freedom of Intimate Association,* 80 YALE L. J. 624 (1980). Karst's reference, however, is to a wider range of cases than simply the substantive due process ones.
117. *See* Griswold v. Connecticut, 381 U.S. 479 (1965); Eisenstadt v. Baird, 405 U.S. 438 (1972); Carey v. Population Services International, 431 U.S. 678 (1977).
118. Moore v. City of East Cleveland, 431 U.S. 494 (1977). *Cf.* Belle Terre v. Boraas, 416 U.S. 1 (1974).
119. Zablocki v. Redhail, 434 U.S. 374 (1978). *Cf.* Califano v. Jobst, 434 U.S. 47 (1977).
120. The following is a sampling of recent cases: Schuman v. City of Philadelphia, 470 F. Supp. 449 (E.D. Pa. 1979) (Police officer may not be fired for refusing to answer

questions about his unmarried cohabitation); Fisher v. Snyder, 346 F. Supp. 396 (D. Neb. 1972), aff'd, 476 F.2d 375 (8th Cir. 1973) (school teacher may not be fired for having men stay overnight with her); Gay Law Students Ass'n v. Pacific Tel. & Tel. Co., 24 Cal. 3d 458, 595 P.2d 592, 156 Cal. Rptr. 14 (1979) (public utility may not discriminate against gays with respect to employment); New Jersey v. Saunders, 75 N.J. 200, 381 A.2d 333 (1977) (New Jersey fornication statute violates federal constitutional right to privacy); People v. Onofre, 72 A.D.2d 268, 424 N.Y.S.2d 566, aff'd, 51 N.Y.2d 476, 434 N.Y.S.2d 947 (1980) (New York sodomy statute violates federal constitutional right to privacy); Cord v. Gibb, 219 Va. 1019, 254 S.E.2d 71 (1979) (woman may not be denied admission to legal profession under "good moral character" standard merely because of her unmarried cohabitation). But see Doe v. Commonwealth's Att'y, 403 F. Supp. 1199 (E.D. Va. 1975), aff'd mem., 425 U.S. 901 (1976) (sustaining Virginia's sodomy statute); Hollenbaugh v. Carnegie Free Library, 439 U.S. 1052, 1054 (1978) (denying certiorari in a case sustaining discharge of two public library employees for "living together in a state of 'open adultery' "). See generally Rivera, Our Straight-Laced Judges: The Legal Position of Homosexual Persons in the United States, 30 Hastings L.J. 799 (1979).

Other substantive due process cases invalidating state action do not concern freedom of intimate association, but neither are they particularly controversial. A sampling includes: Andrews v. Ballard, 498 F. Supp. 1038 (S.D. Tex. 1980) (Texas laws and regulations that effectively ban acupuncture in state by limiting its practice to licensed physicians infringe prospective acupuncture patients' constitutional right to privacy); Jech v. Burch, 466 F. Supp. 714 (D. Hawaii 1979) (parents have right, founded on federal constitutional right to privacy, to give their child any name they wish); Rennie v. Klein, 462 F. Supp. 113 (D.N.J. 1978) (mental patients have right, founded on federal constitutional right to privacy, to refuse treatment under nonemergency circumstances); Satz v. Perlmutter, 379 So. 2d 359 (Fla. 1980) (terminally ill hospital patients have right, founded on federal constitutional right to privacy, to refuse further life-prolonging treatment); In re Eichner, 73 A.D.2d 431, 426 N.Y.S.2d 517 (1980) (terminally ill patient in permanent vegetative coma has common law and privacy-based right to refuse extraordinary medical treatment).

The state and lower federal courts tend to reject controversial substantive due process claims. Again, a sampling: Carnohan v. United States, 616 F.2d 1120 (9th Cir. 1980) (rejecting claim of constitutional right to use laetrile); Alaska v. Erickson, 574 P.2d 1 (Alaska 1978) (rejecting challenge to state statute banning possession and/or use of cocaine) (compare Ravin v. Alaska, 537 P.2d 494 (Alaska 1975) (possession of marijuana by adults at home for personal use is constitutionally protected)); California v. Privitera, 23 Cal. 3d 697, 591 P.2d 919, 153 Cal. Rptr. 431, cert. denied, 444 U.S. 949 (1979) (rejecting claim of constitutional right to use laetrile); Louisiana v. Chrisman, 364 So. 2d 906 (La. 1978) (rejecting claim of constitutional right to possess marijuana).

121. Roe v. Wade, 410 U.S. 113 (1973); Doe v. Bolton, 410 U.S. 179 (1973). See also Planned Parenthood of Central Missouri v. Danforth, 428 U.S. 52 (1976); Belloti v. Baird, 443 U.S. 662 (1979).

122. Bork, supra chap. 1, note 100, at 6. See also J. ELY, supra prologue, note 6, at 44: "[T]here is absolutely no assurance that the Supreme Court's life-tenured members (or the other federal judges) will be persons who share your values."

123. See J. ELY, supra prologue, note 6. See also Monaghan, supra chap. 3, note 74, at 91.

124. J. ELY, supra prologue, note 6, at 75 n. *.

125. Id. at 88–101.

126. See Lynch, Book Review, 80 COLUM. L. REV. 857, 864–65 n. 17 (1980) (reviewing J. ELY, DEMOCRACY AND DISTRUST: A THEORY OF JUDICIAL REVIEW):

> Even if we grant that judicial review should be "participation-oriented [and] representation-reinforcing," this succeeds only in isolating what sorts of issues are

appropriate for constitutional adjudication (or more precisely, what sorts of issues are not). But when the time comes to apply that approach to, say, the problem of legislative delegation [which Ely discusses at pp. 131–34], the question of how much delegation is consistent with the general participationalist principle that decision-makers should be politically responsible (which can be deduced from the constitutional document) is wide open. Other than the judge's own reasoned preferences and what can be gleaned from judicial and political tradition, I don't see what sources of principle are available.

See also Wellington, The Importance of Being Elegant, 42 OHIO ST. L. J. 427 (1981).

127. Ely, Foreward: On Discovering Fundamental Values, 92 HARV. L. REV. 5, 15 (1978).
128. White, supra chap. 1, note 119, at 72, 71. See also Note, supra note 21, at 1177 n. 119:

While review on behalf of open processes and discrete minorities may be important and constitutionally justified, it is not clear that the Constitution demands it more than it demands review to define the appropriate boundary of governmental intrusion upon the lives of individuals. Both themes are a part of our constitutional jurisprudence.

For other, different, and in my view largely successful criticisms of Ely's participational-nonparticipational distinction, see Symposium: Judicial Review versus Democracy, 42 OHIO ST. L. J. 1 (1981); Tribe, The Puzzling Persistence of Process-Based Constitutional Theories, 89 YALE L. J. 1063 (1980).

129. Braden, The Search for Objectivity in Constitutional Law, 57 YALE L. J. 571, 588–89 (1948). See also Lynch, supra note 126, at 863, 864:

Professor Ely complains that the noninterpretivist who would have judges give content to open-ended constitutional provisions by deciding what political decisions are contrary to our traditions is essentially deceiving herself—the judge will in the end be applying her own values to thwart the popular will. But that is just what Mr. Justice Ely himself is doing. Reading such provisions in light of his view of our traditions, he would override majoritarian decisions that conflict with his preferred portion of that tradition, that which favors broad participation and relatively few substantive constraints on majority choices.

. . . .

In the end, Professor Ely is reduced to arguing, just as he predicts the noninterpretivist would be, that judges should adopt his approach because it's a good one—that is, because it represents his own values and ought to represent theirs.

130. J. ELY, supra prologue, note 6, at 103–04 (quoting A. BICKEL, supra chap. 1, note 7, at 24).
131. Fiss, supra chap. 1, note 87, at 9.
132. Id.
133. Id. at 13.
134. Id. at 58.
135. Id. at 16–17.
136. Id. at 12–13.
137. J. ELY, supra prologue, note 6, at 44. Ely goes on to say:

As we proceed through the various methodologies that are [endorsed], however, I think we shall sense in many cases that although the judge or commentator in question may be talking in terms of some "objective," nonpersonal method of adjudication, what he is really likely to be "discovering," whether or not he is fully aware of it, are his own values. Id.

138. See P. SINGER, supra note 58, at 48–71.
139. See Greenawalt, supra chap. 1, note 80, at 1018.

140. See J. Choper, supra prologue, note 9, at 139–40.
141. See J. Ely, supra prologue, note 6, at 48 ("the [Supreme] Court's power . . . probably has never been greater than it has been over the past two decades.").
142. See Brest, supra chap. 1, note 16, at 236.
143. Greenawalt, supra chap. 1, note 80, at 1018.
144. A. Bickel, supra chap. 1, note 7, at 239. Presumably Bickel meant "only such morally correct principles . . . ," but perhaps not. Cf. B. Cardozo, The Nature of the Judicial Process 141 (1921):

> The judge, even when he is free, is still not wholly free. He is not a knight-errant, roaming at will in pursuit of his own ideal or beauty or goodness. He is to draw his inspiration from consecrated principles. He is not to yield to spasmodic sentiment, to vague and unregulated benevolence. He is to exercise a discretion informed by tradition, methodized by analogy, disciplined by system, and subordinated to "the primordial necessity of order in the social life." Wide enough in all conscience is the field of discretion that remains.

145. See Karst, supra note 116, at 673, 691–92:

> I do not expect any court in this country—today or in the foreseeable future—to hold that the Constitution protects the freedom of a brother and sister to marry. The reason, however, lies not in principle [Karst's broad reference is to "the freedom of intimate association"] but in the force of conventional morality as a political constraint on principle's coherent development.
>
> . . . .
>
> Not only does majoritarian morality influence the shaping of constitutional doctrine; it also influences decisions that go to the judiciary's role in the system of government. A judge faced with the question of the validity of an application of a sodomy law to the private consensual behavior of adults may be excused for feeling a momentary enthusiasm for "the passive virtues." Surely some such notion at least partially explains the Supreme Court's summary affirmance of a lower court's decision denying an injunction against such a law's enforcement in those circumstances [Doe v. Commonwealth's Attorney, 425 U.S. 901 (1976)].
>
> Deciding when to decide—a highly discretionary decision in modern practice—is only one of the occasions for influence by conventional morality over the Supreme Court's management of its institutional role. In the sodomy case, which fell within the Court's theoretically obligatory appeals jurisdiction, the institutional decision was whether to write an opinion. Even if the Court had decided to address the constitutional merits of the case, it still would have had a choice as to the scope of such an opinion. Assuming the Court decided to uphold the law, should it take a sweeping position about the state's interest in enforcing morals, or rest decision on a narrow ground limited to sodomy (acts that can be performed by heterosexuals as well) and ignoring the case's implication for homosexuals? Assuming the Court decided to invalidate the law, should it paint with a brush as broad as that wielded by Justice Douglas in Griswold [v. Connecticut, 381 U.S. 479 (1965)], or should it focus closely on the particulars of this couple's apparently stable relationship? Anyone who thinks that conventional morality plays no part in such choices ignores the Court's role as an agency of government in a human society.

146. Greenawalt, Discretion and Judicial Decision: The Elusive Quest for the Fetters that Bind Judges, 75 Colum. L. Rev. 359, 397–98 (1975).
147. A. Bickel, supra chap. 1, note 7, at 177–78. Bickel continued: "But . . . since we are unable to formulate a rule that will ensure performance of the one function while guarding against the assumption of the other, we tolerate both." Id. at 178.

148. J. ELY, *supra* prologue, note 6, at 7.
149. See p. 28, n. *.
150. See, e.g., Dahl, *Decision-Making in a Democracy: The Supreme Court as National Policy-Maker*, 6 J. PUB. L. 279 (1957). *Cf.* Handberg & Hill, *Court Curbing, Court Reversals, and Judicial Review: The Supreme Court versus Congress*, 14 L. & Soc. Rev. 309 (1980). *Cf.* A. BICKEL, *supra* chap. 1, note 7, at 91 ("[t]he effectiveness of the [Court's] judgment universalized depends on consent and administration").
151. Ely writes that "[e]ven this limited claim overlooks the extent to which court decisions themselves help *shape* the majority will." J. ELY, *supra* prologue, note 6, at 206 n. 12.
152. McCleskey, *supra* chap. 1, note 113, at 358. McCleskey continues:

> No, it is simply not enough to assert without satisfactory proof that "ultimately" the popular will always prevails under judicial review. We have known at least since David Hume that all governments—even the dictatorial ones—rest "ultimately" on the consent of the governed, but . . . democratic theory . . . nowhere contemplates "ultimate" popular control. The whole logic of that theory denies the logic of resorting to such a subterfuge—democracy is an attempt to provide popular control here and now, not ultimately. We must therefore reject this justification for judicial review [that ultimately the polity prevails anyway] for the same reasons we would condemn a proposal to schedule national elections only once every quarter century.

Id. See also Hazard, *supra* chap. 1, note 1, at 10.
Ely has written that:

> It may be true that the Court cannot *permanently* thwart the will of a solid majority, but it can certainly delay its implementation for decades—workmen's compensation, child labor, and unionization are among the more obvious examples—and to the people affected, that's likely to be forever.

J. ELY, *supra* prologue, note 6, at 45.
153. See C. BLACK, THE PEOPLE AND THE COURT 117, 178, 183, 209–11 (1960).
154. See L. LEVY, *supra* chap. 1, note 38, at 47:

> The entire line of reasoning is a curious one which reduces to principle that what is, is democratic. Failure of the people to exercise their sovereign power to abolish or impair judicial review implies their approval; their approval provides democratic credentials. By such reasoning slavery until the Thirteenth Amendment was democratic; segregation until recently was democratic; the electoral college remains the democratic way of electing a president. Whether acquiescence and approval are the same constitutes another difficulty. The simple fact is that at no time in our history have the American people passed judgment, pro or con, on the merits of judicial review over Congress. Consent freely given, by referendum, by legislation, or by amendment is simply not the same as failure to abolish or impair.

155. See McCleskey, *supra* chap. 1, note 113, at 362: "In fact, would not Professor Black's reasoning be sufficient to justify malapportioned Congresses and state legislatures, since the people have 'acquiesced' in such practices for decades?"
156. See, e.g., L. TRIBE, *supra* chap. 2, note 10, at 50–51; Fiss, *supra* chap. 1, note 87, at 15, 38. See also Brest, *supra* note 8, at 764.
157. Article V of the Constitution provides in relevant part:

> The Congress, whenever two-thirds of both Houses shall deem it necessary, shall propose amendments to this Constitution or, on the application of the legislatures of two-thirds of the several states, shall call a convention for proposing amendments, which, in either case, shall be valid to all intents, and purposes, as part of this

Constitution, when ratified by the legislatures of three-fourths of the several states, or by conventions in three-fourths thereof, as the one or the other mode of ratification may be proposed by Congress. . . .

158. See McCleskey, *supra* chap. 1, note 113, at 363. *See also* J. CHOPER, *supra* prologue, note 9, at 49 ("there is no more plainly designated antimajoritarian force in our governmental system—or, now that malapportionment is gone, no more clearly operative one—than the constitutionally prescribed amendment procedures."). *But see* Fiss, *supra* chap. 1, note 87, at 15.

159. It is true, of course, that even apart from judicial review majorities of the polity do not always have their way. *See* chap. 1, note 4 and accompanying text *supra*. Neither do majorities of electorally accountable officials always have their way. *See* J. CHOPER, *supra* prologue, note 9, at 16–25). But none of that counts as an argument in support of noninterpretive review: "[I]mpurities and imperfections . . . in one part of the system are no argument for total departure from the desired norm in another part." A. BICKEL, *supra* chap. 1, note 7, at 18.

160. The President, under Article II, § 2 of the Constitution, "shall nominate, and by and with the advice and consent of the Senate, shall appoint . . . judges of the Supreme Court, and all other officials of the United States, whose appointments are not herein provided for, and which shall be established by law. . . ." Professor Tribe reports that "[i]t has generally been accepted that the Senate's power of 'advice and consent' is formally limited to a veto. See 3 Ops. Atty. Gen'l 188 (1837)." L. TRIBE, *supra* chap. 2, note 10, at 50 n. 6.

161. *See, e.g., id.* at 49–50.

162. J. ELY, *supra* prologue, note 6, at 47. *See also* J. CHOPER, *supra* prologue, note 9, at 50–52. *Cf.* Winter, *The Sources of the Growth of Judicial Power,* in THE ROLE OF THE JUDICIARY IN AMERICA (Moore ed., forthcoming 1982):

[T]he expansion of judicial power does not seem as readily alterable by the appointment process as it has been in the past. Candidate and President Nixon made a large issue of the need for appointment to the bench of "strict constructionists," persons not inclined to assert a major policymaking role for the judiciary. No better illustration exists of how well-rooted the expanding judicial role is than the fact that the Burger Court has not undone the work of the Warren Court in major respects but has itself made a number of decisions significantly expanding judicial power. Busing, the extension of due process to teachers and students, the abortion decisions, restrictions on the death penalty, extension of constitutional protection to commercial advertising, the invalidation of legislative classifications based on sex, and the expansion of rights of mental patients are not the work of the Warren Court. In fact, a solid case can be made for the proposition that the Burger Court, although not always with the support of the Chief Justice whose name it bears and notwithstanding the conventional view taken by the media, is as activist or more so than its predecessor.

163. *See, e.g.,* J. ELY, *supra* prologue, note 6, at 46:

Congress's control over the budget of the federal courts . . . has proved an instrument too blunt to be of any real control potential. The country needs functioning and competent federal courts, and everybody knows it does. Despite the two-thirds requirement, impeachment *might* have developed into an effective mode of controlling decision [*see* Hamilton, *Federalist #81,* FEDERALIST PAPERS 481, 485 (Mentor ed. 1961)]. However, in part precisely because of our allegiance to the idea of an independent judiciary, it didn't, and today it is understood to be a weapon reserved for the grossest of cases.

See also J. CHOPER, *supra* prologue, note 9, at 49–50 (discussing power to control budget and power to impeach, saying, with respect to the latter, "that the two-thirds Senate vote required for conviction strips it of any majoritarian pretenses"; McCleskey, *supra* chap. 1, note 113, at 363 (discussing power to impeach). *Cf.* Kaufman, *Chilling Judicial Independence*, 88 YALE L. J. 681 (1979) (criticizing legislative proposal to facilitate removal of federal judges).

164. Article III sets the outer limits of the Court's appellate jurisdiction, but within those outer limits Congress may specify the classes of cases over which the Court may exercise appellate jurisdiction. *See, e.g.,* Ex Parte McCardle, 7 Wall. 506 (1869). *See also* The "Francis Wright," 105 U.S. 381, 386 (1881): "Not only may whole classes of cases be kept out of the jurisdiction altogether, but particular classes of questions may be subjected to reexamination and review, while others are not."

See M. Redish, FEDERAL JURISDICTION: TENSIONS IN THE ALLOCATION OF JUDICIAL POWER 20–21 (1980):

> Most, if not all, of those who have studied the relevant historical materials agree that concern over the review of facts influenced the adoption of the exceptions clause. There is disagreement, however, as to whether this was the sole concern, for there are relevant statements indicating the desirability of a broader scope for the exceptions clause. Perhaps the greatest obstacle to this very limited view of the scope of the exceptions clause is the appellate jurisdiction authorized by the Judiciary Act passed just after ratification. . . . [The Act limited] appellate jurisdiction to a far greater extent than the "review-of-questions-of-fact" view would allow.

See also Sager, *Foreword: Constitutional Limitations on Congress' Authority to Regulate the Jurisdiction of the Federal Courts*, 95 HARV. L. REV. 17, 31 n. 36 (1981).

165. *See id.* at 34–36.

166. *See, e.g.,* Sheldon v. Sill, 8 How. 440 (1850). *See also* P. BATOR, *et al., supra* chap. 1, note 33, at 11–12.

167. J. ELY, *supra* prologue, note 6, at 46.

168. *See* Van Alstyne, *A Critical Guide to Ex Parte McCardle*, 15 ARIZ. L. REV. 229 (1973).

169. Black, *The Presidency and Congress*, 32 WASH & LEE L. REV. 841, 846 (1975). No less a constitutional scholar than Herbert Wechsler has concurred with Professor Black. *See* Wechsler, *The Appellate Jurisdiction of the Supreme Court: Reflections on the Law and the Logistics of Direct Review*, 34 WASH & LEE L. REV. 1043, 1048 (1977): "[T]hat for me is not an overstatement." *See also* Wechsler, *supra* note 93, at 1004–07.

170. C. Black, *supra* prologue, note 10, at 37–39.

171. *Cf.* Sager, *supra* note 164, at 38 n. 61.

172. Sandalow, *supra* chap. 1, note 16, at 1181. *Cf.* Black, *supra* note 169, at 846–47:

> [T]he federal courts take jurisdiction because Congress tells them to, and do not take jurisdiction when Congress tells them not to—as best they can intepret the constitutional command, with Congress free to correct that interpretation. Now suppose Congress, in language of unmistakable clarity, forbade the Supreme Court to hear on appeal some identifiable class of cases, and suppose the Court . . . took jurisdiction nevertheless, holding the exceptive act unconstitutional. And suppose Congress in its turn disagreed, reading the Constitution, as I would read it, to give it full power to make such "exceptions" as it thinks prudent to the Court's appellate jurisdiction. Why should Congress accept the Court's view? Why should any officer of government accept the Court's view? The Congressional view would be that the Court had acted without jurisdiction, in the face of the constitutional language, and without pretense of following Congress' directions, and that a judgment thus outside the Court's jurisdiction was a mere nullity. I fear (and I choose the word carefully) that I would have to agree.

173. *See, e.g.,* Wechsler, *supra* note 93, at 1004–07; Black, *supra* note 169, at 846; Wechsler, *supra* note 169, at 1048; Hazard, *supra* chap. 1, note 1, at 16; C. BLACK, *supra* prologue,

note 10, at 37–39; Gunther, *Comment*, in THE ROLE OF THE JUDICIARY IN AMERICA (Moore ed., forthcoming 1982).

174. Wechsler, *supra* note 93, at 1008.

175. *Id.* at 1008 (*quoting* F. RICHARDSON, MESSAGES AND PAPERS OF THE PRESIDENTS 3206, 3210 (1897)).

176. *See id.:* "When [the chance that a controversial decision may be overruled and never become a precedent for other cases] has been exploited and has run its course, with reaffirmation rather than reversal of decision, has not the time arrived when its acceptance is demanded, without insisting on repeated litigation?"

177. *See* prologue, note 17 *supra*.

178. Congress has unquestioned power, "in all cases to which the judicial power of the United States extends, [to] rightfully vest exclusive jurisdiction in the Federal courts." The Moses Taylor, 4 Wall. 411, 429 (1867). But that is not necessarily to say that Congress may deny to a state court jurisdiction to review federal action where no federal court has jurisdiction to review the action. *See generally* P. BATOR et al., *supra* chap. 1, note 33, at 418–20.

179. *See* 28 U.S.C. § 1257(1), (3).

180. McCleskey, *supra* chap. 1, note 113, at 364.

181. *Cf.* Hazard, *supra* chap. 1, note 1, at 16: "Whether the power is strictly legislative, or is itself a form of extraordinary appellate review wherein Congress judges the Court according to the Constitution is a question that might be worth examining."

182. J. CHOPER, *supra* prologue, note 9, at 382–83 (emphasis added). *See id.* at 380–415.

183. *See* Sager, *supra* note 164, at 22–25.

184. Hart, *The Power of Congress to Limit the Jurisdiction of the Federal Courts: An Exercise in Dialectic*, 66 HARV. L. REV. 1362 (1953).

185. Ex Parte McCardle, 74 U.S. (7 Wall.) 506 (1869).

186. Hart, *supra* note 184, at 1365.

187. Congress did rely on such a proposal in the aftermath of the Civil War, and the Supreme Court sustained Congress's action. *See* Ex Parte McCardle, 74 U.S. (7 Wall.) 506 (1869).

188. *See* J. CHOPER, *supra* prologue, note 9, at 145, 446 n. 56.

189. For a useful list, see Sager, *supra* note 164, at 18 n. 3.

190. J. CHOPER, *supra* prologue, note 9, at 68–69.

191. *See id.* at 16–24.

192. I am referring to S. 158 (97th Cong., 1st Sess.), "A Bill to provide that human life shall be deemed to exist from conception," introduced by Senator Jesse Helms (R-N.C.). For a technical, and in my view tortured, defense of the proposed legislation, see Galebach, *A Human Life Statute*, 7 HUMAN LIFE REV. 5 (1981). *Cf.* Ely & Tribe, *Let There Be Life*, N.Y. Times, March 17, 1981, at A17, col. 4.

193. Black, *supra* note 169, at 847.

194. *Cf.* Fiss, *supra* chap. 1, note 87, at 38–39:

> Some institutions—the legislature, the schoolboard, the police chief—may have a tighter, more direct connection to consent: particular incumbents serve at the pleasure of the people. To insist upon a similar consensual connection for the judiciary would, however, impair its independence and thus destroy its capacity to discharge its constitutional function within our political system.

195. R. McCLOSKEY, *supra* prologue, note 11, at 12–13.

196. A. BICKEL, *supra* chap. 1, note 7, at 24.

197. Bork, *supra* chap. 1, note 100, at 3–4.

198. Grey, *supra* chap. 1, note 9, at 706. *Cf.* C. MILLER, THE SUPREME COURT AND THE USES OF HISTORY 169 (1969):

The principle of popular sovereignty on which the Constitution is based and the legal cast of the American mind will probably always prevent the complete and candid acceptance in the judicial world of the idea that constitutional development is as legitimate in theory as it is manifest in practice.

199. *See also* Brest, *supra* chap. 1, note 16, at 234: "It is simply anti-democratic to conceal something as fundamental as the nature of constitutional decisionmaking—especially if concealment is motivated by the fear that the citizenry wouldn't stand for the practice if it knew the truth. If the Court can't admit what it is doing, then it shouldn't do it." *But see* M. SHAPIRO, *supra* prologue, note 22, at 27:

> The distinction between what the Court tells the public about its activities and what scholars tell one another must be held firmly in mind. The politician is not usually asked to speak the language of political science or condemned for not doing so. Suicide is no more moral in political than in personal life. It would be fantastic indeed if the Supreme Court . . . were to disavow publicly the myth upon which its power rests.

200. R. BERGER, *supra* chap. 1, note 62, at 417–18. *Cf.* Sandalow, *supra* chap. 1, note 16, at 1195: "[M]any students of constitutional law believe that the ability of courts, and especially of the Supreme Court, to perform the functions that our history has thrust upon them depends upon a popular understanding that courts are ultimate expositors of the meaning of the Constitution."

201. R. BERGER, *supra* chap. 1, note 62, at 415–16 (quoting J. LASH, FROM THE DIARIES OF FELIX FRANKFURTER 59 (1975); Mason, *Myth and Reality in Supreme Court Drama*, 48 VA. L. REV. 1385, 1405 (1962)).

202. *See also* Brest, *supra* chap. 1, note 16, at 235:

> [I]t is not plausible that the truth about constitutional adjudication has been successfully hidden in the fact of almost two centuries of continual exposes of the Court's infidelities to the original understanding of the Constitution—criticisms levied by dissenting Justices, lawyers, politicians, and newspaper editors, as well as scholars. The Justices have not pulled the wool over the eyes of anyone who cared to see.

203. Kilpatrick, *Old Failing Hits Court*, Plain Dealer (Cleveland), December 10, 1979. (Kilpatrick was commenting critically on B. WOODWARD & S. ARMSTRONG, THE BRETHREN (1979).)

204. By "popular" press, I mean the nonacademic press, the press beyond the law reviews. *See e.g.*, Compton, Los Angeles Times, February 20, 1977:

> Let's be honest with the public. Those courts are policymaking bodies. The policies they set have the effect of law because of the power those courts are given by the Constitution. The so-called "landmark decisions" of both the U.S. Supreme Court and the California Supreme Court were not compelled by legal precedent. Those decisions are the law and are considered "right" simply because the court had the power to decree the result. The result in any of those cases could have been exactly the opposite and by the same criteria have been correct. . . .
>
> In short, these precedent-setting policy decisions were the product of the social, economic and political philosophy of the majority of the justices who made up the court at a given time in history. . . .

See also Berger, *The Imperial Court*, N.Y. TIMES MAG., October 9, 1977, at 118; Forrester, *Are We Ready for Truth in Judging?*, 63 A.B.A. J. 1212 (1977).

205. *See* B. WOODWARD & S. ARMSTRONG, THE BRETHREN (1979).

206. 431 U.S. 494 (1977).

207. Only Chief Justice Burger did not address the constitutional issue.
208. *See also* Brest, *supra* chap. 1, note 16, at 234–35 & n. 117.
209. R. McCLOSKEY, *supra* prologue, note 11, at 18. *See also* J. CHOPER, *supra* prologue, note 9, at 65. Of course, none of this is to suggest that electorally accountable representatives have never been agents of moral growth, or will not be in the future. *See id.* at 68:

> The momentous legislative and executive efforts at all levels of government that have been undertaken and consummated specifically in behalf of civil rights evidence the contrary. Indeed, in response to some judicial rulings—involving such matters as wiretapping, electronic interception of conversations with the consent of one of the conversants, noncustodial interrogation by law enforcement officials, multiple prosecutions by state and federal government, police searches of newspaper offices, and the privilege of members of the press to preserve the anonymity of their sources—political bodies have been more sensitive to important personal liberties than has the Court.

"But," continues Professor Choper, "the predominant pattern is otherwise." *Id.*
210. *See* W. WILSON, *supra* prologue, note 27, at 56: "[G]overment is not a machine, but a living thing. It falls, not under the theory of the universe, but under the theory of organic life. It is accountable to Darwin, not to Newton. It is . . . shaped to its functions by the sheer pressure of life."
211. Berger, *quoted in* Footlick, *Berger v. Court,* NEWSWEEK, November 14, 1977, at 75.
212. *See* chap. 3.
213. Woods, *The Indictment,* N.Y. REV. OF BOOKS, May 4, 1978, at 23. *See* D. WOODS, ASKING FOR TROUBLE (1981).
214. *But see* J. CHOPER, *supra* prologue, note 9, at 166, 450 n. 148.
215. Rehnquist, *The Supreme Court of the United States: The Ohio Connection,* 4 U. DAYTON L. REV. 271, 274 (1979).
216. *Id.*
217. The platform of the 1980 Republican National Convention provided that: "We will work for the appointment of judges at all levels of the judiciary who respect traditional family values and the sanctity of innocent human life." Several officials of the American Bar Association have expressed what may fairly be termed outrage at that plank, since, in their view, it represents the politicization of constitutional law and, according to Albert E. Jenner, Jr., of Chicago's Jenner & Block, "an extraordinary attack on the judiciary." *See GOP Blasted on Judges' Plank,* NAT'L L. J., July 28, 1980, at 3, col. 1. I find that reaction difficult to understand. Judges are constitutional policymakers, and as such the personal values of judicial candidates are highly relevant.
218. *See* note 40 and accompanying text *supra.*
219. *See* A. BICKEL, *supra* chap. 1, note 7, at 236, 239:

> The function of the Justices . . . is to immerse themselves in the tradition of our society and of kindred societies that have gone before, in history and in the sediment of history which is law, and, as Judge Hand once suggested, in the thought and the vision of the philosophers and the poets. The Justices will then be fit to extract "fundamental presuppositions" from their deepest selves, but in fact from the evolving morality of our tradition.
>   . . . .
> In one sense, we have thus got no nearer to parsing the inexpressible. "These judges," Mr. Justice Frankfurter was reduced to telling the American Philosophical Society in 1954, "must have something of the creative artist in them; they must have antennae registering feelings and judgment beyond logical, let alone quantitative, proof."

220. *See also* A. Cox, *supra* chap. 2, note 85, at 117–18:

> Constitutional adjudication depends, I think, upon a delicate, symbiotic relationship. The Court must know us better than we know ourselves. Its opinions may . . . sometimes be the voice of the spirit, reminding us of our better selves. In such cases the Court . . . provides a stimulus and quickens moral education. But while the opinions of the Court can help to shape our national understanding of ourselves, the roots of its decisions must already be in the nation. The aspirations voiced by the Court must be those the community is willing not only to avow but in the end to live by. For the power of the great constitutional decisions rests upon the accuracy of the Court's perception of this kind of common will and upon the Court's ability, by expressing its perception, ultimately to command a consensus.

221. 410 U.S. 113 (1973).

222. 410 U.S. 179 (1973).

223. *See Catholics in Survey Endorse Abortion*, N.Y. Times, November 11, 1979, § 1, at p. 43, col. 1 (reporting the results of a New York Times/CBS News Poll). "No figure was given for Jews because they constitute only 3 percent of the population and, in such a survey, their percentages would be considered statistically insignificant." *Id. See also* Stacks, *It's Rightward On*, TIME, June 1, 1981, at 12, 13 (indicating that the American people are opposed to making abortions illegal by 56 percent to 35 percent).

224. *See Israel Selects Middle-Ground Abortion Law*, N.Y. Times, § 4, at p. 7, col. 1:

> [A United Nations study published in 1976] found that almost two-thirds of the world's population lived where access to legal abortion was relatively easy, compared with one-third five years earlier. During the last decade, 33 countries have liberalized their abortion laws, and 12 nations now permit abortion on demand during the first three months. "Few social changes have ever swept the world so rapidly," the authors of the study said.

> *See also On Abortion, Italian Voters Are Less Catholic than the Vatican*, N.Y. Times, May 24, 1981, at E3, col. 1.

225. *See, e.g.*, Sandalow, *Federalism and Social Change*, 43 L. & CONT. PROB. 29, 35 (1980): "[M]y own disagreement with [Roe v. Wade] rests upon its undemocratic character."

226. I think Einstein said that.

CHAPTER 5

1. *See* Perry, *The Abortion Funding Cases: A Comment on the Supreme Court's Role in American Government*, 66 GEO. L.J. 1191, 1236–43 (1978).

2. *See* Perry, *The Disproportionate Impact Theory of Racial Discrimination*, 125 U. PA. L. REV. 540 (1977); Perry, *Modern Equal Protection: A Conceptualization and Appraisal*, 79 COLUM. L. REV. 1023, 1040–42 (1979).

3. For a sensitive discussion of total institutions, see E. GOFFMAN, ASYLUMS 1–124 (1961). Goffman defines a *total institution* as "a place of residence and work where a large number of like-situated individuals, cut off from the wider society for an appreciable period of time, together lead an enclosed, formally administered round of life. Prisons serve as a clear example. . . ." *Id.* at xiii.

4. *Cf.* Chayes, *The Role of the Judge in Public Law Litigation*, 89 HARV. L. REV. 1281, 1315 (1976): "[O]ne may ask whether democratic theory really requires deference to majoritarian outcomes whose victims are prisoners, inmates of mental institutions, and ghetto dwellers. Unlike the numerical minorities that the court protected under the banner of economic due process, these have no alternative access to the levers of power in the system."

5. For a sampling of the cases, see Frug, *The Judicial Power of the Purse*, 126 U. PA. L. REV. 715, 718 nn. 15–17 (1978). *See also Lawsuits a Growing Burden for Prison Authorities*, N.Y. Times, June 1, 1980, § 1, p. 1, at col. 4.

6. *See, e.g.*, Note, *Implementation Problems in Institutional Reform Litigation*, 91 HARV. L. REV. 428 (1977); Special Project, *The Remedial Process in Institutional Reform Litigation*, 78 COLUM. L. REV. 784 (1978). Although used primarily with reference to cases involving prisons and institutions for the mentally disabled, "institutional reform litigation" also refers to cases involving juvenile detention facilities, school desegregation, legislative reapportionment, employment discrimination, and discrimination in public housing and municipal services. *See* Frug, *supra* note 5, at 719 n. 18; Special Project, *supra* this note, at 788 & nn. 2–6.

7. For an argument that such litigation does not constitute a radically new development in adjudication generally, see Eisenberg & Yeazell, *The Ordinary and the Extraordinary in Institutional Litigation*, 93 HARV. L. REV. 465 (1980).

8. Glazer, *The Judiciary and Social Policy*, in THE JUDICIARY IN A DEMOCRATIC SOCIETY 67 (L. Theberge ed. 1979). *See also* Frug, *supra* note 5, at 6:

> Compliance with the orders in the institution cases requires action by the legislature to raise or reallocate funds and, once that is accomplished, detailed judicial supervision of the executive's efforts to implement the changes mandated by the court decree. It is the judicial requirement of major legislative action and the detailed judicial supervision of executive implementation—consequences that derive from the scope of the changes involved—that characterize the institution cases. . . .

9. Fiss, *supra* chap. 1, note 87, at 5. Professor Fiss suggests that institutional reform litigation, or "structural reform," as he calls it (*id.* at 2), is an outgrowth of the school desegregation cases. *See id.* at 2–4. Fiss prophesies that "structural reform . . . in the years ahead promises to become a central—perhaps the central—mode of constitutional adjudication." *Id.* at 2. *But see* Weinstein, *Litigation Seeking Changes in Public Behavior and Institutions—Some Views on Participation* U. C. DAVIS L. REV. 231, 231 (1980). "Severe restrictions on resources available at the national, state, and local levels and changing social and political attitudes suggest that [institutional reform litigation] will be less important in the immediate future than it has been in the past."

10. The Court's involvement, as of 1981, has been marginal. *See* Bell v. Wolfish, 441 U.S. 520 (1979); Hutto v. Finney, 437 U.S. 678 (1978). *See also* Frug, *supra* note 9, at 2–4. *Cf.* Pennhurst State School and Hospital v. Halderman, 451 U.S. 1 (1981).

11. *See, e.g.*, Glazer, *supra* note 8; Glazer, *Overseeing Education and Social Services*, in THE ROLE OF THE JUDICIARY IN AMERICA (Moore ed., forthcoming 1982). *See also* D. HOROWITZ, THE COURTS AND SOCIAL POLICY (1977).

12. Frug, *supra* note 5, at 723.

13. *Hell in Texas*, NEWSWEEK, January 15, 1979, at 74. *See also An Added Punishment is Poor Health Care*, N.Y. Times, February 4, 1979, § 4, at p. 10 col. 1 (discussing "the denial of adequate medical care" to prisoners); *Fresh Assault on Old Max*, NEWSWEEK, January 14, 1980, at 90 (reporting on Colorado prison cases, in which federal district judge found "that almost 900 inmates were being held in three dirty, crowded, stinking, poorly lit, dangerous cell blocks where most have literally nothing to do"); *When Will It Happen Again?*, NEWSWEEK, February 18, 1980, at 68 (discussing prison conditions in general and suggesting that "prisons fail in almost every way, and that more riots like Santa Fe's [see note 34 *infra*] seem certain"); *The Scandalous U.S. Jails*, NEWSWEEK, August 18, 1980, at 74; Lieber, *The American Prison: A Tinderbox*, N.Y. TIMES MAG., March 8, 1981, at 26; *Lock 'Em Up—But Where?*, NEWSWEEK, March 23, 1981, at 54; Will, *When Government Fails*, NEWSWEEK, May 11, 1981, at 100; Fiss, *supra* chap. 1, note 87, at 12 (setting forth "examples . . . taken from a single, but protracted case involving the Arkansas prison system"):

the use of torture in all its varieties—the teeterboard, the Tucker telephone, the strap, the failure to provide medical care, the heavy use of armed, mounted, and undisciplined trusties to supervise field labor, and the housing of anywhere from 85 to 150 inmates in a single dormitory room, leaving the weak and attractive to spend each night terrorized by the "creepers" and "crawlers." . . .

14. Note, *supra* note 6, at 429.
15. 325 F. Supp. 781 (M.D. Ala.), *Hearing on standards ordered,* 334 F. Supp. 1341 (M.D. Ala. 1971), *enforced,* 344 F. Supp. 387 (M.D. Ala. 1972), *aff'd in part, remanded in part, decision reserved in part sub nom.* Wyatt v. Aderholt, 503 F.2d 1305 (5th Cir. 1974).
16. Frug, *supra* note 5, at 720. The federal trial judge in Wyatt v. Stickney was Frank M. Johnson, who may truly be said to have spearheaded institutional reform litigation in the early 1970s. *See* R. KENNEDY, JUDGE FRANK M. JOHNSON, JR. (1978). For Judge Johnson's graphic portrait of the shameful conditions disclosed in several of the institutional reform cases over which he has presided, see Johnson, *Observation: The Constitution and the Federal District Judge,* 54 TEX. L. REV. 903, 907–13 (1976). (Johnson is now a judge of the United States Court of Appeals for the Fifth Circuit.)
17. *See* Henkin, *supra* chap. 4, note 72, at 416: "The International Covenant on Civil and Political Rights forbids . . . cruel, inhuman, or degrading treatment or punishment. . . . The Covenant provides that the 'penitentiary system shall comprise treatment of prisoners the essential aim of which shall be their reformation and social rehabilitation.' "
18. Frug, *supra* note 5, at 728. For a discussion of the developing constitutional bases of the right to treatment, see Garvey, *Freedom and Choice in Constitutional Law,* 94 HARV. L. REV. 1756, 1788–89 n. 140 (1981).
19. *See especially* D. HOROWITZ, *supra* note 11; Glazer, *supra* note 8; Glazer, *supra* note 11.
20. *See, e.g.,* Note, *The Wyatt Case: Implementation of a Judicial Decree Ordering Institutional Change,* 84 YALE L.J. 1338 (1975); Chayes, *supra* note 4; D. HOROWITZ, *supra* note 11; Note, *supra* note 6; Frug, *supra* note 5; Special Project, *supra* note 6; Diver, *The Judge as Political Powerbroker: Superintending Structural Change in Public Institutions,* 65 VA. L. REV. 43 (1979); Fiss, *supra* chap. 1, note 87; Weinstein, *supra* note 9.
21. *See generally* Chayes, *supra* note 4; Note, *supra* note 6; Special Project, *supra* note 6; Fiss, *supra* chap. 1, note 87.
22. Chayes, *supra* note 4, at 1307. *See id.* at 1307–09.
23. *See generally* Note, *supra* note 6. *See also* Johnson, *The Role of the Judiciary with Respect to the Other Branches of Government,* 11 GA. L. REV. 455, 471–72 (1977); Friendly, *The Courts and Social Policy: Substance and Procedure,* 33 U. MIAMI L. REV. 21, 40–41 (1978); Tribe, *Seven Pluralist Fallacies: In Defense of the Adversary Process—A Reply to Justice Rehnquist,* 33 U. MIAMI L. REV. 43, 53 (1978); Diver, *supra* note 20, at 61; Fiss, *supra* chap. 1, note 87, at 26–27.
24. *See e.g.,* D. HOROWITZ, *supra* note 11, at 293:

    For every judge who acts on imperfect information, students of Congress can produce three legislators. For every judge who assumes his orders to be effective, students of bureaucracy can adduce untold instances of lack of administrative follow-up. In a period in which the discovery is being made that effective policymaking and implementation are scarce, there is plenty of incapacity for officials to share.

    See also Fiss, *The Jurisprudence of Busing,* in THE COURTS, SOCIAL SCIENCE, AND SCHOOL DESEGREGATION 194, 209 (B. Levin & W. Hawley eds. 1977).
25. Goldstein, *A Swann Song for Remedies: Equitable Relief in the Burger Court,* 13 HARV. CIV. LIB.–CIV. RTS. L. REV. 1, 46 (1978). *See also* Cox, *The Effect of the Search for Equality upon Judicial Institutions,* 1979 WASH. U. L. Q. 795, 804–05:

    But the true question is not whether the court is an ideal forum. Because a plaintiff comes to court to say that the nonjudicial system has broken down and that no one else will fix it, the true short-run question is whether the court will do the job so badly that it is better to let the breakdown continue rather than suffer judicial intervention in desperate last resort. The long-run question for the creators and shapers of institutions is whether some other ombudsman or forum of last resort, equipped with expertise and tools that no court commands, can be created to deal with such disasters.

26. Fiss, *supra* chap. 1, note 87, at 32. *See id.:*

The performance of one function may interfere with another, failures in one domain impair its capacity to perform in others, but there is no reason to believe that the relationship between the structural [*i.e.*, institutional reform] and dispute-resolution models of discharging the judicial function is one of interference, that involvement in the structural litigation will compromise the judiciary's capacity to resolve disputes. The functions may well be independent, or maybe even complementary.

27. Glazer, *supra* note 8.
28. Greenawalt, *Comment*, in THE JUDICIARY IN A DEMOCRATIC SOCIETY 86, 87 (L. Theberge ed. 1979).
29. *Id.*
30. *See* Eisenberg & Yeazell, *supra*, note 7, at 517:

[W]e favor many of the actions of courts in institutional litigation on the ground that they tend to foster rather minimal standards of human dignity, but we do not think that such a preference is susceptible of proof. We would insist, however, that it is such questions, *rather than those of technique and administration*, that the new litigation requires us to confront. (emphasis added)

See also Gunther, *supra* prologue, note 8, at 820: "[T]he legitimacy-rights problem is a deeper and more serious one than the competence-remedies problem."

31. *See* Comment, *Confronting the Conditions of Confinement: An Expanded Role for the Courts in Prison Reform*, 12 HARV. CIV. RTS.–CIV. LIB. L. REV. 367, 379–80 (1970): "The physical conditions in most American prisons do not represent a considered judgment about what correctional facilities should be like; rather, they are often the product of inertia or default."

32. *See* Inmates of Boys' Training Schools v. Affleck, 346 F. Supp. 1354, 1358 (D.R.I. 1972):

[Where some deliberate choices have been made, they are most likely to have been made by lower-level institutional administrators merely trying to stay within external budget constraints, decisions that probably haven't been ratified or reviewed by, or even made known to, high-ranking officials in the state executive branch or legislators acting either singly or jointly.]

See also Justice, *Prisoners' Litigation in the Federal Courts*, 51 TEX. L. REV. 707, 716–17 (1973):

To the extent that judicial forebearance is founded on the notion, often unarticulated, that courts should defer to legislative guidance in determining what punishment is acceptable, I submit that this forebearance is inappropriate to punishment assessed by prison officials. First, many kinds of punishment inflicted are not expressly authorized by the legislature. Rather, prison administrators assess the punishment pursuant to a general delegation of authority. . . . It is hard to believe that any legislature today would draft a statute providing that punishment might properly include confining the prisoner in a dimly lighted cell with one blanket, no clothes, no mattresses, sheets, pillows, and no hot water. Yet the deference to legislative guidance . . . authorizes this kind of punishment even without legislative imprimatur.

33. See chap. 4.
34. Cf. The Killing Ground, NEWSWEEK, February 18, 1980, at 66, 68:

[T]hrough 36 hours of rage last week, the New Mexico State penitentiary near Santa Fe was the site of one of the most brutal prison riots in U.S. history—a sadistic display of convict against convict violence that included beheading, hanging, torching and rape. In the end, 33 inmates were dead—four burned so badly that their race could not be determined. The prison itself was almost destroyed: water from broken pipes flowed through the corridors; walls were blackened from fire; offices were sacked; the kitchen, educational wing, psychological unit and Protestant chapel were trashed beyond repair, and the gymnasium was gutted to its girders. . . .

The New Mexico riot is certain to revive concern about how U.S. society warehouses its felons. . . . The New Mexico pen, praised at its 1954 dedication as "among the most advanced correctional institutions in the world," turned into one of the worst. There were 1,136 prisoners placed into space designed for 800. Young inmates serving time for relatively minor crimes were housed, sometimes five to a cell, along with case-hardened long-termers. The prisoners complained often about rats in their cells, roaches in their food and rough treatment by guards. One diabetic inmate told his father that when he went into insulin shock late at night and pleaded for help, he was ignored.

Despite protests from the inmates and their families, the state government was reluctant to spend money on the facility. . . .

. . . .

In the aftermath of the riot, the state government soon came in for its share of blame. "Obviously, it didn't happen overnight," said [Governor Bruce] King. This spring, he will call a special session of the state legislature to consider emergency prison expenditures that may well wipe out his planned $60 million tax rebate. Quick repairs at the prison along with temporary housing costs will come to an estimated $28.5 million. In addition, King is also pushing for a new maximum security facility that would relieve overcrowding and separate hard-core cons—at a cost of $45 million. "They wouldn't spend the money before," sniffed one inmate's mother last week outside the prison gates. "Now they'll have to spend a goddam lot of money."

35. Note, The Increasing Scene of Federal Judicial Involvement in State and Local Corrections Facilities, 3 NEW ENG. J. PRIS. L. 227, 235 (1976).
36. Comment, supra note 31, at 386.
37. Even conservative columnist George F. Will—who is certainly no enthusiast of judicial activism—has acknowledged as much. See Will, When Government Fails, NEWSWEEK, May 11, 1981, at 100.
38. As opposed to the distinct question of how, in a particular situation, such rights can best be remedied. Cf. Fiss, supra chap. 1, note 87, at 46, 52:

The remedy expresses the judge's desire to give a meaning to a constitutional value that is more tangible, more fullblooded than a mere declaration of what is right.

. . . .

Rights and remedies are but two phases of a single social process—of trying to give meaning to our public values. Rights operate in the realm of abstraction, remedies in the world of practical reality. A right is a particularized and authoritative declaration of meaning. It can exist without a remedy—the right to racial equality, to be free of Jim Crowism, can exist even if the court gave no relief (other than the mere declaration). The right would then exist as a standard of criticism, a standard for evaluating present social practices. A remedy, on the other hand, is an effort of the court to give meaning to a public value in practice. A remedy is more specific, more concrete, and more coercive than the mere declaration of right; it constitutes the actualization of the right.

39. Comment, *supra* note 31, at 380–81.

40. Frug, *supra* note 5, at 728. Frug ádded: "Given the records in a number of the institution cases, the requisite level of degradation, whatever it may be, exists in a number of state institutions." *Id.* (The entire passage is quoted in the text accompanying note 18 *supra*.)

41. Johnson, *supra* note 23, at 474.

42. Frug, *supra* note 5, at 792.

43. Gilhool, *The Uses of Courts and Lawyers*, in Changing Patterns in Residential Services to the Mentally Retarded 155, 156 (Kugel and Shearer eds. 1976). *See also* Denvir, *Towards a Political Theory of Public Interest Litigation*, 54 N. Car. L. Rev. 1134, 1158–59 (1976).

44. One could say much the same thing about noninterpretive review in, say, racial discrimination cases—that it served to make us more fully aware of the problem, thereby allowing us to do something about it (like enact federal civil rights legislation).

   Of course, another prime function of institutional reform litigation is deterrence. *See id.* at 1137:

> [S]ome cases need not even be filed because the very potential of a court challenge will have an effect on an agency decision. Bureaucracies instinctively attempt to shield themselves from monitoring by other agencies such as the courts. Once the threat of a court challenge is credible, the agency feels a significant pressure against illegal action. Therefore, for each suit brought, there may be several that need not be.

See also the discussion by Judith Lachman in The Role of the Judiciary in America (Moore ed., forthcoming 1982).

45. 325 F. Supp. 781 (M.D. Ala. 1971), *aff'd sub nom.* Wyatt v. Aderholt, 403 F.2d 1305 (5th Cir. 1974).

46. Note, *supra* note 6, at 463 n. 178.

47. 42 U.S.C. §§ 6001–6081.

48. *Id.* at § 6010. Section 6010, which is the "bill of rights" provision of the act, provides in relevant part:

> Congress makes the following findings respecting the rights of persons with developmental disabilities:
>
> (1) Persons with developmental disabilities have a right to appropriate treatment, services, and habilitation for such disabilities.
>
> (2) The treatment, services, and habilitation for a person with developmental disabilities should be designed to maximize the developmental potential of the person and should be provided in the setting that is least restrictive of the person's liberty.
>
> (3) The Federal Government and the States both have an obligation to assure that public funds are not provided to any institution [that] . . . (A) does not provide treatment, services, and habilitation which are not appropriate to the needs of such person; or (B) does not meet the following minimum standards. . . .

For a construction of this provision, see Pennhurst State School and Hospital v. Halderman, 451 U.S. 1 (1981).

49. Pp. 112,113 *supra*.

50. *See* 1979 Cumulative Supplement to R. Singer & W. Statsky, Rights of the Imprisoned (1974), 181–82 (discussing actions by states governments, professional groups—including the American Bar Association and the American Medical Association—and the United States Department of Justice aimed at establishing standards of operation for

correctional institutions). *Cf.* Denvir, *supra* note 43, at 1140–43 (discussing public interest litigation in general as a catalyst to legislative action).

51. P.L. 96–247 (96th Cong., 2d Sess.).
52. Glazer, *supra* note 11.
53. Petition of Governor of Alabama for Appointment as Temporary Receiver, filed February 2, 1979. Pugh V. Locke, 406 F. Supp. 318 (M. D. Ala. 1976), *Aff'd sub nom.* Newman v. Alabama, 559 F. 2d 283 (5th Cir. 1977).
54. *Id.* (emphasis added).
55. *See Governor Ends Alabama's Rift with Judge*, N.Y. Times, February 12, 1979, at A14, col. 1. *See also* Johnson, *In Support of Judicial Activism*, THE BRIEF, Fall 1979, at 4, 8 ("[my appointment of] a receiver for the Alabama prison system . . . will not work to diminish state responsibility but to increase it—because . . . the receiver I appointed is the new Governor of Alabama."). (Governor James obviously takes a rather different view of the matter than his predecessor, George Wallace, who reportedly suggested that Judge Johnson be given a barbed wire enema. *Governor Ends Alabama's Rift with Judge, supra* this note.) For a report on the progress Alabama has made, see *Alabama Racing to Avert Order Freeing Prisoners*, N.Y. Times, May 4, 1981, § 1, at 10, col. 2.

   Cf. McCormack, *The Expansion of Federal Question Jurisdiction and the Prisoner Complaint Caseload*, 1975 WIS. L. REV. 523, 536:

   > [T]he tendency of many state officials [is] to punt their problems with constituencies to the federal courts. Many federal judges have grown accustomed to allowing state officials to make political speeches as a prelude to receiving the order of the district court. This role requires the federal courts to serve as a buffer between the state officials and their constituencies, raising the familiar criticism that state officials rely upon the federal courts to impose needed reforms rather than accomplishing them themselves.

56. Glazer, *supra* note 11.
57. Frug, *supra* note 5, at 728–29 (footnote omitted). *See also* D. HOROWITZ, *supra* note 11, at 6; *Fresh Assault on Old Max, supra* note 13.
58. Frug, *supra* note 5, at 735–36. *See also* Eisenberg & Yeazell, *supra* note 7, at 506 (referring to "the allocation of social resources" as "a quintessentially legislative choice"). Frug points out that in general compliance costs in institutional reform cases are significantly greater than those in other sorts of constitutional cases when compliance with the court's decree requires an allocation of public monies—e.g., school desegregation cases. See Frug, *supra* note 5, at 758–74. For one court's view of the problem, see N.Y. State Ass'n for Retarded Children v. Carey, 631 F.2d 162 (2d Cir. 1980).
59. The fact of significantly greater compliance costs also raises and magnifies the problem of competence: How can a court know whether, and to what extent, the required allocation of scarce resources to correct the conditions at a prison or mental health facility will diminish the amount available to satisfy other vital interests, *especially other interests of the poor and other marginal persons?* Critics emphasize the danger that in institutional reform cases, courts may be robbing Peter to pay Paul. See, e.g., Glazer, *supra* note 8, at 73; Frug. *supra* note 5, at 742–43. But that problem, like other problems of competence, is neither inherent nor insurmountable. At the remedy stage of an institutional reform case, the court can enlist the assistance of budget experts, including and indeed especially the state's own, in an effort to ascertain beforehand, and to modify if necessary, the impact of compliance costs on other aspects of the state's budget. See, e.g., Note, *Developments in the Law—Section 1983 and Federalism*, 90 HARV. L. REV. 1133, 1245, 1248 (1977); Note, *supra* note 6, at 440 & n. 61.
60. *See* chap. 4.
61. P.L. 96–247 (96th Cong., 2d Sess.). The text of the act is reproduced at 48 LW 133–35 (June 24, 1980).
62. Frug, *supra* note 5, at 785. *See id.* at 785–88.

63. *See* §§ 3(a), 5(a)(1).
64. The act applies to any facility or institution owned, operated, or managed by, or providing services on behalf of any State or political subdivision of a State, and which is (i) for persons who are mentally ill, disabled, or retarded, or chronically ill or handicapped; (ii) a jail, prison, or other correctional facility; (iii) a pretrial detention facility; (iv) for juveniles held awaiting trial, residing in such facility or institution for purposes of receiving care or treatment, or residing for any State purpose in such facility or institution; or (v) providing skilled nursing, intermediary or long-term care, or custodial or residential care. Section 2(1).
65. Frug, *supra* note 5, at 793. Frug continues:

    Unless the courts are prepared to do what no responsible government official would do—close the institutions, and let the prisoners and the mentally ill, dangerous or otherwise, go free—if the courts are unwilling to play a game of "chicken" with state officials, as they should be, they should face the fact that these orders will be complied with, if at all, voluntarily, absent federal executive action to enforce them.

66. Fiss, *supra* chap. 1, note 87, at 54–55. *See id.* at 55–58.
67. *Cf. id.* at 58:

    [The judge] among all the agencies of government is in the best position to discover the true meaning of our constitutional values, but, at the same time, he is deeply constrained, indeed sometimes even compromised, by his desire—*his wholly admirable desire*—to give that meaning a reality. (emphasis added)

68. 487 F.2d 700 (D.C. Cir. 1973).
69. *Id.* at 112.
70. *See* Cox, *supra* note 25, at 808–09.
71. A threat to cut off funding in the absence of compliance with federally established standards—another conceivable strategy—might be a terribly potent weapon. For a comment favoring such a strategy, see *id.* at 815–16. *Cf.* J. CHOPER, *supra* prologue, note 9, at 152–53 (discussing the efficacy of such threats with respect to school desegregation).
72. Frug, *supra* note 5, at 792.
73. *See* note 66 and accompanying text *supra.*
74. *See* Department of State, COUNTRY REPORTS ON HUMAN RIGHTS PRACTICES FOR 1979 (1980) (submitted to the Committee on Foreign Affairs, U.S. House of Representatives, and the Committee on Foreign Relations, U.S. Senate).
75. *See* Gunther, *supra* prologue, note 8, at 824:

    I am naive enough to think that a court should not shrink from announcing legitimate constitutional rights simply because of remedial concerns. . . . *Worcester v. Georgia,* [31 U.S. (6 Pet.) 536,] the 1832 case that rejected Georgia's claim of authority over Indian lands and held the imprisonment of two missionaries illegal[,] . . . engendered the most threatening consequences for the Marshall Court, and yet I think it represents the Marshall Court's noblest hour. When *Worcester* was decided in the spring of 1832, John Marshall and his colleagues knew that Andrew Jackson's White House and a large part of Congress and a large part of Georgia were ready to defy the Court. When John Marshall and his fellow justices voted in that case, they genuinely believed that the decision might well mean the end of effective Court authority. But they also thought that it was legally right, and so it was. And, unflinchingly, they did their duty: they decided the case on the merits, even though the immediate prospects were anxiety-producing, even though the survival of the Court was truly at stake. I think theirs was the proper judicial stance. If a decision is right on the merits, it *should be* handed down, despite fears about the consequences.

See also In re Grand Jury Subpoena Duces Tecum Issued to Richard M. Nixon, 360 F. Supp. 1, 9 (D.C.C.), *aff'd sub nom.* Nixon v. Sirica, 487 F.2d 700 (D.C. Cir. 1973):

> That the Court has not the physical power to enforce its order to the President is immaterial to a resolution of the issues. [T]he Court has a duty to issue appropriate orders. [I]t would tarnish the Court's reputation to fail to do what it could in pursuit of justice.

EPILOGUE

1. *See* chap. 4.
2. For an overview of the Supreme Court's human rights workproduct in the modern period, *see* J. CHOPER, *supra* prologue, note 9, at 79–122.
3. *See* chap. 4.
4. G.A. Res. 217, U.N. Doc. A/810 (1948).
5. G.A. Res. 2200, 21 U.N. GAOR, Supp. (No. 16) 49, U.N. Doc. A/6316 (1966). *See* note 8 *infra*. The United States officially supports the Universal Declaration, which does not have the status of law, but thus far has refused to subscribe to the International Covenant, the status of which as law is ambiguous (*see* note 9 *infra*). *See generally* Henkin, *supra* chap. 4, note 72, at 420–24.
6. *Id.* at 418.
7. For an attempt to grapple with that question, see Michelman, *Welfare Rights in a Constitutional Democracy,* 1979 WASH. U. L. Q. 659. *Cf.* Henkin, *supra* chap. 4, note 72, at 418–19:

> The division between civil-political and economic-social rights is not sharp; a few of the rights provided in the Covenant on Economic, Social and Cultural Rights are constitutional rights as well. The right to join a trade union, for example, is protected in American constitutional law as an aspect of the freedom of association. The right to choose one's work is an aspect of constitutionally protected liberty. If the government decides to make available economic and social benefits, invidious discrimination in providing them would be a denial of the equal protection of the laws. But, in the main, the rights in the Covenant on Economic, Social and Cultural Rights are not constitutional rights in the United States. The Constitution tells government what not to do, not what it must do. The Framers saw the purposes of government as being to police and safeguard, not to feed and clothe and house. Of the Four Freedoms which Franklin Roosevelt proclaimed to the world, the Constitution guarantees three against abridgment by government—Freedom of Expression, Freedom of Religion, and Freedom from Fear. But there is no constitutional right to Freedom from Want.

8. *See* Scarman, *Fundamental Rights: The British Scene,* 78 COLUM. L. REV. 1575, 1578 (1978).

> The welfare state is in legal terms an attempt to incorporate into the law social and economic rights as fundamental human rights. It confers upon the citizen rights which the state has to find cash to implement. The state is not asked to keep out of the way as in the case of civil rights—for example, freedom from unlawful arrest or freedom of speech—but is under a duty to come in with its basket of benefits. All of these benefits must be paid for by the state—out of taxation, if there be no other funds available.

9. *See* Henkin, *supra* chap. 4, note 72, at 418:

> Although states adhering to the Covenant undertake to realize these rights only "progressively" and "to the maximum of available resources," the document uses the language of right, not merely that of hope, of undertaking and commitment by

governments, not merely of aspiration and goal. Some have asked whether it is meaningful to call what is here promised "rights," since the undertakings are vague and long term; they are unenforceable, if only because they require major governmental planning and programs and are conditioned upon availability of resources. But in international law and rhetoric, they are legal rights, and in many societies, including our own, the language of rights is increasingly used and the sense of entitlement to such benefits is becoming pervasive.

10. From time to time recently it has seemed that China is such a society. *See* Department of State, *supra* chap. 5, note 74, at 437–45. *See also Notes and Comment,* THE NEW YORKER, Jan. 22, 1979, at 25–26; Wang, *China's "Four Big Rights,"* N.Y. TIMES, June 1, 1980, § 4, at p. 21, col. 2. *But see* Kamm, *Is Peking's Liberalization Really Over?,* N.Y. TIMES, May 3, 1981, § 4, at 4, col. 3; *Let a Hundred Flowers Wilt,* TIME, Sept. 21, 1981, at 34. *Cf.* Spence, *China: How Much Dissent?,* THE NEW YORK REVIEW, Aug. 13, 1981, at 32; Jinglun, *China's Reforms,* N. Y. TIMES, Dec. 20, 1981, § 4, at 19, col. 2.

11. *See generally* THE HUMAN RIGHTS READER, *supra* chap. 4, note 62.

12. It appears that the lesson is being learned in Great Britain. *See* Scarman, *supra* note 8; Lester, *Fundamental Rights in the United Kingdom: The Law and the British Constitution,* 125 U. PA. L. REV. 337 (1976).

13. Scarman, *supra* note 8, at 1577.

14. *Cf.* M. WALZER, RADICAL PRINCIPLES 52–53 (1980).

15. *See* Department of State, *supra* chap. 5, note 74, at 675–89. None of this is to dispute the desirability or even necessity of a welfare state in America, only to note the inherent dangers.

INDEX

concerning, 120–21; Universal
Declaration of, 163
Hume, David, 217n152
Hutto v. Finney, 224n10

*Inmates of Boys' Training Schools v.
Affleck*, 226n32
Institutional reform litigation, 7, 146,
147–62
International Covenant on Economic,
Social, and Cultural Rights, 163–64,
225n17. *See also* Human rights
Interpretive review: controversy over, 15;
distinguished from noninterpretive
review, 6, 10, 11, 36, 45, 130; in
federalism cases, 41, 42, 59; functional
justification for, 13, 15–17, 22–23, 36, 38,
46, 50, 57, 92; as judicial enforcement, (of
existing constraints) 22–23, (of value
judgments) 88; legitimacy of, 6, 10, 11–12,
17, 19, 25, 27–28, 36, 130; by lower courts,
13–14, 17; in separation-of-powers cases,
49, 59; by Supreme Court, 10–11, 12–15,
17, 19, 38, 41, 45, 58; as term of recent
coinage, 7
Interpretivism, 21, 23, 28, 33, 74, 90, 104,
141–42; and anti-interpretivism, 30,
31–32, 34, 70, 71; commitment of, to
"majoritarian" policymaking, 30; defined,
11; and equal protection, 66–68, 70;
essential question posed by, 80, 83, 85, 87,
88; and freedom of expression, 64–65, 66,
70; and "illegitimacy" of noninterpretive
review, 11, 37, 40, 45, 57, 60, 61, 65–70
passim, 91; proponents of, 29, 49, 64–65,
66, 67, 86, 117, 119; test of, 41, 49, 59, 60

Jackson, Andrew, 212n96, 230n75
Jackson, Robert, 39, 50–52, 53–54, 55, 112
James, Forrest H., Jr., 156–57, 161
Japanese Exclusion Cases, 113n
Jech v. Burch, 214n120
Jefferson, Thomas, 62, 174n50, 208n38
Jenner, Albert E., Jr., 222n217
Johnson, Frank, 154, 155, 156, 158, 225n16
Judge(s): electorally accountable, 131,
168nn17, 18; function and task of, 96, 99,
123–24, 161; moral culture of, 111, 116,
119; values of, as source of judgment,
123–25, 143
Judicial activism, 25. *See also* Activism;

Noninterpretive review (constitutional
policymaking)
Judicial review: as "culmination of
Revolutionary thinking," 16–17; defined,
6n, 25; in democratic process, 78, 168n14
(*see also* Democracy); and electorally
accountable policymaking, 9–10, 20, 54;
framers' intentions concerning, 42;
legitimacy of, 9–12, 16–17, 25, 27, 33, 35,
54, 74, 128; by lower courts, 17; and moral
responsibility of polity, 19; "neutrality"
of, 26–27, 30, 96; in separation-of-powers
cases, 54, 56; of state action, 64,
(distinguished from federal action) 35–36;
Thayer on "dangers" of, 18; as
"undemocratic," 168n14. *See also*
Interpretive review; Noninterpretive
review (constitutional policymaking)
Judiciary Act (*1789*), 13, 174n50, 219n164
Judiciary branch: acceptance or denial by, of
legislative value or policy choice, 29, 38;
authority delegated to, 20, 23, 42, 175n50;
Congressional power over, 128–29 (*see
also* Congress, U.S.); Council of Revision
proposal rejected, 21; disinterestedness
of, 16; and disputes between President
and Congress, 52 (*see also* Legislative
branch); framers' creation of, 143, 172n19;
Hamilton's observation on, 16; intrusion
by, on legislative function, 18;
requirement of principled explanations
by, 25–27; sole function of, 28. *See also*
Federal courts, lower; States; Supreme
Court, U.S. Justice Department, U.S.,
Justice Department, U.S., 55–56, 155n,
228n50

Karst, Kenneth, 63, 117
Katz v. United States, 181n119
Kilpatrick, James, 141
King, Bruce, 227n34

"Landmark decisions," 221n204
Lane County v. Oregon, 188n51
Least Dangerous Branch, The (Bickel), 35–36
Lee, Richard Henry, 174n50
Leff, Art, 106–07n
Legality concept: and enforceability, 15
Legislative branch, 14; basic function of, 28;
division of authority of, 38, 41, 42, 43, 44;
-executive branch conflict, 49, 50, 54–60;
Hamilton on, 16; judiciary acceptance or
denial of value or policy choice of, 29, 38;